I0419562

EGON SCHIELE

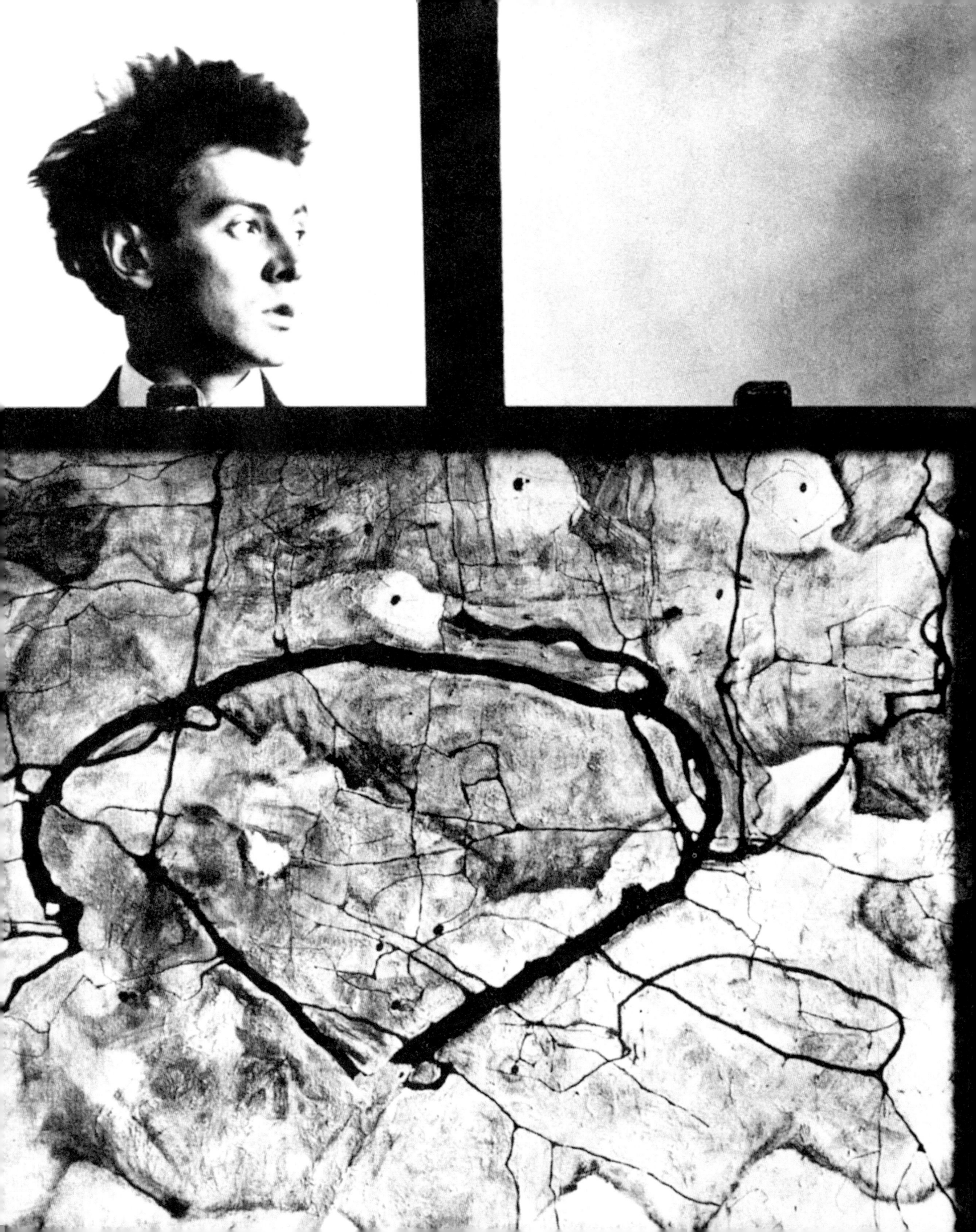

EGON SCHIELE
LIVING LANDSCAPES

Edited by Christian Bauer
Preface by Ronald S. Lauder, foreword by Renée Price

With contributions by

Christian Bauer	Kerstin Jesse	and
Verena Gamper	Kimberly A. Smith	Franz Smola

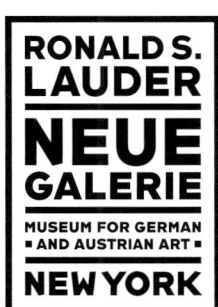

RONALD S. LAUDER
NEUE GALERIE
MUSEUM FOR GERMAN
■ AND AUSTRIAN ART ■
NEW YORK

PRESTEL
MUNICH • LONDON • NEW YORK

This catalogue has been published in conjunction with the exhibition

EGON SCHIELE · LIVING LANDSCAPES

Neue Galerie New York
October 17, 2024 – January 13, 2025

This catalogue is generously sponsored by Marie-Josée and Henry Kravis.
This exhibition is made possible in part by Withersworldwide.

Curator
Christian Bauer

Exhibition Design
William Loccisano

Director of Publications
Scott Gutterman

Managing Editor
Janis Staggs

Editorial Assistant
Liesbet Van Leemput

Book Design
William Loccisano

Translation
Steven Lindberg

Project Coordinator
Cornelia Hübler

Production
Martina Effaga

Origination
Schnieber Graphik, Munich

Printing and Binding
Longo AG, Bolzano

Prestel Verlag, Munich
A member of Penguin Random House
Verlagsgruppe GmbH
Neumarkter Strasse 28
81673 Munich

A CIP catalogue record for this book
is available from the British Library.

Library of Congress Control Number:
2024941639

Paper: 170 g Galaxi Supermat

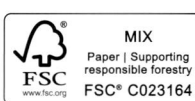

Penguin Random House
Verlagsgruppe FSC® N001967

Printed in Italy

ISBN 978-3-7913-7748-3

www.prestel.com

PAGE 2: Atelier Hanns Ungar,
Neulengbach, Egon Schiele behind
his easel with the painting *Autumn
Tree in Turbulent Air (Winter Tree)*,
Neulengbach, 1912.

ACKNOWLEDGMENTS

Dina Alexander, New York
Marián Aparicio, Madrid
Art Installation Design, New York
Lena Banyan, New York
Sarah Barnard, New York
Vivian Endicott Barnett, New York
Jennifer Belt, New York
Beatriz Blanco, Madrid
Christina Roman Brown, New York
Antonia Bryan, New York
Matti Bunzl, Vienna
Sam Cameron, New York
Jasmine Chen, New Tapei City
Pierre Chen, New Tapei City
Elliot Chu, Washington, D.C.
Alessandra Comini, Dallas
Shawn Digney-Peer, New York
Hermann Dikowitsch, St. Pölten
Fay Duftler, New York
Elisabeth Dutz, Vienna
Martina Effaga, Munich
Jody Egolf, New York
Sonja Eiböck, Vienna
Peter Eisenschenk, Tulln
Christopher Eykyn, New York
Adina Ferber, New York
Eliza Frecon, New York
Verena Gamper, Vienna
Heather Gray, New York
Jeffrey Haber, New York
Katharina Haderer, Munich
Nina Hartl, London
Sandy Heller, New York
Max Hollein, New York
Anton Wolfgang Höslinger, Klosterneuburg
Angela Hsaio, New Taipei City
Catherine Huang, New Taipei City
Wolfgang Huber, Klosterneuburg
Cornelia Hübler, Munich

Kerstin Jesse, Vienna
Barbara Kallir, Venice
Jane Kallir, New York
Cheryl Karim, New York
Suzanne Karsten, Windermere
Evelyn Kelley, New York
Marissa Klein, New York
Samantha Koslow, New York
Daniela Kumhala, Vienna
Armin Laussegger, St. Pölten
Alexandra Leitzinger, St. Pölten
Michael Lesh, New York
Vivienne Lewis, Windermere
Steven Lindberg, Berlin
Reed Liriano, Washington, D.C.
Jill Lloyd, London
William Loccisano, Sarasota
Glenn Lowry, New York
Nicholas Maclean, New York
Edward Manley, Chappaqua
John Manley, Scarsdale
Maya Manley, Chappaqua
Susanne Manley, Scarsdale
Sirena Maxfield, New York
Cassie Mazzucco, New York
Alexandra Morrison, New York
Carmen Müller, Vienna
Richard Nagy, London
Esther Navarro, Madrid
Georg Nebehay, Basel
Stefan Nebehay, Vienna
David Norman, New York
Olaf Peters, Halle (Saale)
Ernst Ploil, Vienna
Ellen Price, New York
Sami Rama, Branford
Jerry Rivera, New York
Stella Rollig, Vienna
Jackie Scalisi, New York

Torben Schnieber, Munich
Klaus Albrecht Schröder, Vienna
Iphigenia Seong, New York
Kimberly A. Smith, Austin
Franz Smola, Vienna
Guillermo Solana, Madrid
Eva Maria Stöckler, Krems
Elizabeth Szancer, New York
Susan Wallach, New York
Heidrun Wenzel, St. Pölten
Nara Wood, Cobb
Yagna Yass-Alston, New York
Susanne Zabehlicky, Vienna
Jack Zinterhofer, New York
Will Zinterhofer, New York
Tom Zoufaly, New York

CONTENTS

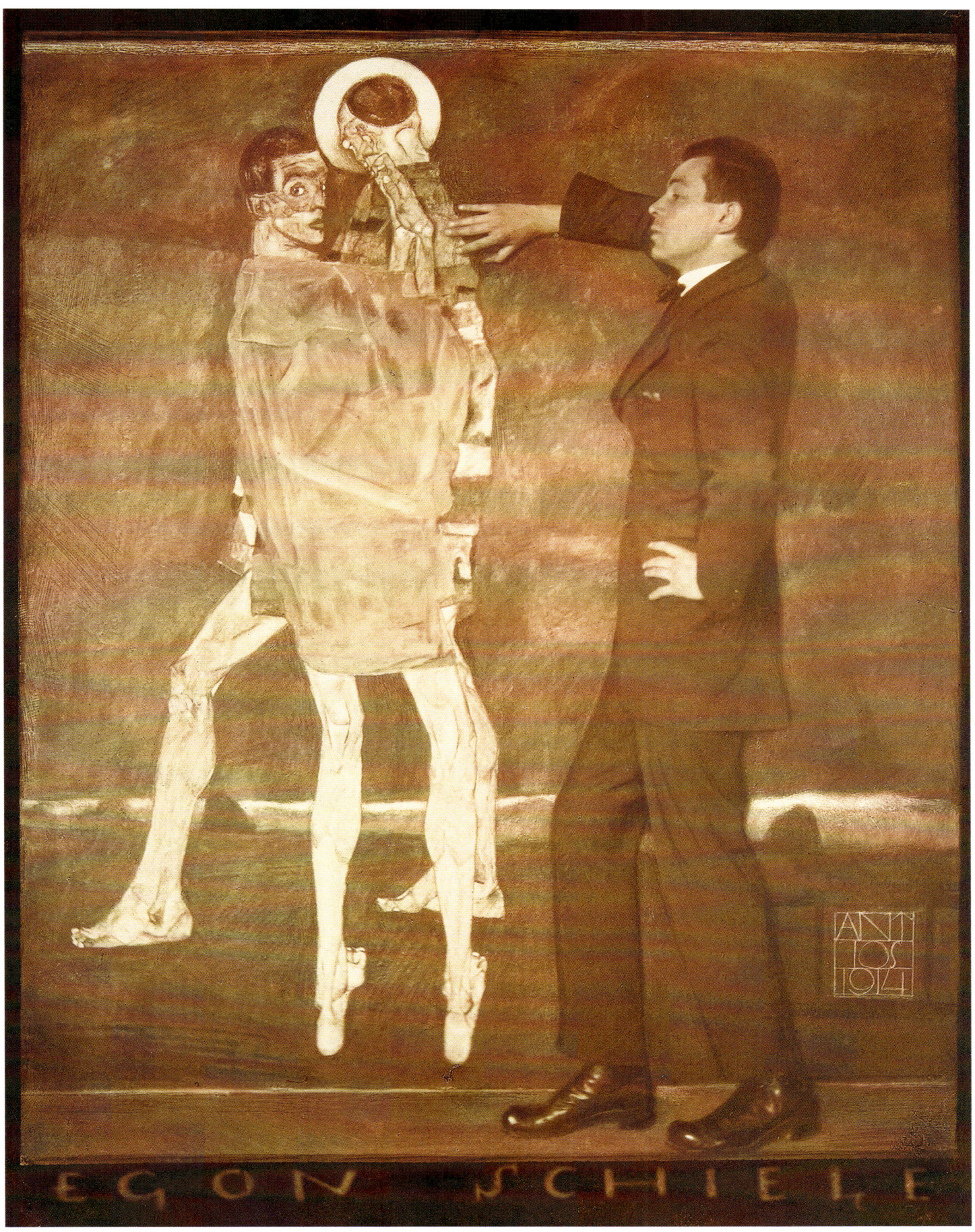

Anton Josef (Antios) Trčka, Egon Schiele photographed with his painting *Encounter (Self-Portrait with Saint)*, 1914 (Kallir P259). Photo: Brandstätter Archive

PREFACE

Egon Schiele is, without question, one of the most important artists in the collection of the Neue Galerie. His work has a power and immediacy that makes it unforgettable.

Schiele first grabbed my attention when I was a very young man. Once I began to learn about him, at the age of thirteen, I sought out every book I could find on the artist. I learned about Schiele's natural abilities, which were recognized by his mentor, the great Gustav Klimt, as well as about his struggles, which included imprisonment. Tragically, Schiele died in 1918 during the influenza epidemic, at the youthful age of 28. Yet despite his rather short career, he managed to achieve so much, and he continues to fascinate me these many decades later. I am very proud to have acquired many important works by this great artist, and to present them in major exhibitions such as this one at the Neue Galerie.

The person most responsible for teaching me about Schiele was my good friend, and the co-founder of the Neue Galerie, Serge Sabarsky. Serge and I spent a lot of time looking at works by this artist, and I consider that time to be a valuable part of my education in art. Every Sunday, Serge and I would get together at his gallery and talk about everything, especially art. Many of the drawings and paintings that I have in my collection came from these Sundays spent with Serge. Whenever I look at art now, I can hear Serge talking to me and saying, "Don't listen to anybody—trust your own eyes."

It is an honor to present this exhibition devoted to Schiele landscapes, and to acknowledge the complex ways the artist used the genre to express his feelings about the world. Dr. Christian Bauer has assembled a number of important works, and he tells a wonderful story with them. I want to extend my thanks to the lenders, without whom the exhibition would not have been possible, and to the staff of the Neue Galerie, led by Director Renée Price, for their hard work and dedication.

I think that Serge would have been pleased to see the Neue Galerie devoting an exhibition to Schiele landscapes. He knew that this artist was uniquely gifted, and that everything he created deserves to be valued and studied. In my view, this exhibition is a tribute to my mentor, Serge Sabarsky. It is also a testament to the lasting power of art.

Ronald S. Lauder
President, Neue Galerie New York

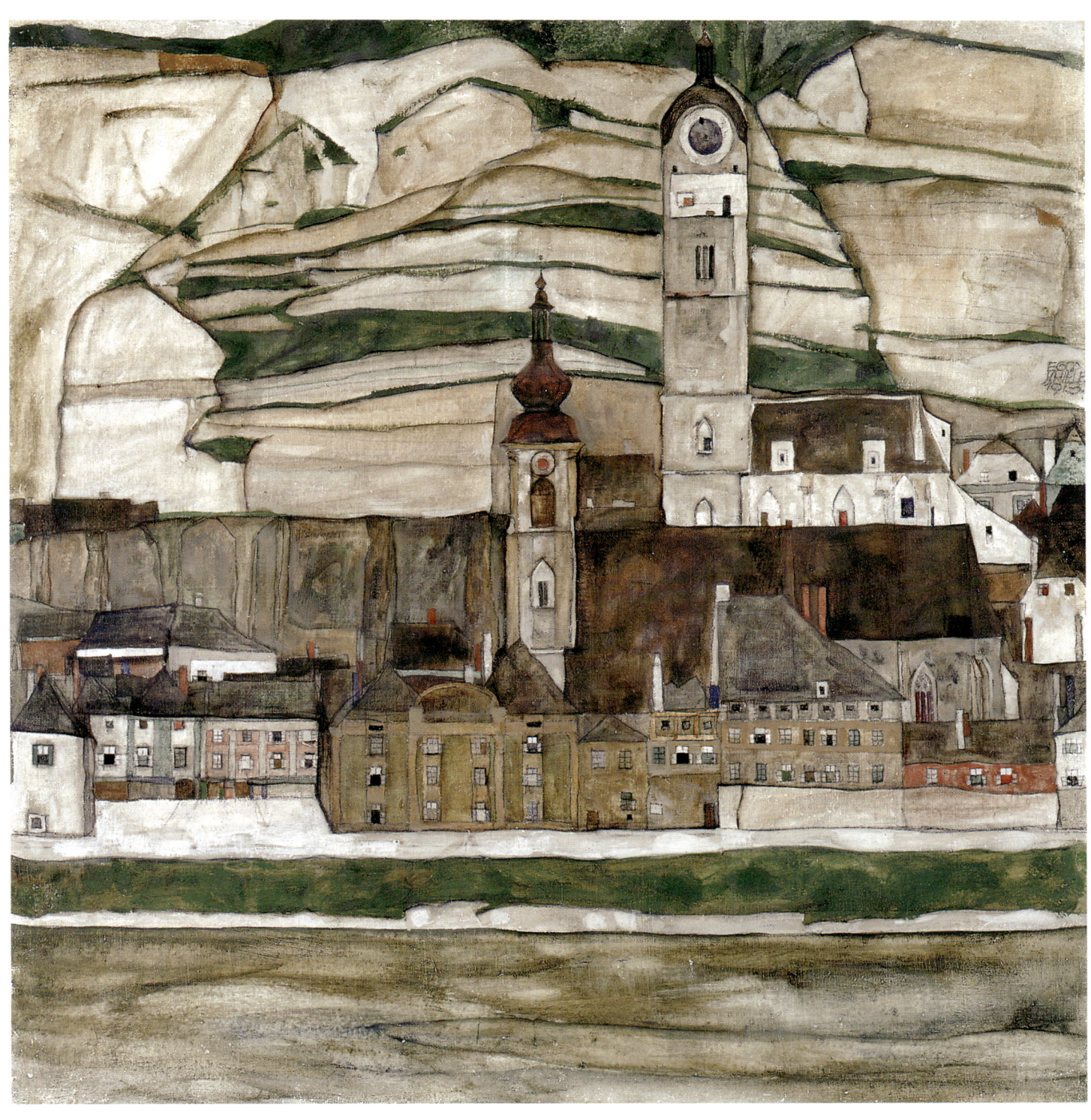

Egon Schiele, *Stein on the Danube, Seen from the South (Large)*, 1913, oil on canvas. Neue Galerie New York. This work is part of the collection of Estée Lauder and was made available through the generosity of Estée Lauder. Photo: Hulya Kolabas

FOREWORD

Although the Neue Galerie New York has been in existence for more than two decades, only in the current year have we focused cur curatorial attention so closely on the great tradition of landscape painting. Earlier in 2024, we surveyed the landscape paintings of the Austrian artist Gustav Klimt. In these lyrical works, we see the beautiful Salzkammergut region in full flower, with Klimt borrowing from masters such as Vincent van Gogh and Claude Monet to portray the lush green countryside and the pristine Attersee. Klimt created these paintings while on his *Sommerfrische* (summer holiday), and they possess an ease and *joie de vivre* that suggests how much he enjoyed his time away from the oppressive summer heat in Vienna. With the current exhibition. we are pleased to focus on the landscapes of an artist Klimt mentored, and another key figure in the history of Austrian art, Egon Schiele.

Klimt and Schiele shared a mastery of painting and drawing, and helped propel fin-de-siècle Viennese art to international prominence decades later. Yet personally, they were a study in contrasts. Klimt was a worldly man, having traveled widely, if somewhat reluctantly, and his artworks were sought out by wealthy and influential individuals. He was a prominent figure in the Imperial City, a founder of the Secession whose artistic development transformed the cultural life of his beloved Vienna.

Schiele, on the other hand, was something of a country boy, a wunderkind who brought his gifts to the Academy of Fine Arts in Vienna when he began to study there at the age of sixteen, but who nonetheless remained close to his rural roots. Born in Tulln, a small town on the banks of the Danube, he rarely traveled in his youth, apart from a short train trip with his sister to Trieste. Once he had established himself as an artist, he still preferred living and working along the Danube in Klosterneuburg or in the village of Neulengbach, in Lower Austria, where he was arrested and jailed at one point by the conservative local authorities, who disliked his provocative and sexually frank art. Later, he returned several times to the rural Bohemian town of Krumau on the Vltava River, the birthplace of his mother, finding solace there, as well.

Schiele, known for his expressive line and striking figures, treated landscape in a different, more modern way than Klimt. He often viewed his subject from unusual angles, and tended to imbue the landscape with symbolic content, in particular exploring the life and death cycle observed in nature. His palette tended toward darker, more somber colors, and his landscapes often convey a mysterious and ineffable sadness. The remarkable paintings and drawings presented in this exhibition and catalogue constitute an important and under-recognized portion of the artist's body of work, and it is our privilege to gather them in this context and offer a more complete picture of the crucial place they hold within his oeuvre.

My own introduction to Schiele came primarily through two mentors: the late Serge Sabarsky, co-founder of the Neue Galerie New York, and Professor Alessandra Comini,

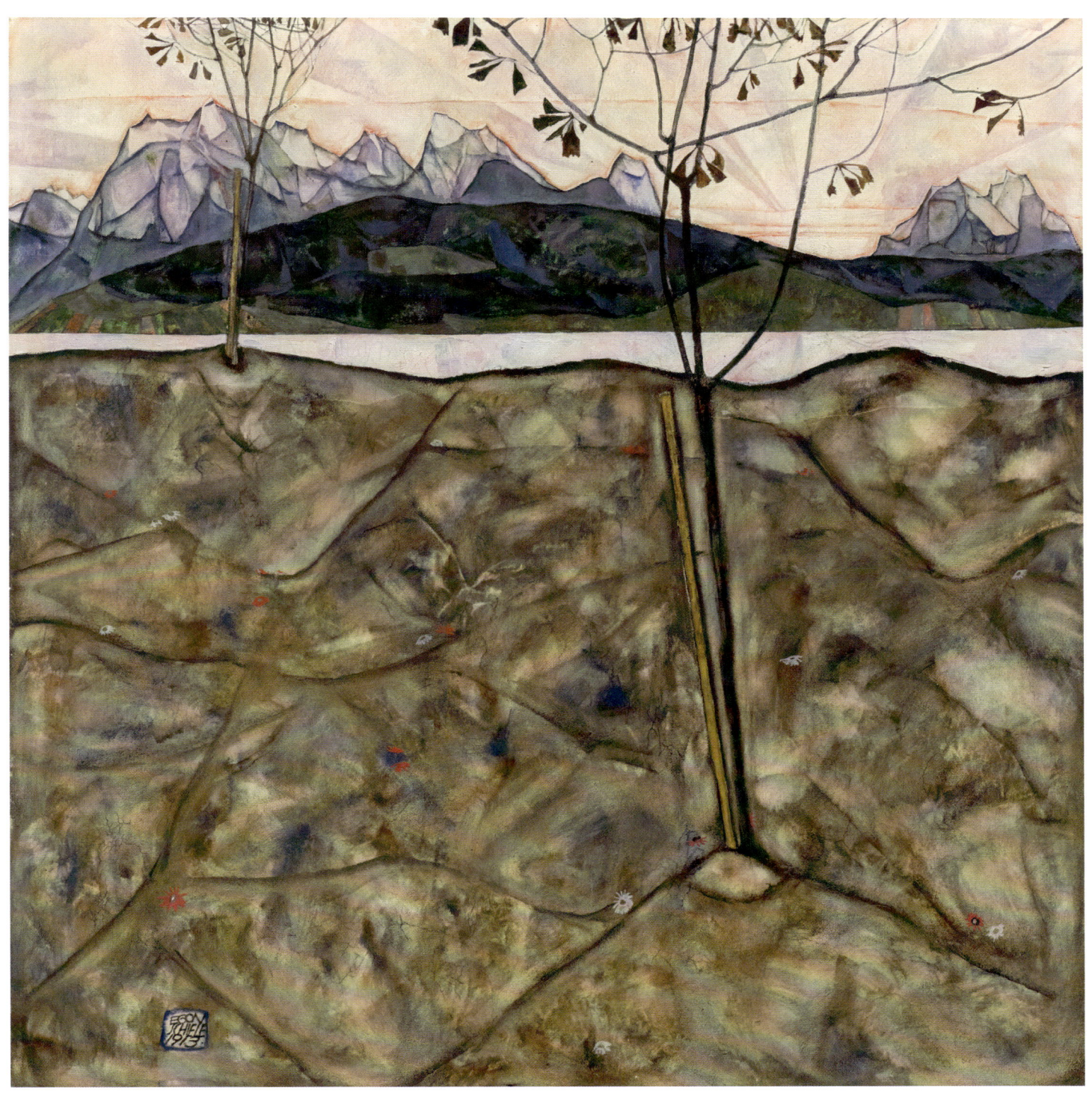

Egon Schiele, *River Landscape with Two Trees*, 1913, oil on canvas. Private Collection. Photo: Alex Jamison

a major Schiele scholar. With Serge, I looked at countless works by Schiele, which was a critical step in my training and helped me to develop an eye. Alessandra made her mark as an American art historian who came to Vienna from Texas as a student in the 1950s and helped foster interest in Schiele through her many publications, including a major study of the artist's portraiture for her dissertation at Columbia University and for the Neue Galerie in 2005. She counts among her achievements the discovery of the Neulengbach prison cell where Schiele was held, as well as befriending and reuniting his two surviving sisters, Gerti and Melanie, which led to still more insights into the artist and his work. I recall nervously hand-carrying the plaster Schiele death mask with me on a flight from Dallas to New York, a cherished gift to the Neue Galerie from Alessandra.

There is another key figure in the history of Schiele's presence n the United States art world who deserves our acknowledgement, and that is the legendary Viennese émigré art dealer Otto Kallir. Through his Galerie St. Etienne, he was the first to present Schiele to American audiences, and his cause was later taken up by his granddaughter, Jane Kallir, who produced a standard-bearing *catalogue raisonné* on the artist as a magnificent labor of love. In addition to these individuals, I wish to thank Christian Bauer,

Curator of the Egon Schiele Museum in Tulln, who organized the present exhibition; William Loccisano, who designed the catalogue and exhibition; as well as the numerous lenders to the show, including the Albertina Museum, Vienna; City Collection, Tulln; Galerie St. Etienne, New York; the Landessamlungen Niederösterreich, St. Pölten; the Monastery Museum Klosterneuburg; Museo Nacional Thyssen-Bornemisza, Madrid; The Museum of Modern Art, New York; Ernst Ploil, Vienna; YAGEO Foundation Collection, Taiwan; various private collections; and as always the staff of the Neue Galerie New York, all of whom made the exhibition possible. Finally, I wish to extend my heartfelt thanks to the President and Co-founder of the Neue Galerie, Ronald S. Lauder. I have witnessed first-hand the love and devotion he maintains for the art of Egon Schiele, a passion that dates back to the first Schiele drawing he acquired with money he received on the occasion of his Bar Mitzvah. It is his commitment to the best of Austrian and German art and design that has made the Neue Galerie a beloved museum, both in our home of New York and with visitors from around the world. His vision and generosity are truly extraordinary, and we reserve for him our greatest thanks.

Renée Price
Director, Neue Galerie New York

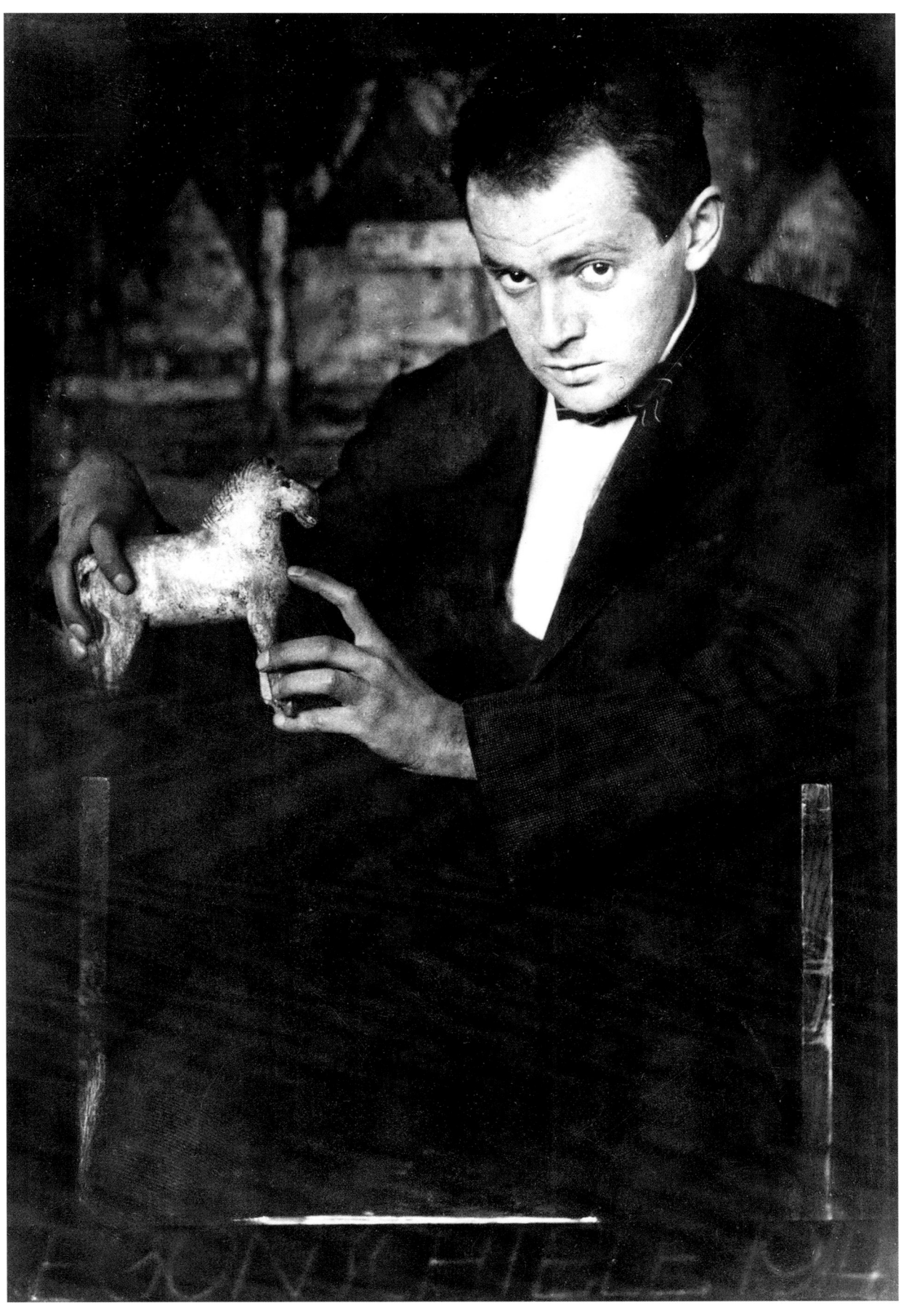

Johannes Fischer (?), Egon Schiele in his studio at 101 Hietzinger Hauptstrasse in Vienna, with *Houses by the Sea (Row of Houses)* in the bac‹ground, 1914. Photo: Brandstätter Archive

"EVERY TREE HAS ITS FACE"

SCHIELE'S LANDSCAPES AS SYMBOLIC PORTRAITS

Christian Bauer

Nature was without a doubt the great love of Egon Schiele's life. Reflection on landscape phenomena occupies a prominent role in the artist's work. When still a boy, Schiele's art began with the outward gaze: his early oil paintings are dominated by landscapes,[1] and his late work also focuses on landscape motifs, which form the largest group in his oeuvre in general.[2] Since the pioneering publication by Kimberly A. Smith,[3] Schiele scholars have reevaluated the importance of his landscapes.

This essay focuses on the relationship of plants, landscapes, and townscapes to the genre of the portrait. It is striking that Schiele separates the themes; the depiction of human beings in a landscape represents the exception—even if those exceptions are central, major works. Schiele could see himself embodying various manifestations, as is evident from numerous writings, including this poem: "I am everything at once but I'll never do everything at the same time."[4] Schiele is expressing here that he finds himself everywhere even when he cannot do everything at the same time; "do" in Schiele's sense refers to artistic work. The system of references between Schiele's self-portraits and landscapes represents a world of its own. Photo-graphs can thus establish a new connection for Schiele to the landscapes and pictorial spaces in a painting. That is demonstrated by the artist's performative engagement with his now-lost painting *Begegnung (Selbstbildnis mit der Figur eines Heiligen)* (Encounter [Self-Portrait with Saint]), captured in a photograph by Anton Josef Trčka [see ill. p. 7]. Here the artist extends the pictorial space by adding a strip of real space. The artist's connection to the painting is reinforced by him touching the work and is concentrated and spiritualized by Schiele's gaze.

Just as Schiele separated artistic genres and usually addressed portraiture and the land-scape individually, he developed a language in his works that is full of references to their subject matter. In the process he related the landscape to the human being and vice versa. This symbolism does not just characterize one period in his creative output but describes nearly all the phases of the artist's career, though the concentration varies. Looking at his oeuvre as a whole, Schiele is more aptly described as a Symbolist rather than as an Expressionist.[5] The stylistic expression in Schiele's art was constantly changing, but that is less true of the validity of a symbolic language that, while

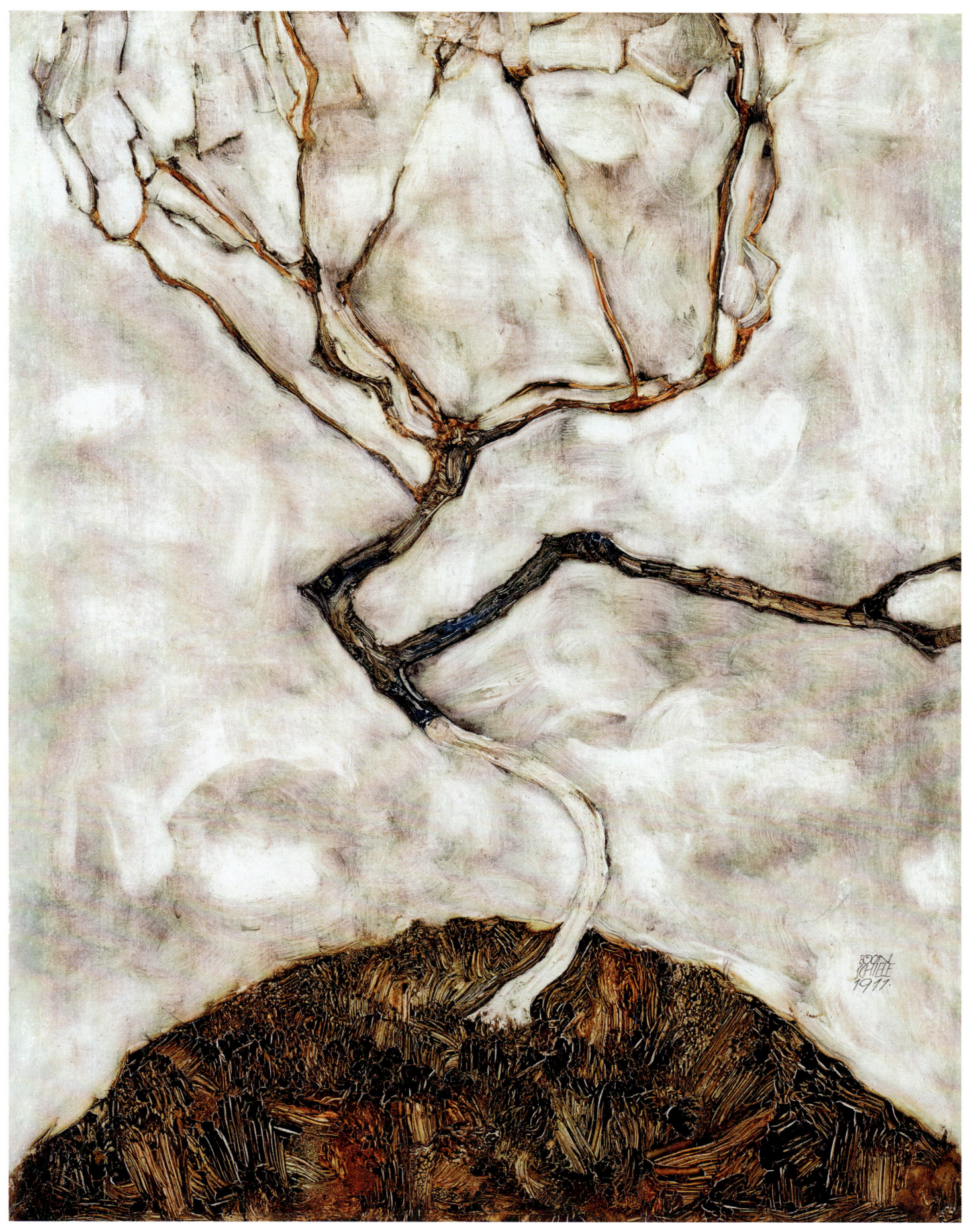

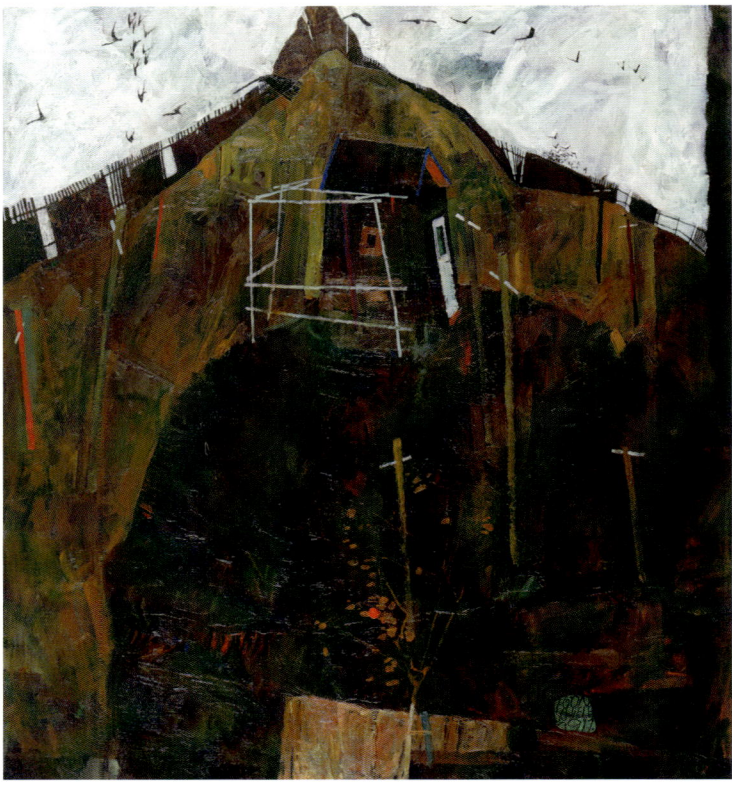

2. Egon Schiele, *Landscape with Ravens*, 1911, oil on canvas. Leopold Museum, Vienna (Kallir P216). Photo: Leopold Museum, Vienna

Opposite:

3. Egon Schiele, *Shrines in the Forest II*, 1915, oil on canvas. Kunsthaus Zug, Stiftung Sammlung Kamm, Zug (Kallir P296). Photo: akg-images

4. Johannes Fischer, Egon Schiele photographed with his painting *Shrines in the Forest II*, 1915. Private Collection

it did change from his early pictures to his final works, always had a determinantal dimension.

Schiele's written statements on landscapes are extensive and focus on subjective feeling, the individual, sensory perception, and they convey a myriad of impressions,[6]—hence there is considerable overlap with the artist's self-portraits. Often his text and his image convey a common idea about the symbolism of the visual works.

SCHIELE AS CHOSEN ONE AND SEER

Schiele's landscapes are to a large extent a mirror of his self-view; indeed, they all but evolve from it. Nevertheless, Schiele usually avoided placing a self-portrait in a landscape. His *Selbstbildnis mit der Pfauenweste, stehend* (Self-Portrait with Peacock Waistcoat, Standing) [Cat. no. 40] of 1911 is presented as

Schiele's most expressive solo self-portrait in a natural landscape[7] that survives.[8] This painting has a programmatic character for Schiele's self-view in general. As if in a manifesto, the artist reveals his perceived role in the world. Schiele confronts the viewer with unheard-of self-confidence, with the nimbus of a saint, in the most elegant clothing, on a meadow with flowers. A letter by Schiele dating from around the same time as the painting has come to light, which provides the opportunity to understand the painting in his own words. "A divine human being always leads the crowd!" Schiele remarked and summed it up: "So let it be said: that the artist is the only one who is the ruler, the dominator, of 100, 1000, and 10,000, that he creates only for himself, because it is the same as breathing."[9] Schiele is defining here a comprehensive claim to leadership and presents himself to the viewer in stately clothing as one of the chosen. The extent to which Schiele was elevating himself is also evident in a poem from 1910 about the "*lebend Primbegabten*" (the ones gifted with life and senses).[10] "An artist above all is the one of great spiritual gifts." For Schiele, it was about expressing "view of thinkable phenomena in nature," which distinguishes only a few artists.

Not only did Schiele see himself as a highly talented person who brought with him a new understanding of the world, but religion and landscape are fundamentally connected in Schiele's work. That becomes clear in a poem from 1910: "The highest sentiment is religion and art. Nature is purpose, but God is there, and I sense him powerfully, very powerfully, most powerfully."[11] Schiele is expressing here his nature-God sentiment, which is also reflected in his artistic work.

That the meadow with flowers in the self-portrait [Cat. no. 40] was not chosen haphazardly and incorporates a divine dimension is also made clear by this nearly contemporaneous text: "For the public, parks […] too raw to sense the divine in everyone; that is why it needs churches to be able to imagine a God, since meanwhile he breathes much more clearly in a field."[12]

The connection of Schiele's self-view to a divine dimension that he perceived in himself and in nature is a key to understanding the artist's work.

THE DIVINE DIMENSION OF LANDSCAPE

Schiele recognized a manifestation of God in nature. Schiele's profound religiousness has little to do with faith in the traditional sense. On the contrary, the artist fundamentally rejected faith in the confessional sense; for him, the common forms of religion were linked to a hated system of rules, as this passage demonstrates: "I do not want to speak or write to people in uniform or with ranks and titles, because they could recognize all of their respective schools in life, like the Catholics their faith and the Protestants theirs. Every believer is thus a weakling!"[13] Schiele viewed socially accepted dogma in the practice of the institutional church and rejected it "What is every rule for?"[14] he asked in that context.

Schiele's religious view of nature was closely connected to the intellectual world of Romanticism and with movements of the period around 1900, as Helena Pereña has convincingly demonstrated. The monism propagated by Ernst Haeckel sought a unity between religion and the natural sciences, in which reflections that set out from Charles Darwin were associated with a concept of nature that is equated with God.[15]

Schiele's *Landschaft mit Raben* (Landscape with Ravens) [Fig. 2] of 1911 illustrates

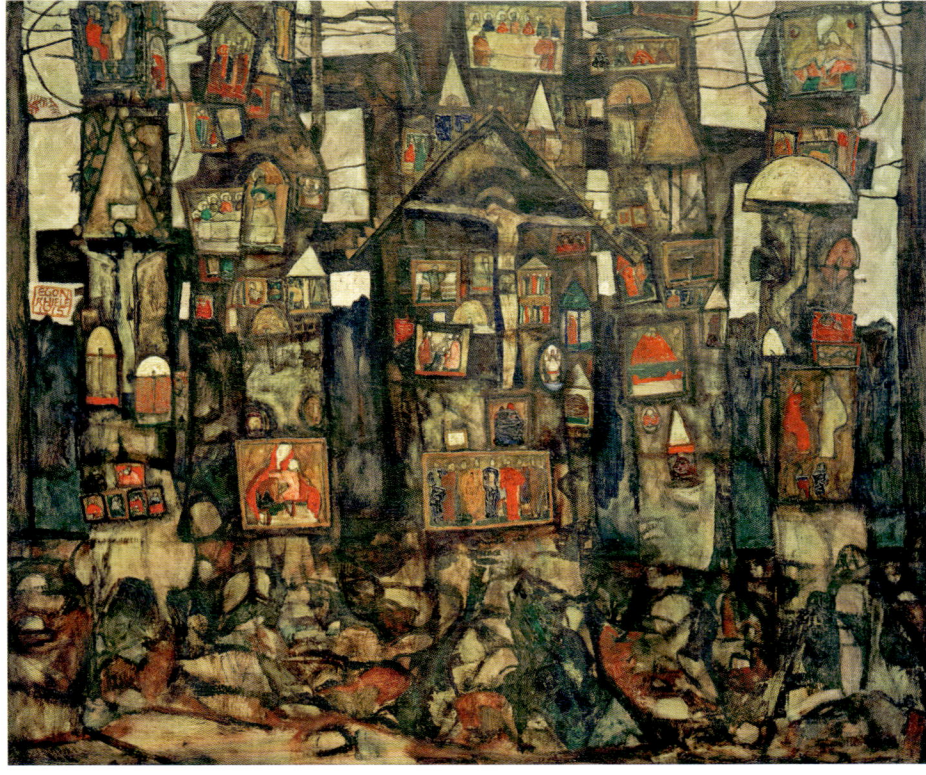

the divine dimension of nature and can be described with a text by the artist: "No, outside in the raging autumn storm or high up on cliffs where rare flowers are for them they can sense God." A hill with a crooked hut; a fence full of gaps in the background; in the pictorial field, stakes like tomb crosses; in the foreground, a nearly leafless autumn tree. All these things are signs of ephemerality and death. "[A] landscape envisioned as a cathedral," as Rudolf Leopold noted.[16]

The forest can also become a cathedral—what Pereña called a five-nave church—as a juxtaposition of the poem "*Tannenwald*" (Fir Woods) with Schiele's painting *Waldandacht II* (Shrines in the Forest II) [Fig. 3] illustrates. With its dense collection of panel paintings, the setting evokes a sacred space. "I enter into the reddish-black cathedral of the dense fir woods,"[17]

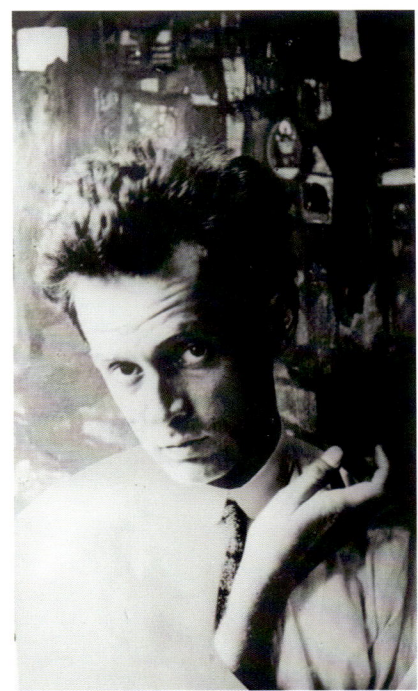

Schiele wrote in 1910. The individual pictures that crowd their way into the forest can be understood as works by Schiele by looking at the composition and coloration. Here, too, Schiele achieved a new dimension of self-presentation—through his paintings. The artist's presence in the woods results from his artistic intervention, not from his self-portrait.

In a photograph from 1915 [Fig. 4], Schiele unambiguously refers to the painting *Shrines in the Forest II*. He looks at the viewer and gestures to the painting behind him. By doing so, Schiele established a connection to the painting that he linked directly to himself. The reference can be considered a clue to the author-

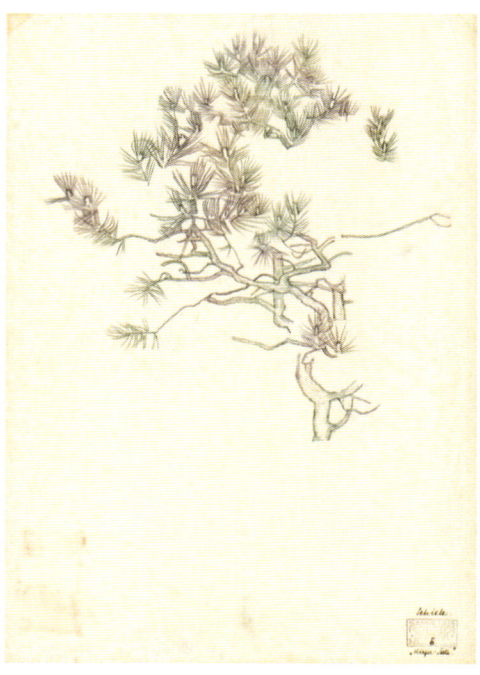

ship of the painting and to the artworks of the forest in the painting.

POSITIVE AND NEGATIVE FORM: THE ABSENT AND REFLECTIONS OF REALITY

The fact that Schiele usually separates genres, keeping landscape and portrait apart, but, very much in contrast to that, employs a symbolism that leads from the one to the other, calls attention to what is missing in his paintings. What is consciously left out? Looking at Schiele's works in this way reveals a principle of the dialogue with the invisible that has a significance for the artist's work that is still underestimated.

A "disconcerting presence of the absent" is recognizable in numerous works by Schiele.[18] This method comes through even in the landscape motifs and includes studies such as *Kiefernäste* (Pine Branches) [Fig. 5] of 1915. The motif represents a puzzle, showing the branches with young shoots and needles that the tree as a whole lacks. The connecting

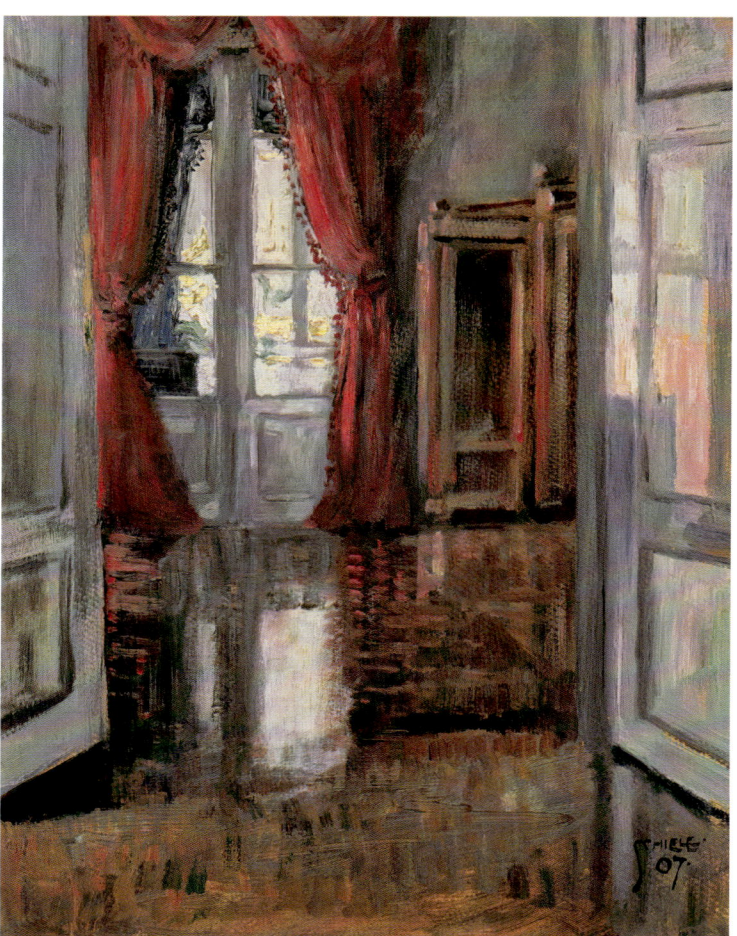

branches are just as much interrupted as their connection to the tree remains mysterious. This approach is a play between the levels of reality of the representation: a back and forth between the projection screen of the sheet of the drawing and the illusion of what it depicts. "The image-intensifying rhetoric of the plane is indebted to the ability to point. And because the elemental linear works also point to the deception of pointing, no illusion of pure being results. Everything seems unfinished and provisional."[19]

This intensity of representing indecisions is indebted to Schiele's concept of ambivalence. The multiple interpretation as signs of lots of solely valid truths is a central insight of the modern era. Schiele responds to it throughout his oeuvre; he leaves the universally valid behind and replaces it with changing gazes—indebted to the subjectivity of the viewer. Now there is no longer any determining reality; reality is broken down into numerous viewing angles and interpretations. In Schiele's case, this insight occurs already in his mid-teens, when he began studying at the academy.

Schiele portrayed no one more frequently than he did Leopold Czihaczek, and nearly all of the portraits of him dispense with any attempt to convey a spatial context. In the painting *Blick in die Wohnung von Leopold und Marie Czihaczek (Interieur)* (View into the Apartment of Leopold and Marie Czihaczek [Interior]) [Fig. 6], Schiele's uncle, godfather, and guardian is depicted by his lifestyle. The opulent salon of his city apartment and draped curtains as a sign of premodern taste mirror a resident who is described but not shown. The center of the image is a void, which is enlivened only by reflections of the exterior—just like the pair of doors in the foreground. Stylistically, the painting is a not very expressive early work, almost a quotidian painting; in its subject matter, the

seventeen-year-old Schiele reveals here an impressive maturity, exploring the limits of the depictable and turning pictorial traditions upside down. The resident is not presented in his interior; the focus is on empty planes that provide for the reflections.

The play between reality and mirror image is taken to the extreme that following year in the painting *Jodokuskirche, sich im Fluss spiegelnd (Krumau)* (St. Jodocus Church Reflected in the River [Krumau]) [Fig. 7], since the image should appear inverted. Two-thirds of the picture plane corresponds to the mirror image in the water, not the actual appearance of the buildings. After completing the painting, Schiele reversed the work, signed it, and thus swapped reality with the mirror image. The reflection has taken the place of the real.

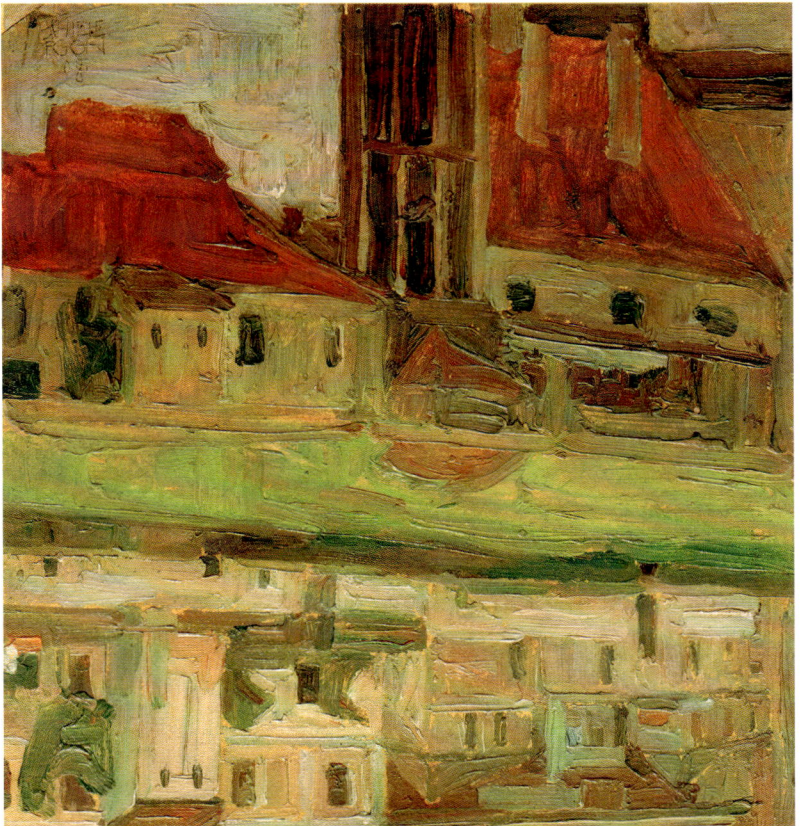

7. Egon Schiele, *St. Jodocus Church Reflected in the River (Krumau)*, 1908, oil on paper. Tiroler Landesmuseen, Innsbruck (Kallir P131). Photo: akg-images

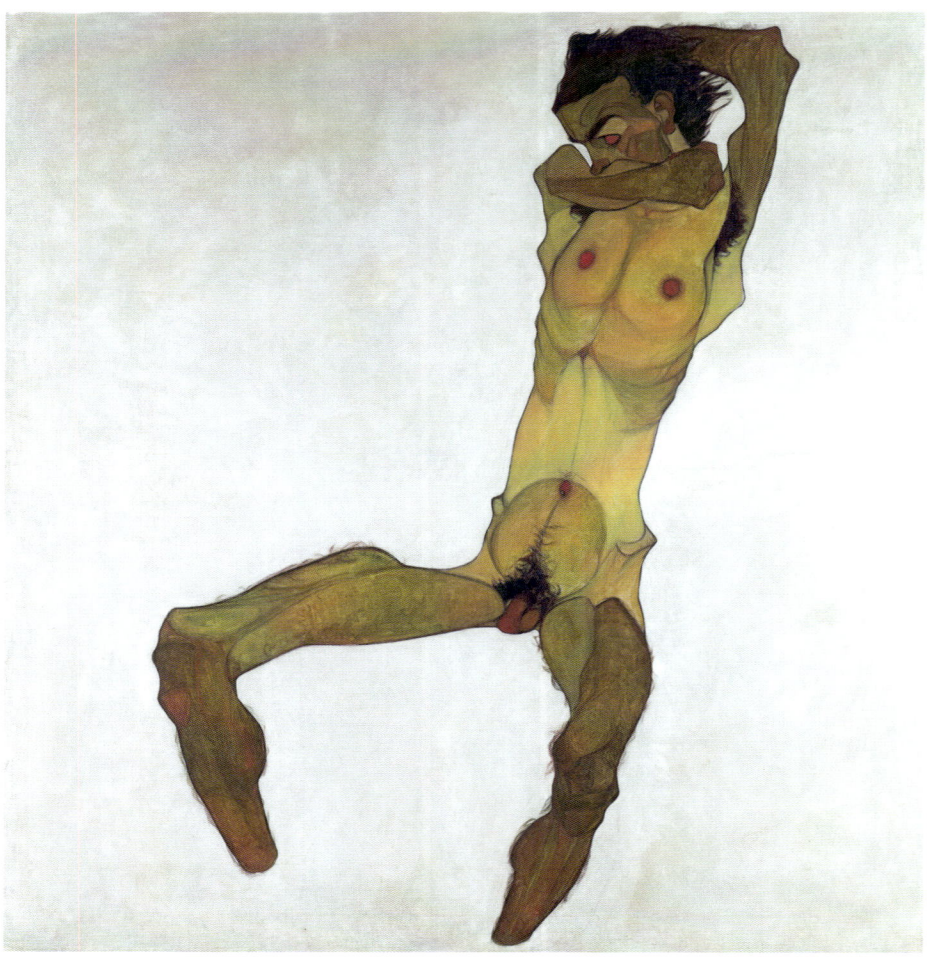

8. Egon Schiele, *Seated Male Nude (Self-Portrait)*, 1910, oil and gouache on canvas. Leopold Museum, Vienna (Kallir P172). Photo: Leopold Museum, Vienna

THE HUMAN IMAGE IN ITS SPATIAL CONTEXT: AMBIGUITIES AND TRANSFORMATIONS

Ambiguities and contradictions also accompany the structure of relationships between human beings and their spatial and landscape surroundings.

Schiele calls into question and blurs pictorial traditions. This is true first and foremost of the topos of portrait likeness, which Schiele buffets. The self-portrait shows most clearly how little Schiele wants to tie himself to the external confines of his body. This leads to blurring the sex characteristics in nudes and is indebted to the principle of not organizing the

characterization of a person around his physiognomic and physical features.

Usually, the placement of the figures is blurred as well: Schiele avoids clear assignment to spatial and landscape contexts. This creates the impression that Schiele is often exploring the choice of pictorial themes and avoiding all unambiguity.

A good example of this is *Bildnis der Gerti Schiele* (Portrait of Gerti Schiele) [Cat. no. 38] of 1909. Not only did the nineteen-year-old Schiele achieve a masterly interplay of showing and conceiving, but he also managed to blur his essential pictorial ideas. The result is a painting that brilliantly evades a clear interpretation and immediately relativizes any determination. The sitter, the artist's sister, is difficult to grasp as a human being here. First, her resting state leads beyond sleep into a lingering, like a natural phenomenon; also borrowed from nature are her brown skin tone and the depiction of her splendid hairdo. It is equally unclear whether she is sitting or leaning; the location of the action enhances these contradictions. Gerti is leaning or sitting on a chair, which, covered with a blanket, is standing on a meadow, which is placed in turn on the white of the picture like an island. Or is the meadow merely the back of the covering of a chair? The piece of a cape over her right shoulder suggests that is the case; the plants on the lower left growing out of it that it is not. This deliberate contrasting of what is depicted with features of an alternative world—here as a play between exterior and interior—is a principle in Schiele's work that is revealed especially in the coexistence of human being and landscape.

The sitter seems to be undergoing a transformation—a state between human being and natural phenomenon—on a meadow with flowers that is spread out like a carpet, a back and forth between different pictorial contexts: the lack of unambiguity is pushed to the extreme.

The situation is similar in a painting that for a long time was mistakenly known as *Danaë* [Cat. no. 37]. Franz Smola has shown that it must be the work *Jugendströmung* (Current of Youth), which Schiele presented in the "Internationale Kunstschau" (International Art Show) of 1909.[20] Against a backdrop of birds sitting on tree branches, a hybrid of carpet and meadow flows like a waterfall in the center of the image and frames a red-haired female figure. Here, too, every unambiguity is avoided, resulting in a wonderful enigma of a painting.

Interiors could also become natural phenomena of formations of materials, as is evident from the monumental painting *Mann und Frau I (Liebespaar I)* (Man and Woman [Lovers I]). [Cat. no. 42] of 1914. This view from above is constructed as a multifaceted landscape that causes the carpet to resemble a formation of fields and the blanket like a mountain massif. The interior is thus defamiliarized as much as Schiele's self-portrait, which lurches out at the viewer like a lifeless and powerless body in a brownish-blue that suggests death and is completely brown down in its linearity. The body seems to be undergoing a transformation, which also affects the position of the arms, which Renée Price has compared to crab claws.[21] The loss of fleshiness was also noticed by contemporaries and the couple described as being in the approximate shape of a scorpion.[22]

THE METAMORPHOSIS OF THE PERSON PORTRAYED

Just how much a self-presentation can become a monumental transformation is demonstrated by Schiele's *Sitzender männlicher Akt (Selbstbildnis)* (Seated Male Nude [Self-Portrait]) [Fig. 8] of 1910. With his legs

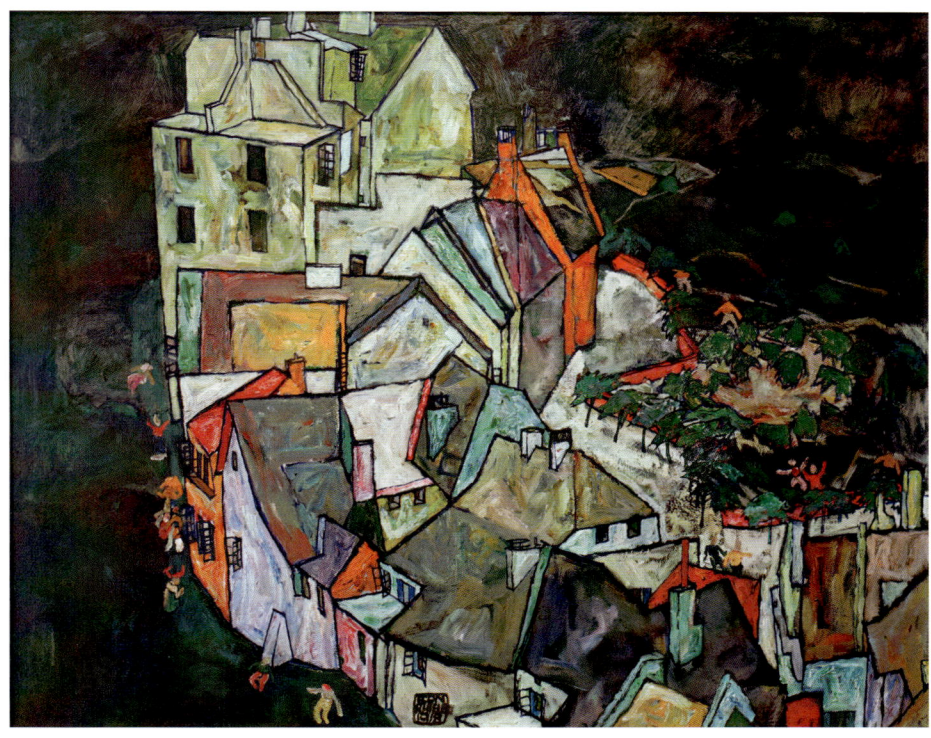

spread wide, his body undergoes a transformation into a hybrid creature that unites plant and insect features. His legs evoke landscape formations; his limbs appear encrusted. Schiele shares this artistic reflection on physical metamorphoses with other artists, as Eva Werth noted with reference to Franz Kafka. In 1912, in his novella *Die Verwandlung* (*The Metamorphosis*), the author gave an account of the transformation of a human being into vermin, the agonizing course of which leads to isolation and death. As different as these works are, both authors dramatically describe sensations over the course of a physical metamorphosis. "Kafka and Schiele intend to present the inside by means of the outside."[23]

At the end of his life, Schiele created an enigmatic work that brings the connection of portrait and landscape into a new dimension. We owe central insights into this painting to Paul Bernhard Eipper, a restorer who

9. Egon Schiele, *Edge of Town (Krumau Town Crescent III)*, 1917–18, oil on canvas. Neue Galerie, Joanneum, Graz (Kallir P331). Photo: akg-images

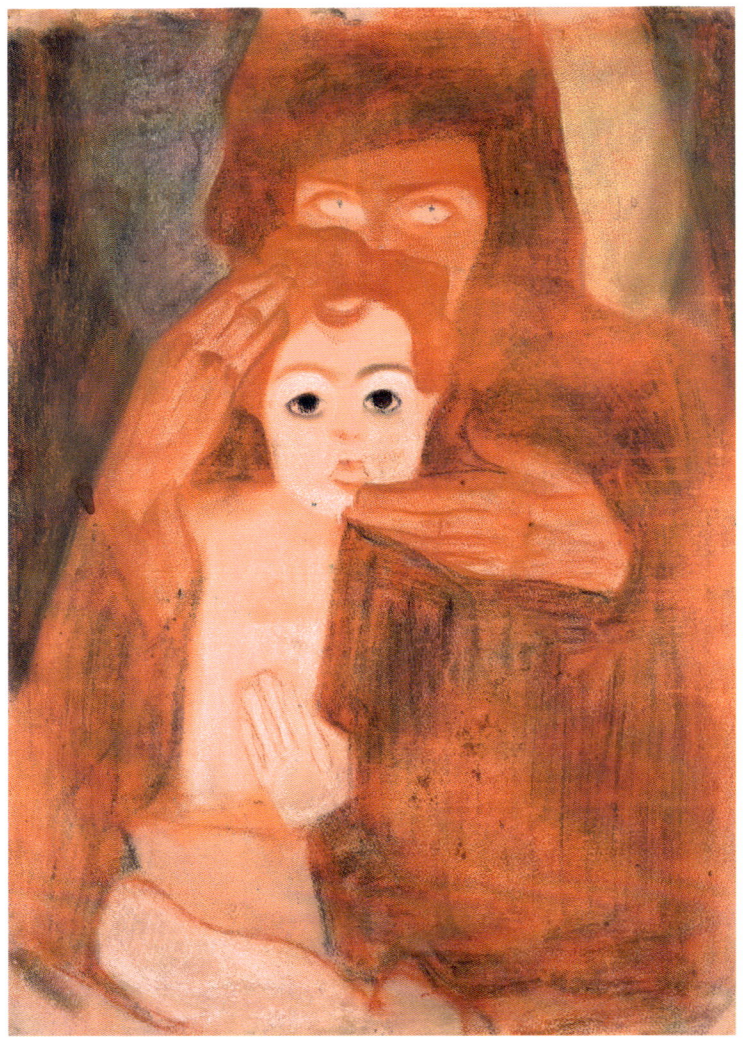

10. Egon Schiele, *Mother and Child (Madonna)*, 1908, sanguine, charcoal, and white chalk on paper. Landessammlungen Niederösterreich, St. Pölten (Kallir D245)

Opposite:

11. Egon Schiele, *Sunflower II*, 1909, oil on canvas. Wien Museum, Vienna (Kallir P159)

the city with the individual houses transitions into the natural landscape in the middle right of the painting, the portrait has been reworked but remains clearly visible.

One is struck by the extent to which Schiele not only retains essential parts of the portrait head but also defaces them with the tops of trees and plants that grow out of the eyes, nose, mouth, and hair. In addition, there are small figures of people, often gesturing powerfully, on the edges, who are very clearly leading to the portrait and marking it.

PLANTS AS ANALOGIES TO THE IMAGE OF THE HUMAN BEING

The connection between the portrait and the depiction of plants in Schiele's work can be grasped more clearly with a recently discovered letter from the artist. Until now, a later letter from Schiele to Franz Hauer from August 1913 has been referred to in this context: "For the most part, I am now observing the physical movement of mountains, water, trees, and flowers. Everywhere one is reminded of similar movements in the human body, of similar stirrings of joy and suffering in plants."[25] This text provides an understanding of landscape motifs in Schiele's visual world, but here it is limited to identifying analogies between human beings and plants.

A letter that Schiele had written to Josef Hoffmann [Cat. no. 20] three years earlier on September 20, 1910,[26] is in many respects even more revealing. It introduces Schiele's most central creative phase and forms the basis for the explosive development of his expressive language of words and images.

The letter is distinguished by its striving for utter clarity in its tone; poetic formulations are linked to a narrative mode of language. After interpreting the facial expressions of peo-

has elucidated uncommonly well the painting *Stadtende (Krumau Häuserbogen III)* (Edge of Town [Krumau Town Crescent III]) [Fig. 9] by examining its materials and painting technique. This work was repeatedly reproduced for nearly a century without being properly understood. The central observation is that there are two portraits that Schiele rejected under the painting.[24] Whereas one of the two portraits was painted over, the second one was not only integrated into the later landscape but illustrated symbolically. The format was rotated and, precisely where the depiction of

ple and a reference to the contemporaneous self-portraits, Schiele notes: "I can speak with all living creatures, even with plants and stones; speak, speak directly into their face, into their essence. Every tree has its face; I recognize its kind of eyes, its kind of arms, its components, its organism. I want to be addressed by everything!—My act is the answer." This is not an analogy but the description of the body parts of plants and a reference to the talent for communication. "My act is the answer" is explained in the subsequent postscript of the letter, in which Schiele says that he wants to offer and exhibit bigger answers. Thus the act is tied to creative work. Speaking with flowers is found only in a poem by Schiele from around the same time, which was incorporated into a letter to Anton Peschka. "I want […] to speak to flowers, flowers."[27]

That Schiele formulates speaking in a new quality as "speaking into" is unique in his writings, but it can be explained quite convincingly by reference to other formulations. Schiele finds in this choice of words a simile of intensity, understanding, and related essence, as a comparison makes clear. "Speaking into" is that kind of speaking that only a few chosen ones are capable of, and Schiele clearly included himself. In two letters from the following year,[28] we see "*hineinschauen*" (looking into) as an instruction to penetrate an image and the explanation of a visual figure that "melts into" another figure.[29]

Analogies and design principles in Schiele's literary and visual work show how much the two genres are intimately connected. Schiele's paintings of people and of landscapes are just as essentially related and connected in a highly differentiated symbolism. Flowers and trees take the place of the human being. Sunflowers play a central role here. They are found throughout Schiele's oeuvre.

SUNFLOWERS AS A FORM OF REPRESENTING LIFE AND DEATH

It begins with the painting *Sonnenblume I* (Sunflower I) [Cat. no. 25] of 1908, which was completed during a period when Schiele was studying in Vienna and was allowed to participate for the first time in a group exhibition in Klosterneuburg, a small town near Vienna.

Comparing this painting to an early work from the same year—*Mutter mit Kind (Madonna)* (Mother with Child [Madonna]) [Fig. 10]— shows not only that sunflowers are grasped as the mirror image of the human being but also exposes a central dimension of the meaning of sunflowers. Both works put the mother-and-child theme in the center. The red chalk drawing reproduces a contrast in the rendering of an almost lifeless maternal figure and the child bursting with energy. The sunflower painting reveals something similar. Once again, the approaching death of the "mother," whose lack of energy is evident from the drooping leaves, is contrasted with the vital life energy of the three young flowers. The freshly opened yellow flowers press against the discolored, heavy leaves and resist decay.

Sonnenblume II (Sunflower II) [Fig. 11] of 1909 is even more closely related to the human image. In this work, the plant appears in an extended vertical format, while numerous elements from the earlier painting have been retained. Once again, the mother flower, wilted in autumn, is shown in the company of young flowers that radiate energy, and the depiction—of the enraptured landscape—is placed against a white background. The later version presents the flower on an island with dense rows of flowers that resemble a pedestal.

Here, the components of the sunflower are formed similarly to human limbs. Two large leaves mimic arms, while the stalk and

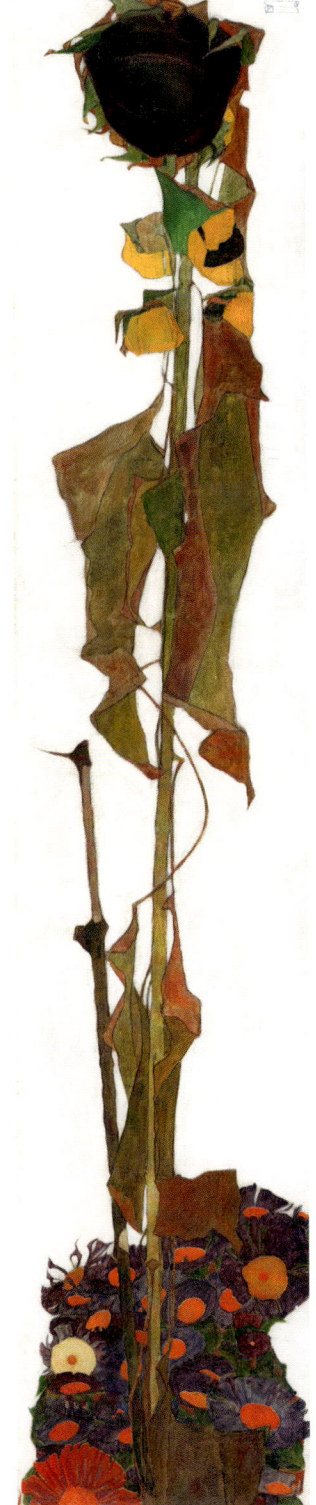

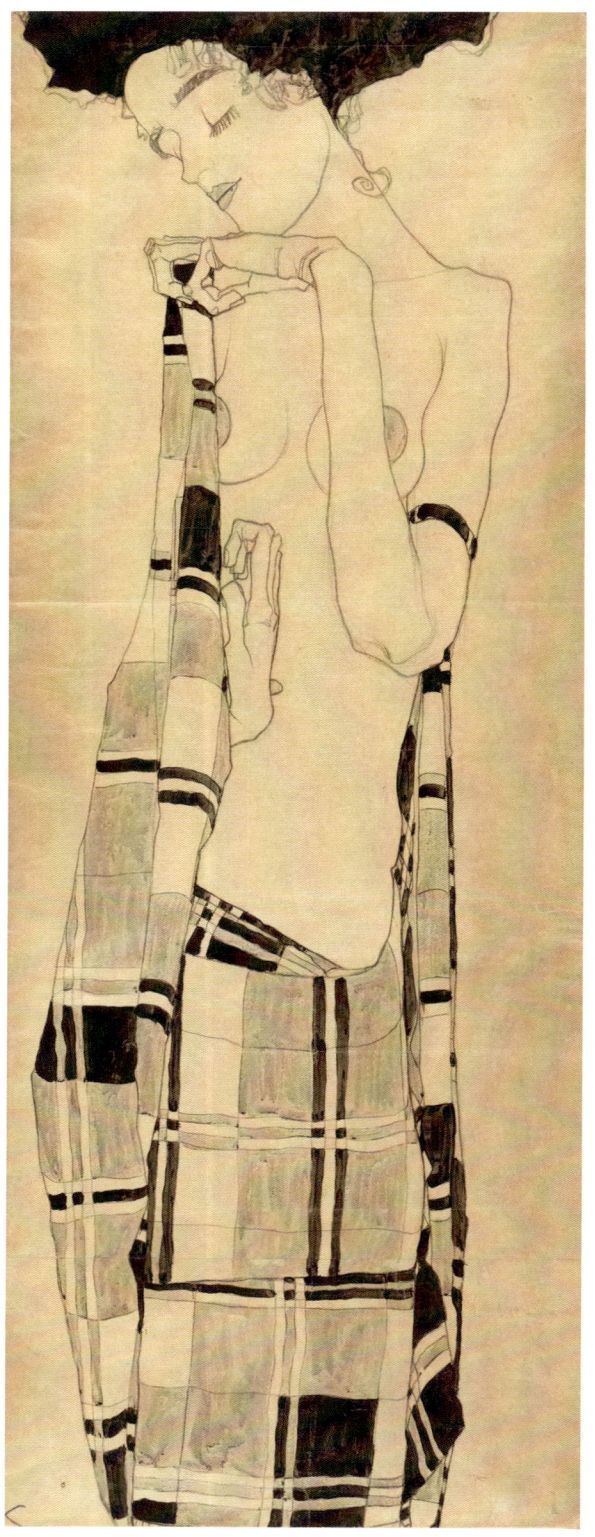

drooping leaves are shaped like legs, suggesting an analogy to the motif of striding. The impression of aging and approaching death is reinforced by the bent stalk, which evokes a crutch. This work can be compared to contemporaneous portraits in an extended vertical format, such as the portrait *Stehendes Mädchen in kariertem Tuch* (Standing Girl in Plaid Garment) [Fig. 12] of 1909–10.

This account already makes it clear that Schiele belongs primarily to Symbolism, and the sunflower should be seen above all as a representative that shows decay. The "death mask communicates the message of mortality, of pain, of anxiety, and of human suffering."[30] The dying of the mother flower contrasts with the growing of the new, strong generation. Without question Schiele saw himself as a chosen one in the transition of generations. That same year, he drafted the manifesto of the Neukunstgruppe (New Art Group) as the declaration of the battle of a new generation of artists against an aging art world.

Two years later, in the painting *Sonnenblumen* (Sunflowers) [Fig. 13], Schiele condensed the drama of the birth and death of generations in a group of flowers swaying the wind, which, pushed together, is exposed to the drama of autumn. Once again, the depiction is removed from any natural context and presented against a white background.

Dying, wilting, and ceasing to exist in contrast with resplendent life remain the central symbolism of this genre in the years to follow, as illustrated by the painting *Welke Sonnenblumen (Herbstsonne II)* (Wilted Sunflowers [Autumn Sun II]) [Cat. no. 30] of 1914. A landscape is suggested by the meadow and mountain on the right side and a feeble autumn sun is visible through the grid of sunflowers. Now the entire group of flowers appears wilted and

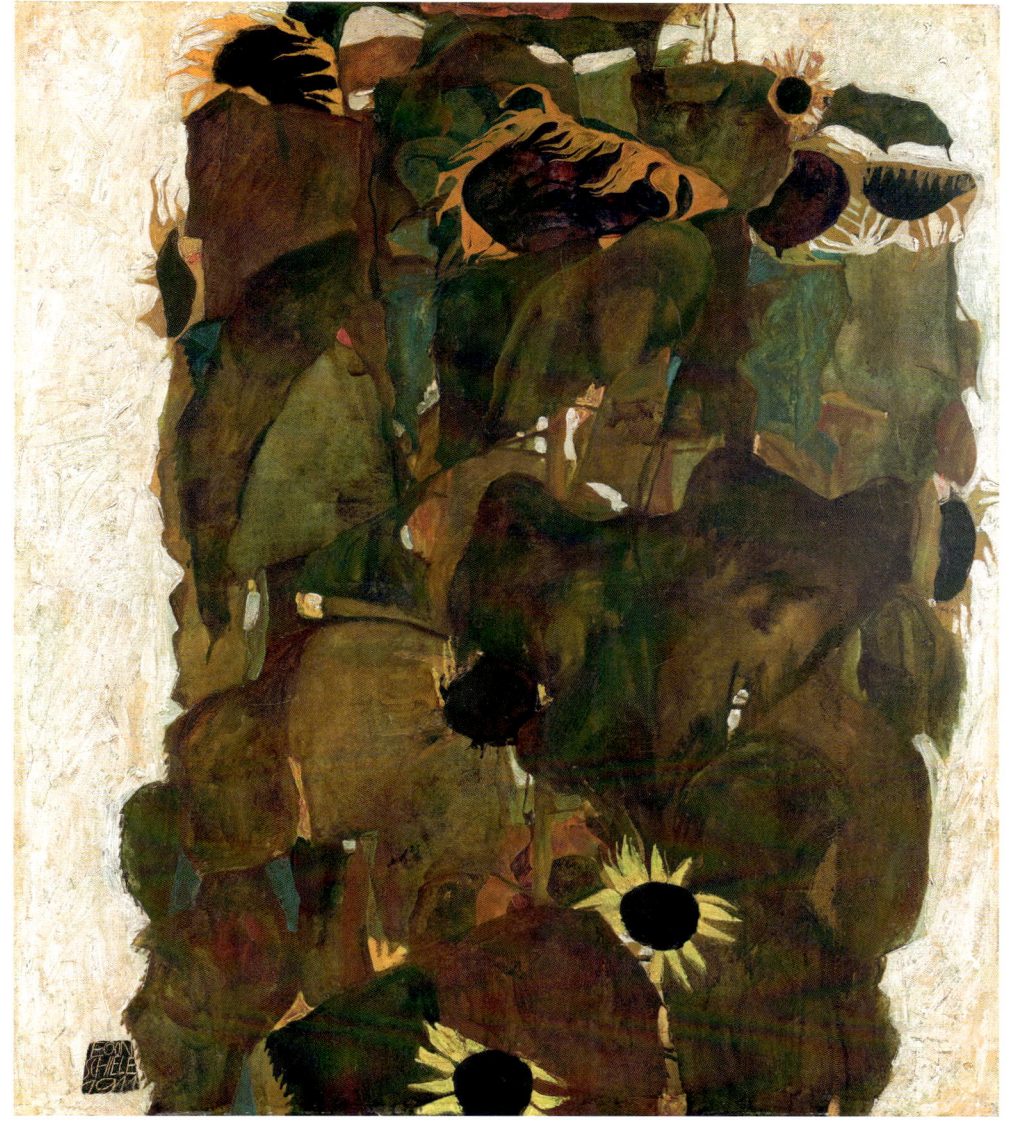

Opposite:

12. Egon Schiele, *Standing Girl in Plaid Garment*, 1909–10, conté crayon and tempera wash over black chalk on wrapping paper. Minneapolis Institute of Art, The John R. Van Derlip Fund and gift from Dr. Otto Kallir (Kallir D541)

13. Egon Schiele, *Sunflowers*, 1911, oil on canvas. Belvedere, Vienna (Kallir P221). Photo: Johannes Stoll / Belvedere, Vienna

doomed to die, whereas the flowers on the meadow are in full bloom.

With the sunflowers and their symbolism, Schiele surpasses his role models. He overcomes the decorative qualities of Gustav Klimt's works and also counters the sunflowers of Vincent van Gogh, with their glorious hunger for life, with a visual language that makes allowance for uncertainty, isolation, exposure, aging, and death as well as for the new generation of "young flowers" to which Schiele himself felt connected.

AUTUMN TREES AS MIRROR OF THE SELF

Schiele also saw the isolated human being in depictions of leafless trees. Schiele described how much he saw them as analogous to the portrait when he said: "Every tree has its face; I recognize its kind of eyes, its kind of arms, its components, its organism."[31]

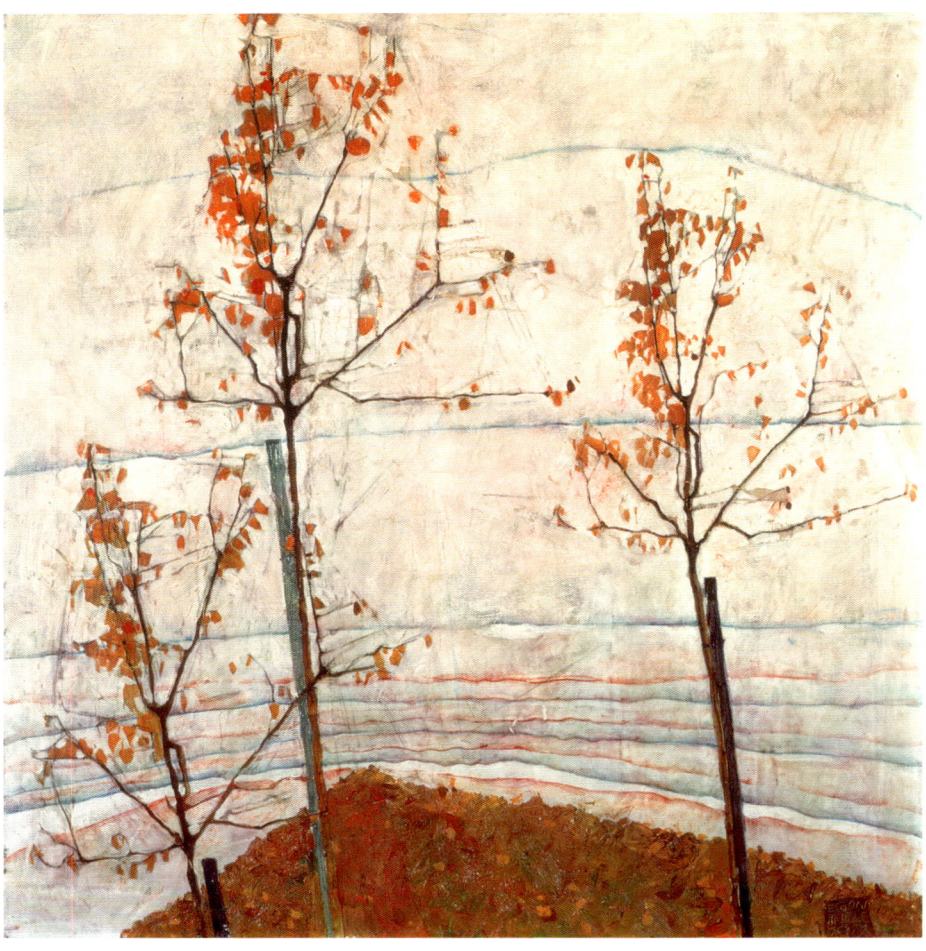

14. Egon Schiele, *Autumn Trees I*, 1911, oil on canvas. Dichand Collection, Vienna (Kallir P218). Image courtesy Kallir Research Institute, New York

Ein Baum im Spätherbst (A Tree in Late Autumn) [Fig. 1] of 1911 can be considered against this backdrop. It has a number of possibilities for comparison to the image of the human being. A slender tree is seen on a hill; its trunk and branches unfold in curves, bends, and gestures. This movement is further heightened by the drama of the background, which flickers menacingly in light and dark fields.

The tree, whose barren isolation becomes the central motif of the painting, appears to stride, dance, or sprain its leg. The analogies to the human image are obvious. Along with the "nakedness" of the tree, numerous

shared features with Schiele's contemporaneous self-portraits are evident—the isolation, the expressive tension, and the nudity. The tree's "anthropomorphic form" takes over "completely the place of the human being; it thus becomes an allegory and a parable of life."[32] In that respect Schiele learns from the example of Giovanni Segantini and Ferdinand Hodler and creates a parable that—borrowed from Romanticism—is transferred to the modern era.

Baum hinter einem Zaun (Tree behind a Fence) (Kallir P238) of the following year intensifies the drama of the motif by the choice of an animated application of paint with thick brushstrokes that underscores an atmosphere of seething unrest. In addition, a fence dominated by yellow encloses the tree on two sides. The strong presence of the fence contrasts with its senselessness, which is evident from its warped form on the verge of collapse.

In addition to depictions of threatened human existence in the subject of the leafless tree in autumn as an analogy to the portrait, repeated images establish a connection to the portrait. The common feature is a multiplication of the subject. The painting *Herbstbäume* (Autumn Trees) [Fig. 14] of 1911 only appears to have three trees as its subject. On closer inspection, a single tree has been tripled in nearly all details. Schiele also applies this multiplicity in portraits and self-portraits as in *Dreifaches Selbstbildnis* (Triple Self-Portrait) of 1913, for example [Fig. 15].

THE TOWNSCAPE AS PORTRAIT AND AS PART OF THE SELF-PORTRAIT

The townscape plays a dominant role in Schiele's oeuvre; it results in works of extraordinary quality whose symbolism, here too, is connected to the artist's self-view.

Schiele presumably participated in the urban life of imperial Vienna, with its theater and opera offerings and diverting entertainments in bars, cafés, and soirées, but his visual world does not reflect that. His remarks on Vienna, too, are often dismissive: "Everybody is envious of me and deceitful; former colleagues look at me with dissembling eyes, in Vienna there is only shadow, the city is black, everything is done by recipe."[33]

One can surely speak of Schiele having a love-hate relationship, but his written rejection of Vienna was nothing more than a contemporaneous fashion, concealing the desire for an alternative life. Nevertheless, Schiele enjoyed the pleasurable aspects of the metropolis on the Danube and spent his entire life within a short distance of Vienna. The centers of the separate phases of Schiele's life—Tulln, Klosterneuburg, Neulengbach—are also located approximate to the capital of the monarchy on the Danube. It was thus more about artistic considerations than about the contexts of his life when Schiele consistently developed his visual world outside of urban centers.

Krumau (Český Krumlov) became a subject as early as 1906. Schiele then traveled to the birth city of his mother every year until 1911.[34] Here, too, Schiele's way of life and artistic reflections diverged. Schiele participated actively in the social life of the town in Bohemia, together with Peschka and Erwin Osen. Schiele was also involved with experiments with flight and was tied to an airplane along with air cushions.[35] None of that—technology and social life—played any role in Schiele's Krumau works. On the contrary, the town is consistently depicted as empty of people and devoid of technology. That confirms once again Schiele's principle of rigorously demarcating the realm of his art from the world of his life. One gets the impression that Schiele saw in Krumau a

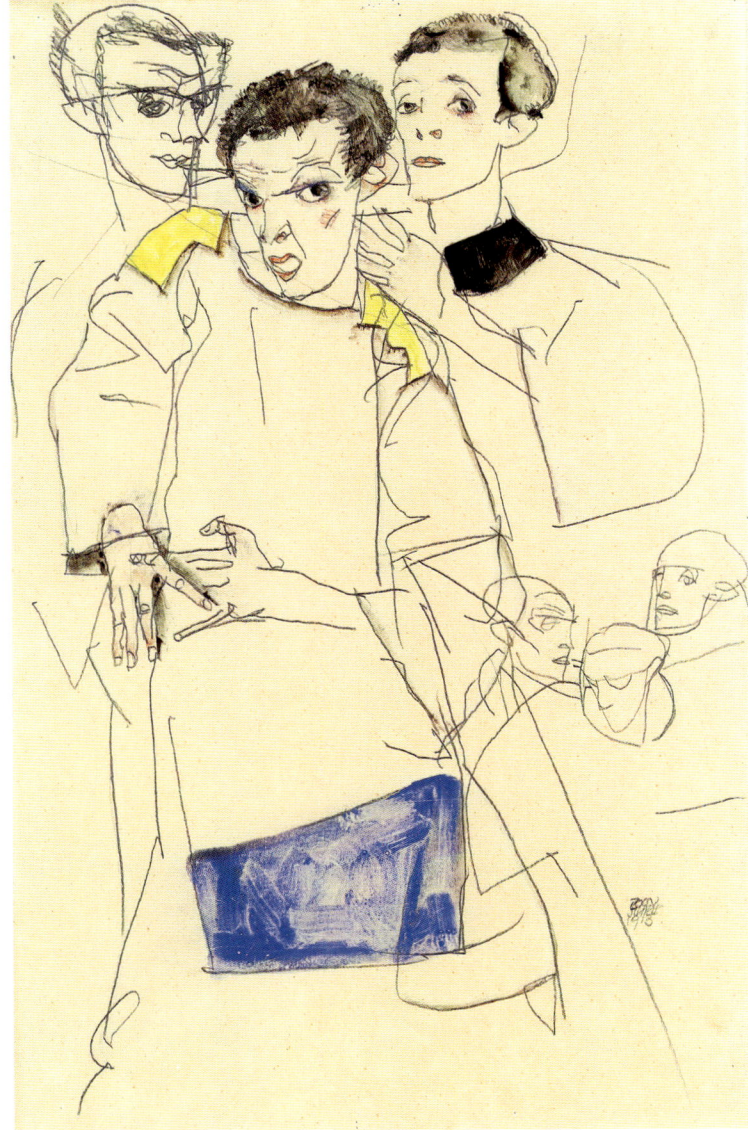

new dimension in the parable of himself and the city: "I affirm that I want to live in Krumau for years, perhaps forever—there where I most see myself."[36] That he saw himself in the town is also suggested by the fact that Schiele symbolically placed depictions of Krumau in the background of two self-portraits that are now lost: *Weltwehmut (Selbstbildnis)* (Melancholia [Self-Portrait]) of 1910 [Fig. 16] and *Delirien* (Delirium) of 1911 [see ill. on p. 58].[37]

15. Egon Schiele, *Triple Self-Portrait*, 1913, gouache, watercolor, and pencil on paper. Private Collection (Kallir D1425)

The paintings of the *Tote Stadt* (Dead City) series represent a culmination of the depictions of Krumau. All of these works capture the city from above; the preferred vantage point is the Krumauer Schloss (Krumau Castle), from which he recorded details of the city. Schiele had already experimented with this view from above in 1908;[38] it becomes the principle for the paintings of the *Dead City* series, most of which are in shades of brown. Schiele justified the view from above to Leopold Liegler in response to a question whether the view had been inspired by Brueghel's works: "Not really, that forced itself on me in Krumau. There you learn to observe the world from above and in the eccentricity of such a view, the usualness of views from above, to appreciate a value in painting and drawing."[39]

Dying, wilting, autumn are all favorite motifs of Schiele across all genres; even in the allegorical self-portraits, the character of ephemerality is omnipresent. It is therefore not surprising that Schiele applied this attitude to the townscape. The first work titled *Tote Stadt* (Dead City) is *Stadt am blauen Fluss I (Tote Stadt I)* (City on the Blue River I [Dead City I]) of 1910 [Cat. no. 44]; five additional versions were produced in the following years. This title was described by Albert Paris Gütersloh in his preface to the catalogue of Schiele's first solo exhibition at the Galerie Miethke in 1911: "He calls a city he sees looking down from above foreshortened 'dead.' Because it becomes that when looked at that way. The meaning behind the bird's-eye view has been guessed unconsciously. The title is of equal value as an insight as the painting it names."[40] Schiele himself pointed to its significance in an autobiographical account from 1910: "then began the times of leisure and the lifeless schools. I came to endless dead cities and mourned for myself."[41] Regardless, from the late nineteenth century onward the description of old towns as dead or dying had not been unusual, as evidenced,

for example, by Georges Rodenbach's novel *Bruges-la-Morte*.[42]

The first work of the series established essential elements. A group of houses around the old town mill, seen from the plateau of the castle, is tightly packed and looks like an island—with the Moldau (now Vltava) River flowing around it. The coloration varies between shades of brown and dark blue; here, too, colors of death dominate. Schiele is not a chronicler of the decline of old towns; he seems to have been less interested in the topography or in documenting the aging town than in a dimension of reflecting on himself.

Just how unimportant precise topography can be is demonstrated by *Häuser am Fluss II (Die Alte Stadt II)* (Houses by the River II [The Old City II]) [Cat. no. 58] of 1914. Although the Jodokuskirche (St. Jodocus Church)—without its spire—is recognizably the center of the painting, the townscape has been reordered. The group of houses has been arranged freely and incorporated into a newly created landscape with a range of hills in the background.

The painting *Stadt im Grünen (Die alte Stadt III)* (Town among Greenery [The Old City III]) [Cat. no. 68] achieves complete freedom in its approach to the topographic facts. A view from the Kreuzberg (Cross Mountain) of Krumau over the row of houses toward the outskirts of the town may have inspired the painting, but ultimately the image breaks completely with that detail of the town.

VIEWS OF KREMS: SELF-VIEW AND PLACES OF YEARNING

Schiele traveled through the twin towns of Krems-Stein all his life and felt the desire "to paint such cities as paintings."[43] As a boy, Schiele had begun his disastrous career as a secondary school student at a gymnasium in

Krems, since there were no college preparatory schools in Tulln. From that point forward, Krems-Stein became a fixture of Schiele's cosmos of towns. In June 1906, Schiele sketched Margarethenstrasse in Krems [see ill. on p. 121] in a manner that anticipates his later views of Stein. This includes both recording the old town when deserted and the purism of a *veduta* of a town purged of modern technology and current events as a projection screen for a yearning for the past that many modern artists shared.

In the years after 1900, the Wachau increasingly solidified the reputation it had achieved as place of yearning for artists. With the rapid growth of Vienna's population to over two million inhabitants, the countryside between Krems and Weissenkirchen evolved into an idyllic alternative to the big city, which had long since become a point of contention for young artists. "They dreamed of a 'South Seas' adventure that brought them closer to the sources of creativity and that they also hoped for […] from a stay […] in the Wachau."[44]

That Schiele saw himself in these depictions of the town of Stein is probably connected not only to his biographic association but also to a love of its medieval—Gothic—character, which Smith has pointed out.[45] Schiele's strong attraction to the Gothic was often emphasized by Arthur Roessler. He reports of Schiele's enthusiasm: "People in the Middle Ages, yes, they had culture! And yet people always stupidly speak of the 'Dark Ages'!—Yes, it was perhaps dark in the streets in those days, but certainly not in the souls of artists. And then I […] found that—quite indisputably—landscape was discovered for the human being by the Gothics. Gothic painters were certainly the first artist to place the human likeness before a landscape background."[46] Schiele produced both the two small Stein *vedute*, including

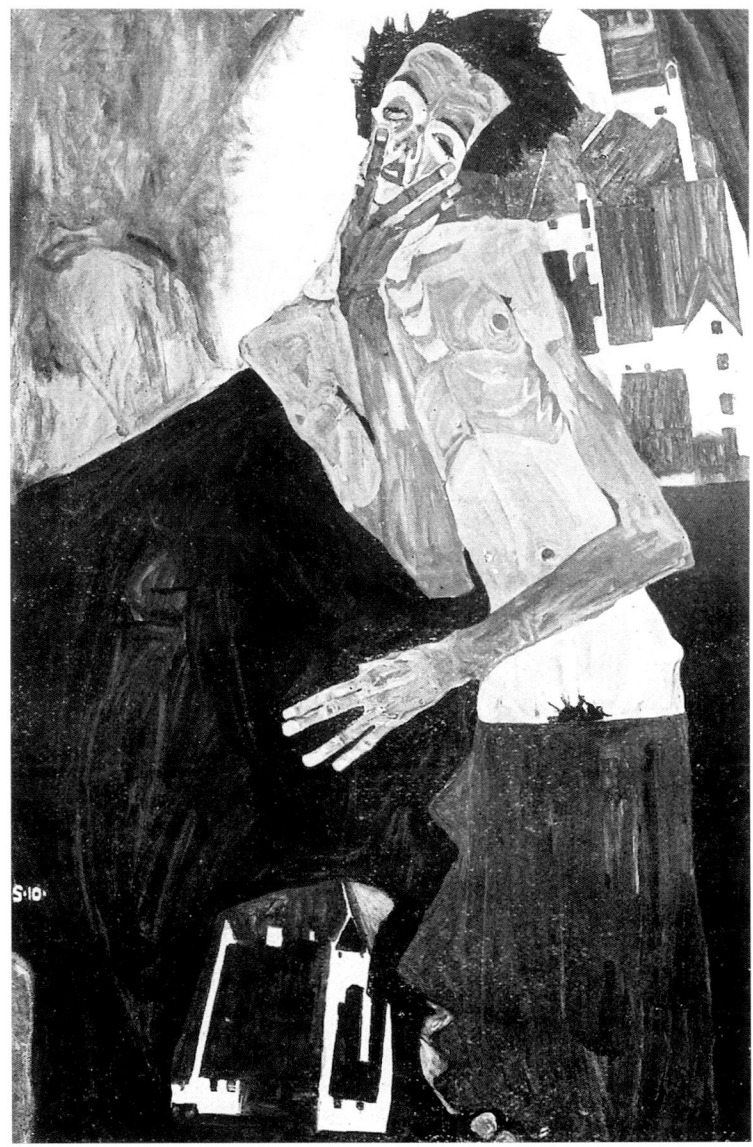

the one that captures the city from the south [Cat. no. 55] and what he called "*Brettlbilder*" (board paintings),[47] with which he was probably consciously seeking continuity with the panel painting of the Gothic era. That Schiele was striving for a medieval character here is clear not least from his effort to "re-Gothicize" the roof of the parish church, which still has a Baroque onion tower today, but reconstructing its original form, as Smith has shown.

16. Egon Schiele, *Melancholia (Self-Portrait)*, 1910. Reproduction from Paris von Gütersloh's *Versuch einer Vorrede* (Vienna: Brüder Rosenbaum, 1911).

The four variations on the townscape of Stein form two pairs of paintings that depict the little town on the Danube in one small and one larger format, either from the opposite shore of the Danube [Cat. nos. 54–56] or from the Kreuzberg.[48] Although he adopts real topographic features, Schiele makes "corrections" to the image of the place in all these *vedute*. They all have in common the central position of the Frauenbergkirche (Mount of Our Lady Church), which penetrates the upper edge in three of the paintings. In general, the church appears in ever new perspectives and contexts. Schiele is applying here the design principles of his experience with the portrait to the townscape. This includes encircling the subject and dispensing with fidelity to the details of the town's physiognomy. Schiele makes striking changes, reducing the number of window axes and stories.

The depictions from the south [Cat. nos. 54–55] combine the motifs of water and countryside by means of colors and using the structure of a grid into a unity with the city.

Viewed in another context, this apparently lightweight handling of content is indicative of (pre-)conscious selection. The colorful, tapestry-like patterning of houses nestling up against each other does not contrast with the landscape; the draughtsmanly arabesques that appear in some corner of an old town do not contrast with the brutal track of a modern road—in other words, the yawning gap between nature and human civilization, between the old and the modern, which Van Gogh and some of the Impressionists had already taken as their theme, is never one of Schiele's concerns. In his landscapes and townscapes there is no industry, there are no smoking factory chimneys or other signs of modern technology.[49]

That is how Reinhard Steiner describes Schiele's modernism, which in terms of landscape is focused entirely on the past without the set pieces of progress.

Modern life is not all these paintings rigorously exclude; Schiele also dispensed with any content that could connect the image of the city to a particular time. Depictions of people are eschewed as well as indications of any specific time. Even reflections in the river, which were still a central component in the early paintings of the Danube and Vltava, are pointedly omitted.

THE DILAPIDATED MILL AS SPECTACLE OF NATURE

Schiele dedicated numerous works to specific architectural motifs. *Zerfallende Mühle (Bergmühle)* (Decaying Mill [Mountain Mill]) [Fig. 17] of 1916 stands out among them.[50] It is in many respects a painting that lies between genres; in any case, it is a magnum opus among his landscapes and the central canvas of the period in which Schiele was doing his military service when he spent every free moment in nature. Schiele himself saw the painting as his "probably best landscape."[51]

In that composition, Schiele addressed the motif of a mill that, long since disused, has been left to decay and, one has the impression, is about to collapse at any moment. The painting reflects "the unequal battle between an artificial world created by man and the power of nature that is always both renewing and destructive."[52] This intertwining of nature and architecture is also reflected by the moss-covered wooden plans on the upper edge of the water, which are executed like a row of landscapes.[53] In the upper right end of the picture, the crumbling plaster looks like a mountain chain that establishes the horizon. The system of connections between a building and (the force of) nature could not be depicted more impressively. Not only in its premonition

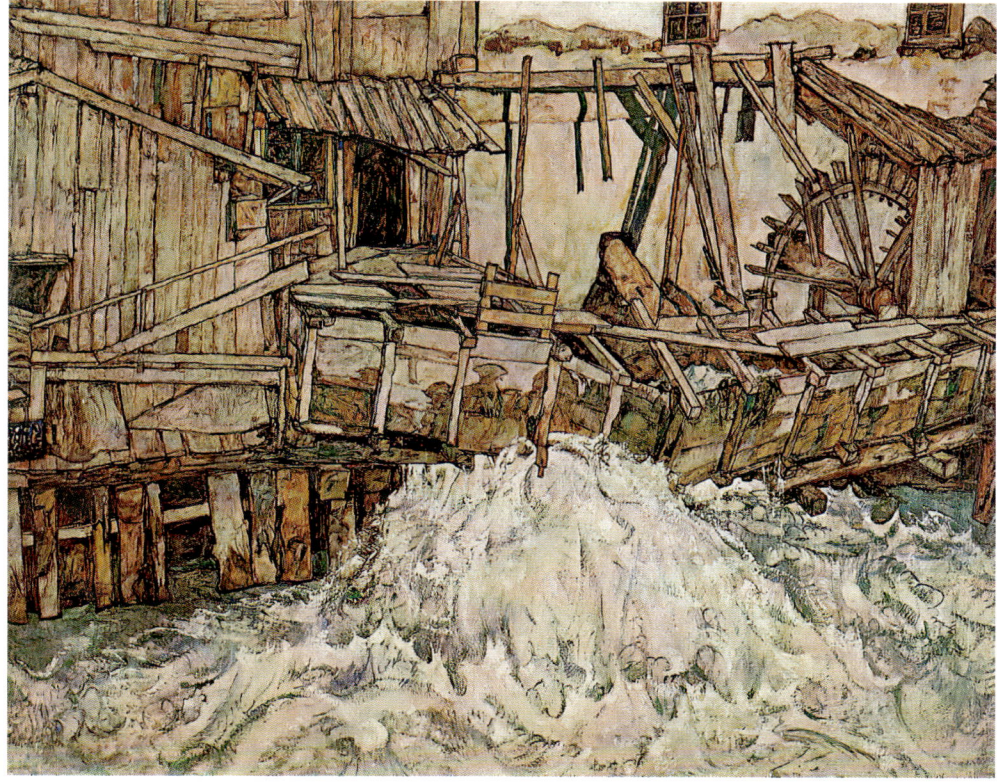

17. Egon Schiele, *Decaying Mill (Mountain Mill)*, 1916, oil on canvas. Landessammlungen Niederösterreich, St. Pölten (Kallir P301). Photo: Artefact/Alamy Stock Photo

of death, the motif is a condensation and metamorphosis that turns everything into nature.

SCHIELE'S WORLD: A MICROCOSM AS DETAIL OF THE EARTH WITH A CLAIM TO LEADERSHIP

For all the significance that Schiele's landscapes and townscapes have in the artist's work, the question of his geographical cosmos still arises. Schiele developed early on a great interest in faraway countries and would have liked to live in London or New York after World War I. Nevertheless, all of his life he remained within a geographically modest cosmos.

Schiele's world, the space of his life and work—Vienna and nearby small towns—is so compact that it could be covered by bicycle. Klosterneuburg and Neulengbach are around fifteen miles from Tulln; the distance to Krems and the former imperial and residence city of Vienna is hardly more than twice that far. The international innovation of train travel shrunk such distances to meaningless around 1900. That a child of train stations and a railroad fanatic like Schiele did not travel further on his few trips than Krumau, Trieste, and Munich is surprising. How can someone participate in so much world history and at the same time be so regionally rooted? Anton Faistauer offered a possible explanation for this shortly after Schiele's death, saying that Austria was in relative terms the most international country on the continent: "Its capital houses all nations in proportionally higher numbers than any other world city."[54]

Austria, as Schiele knew it under the monarchy, was more than just a representative cross section of the world. At the start of the

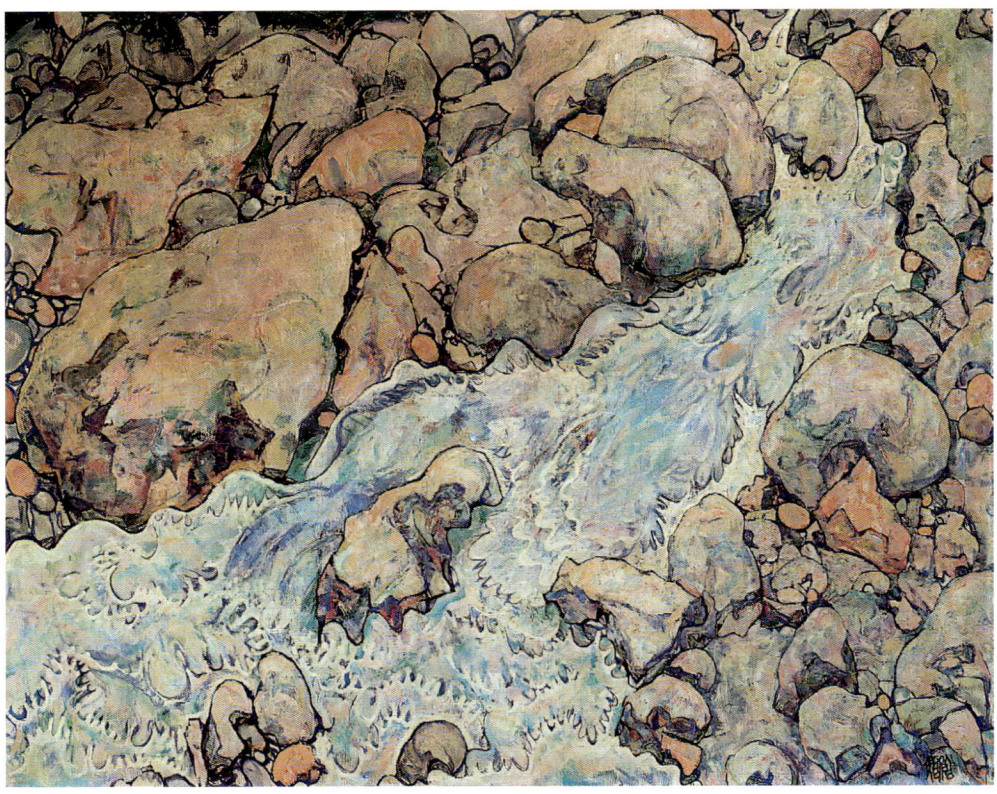

18. Egon Schiele, *Mountain Torrent (Waterfall)*, 1918, oil on canvas. Private Collection (Kallir P332). Photo: Artefact/Alamy Stock Photo

twentieth century, there was a strong trend to assert that Austria had a claim to be a leader of international culture. Not infrequently, artists combined nationalism with the desire for a united Europe.[55] The gigantic project of a world cultural academy, with Oskar Kokoschka as its president, was part of the Weltkulturgesellschaft (World Cultural Society) of Erwin Hanslik, the founder of the Institut für Kulturforschung (Institute of Cultural Research) in Vienna, to which essential figures of Vienna's artistic elite—Klimt, Schiele, Josef Hoffmann, Adolf Loos, and many others—belonged.

Schiele was, as Smola has shown, not just an admirer of Hanslik;[56] he also collaborated on his book *Wesen der Menschheit* (The Essence of Humanity), provided a standardization of skull forms, which in the chapter "Talent" are classified from "weak" by way of "medium" to "strong" [Cat. no. 69]. These head types are said to have been influenced by the corresponding geographical area. Not coincidentally, the form of head chosen for "strong" recalls Schiele's contemporaneous self-portraits. Such pseudoscientific classifications led to horrible historical events two decades later. For Schiele, who was convinced of a deep connection between people and the surrounding landscape, Hanslik's theories were fascinating.

As the Austrian state increasingly declined, Hanslik continued to advocate the concept of a larger Habsburg empire extending eastward. For Hanslik, Austria was a guarantor and mediator of a Europe that would connect nations.

Schiele was presumably especially taken with Hanslik's book *Österreich als Naturforderung*

(Austria as Natural Challenge), since he had two copies of the book in his library,[57] one of which even had a personal dedication by the author.[58] That work extends to the extreme the connection of human being and surrounding landscape: "In Austria, humanity and society can be discovered. Humanity as it truly is, as an earth person, as a powerful, earth-bound spiritual being, as a formation that can be traveled, appears here with the power of the senses."[59]

INDIVIDUALITY AND TYPE

With Hanslik, a typological dimension becomes important in Schiele's late paintings, as is evident from his portraits: "In several symmetrically constructed double portraits produced in 1917, Schiele appears to be more interested in a type than in the subjective disposition of the model."[60]

In his townscapes, Schiele had previously—for example, in the *Dead City* series—created a town type whose totality is superior to all urban details. In his final phase, the fidelity to details is further reduced. Schiele's final landscape, produced months before his death in 1918, is the monumental painting *Wildbach (Wasserfall)* (Mountain Torrent [Waterfall]) [Fig. 18]. The motif was taken from an excursion to the Stubai Valley in 1917.

As is often the case in his landscapes, Schiele chooses a view from above, so that the depiction extends without a horizon in the rendering of the soil. The stony ground is almost monochrome in pallid shades of gray and brown, whereas the river cuts through the painting diagonally in blue and gray with the edges of the waves tipped with white.

The landscape loses any connection to a temporal dimension. That impression is further reinforced because the dynamic wave formations appear frozen. Even more than that, an almost metallic quality accompanies the movement of the water. Everything is frozen; no sign of life populates the picture plane. This is a painting in which everything is relativized; the realism of the stones becomes an image of death; spatial illusion becomes the pattern of the picture plane; the living course of the river is frozen and sent into deep sleep.

Is this a hint of the direction in which Schiele's landscapes would have evolved? We cannot know, because Schiele died soon thereafter, at the age of only twenty-eight, as a result of the international flu pandemic.

Translated from the German by Steven Lindberg

1 On this, see Christian Bauer, "'I, Eternal Child': The Early Work as a Harbinger of Maturity," in idem, ed., *Egon Schiele: The Beginning*, trans. Matthias Goldmann and Michael Strand (Munich: Hirmer, 2013), 8–22.

2 Franz Smola counts 167 paintings with landscape and townscape motifs, as opposed to 131 Symbolist-allegorical works, nudes, and portraits. See Franz Smola, "Egon Schiele's Landscapes and Cityscapes," in *Egon Schiele, Jenny Saville*, ed. Zürcher Kunstgesellschaft, exh. cat. Kunsthaus Zürich (Ostfildern: Hatje Cantz, 2014), 89–91, esp. 89.

3 Kimberly A. Smith, *Between Ruin and Renewal: Egon Schiele's Landscapes* (New Haven, CT: Yale University Press, 2004).

4 Egon Schiele, "Self-Portrait," in idem, *I, Eternal Child: Paintings and Poems*, trans. Anselm Hollo (New York: Grove Press, 1985), 44; cf. Egon Schiele, "Ein Selbstbild," May 1910, Private Collection; Leopold Museum, Vienna, Egon Schiele Datenbank der Autografen (hereafter ESDA), ID no. 292.

5 Jane Kallir also concludes one could call Schiele "a late Symbolist"; Jane Kallir, *Egon Schiele's Women* (Munich: Prestel, 2012), 13.

6 See the essay by Verena Gamper in the present publication, with references to the research of Ursula Storch, Sandra Tretter, and Eva Werth.

7 Even if the interplay of figure and landscape follows more the idea of representation than that of illusion, this painting goes beyond the use of plant set pieces—as, for example, found in *Selbstbildnis mit schwarzem Tongefäss und gespreizten Fingern* (Self-Portrait with Black Clay Vase and Spread Fingers) (Kallir P204) and *Selbstbildnis mit Lampionfrüchten* (Self-Portrait with Chinese Lantern Plant) (Kallir P233).

8 The lost painting *Weltwehmut* (*Selbstbildnis*) (Melancholia [Self-Portrait]) (Kallir P175) [Fig. 16] combines elements of townscape and landscape in the background.

9 Egon Schiele to an unknown person, July 17, 1911, Private Collection; ESDA, ID no. 2764.

10 Egon Schiele, "Who of the ones given life and senses" (1910), in *I, Eternal Child* (see note 28), 12–14, esp. 12; cf. Egon Schiele, "Wer von lebend Primbegabten," whereabouts unknown; ESDA, ID no. 297.

11 Egon Schiele, "Künstler," 1910, Albertina, Vienna, inv. no. 39881; ESDA, ID no. 1933.

12 Egon Schiele to an unknown person, July 17, 1911 (see note 9).

13 Egon Schiele to Josef Hoffmann, September 20, 1910, Nebehay Family Collection; ESDA, ID no. 2762 [Cat. no. 20].

14 Ibid.

15 Helena Pereña, "Nature, Religion, and Art," trans. Christopher Jenkin-Jones, in *Egon Schiele: "Das unrettbare Ich'; Werke aus der Albertina* (Cologne: Wieland, 2011), 110–26, esp. 112–13.

16 On this, see Rudolf Leopold, *Egon Schiele: Landscapes*, trans. John Gabriel, exh. cat. (Munich: Prestel, 2004), 86.

17 Egon Schiele, "Fir Woods" (July 1910), in *Egon Schiele: Poems and Letters, 1910–1912*, ed. Elisabeth Leopold, trans. Jeff Tapia (New York: Prestel, 2008), 37 (translation modified); cf. Egon Schiele, "*Tannenwald,*" Leopold Private Collection; ESDA, ID no. 1.

18 Klaus Albrecht Schröder, *Egon Schiele*, exh. cat. (Munich: Prestel, 2005), 80.

19 Matthias Haldemann, "Rhetorik der Fläche: Zeigen und Entziehen in Schieles Bildkunst," in Hans-Peter Wipplinger, ed., *Conference Volume on the First Egon Schiele Symposium at the Leopold Museum* (Vienna: Leopold Museum, 2017), 46–59, esp. 51.

20 Franz Smola, who is organizing an exhibition on the "Internationale Kunstschau" of 1909 for the Belvedere, has found a photograph that confirms the presence of this painting in Schiele's first group exhibition in Vienna.

21 On this see Renée Price, ed., *Egon Schiele: The Ronald S. Lauder and Serge Sabarsky Collections* (Munich: Prestel, 2005), 188.

22 Dr. R. H., "Kollektivausstellung," *Fremden-Blatt (Abend-Ausgabe)*, January 9, 1915, 2, quoted in Tobias G. Natter, ed., *Egon Schiele: The Complete Paintings, 1909–1918* (Cologne: Taschen, 2017), 551.

23 Eva Werth, "Egon Schiele und Franz Kafka: Identität und Alerität, in den Metamorphosen Franz Kafkas und Egon Schieles," in *Egon Schiele Jahrbuch II/III 2012/2013* (Vienna: REMA-Print-Littera, Druck- und Verlagsgesellschaft m.b.H., 2014), 232–46, esp. 243.

24 Paul-Bernhard Eipper, "Vier Bilder in einem Bild: Zur Restaurierung von Egon Schieles 'Stadtende/Häuserbogen III,'" in ibid., 71–94, esp. 71.

25 Egon Schiele to Franz Hauer, August 25, 1913, Albertina, Vienna, inv. no. ESA 107 c; ESDA, ID no. 674.

26 Egon Schiele to Josef Hoffmann, September 20, 1910, Nebehay Family Collection; ESDA, ID no. 2762.

27 Egon Schiele to Anton Peschka, ca. 1910, in *Egon Schiele: Poems and Letters* (see note 17), 13–14; cf. Egon Schiele to Anton Peschka, prior to May 12, 1910, Leopold Private Collection; ESDA, ID no. 33.

28 Egon Schiele to an unknown person, July 17, 1911, Private Collection; ESDA, ID no. 2764.

29 Egon Schiele to Hermann Engel, September 1911, in *Egon Schiele: Poems and Letters* (see note 17), 87; cf. Egon Schiele to Hermann Engel, September 1911, Leopold Museum, Vienna; ESDA, ID no. 141.

30 Kimberly A. Smith, "I paesaggi di Egon Schiele: Dalle raffigurazioni di alberi alle vedute urbane," in Rudi Chiappini, ed., *Egon Schiele*, exh. cat. Museo d'arte moderna, Lugano (Milan: Skira, 2003), 79–102, esp. 86.

31 Egon Schiele to Josef Hoffmann, September 20, 1910, Nebehay Family Collection; ESDA, ID no. 2762.

32 Ralph Gleis, "Schiele, Hodler und Segantini: Die beseelte Natur im Symbolismus und Expressionismus," in Hans-Peter Wipplinger, ed., *Conference Volume on the First Egon Schiele Symposium at the Leopold Museum* (Vienna: Leopold Museum, 2017), 16–31, esp. 28.

33 Egon Schiele to Anton Peschka, ca. 1910 (see note 27), 13.

34 There are entries for Schiele in the years 1909 (May 9, 1909) and 1911 (May 13, 1911) in the tourist book of the town of Krumau; ESDA, ID nos. 2470 and 2620.

35 Anton Peschka to Gertrude Schiele, postcard, May 1910, whereabouts unknown; ESDA, ID no. 1930.

36 Egon Schiele's confirmation to Anton Peschka, August 1910, whereabouts unknown; ESDA, ID no. 1931.

37 Kallir P175 and Kallir P190.

38 Kallir P134.

39 Leopold Liegler's contribution to the *Erinnerungsbuch Egon Schiele*, Alberta, Vienna; ESDA, ID no. 2565.

40 [Albert] Paris von Gütersloh, "Egon Schiele: Versuch einer Vorrede," in *Egon Schiele*, exh. cat. (Vienna: Galerie H. O. Miethke, 1911).

41 Egon Schiele, "I have seen first of all the eternal avenues of spring" (July 1910), in idem, *I, Eternal Child: Paintings and Poems*, trans. Anselm Hollo (New York: Grove Press, 1985), 10; cf. Egon Schiele "Ich habe die ewigen Frühlingsalleen...," Albertina, Vienna; ESDA, ID no. 290.

42 See Wolfgang Georg Fischer, *Egon Schiele, 1890–1918: Pantomimen der Lust; Visionen der Sterblichkeit* (Cologne: Taschen, 2007), 183.

43 Egon Schiele to Carl Reininghaus, March 23, 1913, Private Collection; ESDA, ID no. 57.

44 On this, see Nikolaus Schaffer, "Sehnsucht nach Grösse," in *Anton Faistauer, 1887–1930*, exh. cat. (Salzburg: Salzburger Museum Carolino Augusteum, 2005), 55.

45 Smith, *Between Ruin and Renewal* (see note 3), 71.

46 See Arthur Roessler, *Erinnerungen an Egon Schiele*, 2nd ed. (Vienna: Wiener Volksbuchverlag, 1948), 35.

47 Schiele used the word "*Brettlbild*" repeatedly for landscapes; for example, he used it for the two small landscapes of Klein in a letter to Carl Reininghaus; see Egon Schiele to Carl Reininghaus, March 26, 1913, Private Collection; ESDA, ID no. 59.

48 Kallir P267 and Kallir P269.

49 Reinhard Steiner, *Egon Schiele, 1890–1918: The Midnight Soul of the Artist*, trans. Michael Hulse (Cologne: Taschen, 1981), 91.

50 See Wolfgang Krug, "Landscapes on the Brink of War," in Christian Bauer, ed., *Egon Schiele: Almost a Lifetime*, trans. Matthias Goldmann and Camilla R. Nielsen (Munich: Hirmer, 2015), 100–113, esp. 101.

51 See Egon Schiele to Guido Arnot, September 7, 1916, Tiroler Landesmuseum Ferdinandeum, Innsbruck; ESDA, ID no. 1189.

52 Krug, "Landscapes on the Brink of War" (see note 50), 103.

53 I am grateful to the great Schiele pioneer Alessandra Comini for a conversation I was fortunate to have with her in Krems in June 2019, which resulted in this observation.

54 See Anton Faistauer, *Neue Malerei in Österreich: Betrachtungen eines Malers* (Zurich: Amalthea, 1923), 5.

55 Kurt De Boodt and Paul Dujardin, "*Gesellschaft* or *Gemeinschaft*? Visions for Europe; Erwin Hanslik, Otto Neurath, and Richard von Coudenhove-Kalergi," trans. Alison Mouthaan, in *Klimt ist nicht das Ende: Aufbruch in Mitteleuropa*, ed. Stella Rollig and Alexander Klee, exh. cat. (Munich: Hirmer, 2018), 350–57, esp. 351.

56 On this, see, most recently, Franz Smola, "Portrait of Dr. Victor Ritter von Bauer, 1918," in *Egon Schiele: The Making of a Collection*, ed. Stella Rollig and Kerstin Jesse, trans. Rebecca Law, Nick Somers, and Jessica West, exh. cat. Belvedere, Vienna (Munich: Hirmer, 2018), 265–71, esp. 265-67.

57 One copy is in the so-called Peschka-Nachlass of the Wien Museum; another is in a Private Collection.

58 The book with the stamp of the Instituts für Kulturforschung and the handwritten entry "Egon Schiele gewidmet. Erwin Hanslik" (Dedicated to ES. EH) is in a Private Collection.

59 Erwin Hanslik, *Österreich als Naturforderung* (Vienna: Brauns, 1917), 39.

60 De Boodt and Dujardin, "*Gesellschaft* or *Gemeinschaft*?" (see note 55), 353.

AUTUMN LANDSCAPES AND FADED TOWNS

EGON SCHIELE'S ANIMATED PLACES AND SYMBOLIC SPACES

Franz Smola

INTRODUCTION

Landscapes and townscapes represent an important emphasis in Egon Schiele's brief creative period of just over ten years.[1] Purely in terms of numbers, they dominate: nearly 170 paintings with country or urban motifs as opposed to around 130 with nude, portrait, or symbolic motifs.[2] Yet Schiele's landscapes and townscapes are considerably less well known than his nudes and portraits. That may be because the nudes and portraits still captivate viewers even today thanks to their radical and psychologizing attributes, whereas the landscapes and townscapes are perhaps perceived as more closely tied to their era and thus less appealing.

The connection of Schiele's landscapes and townscapes to his lifetime is often expressed in the strong symbolic character these works usually have. Schiele frequently seems to be trying in his art to create projection spaces that function like a mirror of his own emotional states. Schiele rarely provided information about his subjects and the feelings they evoked. Especially in his poems and prose, nearly all of which were written in the years 1910 and 1911, the artist made use of expressive terms in which he established, among

other things, pan-vitalist connections to nature and to his immediate surroundings.[3] He did not, however, address specific works in these poems or in his letters and other writings. Schiele's self-statements are generally only of limited use as guidance to interpreting his landscapes and townscapes.

In such pictures, the artist was surely primarily interested in atmospherically dense representations of nature and not, for example, in communicating specific literary subject matter. In general, Schiele operates on a highly emotional level, which he himself sometimes described using the word *Empfindung* (sentiment, feeling, emotion). For example, in the substantive letter he wrote to the collector Carl Reininghaus in which he explained in detail his just-finished painting *Die Eremiten* (The Hermits), he used the term "*Empfindungsmensch*" (person of sentiment).[4] In a letter to collector Oskar Reichel, the artist explicitly offers directions to achieve such an *Empfindung*, namely, by way of an attentive, almost meditative observation of his works, which the artist describes with the word "*hineinschauen*" (look into): "Soon you will be absolutely convinced by it, as soon as you

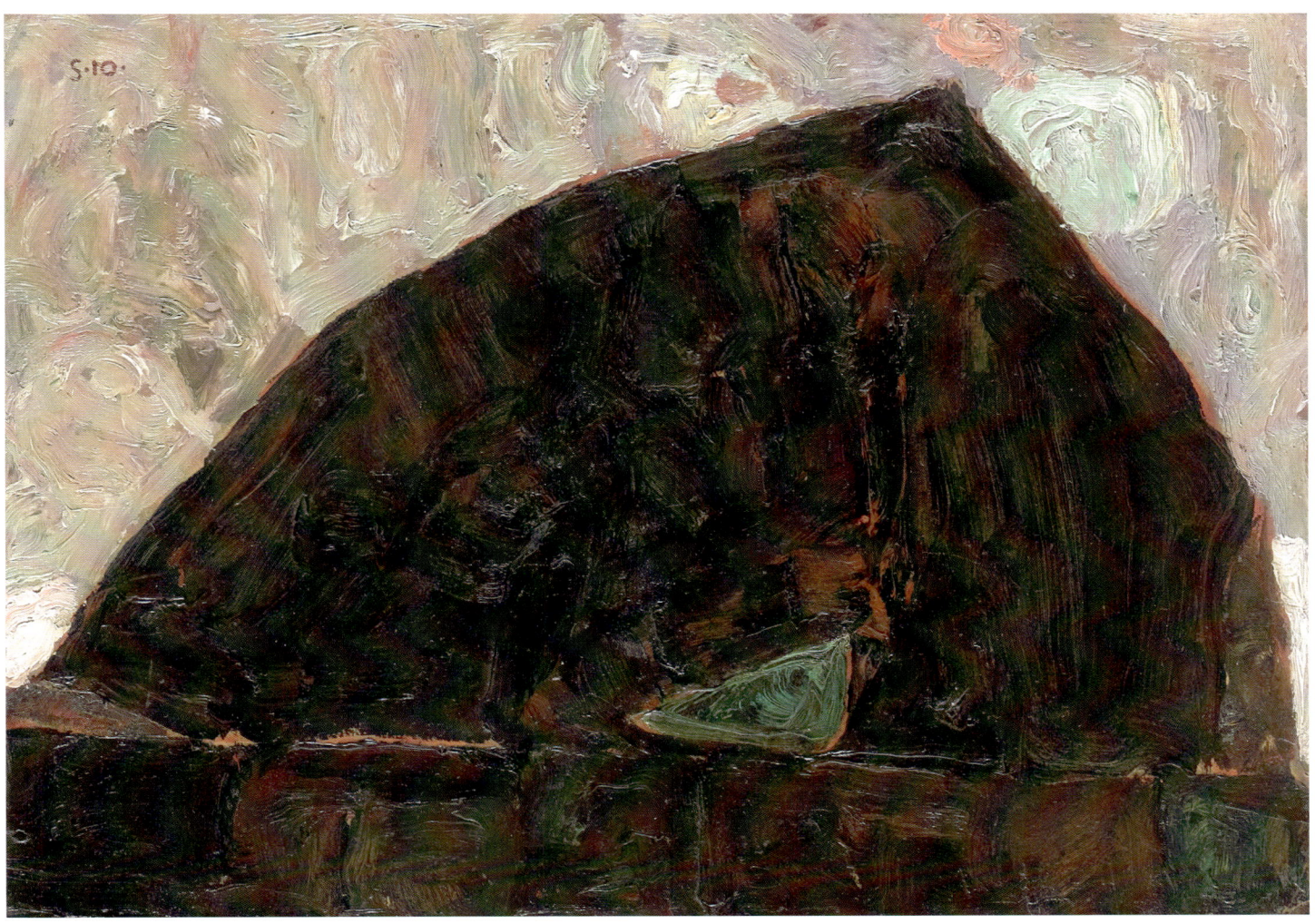

begin, not to look at it, but to look into it."[5] This emphasis on attentive feeling is probably the result of Schiele's study of the philosophical and aesthetic writings of his time, which were intensely discussed and debated under the heading "*Einfühlungsästhetik*" (aesthetic of empathy).[6]

AUTUMN LANDSCAPES

It is no coincidence that such programmatic passages in his letters and the majority of the aforementioned Expressionist poems date from 1910 and 1911. In those two years, the young artist succeeded in radicalizing his artistic expression; he invented himself, as it were, and in the process raised himself above everything that fine art in Vienna had to offer until then. Not only in the area of narrative figure painting, portraiture, and the nude, from

1910 onward Schiele developed a completely autonomous Expressionist style; from the outset, landscapes and townscapes formed an essential part of the then just twenty-year-old artist's stylistic departure, which remains as mysterious and astonishing today as it was at the time.

The radicalness of this development can be traced particularly well in the landscapes and townscapes. During Schiele's academic years, from 1906 to 1909, in addition to his nude and portrait studies, the young student produced explicitly as part of his education, he also made small-format oil pictures with topographical views of sites and places of his immediate surroundings, such as Klosterneuburg, where his family was living at the time, or in Neulengbach and Krumau

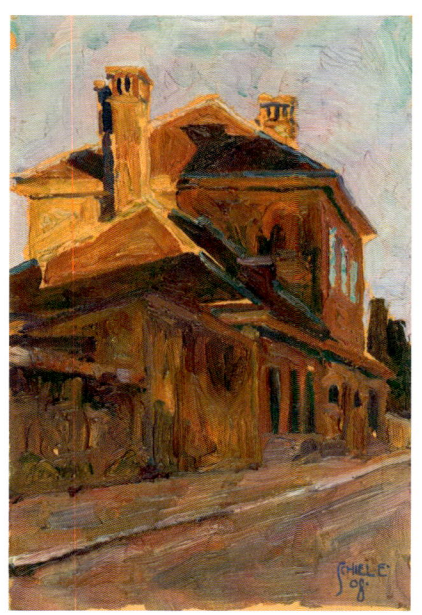

2. Egon Schiele, *Houses in Oberdöbling*, 1908, oil on board. Landessammlungen Niederösterreich, St. Pölten (Kallir P130)

(Český Krumlov), where they spent their summers early on; these were among the most common motifs of his early paintings. All of these paintings which were made in his free time independently of his studies, are rather pleasant works that focus on the picturesque character of the motifs. *Haus Oberdöbling (Wien)* [House in Oberdöbling (Vienna)] [Fig. 2] of 1908 is a typical example in this vein; Schiele ably captured the shadowy atmosphere of a narrow street in Vienna's suburb with reduced planes of contrasting color.

These cheery landscape studies are diametrically opposed to the Expressionist landscapes and townscapes he made from 1910 onward, which produce a completely new and unusual effect with their intensification of the composition and color. Schiele did not shy from distorting natural motifs, often with bizarre and grotesque effects. One example of this is *Berg am Fluss* (Mountain by the River) [Fig. 1], which features a striking silhouette of a mountain seemingly stripped of all vegetation and creating a cuttingly sharp, abruptly rebuffing effect. The impenetrably dark color of the painting contributes to that impression. Despite its striking form, no one has yet identified the mountain. It seems likely that it is a motif from the area around Krumau, where the young artist spent the summer months of 1910. Schiele's mother was from this town in southern Bohemia; her father was a respected building contractor there. Schiele traveled to visit relatives in Krumau regularly from childhood, and it became a second home for the artist through several periods of his life.

Many of Schiele's other early landscapes are, like *Mountain by the River*, marked by a dark, gloomy coloration that presumably reflects the artist's preference for seasons with reduced light: late autumn, winter, and early spring. It

is also possible that they are depictions of twilight or night, not associated with a specific season, but in that case Schiele would presumably have worked much more with the effects of natural and artificial light. For example, the mysterious painting *Rote Erde* (Red Earth) [Cat. no. 35] appears to be completely immersed in the colors of autumn. This work, which was probably painted in late 1910, shows an imposing mountain slope in shades of brown and ocher, against which several parts of a wall standing at the foot and on the ridge of a mountain stand out in bright red. Looming behind the mountain is a rock face that appears to be much taller and hermetically terminates the painting at the top. The bright gray of the sky is visible only in the upper left corner. Tall bars in a grate-like structure also loom out of the red wall on the mountain. It is perhaps the scaffold of a construction site, or a railroad line or a viaduct under construction in the high mountains. Schiele may have encountered such construction areas on his occasional train trips through the Alpine valleys of Tyrol and northern Italy.

It is surely no coincidence that the young Schiele chose *Red Earth* as one of the few landscapes for his first solo exhibition, which was on view in the Viennese gallery of Hugo Othmar Miethke from late May to early June 1911.[7] The exhibition catalogue contains Albert Paris Gütersloh's famous programmatic text *Versuch einer Vorrede* (Attempt at a Preface) and illustrations of nine works by Schiele.[8] Most of the latter are Symbolist figure paintings and self-portraits, evoking a gloomy, dusky general atmosphere. *Red Earth* fits seamlessly into this selection of nocturnal images. It is notable that in these early expressive works Schiele was striving not for shrill, strident color, as was the case with the contemporaneous German Expressionists, but preferred at this time a radically somber coloration.

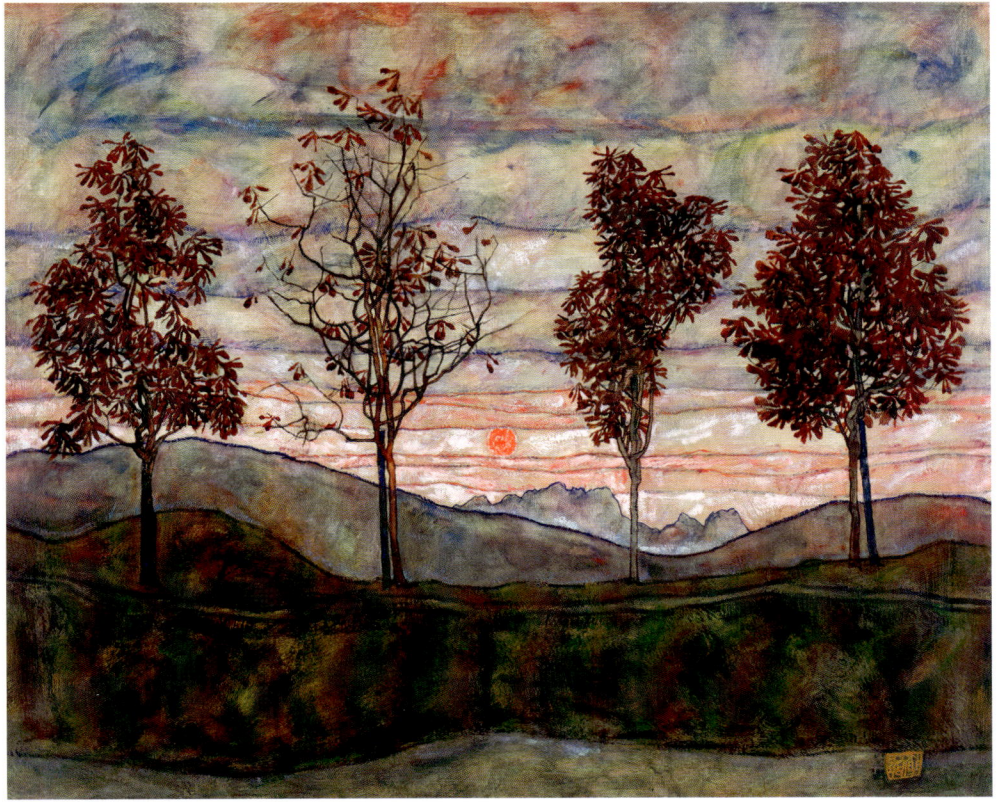

3. Egon Schiele, *Four Trees*, 1917, oil on canvas. Private Collection (Kallir P310). Formerly Belvedere, Vienna, this painting has been restituted to the legal heirs of Josef Morgenstern in 2020. Photo: Johannes Stoll/ Belvedere, Vienna

Characteristically, Schiele's other work from 1910 and 1911 frequently includes landscapes with autumnal motifs. One example is *Landschaft mit Raben* (Landscape with Ravens) [see ill. on p. 16] of 1911. The focus is on a hill, crowned by a garden fence. Its dim lighting reduces the colors of the hill to dark shades of brown, against which motifs such as the garden shack and the fragile laundry poles stand out only weakly. The flock of ravens points to the painting's title and implicitly to the season, standing out against the cold, white sky. Ravens normally assemble in large flocks in late autumn. The work was probably painted in the area around Neulengbach, where Schiele had moved in September 1911, after having to hastily leave his beloved Krumau that summer due to conflicts with the local population.

Landscape with Ravens is one from a group of landscapes, some of which are identified as autumn images by their titles, that were probably also painted in the area around Neulengbach: close-ups of meadows on which small, isolated deciduous trees stand. Some of them still have foliage in autumnal colors, while the leaves on others have already fallen. This presented the artist with the opportunity to explore fully the graphic effect of their bare branches and trunks. One impressive example of this is the painting *Herbstbäume I* (Autumn Trees I) [see ill. on p. 26]. Here Schiele even repeats three times the motif of a bare autumnal tree: all three trees appear almost identical. The artist produces an impressively complex composition, as well as a highly emotional tension, both in the way the trees rise at a slight slope across a narrow strip of meadow that forms a sharp angle and through how their few thin branches interlock with the delicate horizontal stripes that color the grayish sky. For Kimberly A. Smith, Schiele's depictions of trees can be read as geometric grid structures in which centrifugal and centripetal forces counteract each other.[9]

Probably the most imposing effect of an autumnal atmosphere in Schiele's work is conveyed by the large-format painting *Vier Bäume* (Four Trees) [Fig. 3], which the artist produced a few years later in 1917. Strangely, the sober title of the painting, which has been associated with it from the beginning, in no

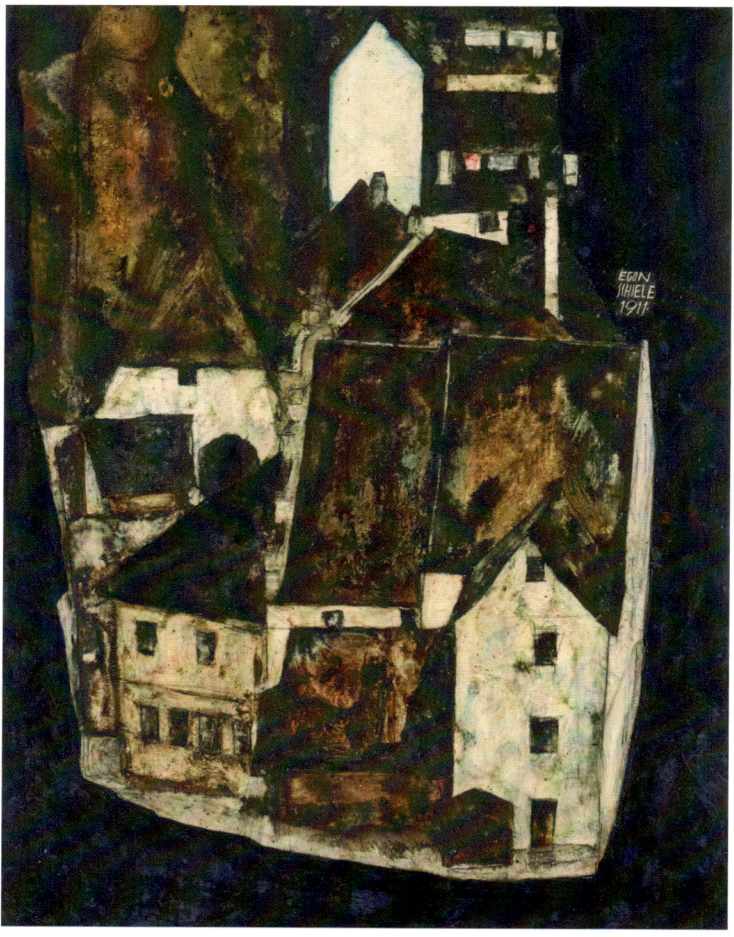

way reflects the prosaic effect this painting radiates. The work was completed at a time when the artist was already fulfilling his military service. After a period of training in the summer of 1915 that he found horrible, Schiele led a relatively calm life as a soldier in various companies, escorting war prisoners and doing office work, among other tasks. He was primarily stationed in the area around Vienna and in towns in Lower Austria, which enabled him to return occasionally to his studio in Vienna and work there for extended periods. From May 1916 to January 1917, he was stationed in a prisoner-of-war camp in Mühling in Lower Austria. There Schiele found himself in the charming landscape of the so-called Prealps, from where he had good views of the mountain ranges of the Alps beginning from their rise, with the Ötscher as their first prominent peak. In diary entries in May and June 1916, he noted in graphic words the magic of the colors of the sky and of nature there: "Saw a fire-red sun—in front of it, conifers and broad-leaved trees in dark purple—violet-transparent clouds above."[10] These intense impressions of nature probably influenced the painting *Four Trees*; the peak depicted in the background is presumably the Ötscher. The flaming-red ball of the sun is setting between four young chestnut trees whose leaves have taken on autumnal colors; one of them has already lost most of its leaves—an impressive allegory of life's transience.

FADED CITIES: KRUMAU AN DER MOLDAU

Autumn colors and moods dominate not only many of Schiele's landscapes but also a fair number of his townscapes. In his aforementioned exhibition at the Galerie Miethke in 1911, Schiele also exhibited a *veduta* of Krumau in gloomy twilight. In 1911 and 1912, the artist created an entire series of views of Krumau, all of which are titled *Tote Stadt*

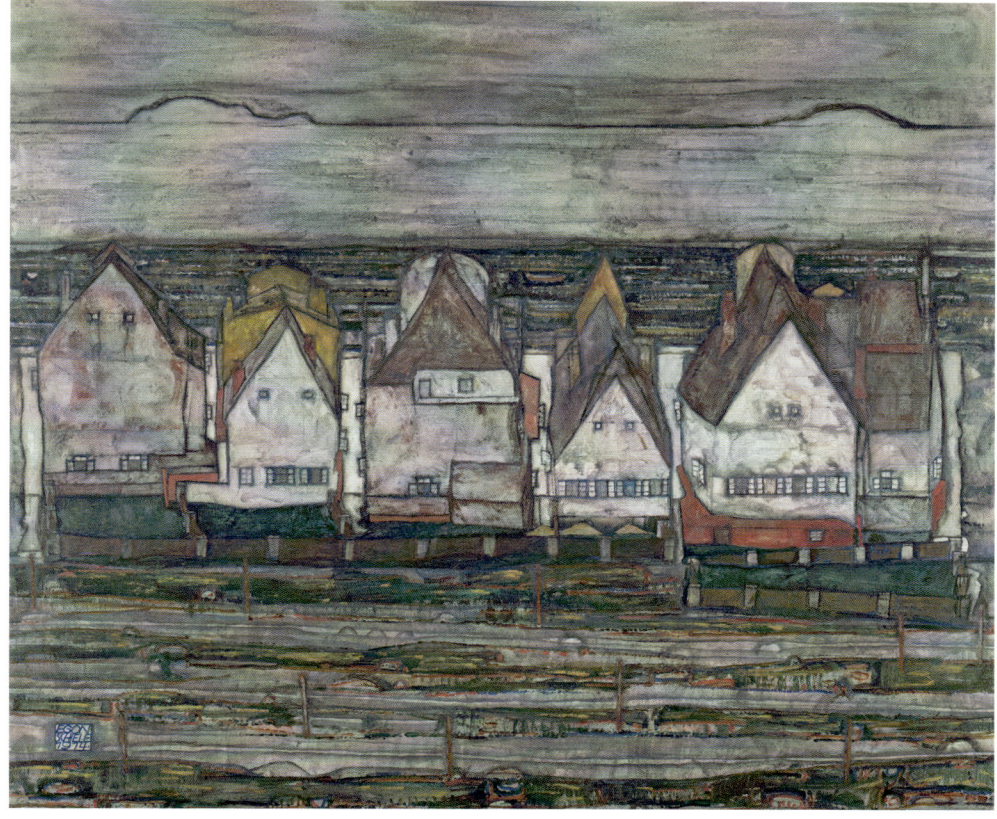

5. Egon Schiele, *Houses by the Sea (Row of Houses)*, 1914, oil on canvas. Leopold Museum, Vienna (Kallir P281). Photo: Leopold Museum, Vienna

(Dead City).[11] The origin of these consistently small-format *vedute* of Krumau, some of which are very similar, can be traced back to the initiative of Schiele's mentor and supporter, the journalist and art writer Arthur Roessler, who probably also came up with the idea to title the series *Dead City*. That term alludes to the famous novel *Bruges-la-Morte*, which was published by the Belgian writer Georges Rodenbach in 1892 and would lend a key concept of Symbolism. The city of Bruges adopts human features and serves as a projection screen for a pessimist aura of silence, mysticism, and death.[12]

There is no trace of this literary model in Schiele's paintings, but he, too, immerses the small town of Krumau in the mysterious, gloomy mood characteristic of Rodenbach's Bruges. In Schiele's works, Krumau lies in a shadowy realm and recalls the city of Pearl, the location of Alfred Kubin's 1909 novel *Die andere Seite* (translated as *The Other Side*), which lies "in permanent twilight."[13] Characteristically, Schiele chose for his paintings not the architectural jewels of Krumau, which date from the height of the Bohemian Renaissance and Baroque from the sixteenth to the eighteenth century, but instead depicted exclusively the simple houses of the bourgeoisie, on which the centuries had left their traces. In principle, Schiele followed rather precisely the existing topography of the city, but he changed and manipulated it as desired with a refined artistic sleight of hand. In the painting *Tote Stadt III (Stadt am blauen Fluss III)* (Dead City III [City on the Blue River III]) [Fig. 4], for example, the artist

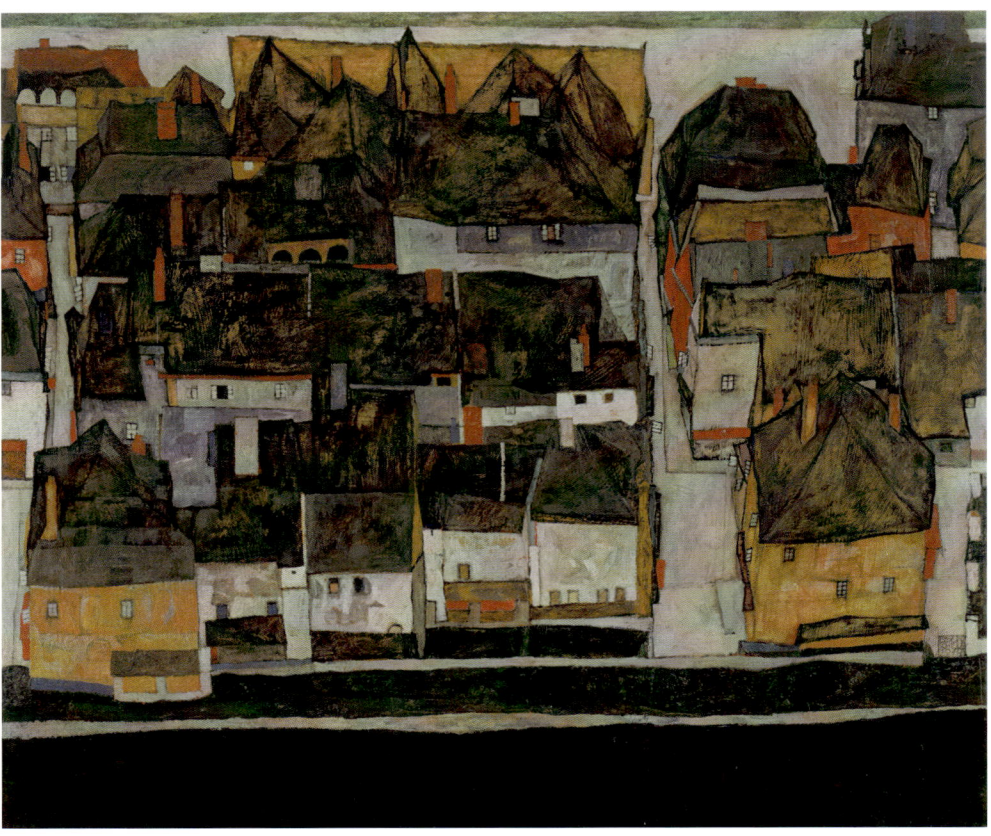

6. Egon Schiele, *The Small City IV*, 1914, oil on canvas. Leopold Museum, Vienna (Kallir P278). Photo: Leopold Museum, Vienna

looked down from a bird's-eye perspective on a group of houses; in Schiele's work, they are surrounded on three sides by the black of the Moldau (now Vltava) River, making them seem almost island-like. The group of houses can, in fact, largely be verified as extant buildings, but the course of the river is a product of the artist's imagination.[14] But precisely by means of this striking bend in the river, Schiele achieves an oppressive effect of the scene being hermetically sealed. The dense group of houses resembles a slumbering organism with the black river menacingly approaching it.

In other paintings from the *Dead City* series, such as *Die kleine Stadt I (Tote Stadt VI)* (The Small City I [Dead City VI]) [Cat. No. 45] of 1912, the artist brings the houses closer to the viewer, so that they seem less like a group

and more like individual objects. As such, they appear highly organic; their rows of windows turn into facial features; eyes peer out of the nocturnal façades, which become grinning masks. Schiele proceeds very modestly with his pleasure in animating them: the anthropomorphic effect is palpable but never inexorable. In this way, the artist avoids the risk of his works lapsing into bizarre fantasies or even caricatures.

In some of the motifs from Krumau, Schiele intensified this anthropomorphic effect by removing the houses from their real topography and placing them in freely invented, suggestive surroundings. For example, in the painting *Häuser am Meer (Häuserreihe)* (Houses by the Sea [Row of Houses]) [Fig. 5] of 1914, he shifted an entire row of houses to a bleak, flat landscape. The sea of the title is only suggested; Schiele was probably thinking of a mud flat by the sea that is regularly flooded with water. The barren landscape formations, designed as horizontal stripes, rise like islands out of this deserted wasteland. The broken, muted colors of the painting reinforce this impression of being abandoned and left exposed. Schiele hardly ever placed composition and color in the service of mood and symbolism as much as he did in this work.

In addition to such symbolic presentations, motifs from Krumau inspired the artist to create paintings of the town focused more on the formal design. In these, Schiele's penchant for geometric structures, which reach a climax in his work in the years around 1913 and 1914, becomes unmistakable. In several of his Krumau scenes, Schiele presents the cramped bustle in the town's streets as a system of orthogonal lines and planes that is harnessed into the picture plane and extends out to the edges of the painting in parallel with them. Even in these geometrically sober-looking *vedute*, however, the suggestive effect of certain motivic elements is surprising. In the painting *Die kleine Stadt IV* (The Small City IV) [Fig. 6], for example, the rows of houses in Krumau are abruptly terminated in the lower half of the painting by the broad black band of the Vltava River, whose unexpected appearance here has an oppressive effect.

In the following years as well, Schiele repeatedly worked with motifs from Krumau. He visited the city for shorter periods, for example, in May and June 1913, in November 1914, and in September 1917.[15] During such brief stays, he executed studies that he made directly in front of the motif in question, sometimes using watercolors on paper. In these studies, Schiele revealed an incredible precision in his topographic reproduction, as is impressively demonstrated, for example, by the sheet *Alte Häuser in Krumau* (Old Houses in Krumau)

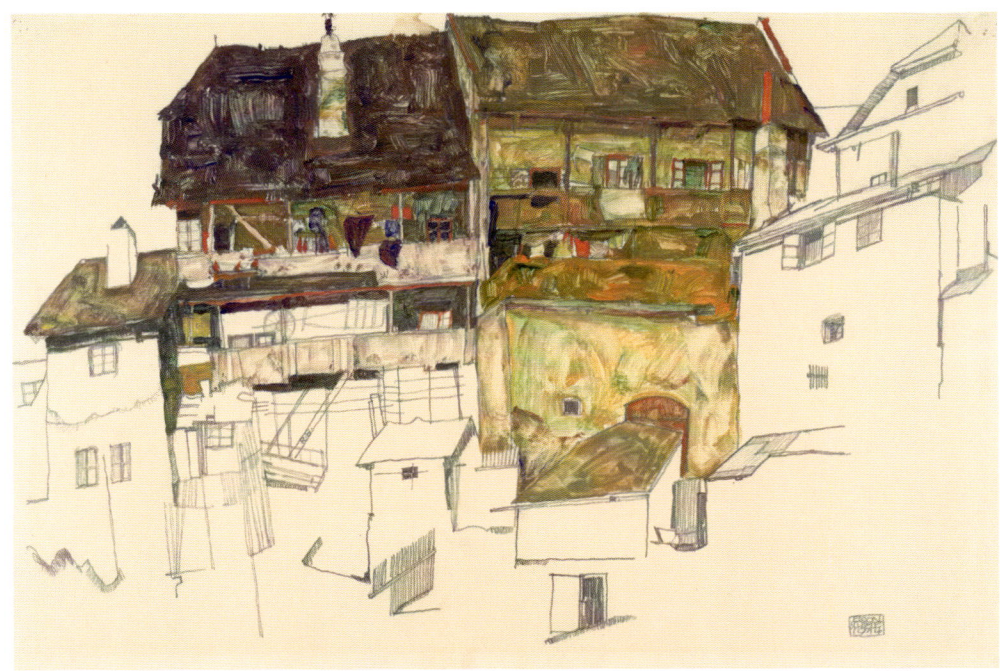

7. Egon Schiele, *Old Houses in Krumau*, 1914, pencil and gouache on Japanese paper. The Albertina Museum, Vienna, (Kallir D1691)

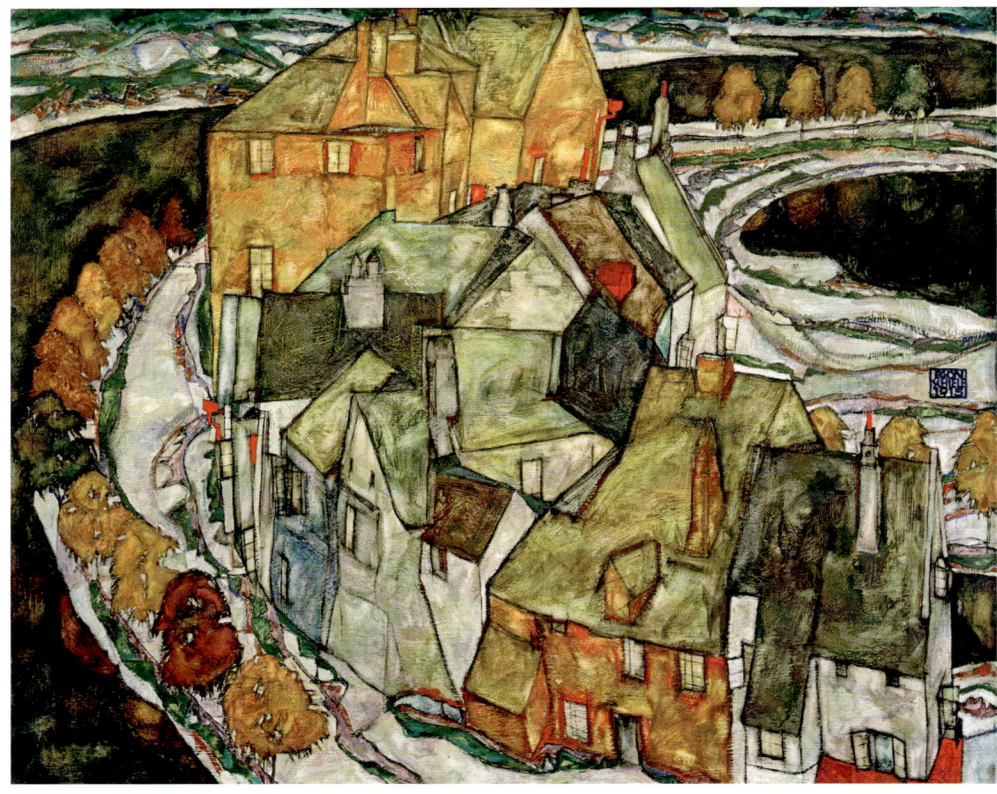

8. Egon Schiele, *Island Town (Krumau Town Crescent II)*, 1915, oil, gouache, and black chalk on canvas. Leopold Museum, Vienna (Kallir P293). Photo: Leopold Museum, Vienna

[Fig. 7] of 1914. This pencil drawing is partially colored, and some of the white patches have notations for colors, with which the artist was clearly hoping to remind himself of the exact colors needed later.[16]

In a series of large-format *vedute* from Krumau, which belong to Schiele's late period, that is, the years from 1915 to 1918, and are titled *Häuserbogen* (Town Crescent), the artist once again brought formal, compositional aspects to the fore. In the version of *Inselstadt (Krumau Häuserbogen II)* (Island Town [Krumau Town Crescent II]) [Fig. 8] from 1915, a section of the town is delimited on two sides by the arc-shaped course of the Vltava River. Within a tree-covered shore landscape, the insularly isolated, closely packed group of houses also follows the curve of the river. As a result, the staggered, often slanted façades

unfold a special dynamic as they recede. Whereas in this painting the city is present in autumnal shades of ocher and gray, in a later version of the *Town Crescent* motif—namely *Stadtende (Krumau Häuserbogen III)* (Edge of Town [Krumau Town Crescent III]) [see ill. on p. 21] of 1917–18—individual façades also have colorful accents. In these geometrically splintered compositions, Schiele may have been assimilating indirect influences from Cubism. He was perhaps inspired by French and German artists close to Cubism, whom Schiele had met in the milieu of the Goltz and Thannhauser galleries in Munich.[17] It is also conceivable that he had contacts with proponents of Czech Cubism, since he had exhibited with them at the Sonderbund exhibition in Cologne in 1912, for example. Such influences are not documented, however, so these reflections represent mere suppositions.

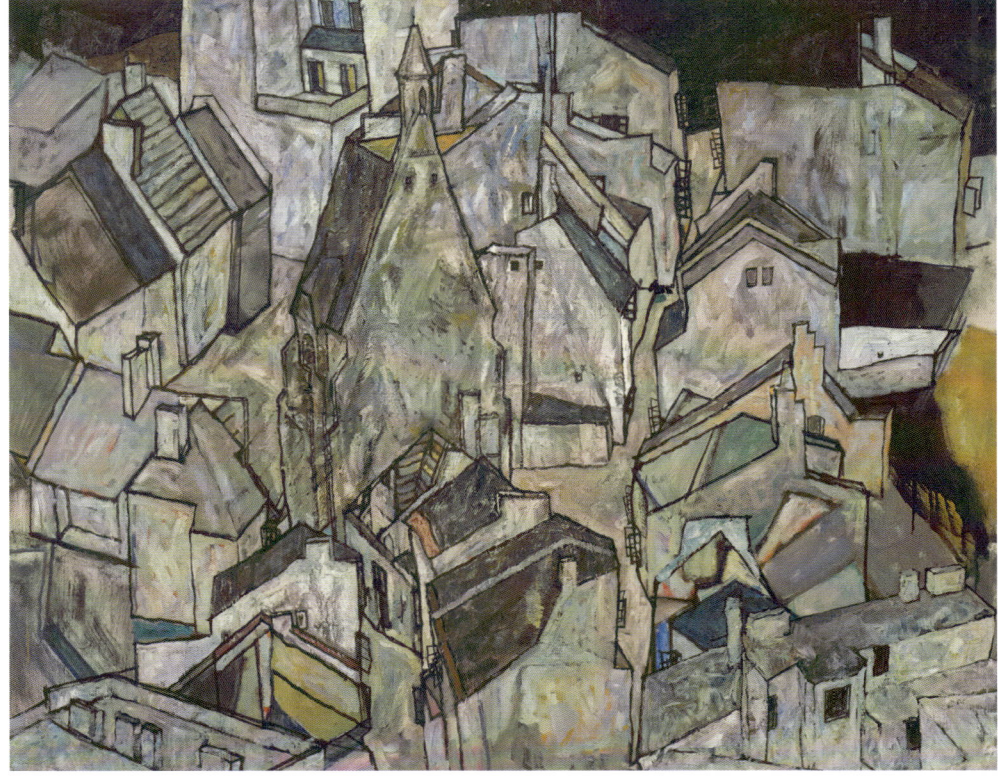

9. Egon Schiele, *Mödling II*, 1918, oil on canvas. Wien Museum, Vienna (Kallir P333). Photo: Birgit and Peter Kainz, Wien Museum

STEIN AN DER DONAU

In a letter to Reininghaus, Schiele explained his motivation for choosing the town of Stein as a motif: "I spent the day before yesterday in Krems and Stein a.d. [an der] Donau because I have long-standing memories of these towns and because I feel a yearning to paint pictures of such towns."[18] By "such towns" he presumably meant towns in an especially picturesque location that look old, which was the case with Krumau and now applied to the small town of Stein, located around thirty miles west of Vienna in a charming location on the Danube River. Unlike in the *vedute* of Krumau, in the depictions of Stein that Schiele painted in the spring of 1913 he did indeed choose the most striking buildings in the city, that is to say, focusing on its medieval churches and several picturesque houses whose locations deviate only slightly from reality. Four paintings with views of the city are securely attributed today; Tobias G. Natter proposes that there was a fifth, large-format scene of which every trace has been lost.[19] Schiele recorded the city from two different viewpoints: one looking from the vineyard slopes down on the city with the Danube in the background and one from the opposite bank of the river with the vineyard terraces visible behind the city. The view with the vineyards in the painting *Stein an der Donau, von Süden gesehen (gross)* (Stein on the Danube, Seen from the South [Large]) [Cat. no. 54] in particular reveals Schiele's decided interest in formal reflection, for example, when he repeats the horizontal lines of the riverbank in the horizontal but organically curved edges of the vineyard terraces and effectively contrasts them with the vertical lines of the towers.

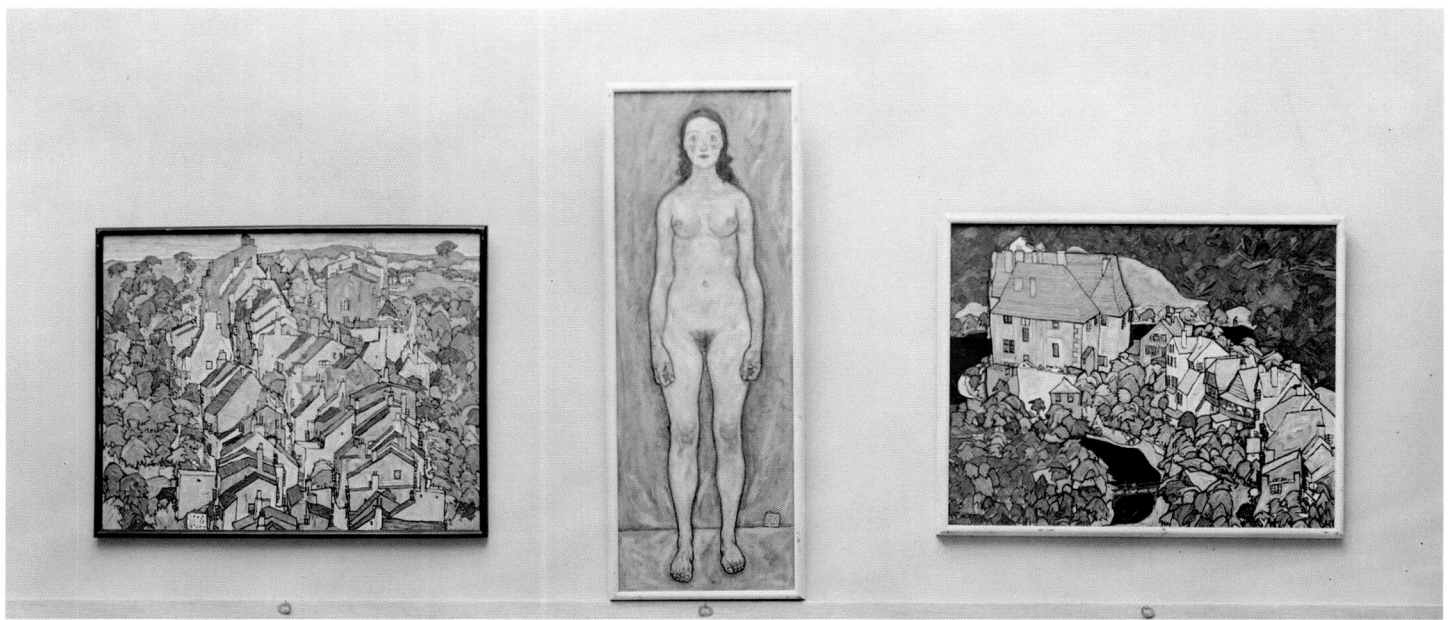

MÖDLING BEI WIEN

Another locale Schiele selected for a townscape is Mödling, near Vienna. The artist probably produced three scenes of it in total. The charm of this little town may have come to Schiele's attention during his military service, which frequently took him to the areas around Vienna. For the view *Mödling II* [Fig. 9] of 1918, the artist chose an elevated perspective similar to that of many of his Krumau *vedute*. And much as he did there, here too he presents a closely packed group of houses that extends to the edge of the painting and therefore seems strangely hermetic. The Gothic Spitalskirche rises in the center of the painting; its pointed roof gable is echoed a number of times in those of the neighboring buildings. With its wan, gray coloration, extending across façades and roofs equally, the Mödling pictures unfold again in the same gloomy mood that was typical of the Krumau *vedute* of his early years. And it seems that with this strikingly angular, "Gothic" confusion of planes of the houses in Mödling, even more so than with the Krumau *vedute*, Schiele earns

the appellation "Neo-Gothic" that Roessler had applied to the artist at the very beginning of their friendship.[20] What is new about the Mödling scenes, however, are the broad, often irregularly drawn, strong contour lines, whose overall effect conveys a peculiar organism and, in tandem with the sparse colors, an almost abrupt archaism.

FICTIVE TOWNSCAPES

Especially in Schiele's final creative years, there is an increasing number of views of cities and groups of houses that cannot be assigned to any particular topography. Although some motifs can be connected with Krumau, the overall composition appears to have been freely invented. For example, the crowded group of houses in the large-format painting *Stadt im Grünen (Die alte Stadt III)* (Town among Greenery [The Old City III]) [Cat. no. 68] of 1917 cannot be related to any specific, identifiable place. One is struck by the comparatively reduced formal design in this way, which essentially concentrates on a group of densely packed, staggered houses

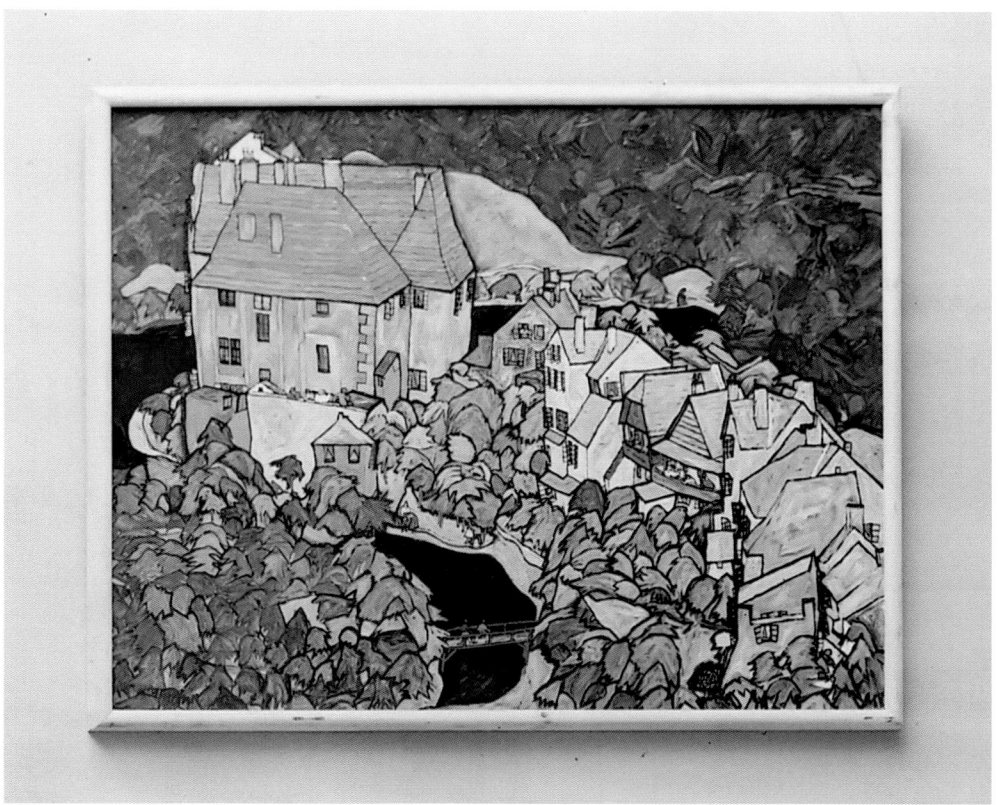

facing the same direction. This homogeneity is disrupted by the surprisingly bright colors on several of the walls of the houses, which in combination with the intense green of the lush stand of trees that generously frames the group of houses lends the painting a surprisingly cheery atmosphere. Whereas Schiele's townscapes of the early years convey an overwhelmingly autumnal-cool impression, in this example he embeds the *veduta* in a summery landscape. Over the course of his development as an artist, Schiele clearly managed to leave behind the symbol-laden melancholy of his early period and open up to a carefreeness that is new in his work.

A similar atmosphere of summery colors may have been associated with a townscape that is known today only from a black-and-white illustration. Only recently, Kerstin Jesse identified one of the nine Schiele paintings shown in the "*Österrikisk* konstutställning" (Austrian Art Exhibition) at the Liljevalchs Konsthall in Stockholm in September 1917 as a work previously unknown to Schiele scholars.[21] At the latest since the commendable publications of Elizabeth Clegg regarding that show, which is thoroughly documented in excellent photographs, unlike most other exhibitions from the period,[22] it was possible to gain a number of insights from it for more detailed research into Viennese painting of the early twentieth century. Without a doubt, the discovery of a new work by Schiele represents a minor sensation. In terms of its format and motif but also its style, this previously unknown townscape, identified in the catalogue of the Stockholm exhibition only as *Landskap* (Landscape) [Fig. 11], adopts directly the aforementioned work *Town among Greenery (The Old City III)*, and in the show in Stockholm it was hung in its immediate vicinity [Fig. 10]. The painting *Landscape (Krumau Town Crescent)* can therefore also be dated to around 1917. A study drawing for the painting has survived, which has been dated to 1917, probably based on style.[23] Both the drawing and the painting show a group of houses surrounded by an arching river, recalling the *Krumau Häuserbogen* series. But here a striking, castle-like building joins the

11. Egon Schiele, *Landscape (Krumau Town Crescent)*, ca. 1917, oil on canvas, whereabouts unknown, (Kallir P313a). Photo: Archives of the Liljevalchs Konsthall, Stockholm

group of houses. It may be part of Krumauer Schloss (Krumau Castle), specifically the portion immediately adjacent to its round tower, which is characterized by a tall hipped roof. The dark plane in the background visible in the black-and-white photograph might be a wooded mountain ridge. The landscape element thus dominates in the overall impression, which would explain the title assigned to the painting in the catalogue. The individual houses that also appear in this photograph, some of which also recall motifs from Krumau, presumably had bright colors similar to those seen in the aforementioned painting *Town among Greenery (The Old City III).*

CONCLUSION

Schiele was an exceptional artist in many areas. His art was part of the Expressionist movement that seized many European artists around 1910. Fascinated by experiences that verge on the mystical, Schiele also penetrated the abysses of Symbolism. With his unmistakable manner of representation and highly unusual pictorial subjects, Schiele rose far above the mainstream of his time. In addition to provocative self-portraits and portraits, taboo-violating nudes, and allegorizing figurative works, the uniqueness of his lifework is manifested above all in his landscapes and townscapes. Yet Schiele was no landscape painter in the traditional sense. His landscapes are not snapshots of nature but rather manifestations of a lyrical, melancholic experience of nature. Pulsating urban life is not encountered in his townscapes but rather timeless reflections of the mystically inclined artist's soul. His landscapes and towns are largely devoid of human beings but inhabited rather by the dreamlike, visionary moods and emotions that the artist projected into them.

Translated from the German by Steven Lindberg

1 Franz Smola, "Egon Schiele's Landscapes and Cityscapes," in *Egon Schiele, Jenny Saville*, ed. Zürcher Kunstgesellschaft, exh. cat. Kunsthaus Zürich (Ostfildern: Hatje Cantz, 2014), 89–91.

2 Kimberly A. Smith, *Between Ruin and Renewal: Egon Schiele's Landscapes* (New Haven, CT: Yale University Press, 2004), 174.

3 Helena Pereña Sáez, *Egon Schiele: Wahrnehmung, Identität und Weltbild* (Marburg: Tectum, 2010), 240–50.

4 Egon Schiele to Carl Reininghaus, February 27, 1912, Private Collection, quoted in *Egon Schiele: Poems and Letters, 1910–1912*, ed. Elisabeth Leopold, trans. Jeff Tapia (New York: Prestel, 2008), 101; cf. Christian M. Nebehay, *Egon Schiele, 1890–1918: Leben, Briefe, Gedichte* (Salzburg: Residenz, 1979), no. 320; Leopold Museum, Vienna, Egon Schiele Datenbank der Autografen (hereafter ESDA) ID no. 45.

5 Egon Schiele to Oskar Reichel, January 31, 1911, quoted in *Egon Schiele: Poems and Letters* (see note 4), 73, ESDA ID no. 113; http://www.schiele-dokumentation.at; cf. Pereña Sáez, *Egon Schiele* (see note 3), 229.

6 Pereña Sáez, *Egon Schiele* (see note 3), 229–40.

7 [Albert] Paris von Gütersloh, *Egon Schiele*, exh. cat. (Vienna: Galerie H. O. Miethke, 1911); Tobias G. Natter, *Die Galerie Miethke: Eine Kunsthandlung im Zentrum der Moderne*, exh. cat. (Vienna: Jüdisches Museum, 2003), 218; Elisabeth Leopold, "Die frühen Schaffensjahre Schieles: Die Ausstellung in der Galerie Miethke," in *Egon Schiele: Melancholie und Provokation*, Elisabeth Leopold and Diethard Leopold, exh. cat. Leopold Museum, Vienna (Vienna: Brandstätter, 2011), 12–31, esp. 15–18.

8 Gütersloh's preface had been published by Arthur Roessler only shortly before in the third issue of the short-lived journal he edited: *Bildende Kunst*. See Nebehay, *Egon Schiele* (see note 4), 151.

9 Smith, *Between Ruin and Renewal* (see note 2), 51–57.

10 Egon Schiele, war diary, May 10, 1916, Albertina, Vienna, ESDA ID no. 978; http://www.schiele-dokumentation.at, quoted in Kerstin Jesse, "Egon Schiele: Four Trees, 1917," in *Egon Schiele: The Making of a Collection*, ed. Stella Rollig and Kerstin Jesse, trans. Rebecca Law, Nick Somers, and Jessica West, exh. cat. Belvedere, Vienna (Munich: Hirmer, 2018), 195–200, esp. 196.

11 Franz Smola, "City on the Blue River II, 1911," in Rollig and Jesse, *Egon Schiele* (see note 10), 165–68.

12 Gisèle Ollinger-Zinque, catalogue entry for Fernand Khnopff, "Avec Georges Rodenbach: Une ville morte," in *Fernand Khnopff*, exh. cat. Royal Museums of Fine Arts of Belgium, Brussels; Museum der Moderne, Salzburg; McMullen Museum of Art, Boston (Ostfildern-Ruit: Hatje Cantz, 2004), 225.

13 Alfred Kubin, *The Other Side*, trans. Mike Mitchell (Sawtry, UK: Dedalus, 2000), 191.

14 Rudolf Leopold, *Egon Schiele: Paintings, Watercolours, Drawings*, trans. Alexander Lieven (London: Phaidon, 1973), 641–43.

15 Franz E. Wischin, *Die Stadt am blauen Fluss: Egon Schiele und Krumau* (Vienna: Wirtschaftstrend Zeitschriften, 1994), 49–50.

16 Franz Smola, "'Shall I color it?': On the Special Features of Schiele's Colored Works on Paper," in the *Conference Volume on the First Egon Schiele Symposium at the Leopold Museum*, ed. Hans-Peter Wipplinger (Vienna: Leopold Museum, 2017), 61–81, esp. 74–75.

    The Galerie Hans Goltz in Munich tried to sell Schiele's works in Germany from 1911 to 1914. In the spring of 1918, in connection with the artists' group Neue Secession Wien that he had formed, Schiele again worked closely with Goltz. On this, see Franz Smola, "Egon Schiele and the Artists' Associations Neue Secession Wien and Sonderbund," in *Egon Schiele: Expression and Lyric; Conference Volume on the Second Egon Schiele Symposium at the Leopold Museum*, ed. Verena Gamper and Hans-Peter Wipplinger (Vienna: Leopold Museum, 2018), 153–69.

17 Franz Smola, "Der österreichische Beitrag zur Kölner Sonderbundausstellung 1912," in *1912: Mission Moderne; Die Jahrhundertschau des Sonderbundes*, ed. Barbara Schaefer, exh. cat. Wallraf-Richartz-Museum and Fondation Corboud, Cologne (Cologne: Wienand, 2012), 177–91, esp. 184–88; Franz Smola, "Egon Schiele und der Österreich-Beitrag der Kölner Sonderbundausstellung 1912," *Egon Schiele Jahrbuch*, ed. Johann Thomas Ambrózy et al., vols. IV–VIII, Vienna, 2014–18 (Vienna: REMAprint, Druck- und Verlagsgesellschaft m.b.H, 2019), 58–71, esp. 67–71.

18 Egon Schiele to Carl Reininghaus, March 23, 1913, ESDA ID no. 57; http://www.schiele-dokumentation.at, quoted in Christian Bauer, "Places of Desire and Townscapes: Egon Schiele's Paintings of Krems and Stein," in *Egon Schiele: Almost a Lifetime*, ed. Christian Bauer, trans. Matthias Goldmann and Camilla R. Nielsen (Munich: Hirmer, 2015), 83–91, esp. 83.

19 Tobias G. Natter, ed., *Egon Schiele: The Complete Paintings, 1909–1918* (Cologne: Taschen, 2017), 542, cat. no. 141.

20 Arthur Roessler, "Egon Schiele: Mt 9 Reproduktionen nach Bildern und Zeichnungen," *Bildende Künstler: Monatsschrift für Künstler und Kunstfreunde* (1911), 104–18, reprinted in Nebehay, *Egon Schiele* (see note 4), 171.

21 I am sincerely grateful to Kerstin Jesse of the Leopold Museum, Vienna, for permission to publish this discovery for the first time in this essay.

22 Elizabeth Clegg, "'Austrian Art' on the Move: The Cultural Politics of International Exhibiting 1900–1918," in *Gustav Klimt: Painting, Design and Modern Life*, ed. Tobias G. Natter and Christoph Grunenberg, exh. cat. Tate Liverpool (London: Tate Publications, 2008), 52–57, esp. 56; Elizabeth Clegg, "War and Peace at the 1917 Stockholm "Austrian Art Exhibition" of 1917," *Burlington Magazine*, no. 1315 (October 2012): 676–88.

23 Jane Kallir, *Egon Schiele: The Complete Works*, exp. ed. (New York: Harry N. Abrams, 1998), cat. no. 2136.

LOST IN LANDSCAPE

HUMAN BEINGS IN THEIR SURROUNDINGS

Kerstin Jesse

LANDSCAPE VERSUS HUMAN BEING
From December 1914 to January 1915, the Galerie Arnot in Vienna presented a solo exhibition by Egon Schiele at its premises on the Kärntnerring. In addition to watercolors and drawings, sixteen paintings from the years 1911 to 1914 were presented, including nine landscapes and townscapes.[1] "The area in which Schiele could effortlessly have achieved a certain importance is clearly the landscape […]," wrote the critic Rudolf von Enderes during the exhibition, "but a truly diabolical imagination that cannot do enough when it comes to showing the dark sides of the human passions compels him again and again to the area of the figurative," he continued, disappointed.[2] He saw "healthy efforts" in the *vedute* of the town of Stein, quite the opposite of the "perverse abomination" of the painting *Mann und Frau I (Liebespaar I)* (Man and Woman I [Lovers I]) [Cat. no. 42].[3]

In general, at the time there seemed to be a recognition of Schiele's sometimes decorative townscapes and landscapes than of his way of depicting the human being. His drawing talent was recognized unanimously by the most prominent critics, but generally there was little appreciation for his radical exposure of human plights, desires, and fears and his extreme

view of the body and his questioning of the self in the form of an unfamiliarly new and consciously exaggerated dramaturgy.

In the spring of 1912, nearly three years before Endere's comment, the painter and art critic Adalbert F. Seligmann expressed a similar viewpoint. In addition to exhibitions in Germany and Budapest, Schiele participated in the thirty-fifth Hagenbund (Hagen Union) exhibition from March to April with eight oil paintings, five of which were townscapes or landscapes.[4] Seligmann, conservative and antimodernist in his basic stance, emphasized, on the one hand, the "refined, playful virtuosity of the draftsmanship" of the then twenty-two-year-old; on the other hand, he described Schiele's renderings of figures as "gruesome-fantastical caricatures […], ghostly lemurs with bloody spider fingers, mutilated, half-decomposed corpses, as if caught in a distorting mirror" and "even the painting seems to have been taken from thousand-year-old graves."[5]

Hans Tietze, by contrast, felt that the spring exhibitions of 1912 necessitated reflection on "Neue Richtungen in der Landschaftsmalerei" (New Directions in Landscape painting).[6] The art historian wrote:

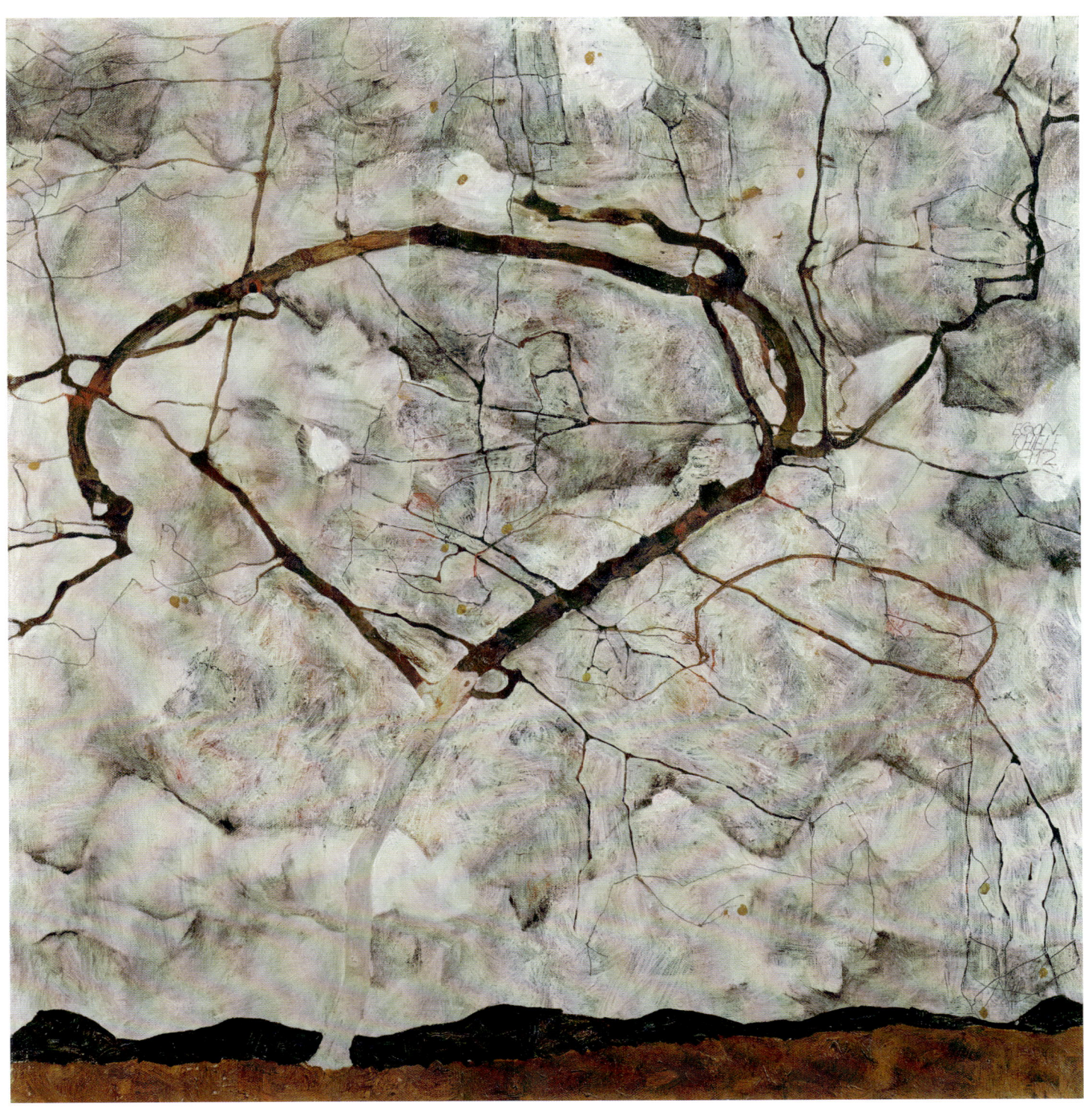

Perhaps it is most important for landscape painting in particular to make general observations now and again, since it is characteristic of this field [...] that the idea is widespread so that the artist is simply supposed to copy a piece of nature. In fact, however, there is no art that does such a thing; it is always a creative engagement with nature for a beauty that exists only when the artist sees it, indeed, when he first forms it.

Setting out from Impressionist landscape painting, which he says strove for a "uniform spatial impression [...] at a specific moment," Tietze switched to a "new conception of the world" that "begins to make itself clearly noticeable" above all among "younger painters." Whereas previously it had been the "individual standpoint" to which everything depicted was "subordinated," now the individual objects begin "to possess a separate life; a stream of life goes through the landscape paintings, in which otherwise only light and color had done all the talking. [...] [E]ither we insert something of our life into them, or we assume that all of nature is permeated by a soul of which ours is just one part and that is also expressed in every other natural object." A heightening of the effect results from "anthropomorphizing expressions that attribute human action and feeling to things," Tietze analyzed.

One of the works exhibited in the Hagenbund show was *Herbstbaum in bewegter Luft (Winterbaum)* (Autumn Tree in Turbulent Air [Winter Tree]) [Fig. 1].[7] Against a deep, hilly horizon, a thin, leafless tree grows out of barren, brown earth; its filigreed branches ramify in all directions like delicate veins against a sky that is sometimes creating and sometimes breaking down forms.[8] Tietze continues:

To Schiele's landscapes, too [...] we come closer in this way; if one senses in the two tree studies only the charm of the lines and regards their delicate veins against the milk-white ground as a decorative spot—something like an agate—one satisfies the painter's intention only unsatisfactorily, I believe. He doubtless wants to express and trigger powerful and specific emotions in these twitching branches, [...] or with these trembling leafless stems and with the pale harmony of the colors.

SOULFUL LANDSCAPE

Tietze approached Schiele's tree landscapes, several of which were painted in 1911 and 1912,[9] in the artist's spirit. Schiele's letter from August 1913 to collector Franz Hauer seem like an extended confirmation of Tietze's remarks:

I find and know that drawing from nature is meaningless for me, because I paint paintings better from memory, as a vision, of the landscape.— For the most part, I am now observing the physical movement of mountains, water, trees, and flowers. Everywhere one is reminded of similar movements in the human body, of similar stirrings of joy and suffering in plants. [...] Most sincerely and with being and heart, one senses an autumnal tree in the summer; I want to paint this melancholy.[10]

Autumn Tree in Turbulent Air was acquired in December of the same year by the artist Magda Mautner-Markhof, who expressed herself openly to Schiele: "I much prefer, namely, [...] your landscapes to your figural works, which are often rather alien to me."[11] Yet the work does not avoid a human presence. The anthropomorphic or "soulful" landscape is a kind of hybrid form of depicting nature and human being. The human presence is brought into the picture by way of the artistic design of a landscape motif, and human sensations and feelings are expressed through natural elements.

The anthropomorphizing of the landscape is a central aspect of Schiele's oeuvre. His inner connection to nature is well known and omnipresent in his work as well as in his poems and letters. He was no "*Stubenhockerhäusler*"[12] (stay-at-home homebody) but rather had since childhood spent lots of time in nature. "Every free moment, Egon was out in the meadows, on the slopes, at the streams and drawing sheet after sheet," recalled the art historian and librarian Otto Kunz in 1929.[13]

"In nature, the artist felt and found the divine: Nature is purpose, but God is there, and I sense him powerfully, very powerfully, most powerfully."[14] Schiele's image of the world was a pantheistic one. Questioning and analyzing himself, his existence—"of what enigmatic substances am I composed"—life and death, led him to the conviction that the earth and every living being consist of individual elements that are in part immortal and repeatedly sprout anew—an everlasting cycle:

> *Earth breathes, smells, hears, feels in all its small parts; acquires, pairs, decays, and finds itself, [...] everything in everything; [...]. The ephemerality of the material in the sense of an existence is destined; a certain birth and death, coming; living, which should be understood to mean unceasing disintegration, [...] so that there [...] can be no complete death.*[15]

Depicting visually the profound impressions and insights of life and getting to the "seed of the divine shoot" in nature is, according to Schiele, reserved only for the chosen.[16] "I know that among a thousand there is but one [...] who recognizes the organism of all things, who sees in the soul life of plants and in their visage

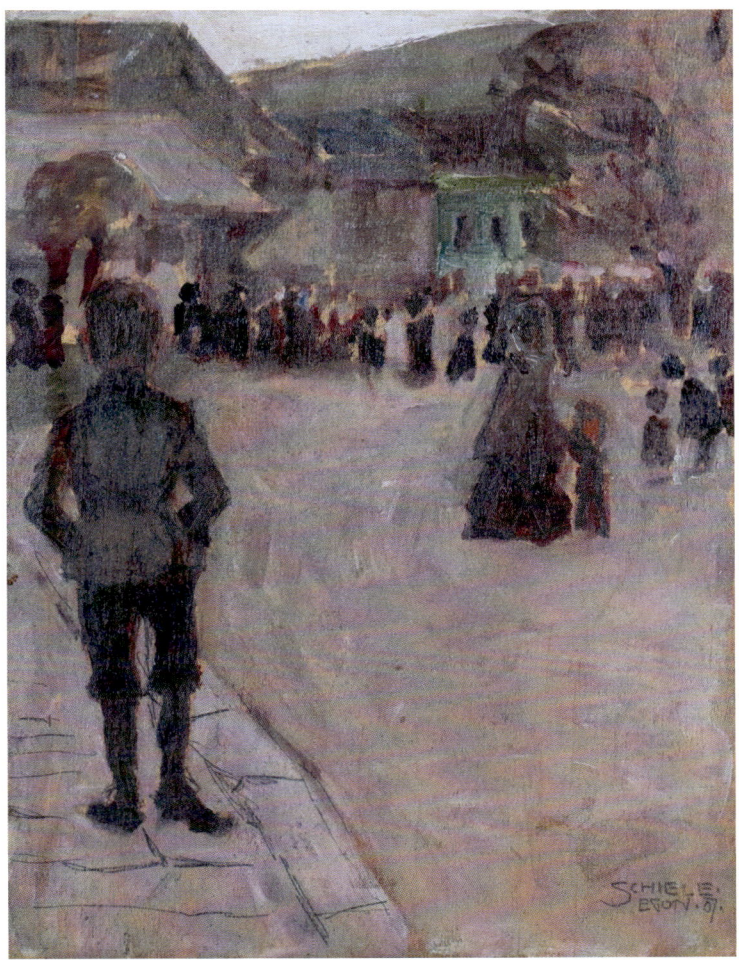

the living breath of their face."[17] True artists number among them; they are those of great spiritual gifts, discoverers, who can express the manifestations in nature that they fathom. They are "closely tied to the world. [...] [T]hey are discoverers. Godlike, highly gifted, all rounded, all knowing—humble living beings."[18]

The works, which are often full of meaning and visionary, found their point of departure in Schiele's aims to depict visions of landscapes, spiritual life, his worldview and impressions; to grasp the essence, the soul of things.[19] Landscape *vedute* without these connotations were irrelevant to the artist.[20]

2. Egon Schiele, *Before the Feast of St. Leopold in Klosterneuburg*, 1907, oil on panel. Private Collection (Kallir P82). Photo: Leopold Museum, Vienna

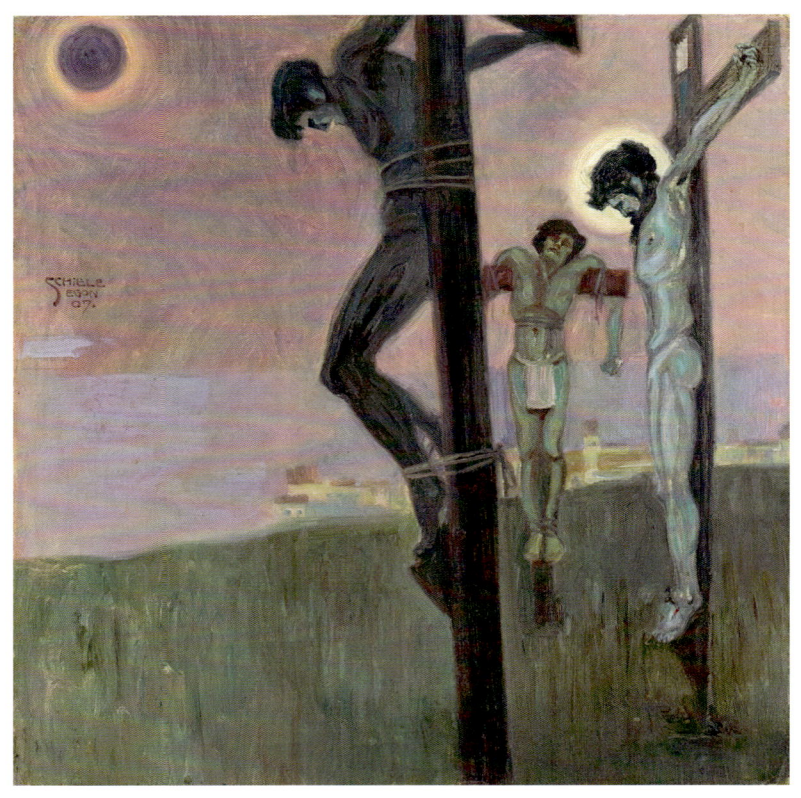

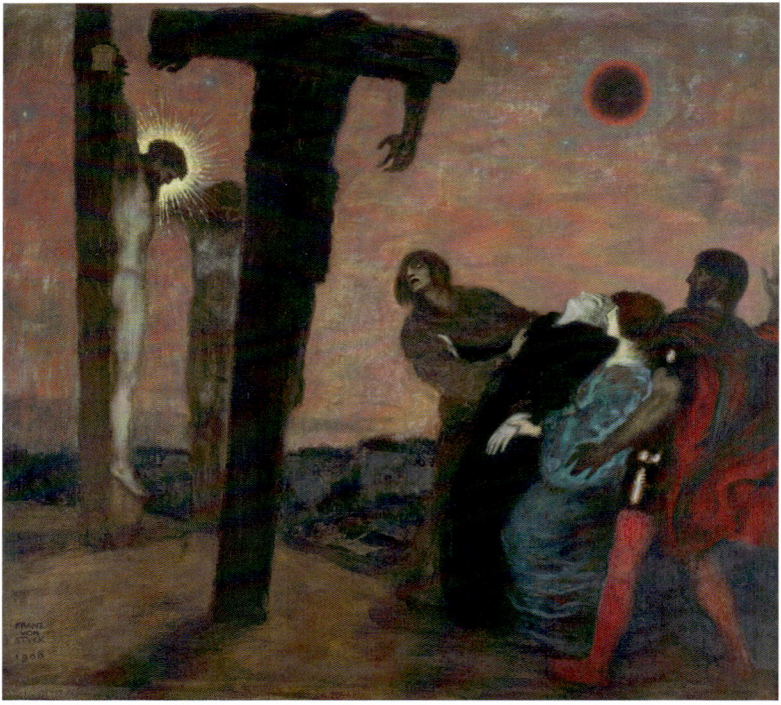

HUMAN BEING AND LANDSCAPE

The human being and townscapes and landscapes are the main motifs of his pictorial compositions, whereby his intense engagement with landscape motifs has received little attention thus far.[21] The discussion that follows represents an attempt to examine the spatial surroundings of Schiele's protagonists with a focus on the landscape. In addition to general remarks, specific works will be studied more closely.

People embedded in landscape surroundings or interacting in a natural environment are rare in Schiele's work, and genre scenes in general are avoided in his artistically essential oeuvre. There are exceptions primarily in his early years in school and at the academy, in a phase of learning and finding himself artistically. Naturally, these sometimes rather traditional works are often very different in expression, style, and painting technique; sometimes Schiele found other works from which he took orientation.[22]

Strikingly many townscapes and landscapes were produced in his early paintings in 1907. Schiele was already a student at the art academy in Vienna and met Gustav Klimt that year. There are several motifs of people in everyday activities: painting, sitting in the garden, working, on a walk or canoe ride.[23] The small-format easel painting *Vor dem Leopolditag in Klosterneuburg* (Before the Feast of St. Leopold in Klosterneuburg) [Fig. 2] reveals an unusually large—for Schiele—assembly of the population of Klosterneuburg. A single person in the foreground separated from the lively bustle a distance observes and perhaps contemplates joining it.

In his search for his own, stylistically unmistakable expression, the outmoded academy hardly played any role, but instead early supporters, such as Karl Ludwig Strauch and, in Vienna, the circle around Klimt and the formal idiom of the Wiener Werkstätte were of critical influence. Schiele was searching for the new, the unfamiliar; and it drove him to be active creatively. He also took inspiration even further afield and took inspiration from artists such as, briefly, Franz von Stuck. We owe to that source a painting of a Biblical scene outdoors—a rare exception.

CRUCIFIXION

In 1907, 1912, and in 1915, as well as in several sketches, we encounter the subject of the Crucifixion.[24] The small painting *Kreuzigung mit verfinsterter Sonne* (Crucifixion with Darkened Sun) [Fig. 3] explicitly follows the work *Am Kreuze* (On the Cross) [Fig. 4] by Franz von Stuck, as Christian Bauer convincingly demonstrated.[25] The artist, who was from Tettenweis, made a powerful impact on the Viennese art scene around 1900: from 1892 to 1914, Von Stuck was represented almost annually in exhibitions at the Künstlerhaus, the Secession, or the Galerie Miethke; so it was in 1907.[26] In that year, moreover, Schiele took a study trip to Munich, during which he had an opportunity to see four works by Stuck at the "Internationale Kunst-Ausstellung" (International Art Exhibition) of the local Secession, including this Crucifixion.[27] The somber, emotional depiction of the scene, the darkening black sun, the drama of the moment, and the "memorable compositions" made a lasting impression on Schiele.[28] As Robert Schmidt describes it:

> Stuck tried to lend new form to the old theme of the Crucifixion […]. A gruesome scene was the result. The one cross with the thief is hanging crooked as a black mass against the red sky, which is spanned like a blood-soaked curtain. […] It is not lasting pain but rather a spontaneous horror that shoots through the four

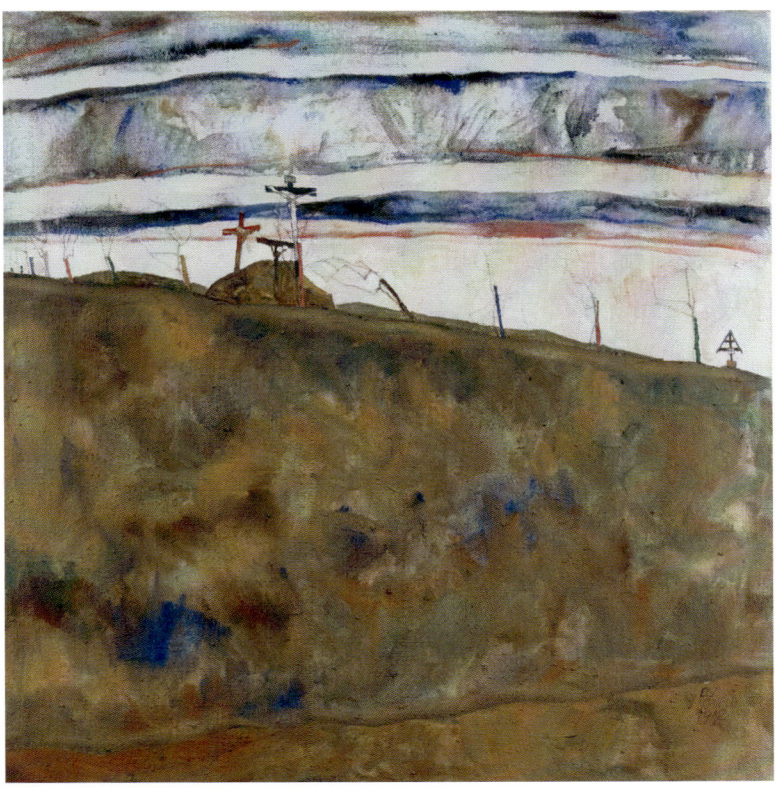

people, provoked by the sudden flare up of a sulfur-yellow halo around the head of the crucified man.[29]

Schiele stuck relatively closely to Stuck's model: he reversed the motif, reduced somewhat the sinister quality of the scene both in terms of colors and by eliminating the group of excited figures and moved the crucifixion to a green landscape near a village.

The same theme was rendered very differently later, in 1912, in the artistically relevant work by Schiele. In *Kalvarienberg* (Calvary) [Fig. 5], the Crucifixion group is moved to the far distance. The place for worshipping the Passion of Christ is emphasized by the title; in the painting, the design of the elevation and the dramatic execution of the sky play a dominant role.[30] The group itself merges into a row of

5. Egon Schiele, *Calvary*, 1912, oil on canvas. Leopold Museum, Vienna (Kallir P240). Photo: Leopold Museum, Vienna

Opposite:

3. Egon Schiele, *Crucifixion with Darkened Sun*, 1907, oil on canvas, mounted on cardboard. Private Collection, Austria (Kallir P30)

4. Franz von Stuck, *On the Cross*, 1906, tempera on canvas. National Museum, Poznań

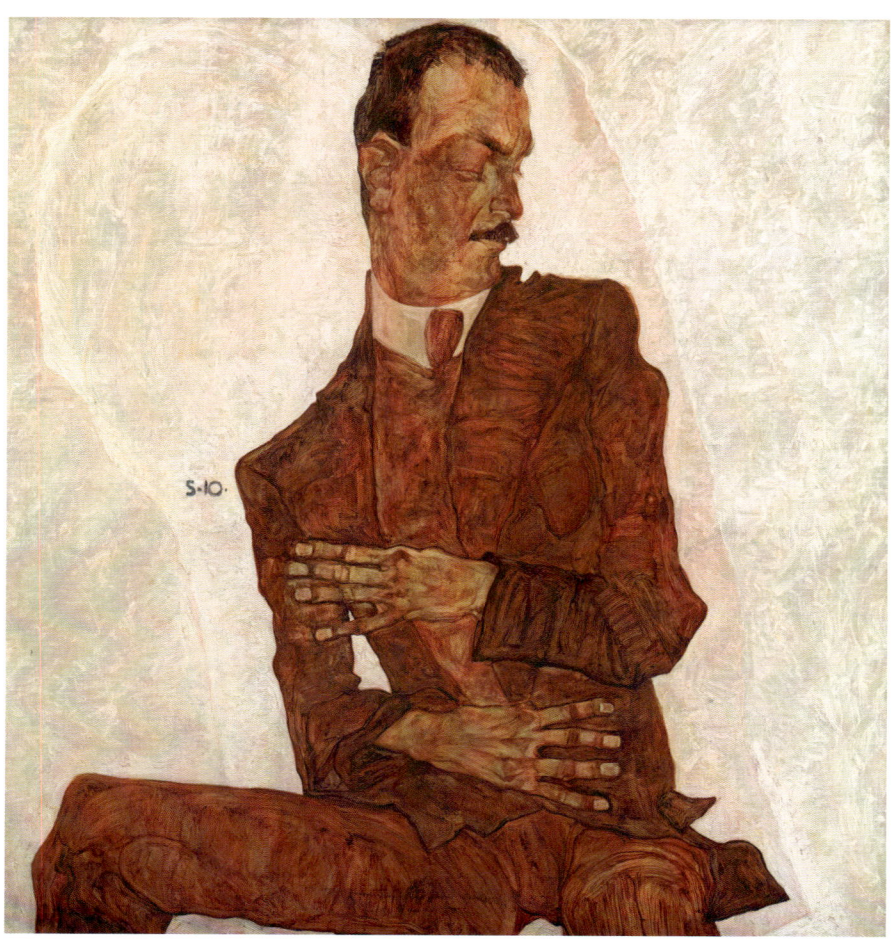

6. Egon Schiele, *Portrait of Arthur Roessler*, 1910 oil on canvas. W en Museum, Vienna (Kallir P163)

the Neukunstgruppe (New Art Group), which presented its works at the Galerie Pisko at the end of that year. He met his most important supporter, Arthur Roessler there.

Paintings such as *Current of Youth (Danaë)*, the portraits of his fellow students Hans Massmann and Anton Peschka, and *Selbstbildnis mit gespreizten Fingern* (Self-Portrait with Spread Fingers) (Kallir P153) completely speak the language of the Secession. His two artist colleagues are sitting on a comfortable fauteuil; spatial depth is negated; the background is formed by patterned planes. The reference to Klimt's portraiture is obvious (cf. *Fritza Riedler*, 1906). Nevertheless, several works, such as the portrait of his sister Gertrude [Cat. no. 38] and *Herbstbaum mit Fuchsien* (Autumn Tree with Fuchsias) (Kallir P158) point to Schiele's future handling of space: a striking void spreads out, a spatial context is lacking, and precise location is precluded. Gerti is sitting in or on a floral area that perhaps connotes a small landscape; on the left side, it rises up approximately to her waist. It cannot be said with certainty whether this is intended to indicate an exterior—and that seems irrelevant. All attention is focused on the sitter, who is surrounded by a mysterious void.[31] Schiele stretches the sitter across the center of the square format and demonstrates his connoisseurship in the balanced treatment of positive and negative space, which will continue to find expression, especially in countless works on paper, until his death.

In 1910, Schiele's artistic output was particularly productive, and his own stylistic signature is evident on sheet after sheet. Jugendstil complaisance gives way to an angular and bony, more expressive visual idiom. As in the portrait of Gerti Schiele, the space is left undefined in the portraits of Erwin von Graff, Karl Zakovšek, Eduard Kosmack, Oskar

barren, supported, leafless trees planted at regular intervals. The emphasized hilltop and the tree to the right of it, which is bent toward the Crucifixion group and nearly snapped by the wind, draws attention to the true subject only on closer inspection. By dramatically designing the landscape, Schiele was trying to evoke in the viewer the emotions inherent in the ominous Crucifixion.

TURNING POINT, 1909–10

The year 1909 was one of great and formative changes in Schiele's life: he celebrated his debut on Vienna's exhibition scene, left the academy after three years with some like-minded students, and cofounded with Anton Faistauer

Reichel, Herbert Reiner, Arthur Roessler [Fig. 6], and in several nudes. Yet the background is not a white, monochrome plane but a more or less subtly designed painterly solution. Careful study of the lively design of backgrounds in general is worthwhile, especially in the portraits of Kosmack, Reiner, and Roessler. Roessler is even backed or surrounded by a kind of "bubble." Similar outlining or distinguishing and hence emphasizing of a depiction are found in works from Vienna's Kunstgewerbeschule (School of the Applied Arts) and the Wiener Werkstätte, which Schiele knew well.[32] A design by Koloman Moser is offered here as an example [Fig. 7]. In the book *Die träumenden Knaben* (The Dreaming Boys), written and designed by Oskar Kokoschka for the Wiener Werkstätte, certain depictions are emphasized by an outlined area. The book, a copy of which Schiele owned,[33] was presented at the first "Kunstschau" in Vienna in 1908 and dedicated by Kokoschka to Klimt "in admiration."[34]

WORKS UNTIL 1914

With few exceptions, the natural surroundings of the human being played hardly any role until around 1914. In his *Selbstbildnis mit Pfauenweste, stehend* (Self-Portrait with Peacock Waistcoat, Standing) [Cat. no. 40] of 1911, a narrow strip of meadow with ciphers of flowers can just be seen, while the remainder of the background is immersed in a conglomerate of dark colors.[35] For the most part, Schiele's people are placed in a space that is not more closely defined, such as for example, in *Prozession* (Procession) [Cat. no. 41]. The title infers that the scene is outdoors. The enviroment in which the religious, celebratory procession of the group occurs is not, however, recognizable. Rather, it can be said that the geometrical, contoured forms to which the figures are essentially reduced are replicated in their surroundings: the figures and the surrounding space merge, and the individual forms are "perceived as parts of a whole."[36]

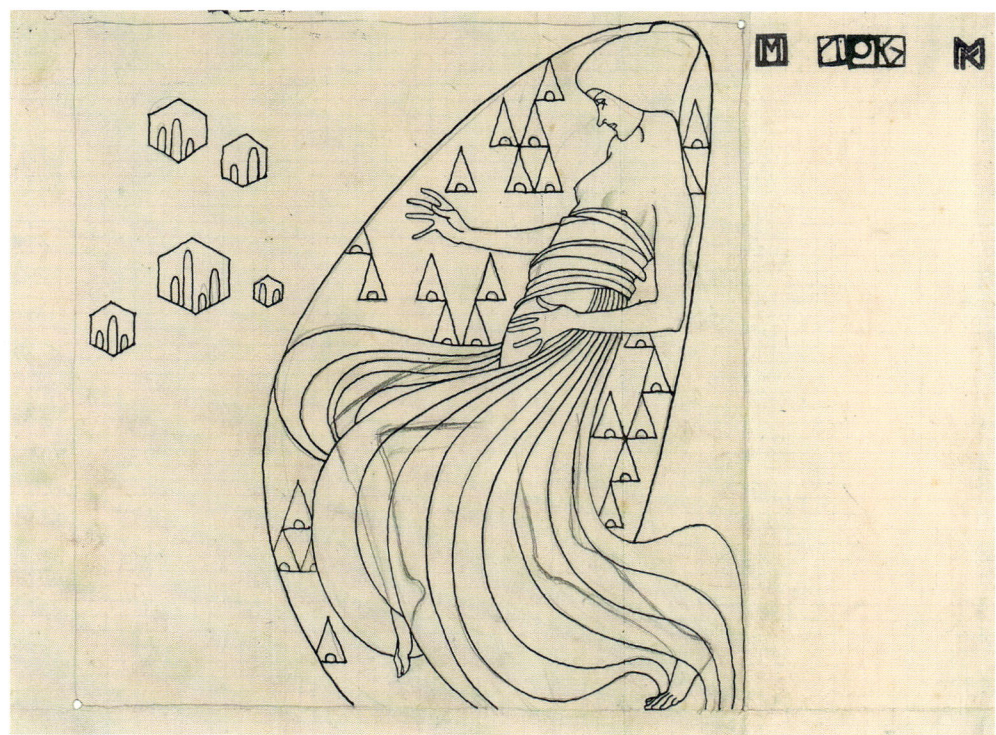

7. Koloman Moser, *Dancer*, design of a metal relief, 1904, pencil and ink on paper. Leopold Museum, Vienna. Photo: Leopold Museum, Vienna

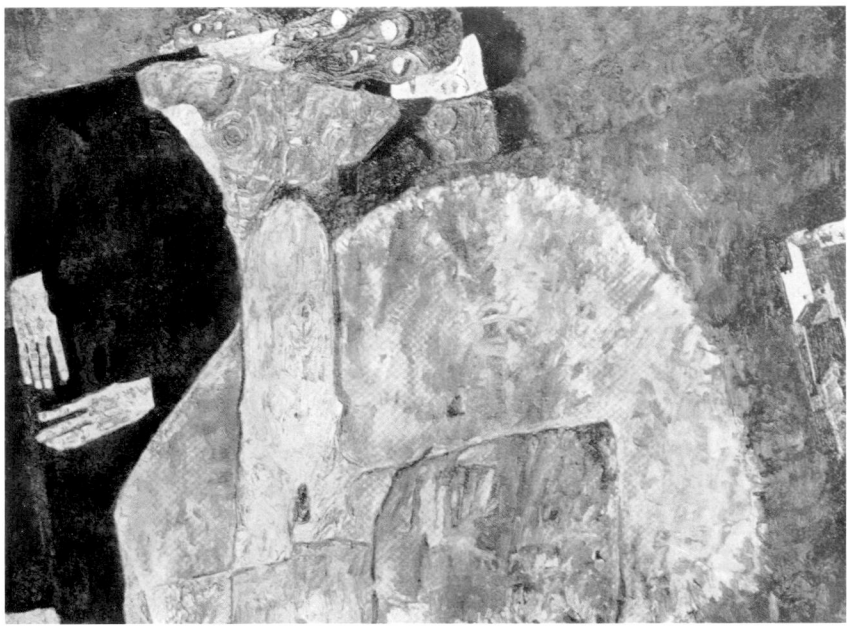

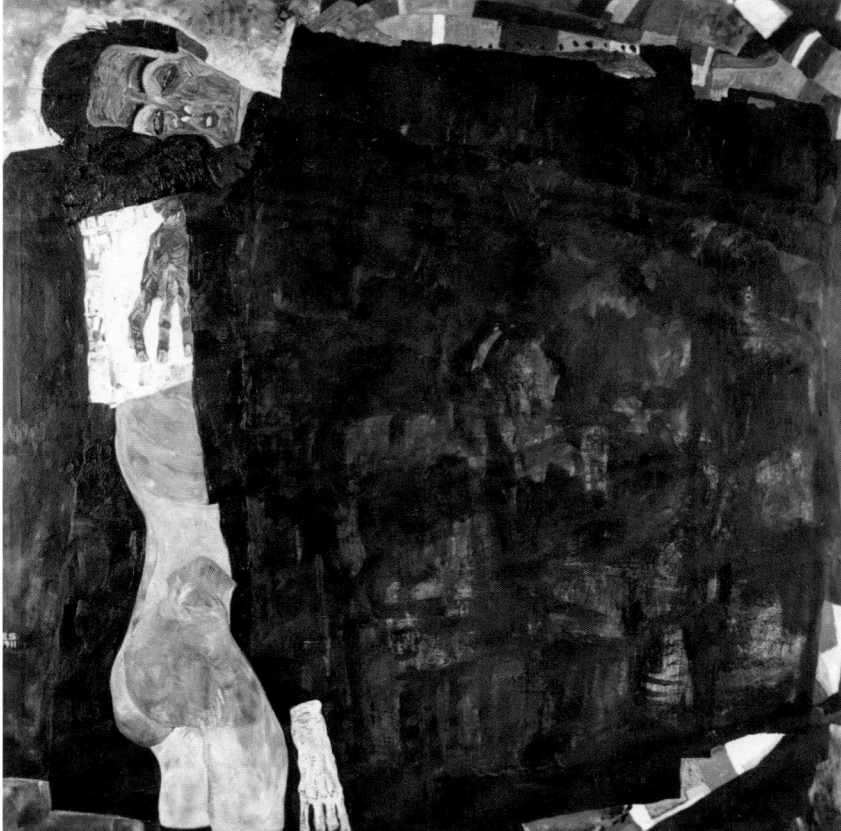

Increasingly, his painting accentuates form: a "geometry elevated to a container of psychological facts," as Otto Benesch remarked.[37]

Three works from 1910–11 that one is tempted to say belong together, which are probably concerned with Schiele's self-questioning, his anxieties, dreams, and wishes, reveal another variation on Schiele's design of space.[38] The people are found in visionary surroundings in which citations from townscapes and landscapes appear; their titles: *Weltwehmut* (Melancholia) [see ill. p. 29], *Delirien* (Delirium) [Fig. 8], and *Vision und Schicksal* (Vision and Destiny [Self-Portrait]) [Fig. 9].[39] In the first two, Schiele depicts a citation from a neighborhood in Krumau on the right edge.[40] In *Vision and Destiny*, as near as one can discern from the black-and-white photograph, there are planes of different colors in the upper and lower right that may represent landscape fields. This interpretation is supported by the small trees visible on the upper edge.[41] Unfortunately, no color photographs of these paintings are known, and they cannot be studied in the original. As Rudolf Leopold noted in 1972, the first of them was cut down and painted over with *Die kleine Stadt IV (Krumau an der Moldau)* (The Small City IV [Krumau On The Moldau]) (Kallir P278) in 1914;[42] the whereabouts of the other two are unknown. These enigmatic paintings are the only ones in which Schiele integrated such urban and landscape set pieces.

Schiele's subjects are often very complex and usually represent "not illustrations of reality but expressions of eternal subject matter," often allegories.[43] Many of his paintings pose puzzles even today and invite diverse, often imaginative interpretations. This is true of *Die Eremiten* (The Hermits) of 1912 [Fig. 10],[44] in which the figures are indeed found in a landscape ambience. Two visually fused men dressed in habits are seen on a narrow strip of earth, against a gray, brown, and reddish background. A small, withered rose in the barren strip of landscape radiates two bright rays and seems to hold the pair in balance. Schiele's brief explanation of this painting is a rarity that offers insight into the world of his thinking:

It is not a gray sky, rather a mourning world in which the two bodies find themselves, they grew up alone in it, came organically from the ground; together with the figures, the entire world should represent the "decrepitude" of all beings; one sole withered rose that exhales its white innocence, opposed to the wreath-flowers on both heads.—

The left one is the one who is bending over in front of such a serious world [...]. [T]he way I painted them so pale is intentional, otherwise the poetic idea and vision would be lost, just like how the figures remain indeterminable, they were intended to look buckled under, the bodies of those who are tired of life, suicidal, and yet bodies full of sentiment.—Think of the two figures as a cloud of dust similar to the earth which desires to amass and must collapse for lack of power. [...] I had to paint the picture, [...] if you knew just how the world appears to me and how people have treated me up to now, by which I mean insincerely, then this is just the direction I have to take and paint pictures which are of value only to me.[45]

Schiele's discussions bring us closer to the melancholic, painful quality of this painting and to its intellectual depth. The black-blue-red-brown earth represents the basis of the everlasting cycle: the bodies of the two men have come out of the ground, to which they return as a "cloud of dust" breaking apart. This description recalls the consequences of the Fall: "In the sweat of thy face shalt thou eat bread, till thou return

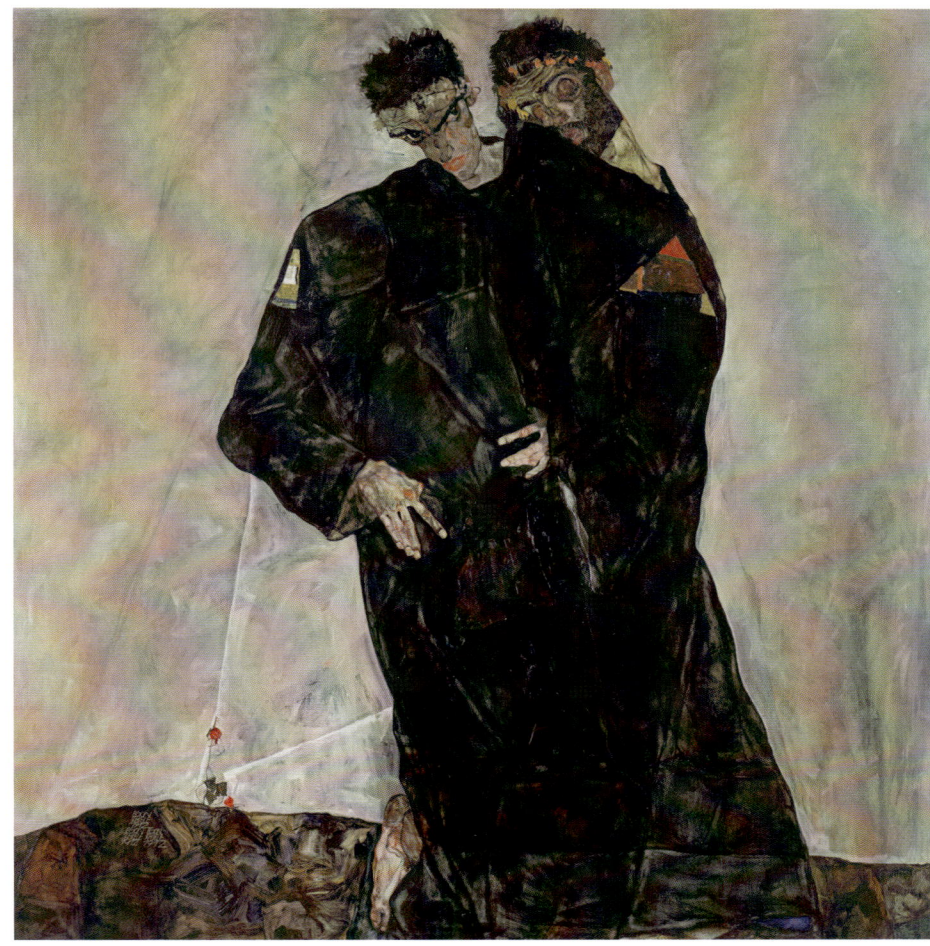

unto the ground; for out of it wast thou taken: for dust thou art, and unto dust shalt thou return."[46] The closely nestled bodies of the sensitive "people of sentiment" are bent together, bent by a false and unjust world, and are weary of life. The quintessence of the overall depiction, as Schiele observes, is the "'decrepitude' of all beings." The essential—among others, the people of sentiment—become powerless and ultimately lifeless; they return to where they came from—but there one also finds the seed of what will become, the new.

"Everyone who is an artist will encounter on his paths, stony and thorny as they are, [...] resistances, will be struck by hard strokes of

10. Egon Schiele, *The Hermits*, 1912, oil on canvas. Leopold Museum, Vienna (Kallir P229). Photo: Leopold Museum, Vienna

Opposite:

8. Egon Schiele, *Delirium*, 1911, oil on canvas. Whereabouts unknown (Kallir P190). Photo courtesy Kallir Research Institute

9. Egon Schiele, *Vision and Destiny (Self-Portrait)*, 1911, oil on canvas. Whereabouts unknown (Kallir P194). Photo courtesy Kallir Research Institute

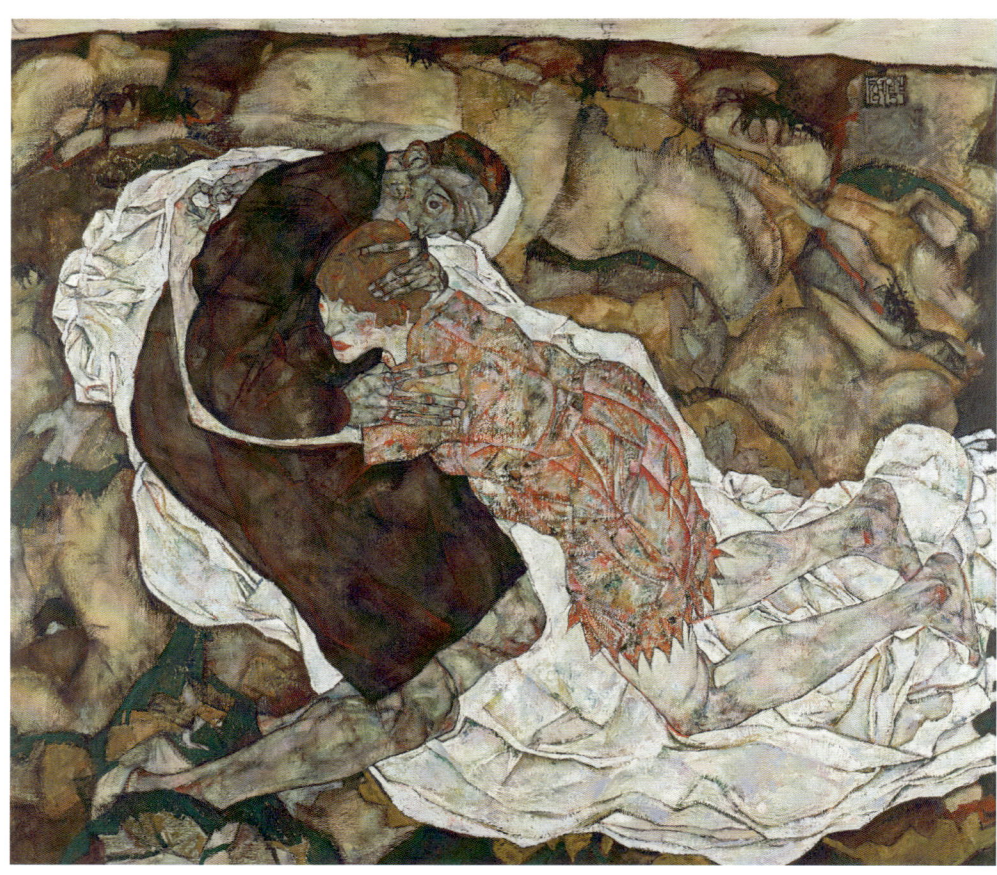

fate, and will perhaps be forced to the ground and so, broken for a time, fear succumbing entirely. But he will pull himself up again, because the soul is a power, stronger than fate," Schiele is purported to have said.[47] The landscape elements are not earth or sky per se but rather stand as metaphors for certain worlds or moods.

LATE YEARS

The outbreak of war in the summer of 1914 also placed Schiele in a world out of joint. Although he was spared armed conflict, it turned his life upside down. Sentry and office duty responsibilities took valuable time from his creative activity. In 1915, Schiele broke up with Wally, and married Edith Harms with lightning speed, and he was drafted.

Bildnis seiner Frau (Portrait of His Wife) (Kallir P290), 1915, presents Edith standing in bright, subtly painted surroundings. In 1916, Schiele portrayed his father-in-law, Johann Harms, seated in one of the armchairs in his studio; in the dark brown surroundings, the edges of the room can be seen. Subsequent portraits will follow this composition of the interior.[48] From 1917 onward, some depictions obtain volume, and Schiele's line becomes more curved, more organic.

"TOD UND MÄDCHEN" AND "ENTSCHWEBUNG"

The paintings *Tod und Mädchen* (Death and Maiden) [Fig. 11] and *Entschwebung (Die Blinden II)* (Transfiguration [The Blind II]) [Fig. 12] are linked by an essential quality that is not found in this form elsewhere in Schiele's work. In the former and the latter, a backdrop-like landscape forms the ground for a pair of people. Ferdinand Hodler, whom Schiele admired, and his articulated and sometimes high-horizon landscapes has often rightly been mentioned as a role model [Fig. 13].[49] Both works, which were produced in the first half of 1915 and share features, reveal in their execution a close interplay between people and surroundings. At the first presentation of these works at the Galerie Arnot, it was important to Schiele that the two works should hang in one room.[50]

Along with *Mutter mit zwei Kindern III* (Mother with Two Children III) (Kallir P303), the paintings were on view in the "Wiener Kunstschau" exhibition at the Berliner Secession in 1916.[51] The large-format canvases were positioned prominently to the left and right of a hallway, each flanked by a work by his fellow painter Felix Albrecht Harta (*Judith* and *Das Boot* [The Boat]) and with a view of Anton Faistauer's *Junge Frau auf rotem Sofa* (Young Woman on Red Sofa) in the next room, as a historical photograph proves [Fig. 14].[52] Although the catalogue indicates that ninety-five works by twenty-four artists were shown, all three of Schiele's works are found among the twenty-one illustrations.

Schiele's melancholic and visionary works usually overwhelmed his contemporaries. "Even more daring [than Kokoschka] is the production of Egon Schiele, who with his three paintings manages to cause an unholy confusion. Standing before these objects, one is baffled and helpless without commentary," wrote the journalist and author Leo Heller.[53] Even today, several paintings evade any unambiguous statement. Whereas the majority of scholars believe that *Death and Maiden* depicts Egon and his muse and partner Wally Neuzil,[54] the

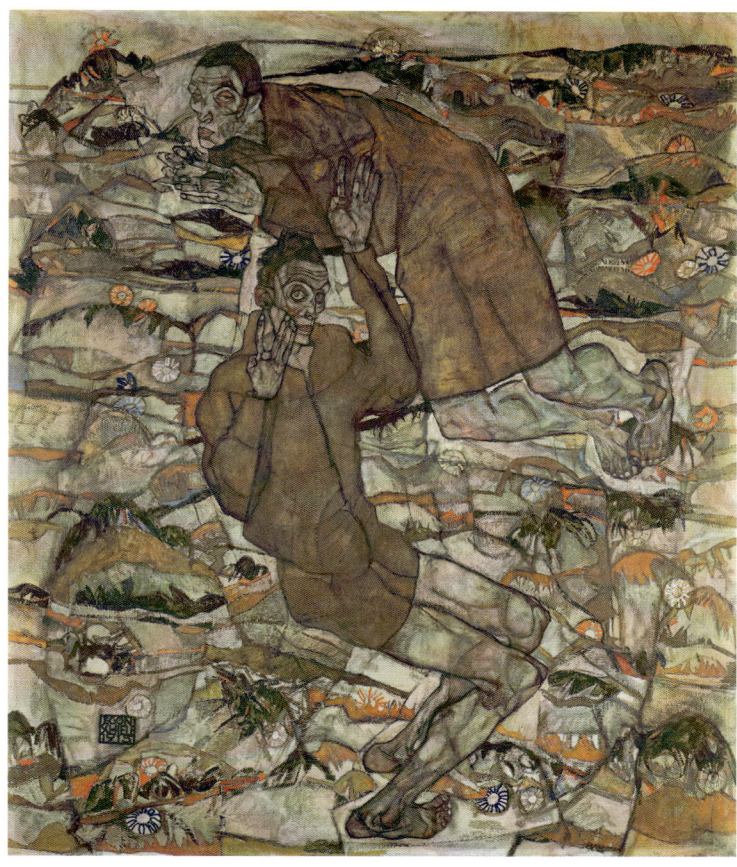

interpretations of other paintings, including *Transfiguration*, differ.[55] In general, it must be said that Schiele's motifs usually have an overarching, universally valid message but not infrequently there is an ambiguity.

In both *Death and Maiden* and *Transfiguration*, a carpet-like landscape is built up from the bottom almost to the upper edge; in each, a horizon line is retained and a narrow strip of sky remains visible; spatial depth is negated; Schiele keeps his depictions more or less in the plane. The violation of the rules of perspective leads to confusion about the viewer's standpoint. The postures of the figures are also similar: the S-shaped line results from the moment of kneeling in *Death and Maiden*, on the one hand, and by the raising up or

12. Egon Schiele, *Transfiguration (The Blind II)*, 1915, oil on canvas. Leopold Museum, Vienna (Kallir P288). Photo: Leopold Museum, Vienna

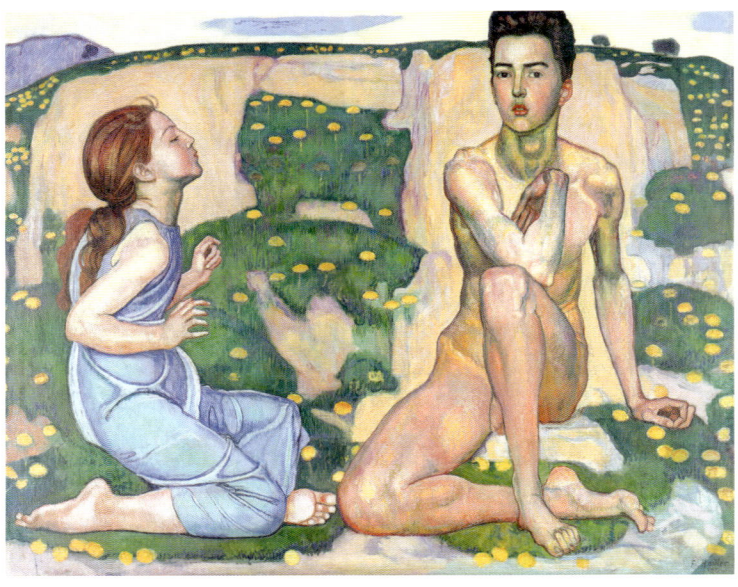

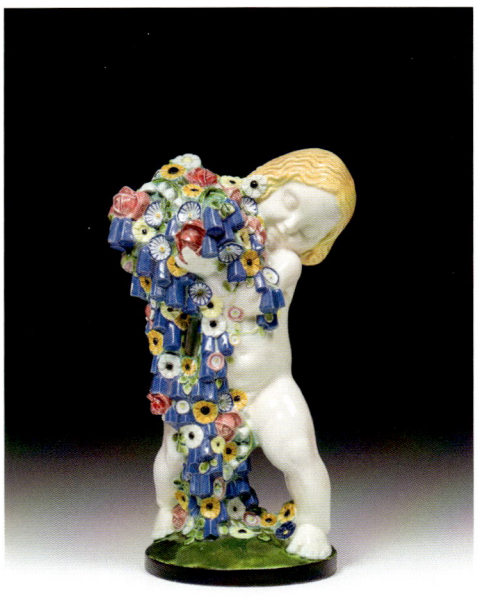

13. Ferdinand Hodler, *Spring*, 1901 oil on canvas. Museum Folkwang, Essen. Photo: Museum Folkwang Essen - ARTOTHEK

14. View of the "Wiener Kunstschau" exhibition at the Berlin Secession, 1916, from *Der Tag* (Berlin) (January 14, 1916). Photo: Zander & Labisch. Salzburg Museum

15. Michael Powolny, *Spring (Putto with Flowers)*, ca. 1907, painted ceramic. MAK—Museum für angewandte Kunst, Vienna

bending of the legs in *Transfiguration*, on the other. Each of the male protagonists wears a habit and has Schiele's physiognomy.[56] The presumed pair of lovers is embedded into a rocky and coarser landscape comprised of building blocks with occasional greenery; the two transfigured ones are also provided with an inhospitable but more intricate and powerfully graphic, furrowed, and partially overgrown landscape. Distributed above it are stylized flowers in blue, yellow, red, and white, most of which have a circular linear border.

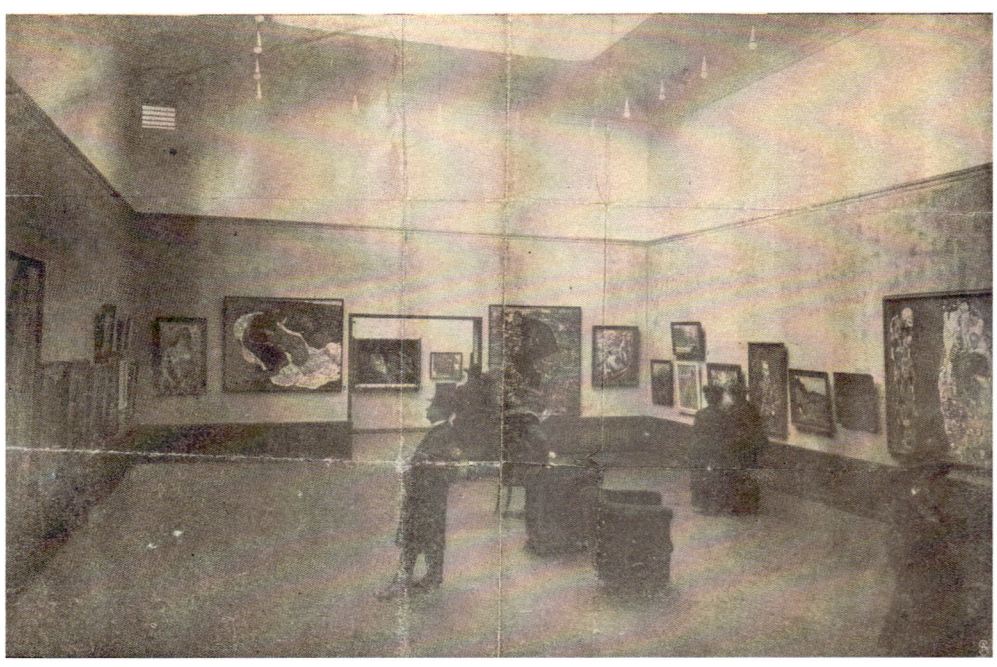

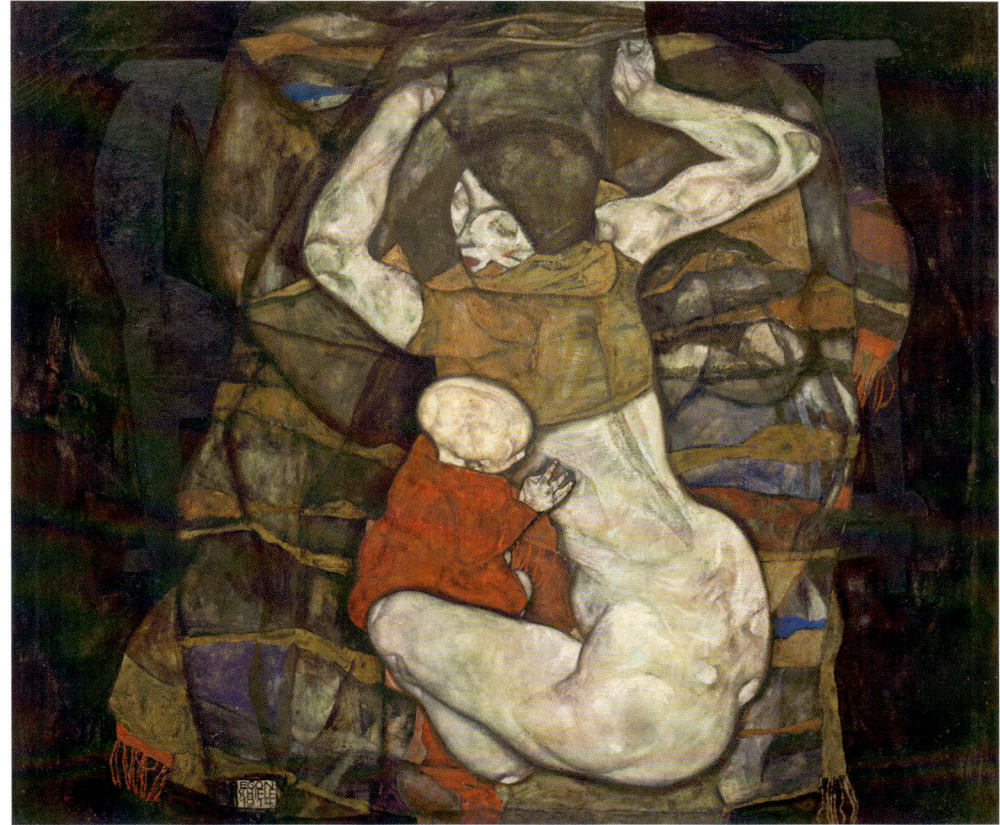

The schematically rendered ciphers of flowers recall the formal vocabulary for flowers employed by artists affiliated with the Wiener Werkstätte (Vienna Workshops). On postcards, fabrics, prints, and ceramics [Fig. 15], one encounters stemless flowers of very similar design.[57] The radial flowers recall asters, whose name is the Greek word for "star." Revealingly, Schiele wrote to his future brother-in-law Anton Peschka in July 1913: "Flowers! Plant asters! Very close together."[58]

It seems more crucial that Schiele may have been thinking here of the ephemeral aspect. Flowers in general are a sign of the vitality of life and, because of their short life, common vanitas symbols.[59] The dual meanings of flowering and wilting, birth and death—the eternal cycle of life—may have played a role in *Transfiguration*. Or the transfigured ones rely on the "anthropoid flowers" that have been left behind on earth: "Outside, in a meadow of colors, the colorful figures have melted away, brown, bushy farmers on the brown road and yellow girls in the meadow of mayflowers."[60] In his compositions, Schiele sometimes distributed in the painting flowers or other elements, such as smokestacks or wooden stakes with accents of color,[61] sometimes at regular distances and sometimes in close proximity to one another, carpet-like, decoratively.[62]

In the case of *Death and Maiden*, the main lines of the rock formations, especially in the upper part of the painting, follow the dynamic of the direction of the primary motif and reinforce it. The round forms of the stones sometimes recall forms of the human

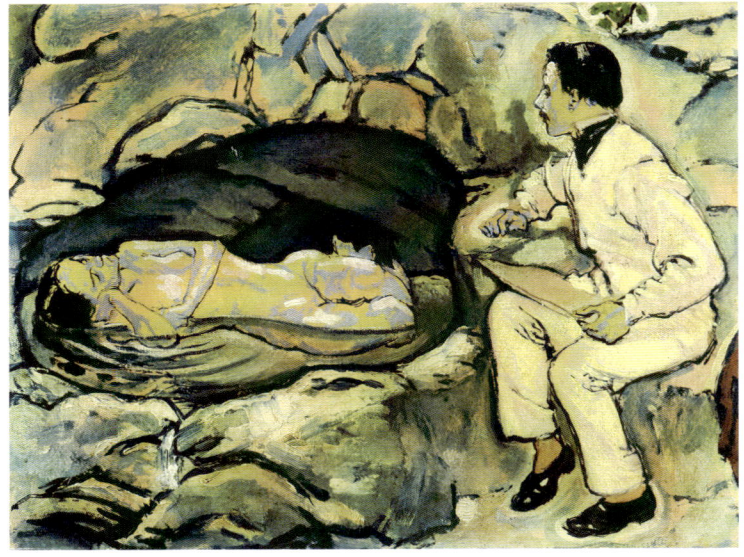

17. Koloman Moser, *Self-Portrait with Mermaid in Cliff Grotto*, 1914, oil on canvas. Private Collection of Josef Schütz, Vienna

18. Egon Schiele, *Transfiguration (The Blind II)* (detail of the outlined area around the figures; on the left-hand side of the image, the highlighted area can be enlarged by adding another visible border), 1915, oil on canvas. Leopold Museum, Vienna (Kallir P288). Photo: Leopold Museum, Vienna

body. In *Transfiguration*, a reinforced net- or grid-like structure is revealed. From 1910 or 1911 onward, his landscapes feature an emphatically horizontal and vertical articulation. Pereña points to Schiele's "search for hidden laws of nature," which is reflected in this pictorial arrangement.[63] Kimberly A. Smith draws attention to a feature of the paper of his sketchbooks, which is usually squared.[64]

The intricate, restless structure of the landscape in *Transfiguration* reveals a striking relationship to the formal vocabulary of the blanket in *Junge Mutter* (Young Mother) of 1914 [Fig. 16]. It would appear he adopted the pattern of the textile for the landscape in the later painting. Schiele drew on a growing repertoire of forms that he employed with variations.

One obvious difference from *Transfiguration*, is the white, elaborately draped sheet in *Death and Maiden*, which causes the couple to stand out, island-like, from the inhospitable landscape.[65] The aforementioned halo-like emphasis of the depictions is here performed by the sheet. Whereas the woman's body is located entirely within the area of the sheet, the head

and lower leg of the man extend beyond it. His feet are also visually anchored between the stones and hence closely connected to the earth. The left arm of "Wally" is largely covered by the material of his habit, with only a thin area remaining visible. Moreover, the fragile interlocking of her fingers conveys that she can no longer keep Death with her. The positions of the man's hands also seem to indicate a pulling-toward and a cautious pushing-away. The emphatically colorful, erotic undergarments of the woman do not place her in the realm of death either.

Although it is, unfortunately, not possible to establish whether Schiele was familiar with Moser's *Selbstbildnis mit Meerjungfrau in Felsengrotte* (Self-Portrait with Mermaid in Cliff Grotto) of 1914 [Fig. 17], which remained in the artist's possession until his death, a comparison is interesting. He was essentially familiar with the works of the founder of the Wiener Werkstätte, who had drawings by Schiele in his collection from 1911 at the latest. From 1913

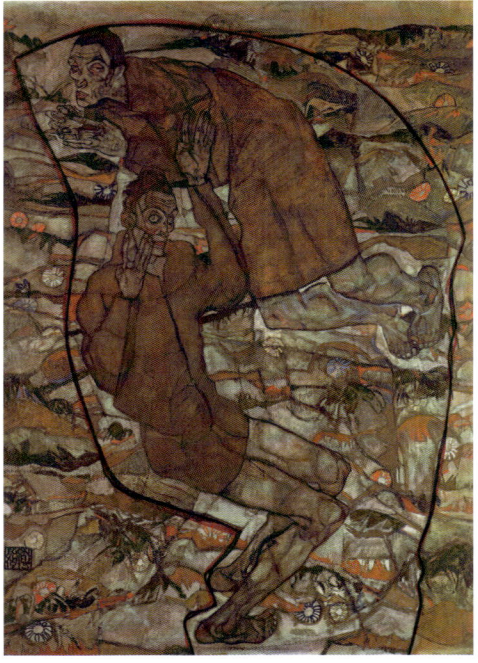

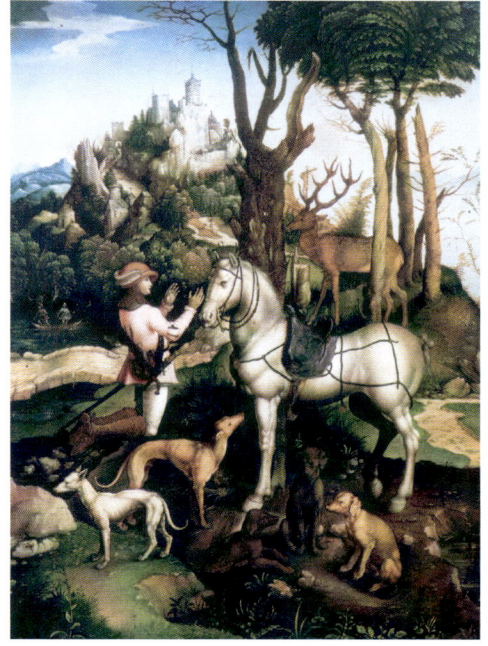

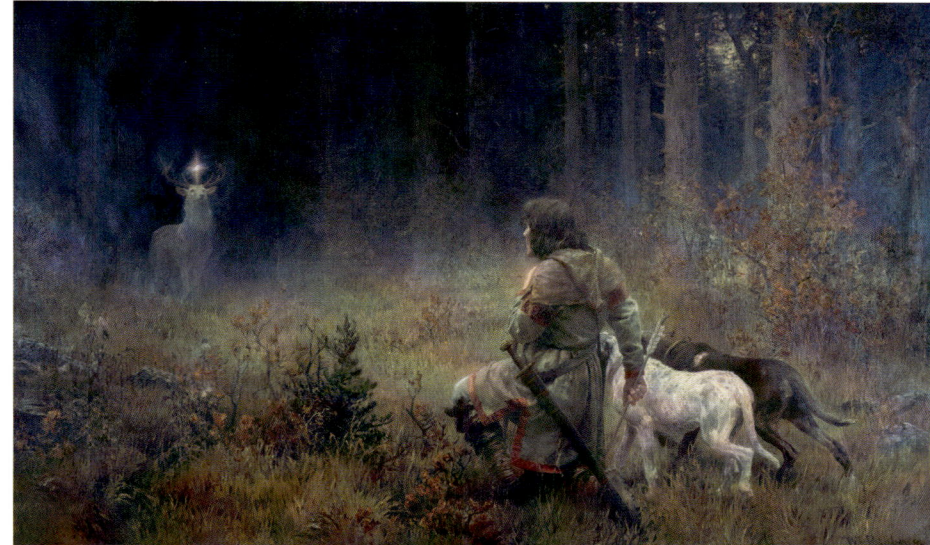

to 1915, Moser painted several landscapes, which he based on the work of Hodler, whom he visited in Geneva in 1913.[66] In his—sometimes allegorical, mythical—figure paintings, one is struck by the frequency of depictions in a protective grotto or an embracing enclosure of a figure by a cloth in an otherwise rather austere landscape.[67] This painting emphasizes the female nude in rocky surroundings by placing her in a protective cave; the artist is sitting next to her, with a sheet of paper in his left hand. The stony landscape, the halo-like emphasis, and the S-form of the figure, here seated, are striking similarities.

The subtle interplay of figure and landscape is also manifested in *Transfiguration*. The lower figure has his eyes wide open with his right hand positioned on his cheek underscoring the importance of seeing—"not to look at it, but to look into it," as the artist emphasized to Oskar Reichel in 1911.[68] A loose connection to the upper figure, whose eyes are half-closed, is made by his raised left arm. This tension is also accentuated by the inner seam of the sleeve of the lower figure, whose line continues both upward in the garment and down-

ward in the right thigh of the other figure. The line of the long hems of the habit is continued into the landscape and thus establishes a correspondence of the people to it. Although not visible at first glance, a "protected" area for the couple is defined directly in the landscape by means of a line or emphasis and in part differences in color [Fig. 18]. Specific forms in the landscape, especially in the area of their legs, feet, and heads react in form and color to their bodies.

In both paintings, the landscape forms refer to the protagonists. It is obvious that the nearly allover landscapes make an essential contribution to conveying the content of the visionary images and triggering a basic mood in the observer. Viewing "Schiele's art from the perspective of the aesthetics of reception" enables us to perceive his "pictorial method as part of an artificial staging deliberately constructed for the viewer," according to Pia Müller-Tamm.[69] Schiele appreciated the "value for painting and drawing"[70] of unusual perspectives, and decorative aspects continue to be inherent even in his late work. "He was a hymnalist of curves and intersections, a

19. Albrecht Dürer, *Saint Eustace*, 1498, oil on panel. Galleria Doria Pamphilij, Rome

20. Wilhelm Carl Räuber, *The Vision of St. Hubert*, 1892, oil on canvas. Bayerische Staatsgemälde-sammlungen—Neue Pinakothek, Munich. Photo: Bayer & Mitko - ARTOTHEK

lyricist of line, and he taught us to perceive his musicality once again," according to the writer Leopold Liegler.[71]

ST. HUBERT IN THE LANDSCAPE

In the artistically unproductive year of 1916, one painting falls completely outside of Schiele's thematic repertoire: the small panel painting *Die Vision des heiligen Hubertus* (The Vision of St. Hubert) [Cat. no. 66], which depicts the patron saint of hunters, foresters, and hunting clubs. It has received essentially no attention in the scholarship on Schiele. That is because it is an atypical, commissioned work that does not conform to Schiele's artistic idiom.

In early May 1916, Schiele was assigned to the Austro-Hungarian officer prisoners' station in Mühling, near Wieselburg. There he met Oberleutnant (First Lieutenant) Gustav Herrmann, who accommodated and supported Schiele in artistic matters. For example, he made room for a temporary studio in the camp.[72] Herrmann is also said to have commissioned the painting from Schiele.[73]

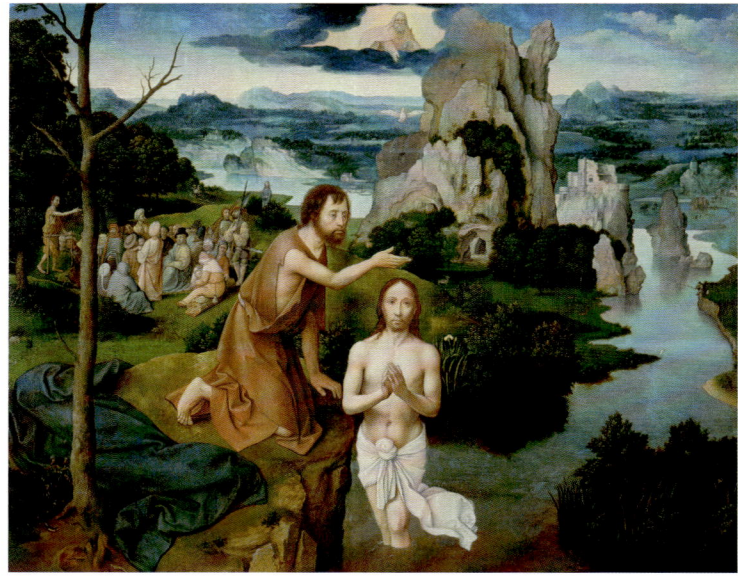

There are various versions of the legend of St. Hubert, which is closely connected to that of St. Eustache.[74] The legend relates that Hubert of Maastricht and Liège "while hunting on a Good Friday saw a stag between whose antlers a cross was glowing."[75] Numerous artists, such as Albrecht Dürer [Fig. 19], Hans von Marées, and Antonio Pisanello, have addressed this legend.

Although we do not know how Herrmann, an "ardent hunter,"[76] formulated his ideas or wishes for this painting, it is interesting that when executing it Schiele referred to a specific oil painting; though he altered it in several ways, it undeniably served as a model. His point of departure was the monumental *Vision des Hl. Hubertus* (The Vision of St. Hubert) of Wilhelm Carl Räuber [Fig. 20], a work that has been in the Bayerische Staatsgemäldesammlungen since it was purchased at the annual fair at the Glaspalast in Munich in 1892. Prior to 1916, Schiele had been represented in exhibitions in Munich several times and had visited there already in 1907 and again in August 1912, when he used the opportunity to tour exhibitions and galleries.[77] Moreover, he had the opportunity to study a print of this work by Räuber, who earned "his popularity in Munich" with this painting.[78] Schiele could have done so, for example, in the standard work edited by Friedrich Jansa in 1912: *Deutsche bildende Künstler in Wort und Bild* (German Visual Artists in Words and Pictures).[79]

Be that as it may, several details of Schiele's work prove that this painting was the template for his small wood panel. They include, for example, the arrangement of the stag, man, and dog within the overall composition and, also the identical poses and depiction of the animals. The head of the white dog is covered by the figure, as in the model; Schiele leaves out the black dog. Hubertus himself is consid-

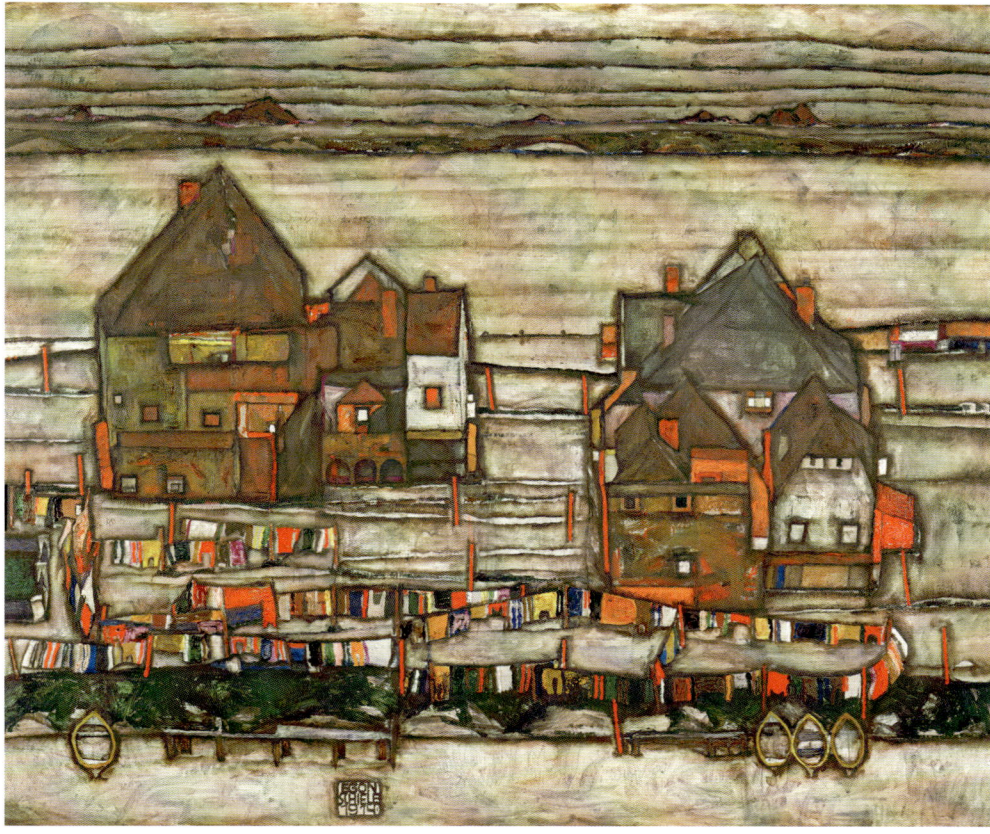

22. Egon Schiele, *Houses with Laundry (Suburb II)*, 1914, oil on canvas. Private Collection (Kallir P283). Photo: Erich Lessing/Art Resource, NY

erably older, wearing a white beard and a cap and kneeling with both legs on the ground; his sword or bow and arrow, respectively, is replaced by a crossbow. The saint's clothing is oriented around that of the model, with the same cape with a cap, the same top tied at the waist, as well as the red seam and side slit, which were partially adopted. Schiele followed the model for the legging straps. In general, he goes into less detail and simplifies the execution; his painting is more graphic and less painterly; the application of the paint is thin and in places transparent.

The complete redesign of the surroundings is striking: Whereas in Räuber, there is a small clearing with grasses and delicate bushes with a view into the dense forest in front of the stag, Schiele transfers the action to a somewhat rocky elevation with a steep, craggy mountain peak. The stag is positioned in front of that alongside a few small trees and some more voluminous tree trunks. At the upper right, Schiele opens the view onto a spacious landscape with a river and mountains in the background. The connection between the middle ground and the background that extends far into the distance is an autumnal, typically filigreed Schielesque tree (cf. *Herbstbäume* [Autumn Trees], 1911).[80] The use of a tree as a connecting element between a landscape in the foreground and a prospect in the background is commonly found—for example, in works by Joachim Patinir, one of the most important, earliest landscape painters, and by other Renaissance artists as well.[81] Some of the paintings Schiele could have known, and which might have inspired him here, are, among others, Patinir's *Taufe Christi* (The Baptism of Christ) in the Kunsthistorisches Museum [Fig. 21] and *Lamentation of Christ* by the Master of the Von Groote Adoration in the Gemäldegalerie of the Akademie der bildenden Künste (Academy of Fine Arts) in Vienna, where Schiele studied for three years: the view from a distance into a spacious foreground, the steeply rising rock formations, and the withered tree as linking the separate levels of the painting may have given him ideas.

ANIMATED TOWNS

Already in Schiele's early work, houses, façades, and roofscapes play a role and are often the main theme. The consistency of the complete absence of people is a striking feature of most of his townscapes.[82]

Yet the way several of these ghost towns are filled with a life of their own in the way they are depicted, such as the restless brushwork, the unusual bird's-eye perspective, and the painting techniques applied. Analogously to the tree landscapes with souls, the human presence is palpable in every corner. Anton Faistauer wrote in 1923:

> The townscapes of Krumau [...] are given a penetrating physiognomy. The houses reveal the spirit of their inhabitants; they turn their interiors outward. They are seen through. Their silhouette, their foundation, reveals the character of their builders, their purpose, their history, and their death.[83]

From 1914 onward, Schiele introduced representatives of the human into several townscapes by depicting colorful laundry or boats.[84] *Häuser mit Wäsche (Vorstadt II)* (Houses with Laundry [Suburb II]) of 1914 should be men-

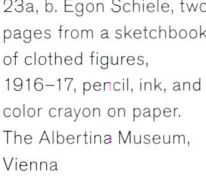

23a, b. Egon Schiele, two pages from a sketchbook of clothed figures, 1916–17, pencil, ink, and color crayon on paper. The Albertina Museum, Vienna

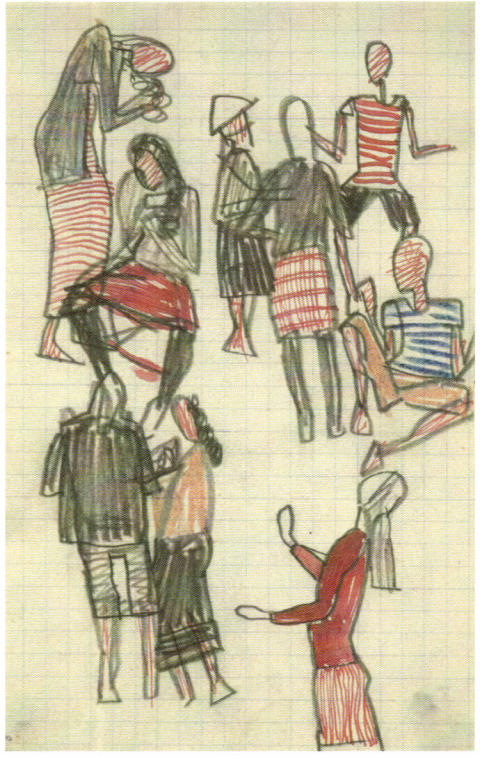

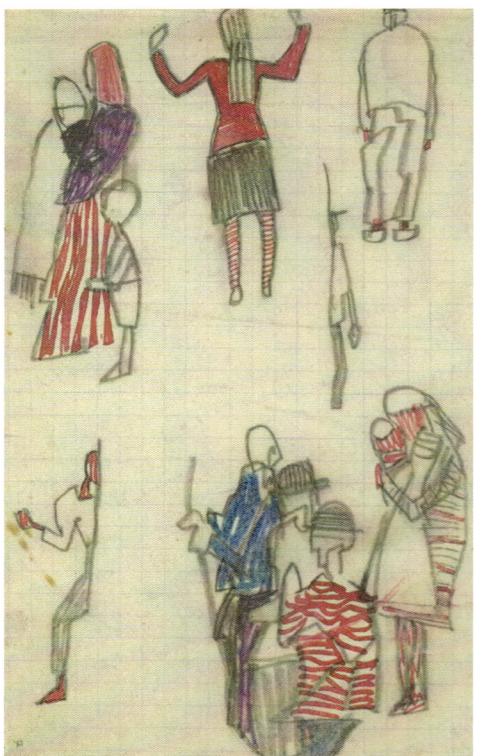

tioned here as an example of other works of a quite decorative character [Fig. 22].[85]

Franz Smola has emphasized the increasingly bright and colorful palette of the townscapes of Schiele's final years.[86] From 1917, he populated in a previously unfamiliar way some of his townscapes with vividly attired people, whom he distributed throughout the picture plane, in narrow streets, adjacent to houses, or on bridges.[87]

Four works should be mentioned in which Schiele employed such staffage figures, including an only recently discovered painting of a landscape in Krumau [see ill. on p. 47],[88] *Landschaft (Häuser in Krumau)* (Landscape [Houses in Krumau]) and *Stadt im Grünen (Die alte Stadt III)* (Town among Greenery [The Old City III]) [Cat. no. 68 of 1917, and *Stadtende (Krumau Häuserbogen III)* (Edge of Town [Krumau Town Crescent III]) of 1918 [see ill. p. 21]. A sketchbook from 1916–17 has several dressed figures, some of whom are gesticulating wildly, who were perhaps intended for that purpose [Figs. 23a, b]. One or another of these figures reoccurs in the paintings, for example, such as the woman with raised arms and the man rounding the corner of a house in *Town among Greenery*, in which a total of twenty figures romp about.

These paintings now lack the usual representatives of people. Whereas *Island Town (Krumau Town Crescent II)* of 1915 [see ill. on p. 44] still had a full clothesline stretching along the crescent of houses,[89] *Edge of Town (Krumau Town Crescent II)* [see ill. on p. 21] depicts people moving erratically as if panicking. They recall the unnatural and exaggerated gestures that Schiele generally tried out in all their variations in his presentations of people.

The surroundings of the neighborhood are rendered as dramatic and gloomy. We can only

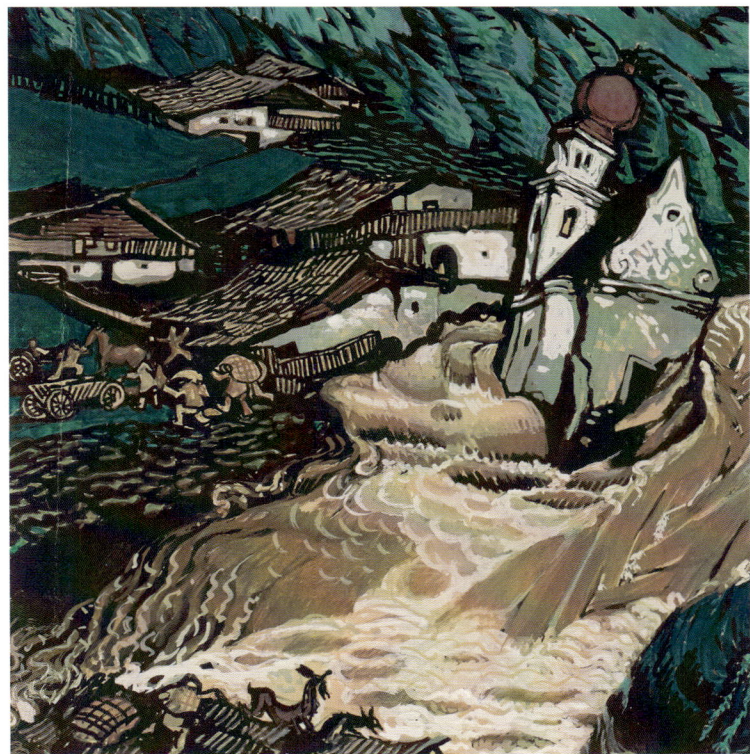

guess whether Schiele found inspiration for this version in Ludwig Heinrich Jungnickel's versions of storms [Fig. 24] or of the Flood. The similar treatment and distribution of small figures in Jungnickel's dramatic works—of which there are several versions—can be compared to those of Schiele. Schiele was in Krumau with Jungnickel and friends in the autumn of 1914; moreover, from 1916, Schiele had increased contact with the artist.[90] A version of *Überschwemmung* (Flood) was in the Berlin Secession in 1916, where Schiele was also represented, and illustrated in the catalogue.[91] Schiele must therefore have known this work. By donation, the tempera work *Das Gewitter* (The Storm) from this series entered the collection of the Österreichische Staatsgalerie (now known as the Belvedere) in 1914. Interestingly, Natter independently described Schiele's *Edge of Town* as a flood-like "nocturne."[92]

24. Ludwig Heinrich Jungnickel, *The Storm*, 1913 (detail), tempera on paper. Belvedere, Vienna

The hopelessness and tragedy of the war, which intensified in 1917 when the United States entered it and reached an unmeasurable scale with the global flu pandemic from the spring of 1918 onward—which would be Schiele's own undoing—perhaps played a role in giving Krumau this gloomy atmosphere. But we can only speculate about what suddenly motivated Schiele to populate certain neighborhoods.

ATMOSPHERIC WORLDS

The human being and the townscape or landscape are connected in different ways in Schiele's art: by a soulful and anthropomorphic nature, by urban and rural set pieces or human representatives in the surroundings, or by a landscape background as backdrop. No matter how human being and landscape meet, the latter is always the one imparting atmospheres and supporting the visionary content of the paintings. It is never landscape per se but always an emotional mediator and conveyor of profound subjects that correspond to the protagonists and transport emotions. Schiele, with his sure sense of line, color, form, and ornament, manages to achieve a gripping, living, and emotional overall effect.

He is [...] not only the greatest medium of thought, but he also says what he wants to say most completely. How many lies are concealed behind the philistine naivete and embellished sincerity of many an average work! How unreal and sprouted from within his landscapes are! How they turn the colorful dead silence of autumn, with its smoldering and rusting foliage, its black, slumbering trees, and colorful sinking clouds, into an inward examination of cravings remote from the world![93]

Translated from the German by Steven Lindberg

1 *Kollektiv-Ausstellung Egon Schiele, Wien*, exh. cat. (Vienna: Galerie Arnot, 1914), 3.

2 R. v. Enderes, "Kunstausstellung," *Neuigkeits-Welt-Blatt*, January 10, 1915, 15.

3 Kallir P275.

4 *Hagenbund. Frühjahrsausstellung*, exh. cat. (Vienna: Hagenbund, 1912), 53.

5 A.F.S., "Kunstausstellungen. 'Hagenbund,'" *Neue Freie Presse*, April 13, 1.

6 Hans Tietze, "Neue Richtungen in der Landschaftsmalerei," *Fremden-Blatt*, March 27, 1912, 19, 20.

7 Kallir P239.

8 Formal inspirations can be found in Giovanni Segantini's *Le cattive madri* (The Evil Mothers), 1894, and in Japanese art. See *Ver Sacrum*, no. 2 (1901): 42; no. 11 (1901): 183; Ralph Gleis, "Schiele, Hodler und Segantini: Die beseelte Natur im Symbolismus und Expressionismus," in *Conference Volume on the First Egon Schiele Symposium at the Leopold Museum*, ed. Hans-Peter Wipplinger (Vienna: Leopold Museum, 2017), 16–31. Tayfun Belgin, "Viennese Japonisme: From the Figured-Perspective to the Ornamental-Extensive Style," in *Japonisme and the Rise of the Modern Art Movement: The Arts of the Meiji Period;*

The Khalili Collection, ed. Gregory Irvine, (New York: Thames & Hudson, 2013), 90–103.

9 See Kallir P218, P222, and P236–42.

10 Egon Schiele to Franz Hauer, August 25, 1913, Albertina, Vienna; ESDA, ID no. 674.

11 Magda Mautner-Markhof to Egon Schiele, October 9, 1912, Albertina, Vienna; ESDA, ID no. 541.

12 Egon Schiele to Arthur Roessler, October 17, 1910, Wienbibliothek im Rathaus, Vienna; ESDA, ID no. 261.

13 Otto Kunz, "Erinnerungen an Egon Schiele," *Salzburger Volksblatt*, May 18, 1929, 7.

14 Egon Schiele, "Skizze zu einem Selbstbildnis" (Sketch for a Self-Portrait), July 1910 (based on content), whereabouts unknown; ESDA, ID no. 291.

15 Egon Schiele to Oskar Reichel, September 1911 (based on content), whereabouts unknown; ESDA, ID no. 388. On the parallels to Friedrich Nietzsche's reflections on "ewige Wiederkunft" (eternal return) and the "Übermenschen" (superman), see Hans Bisanz, "Egon Schiele: Kunst und Gedankenwelt," in *Egon Schiele: Zeichnungen und Aquarelle aus den Beständen des Historischen Museums der Stadt Wien und aus amerikanischem Privatbesitz*, ED. Serge Sabarsky, exh. cat. (Vienna: Historisches Museum der Stadt

Wien, 1981), 10–15, esp. 11; Helena Pereña Sáez, *Egon Schiele: Wahrnehmung, Identität und Weltbild* (Marburg: Tectum, 2010), 17–25.

16 Egon Schiele to Erich Lederer, October 3, 1914, Gustav Klimt | Wien 1900-Privatstiftung, Wien; ESDA, ID no. 2692.

17 Egon Schiele to Carl Reininghaus, February 13, 1913, Leopold Museum, Vienna; ESDA, ID no. 55.

18 Egon Schiele, "Who of the ones given life and senses" (1910), in *I, Eternal Child: Paintings and Poems*, trans. Anselm Hollo (New York: Grove Press, 1985), 12–14, esp. 13–14; cf. Egon Schiele, "Wer von lebend Prim-begabten," whereabouts unknown; ESDA, ID no. 297.

19 Egon Schiele to Erich Lederer, October 3, 1914 (see note 16).

20 In Schiele's later works, there are drawings of houses and (roof) landscapes that have a stronger connection to reality. See for example Kallir D1803, D1807, D1809, D2135, D2137, and D2152.

21 There are only three extensive publications focusing on Schiele's landscape; for its outstanding content, see Kimberly A. Smith, *Between Ruin and Renewal: Egon Schiele's Landscapes* (New Haven, CT: Yale University Press, 2004).

22 Egon Schiele to Max Karpfen, September 4, 1905, Sammlung Gradisch; ESDA, ID no. 201.

23 Kallir P34, P49, P78, P89, and P123 (1908); drawings: D31, D32, D33, D43 (1906), D156, and D157.

24 Kallir P30, P240, and P296.

25 Christian Bauer, "A Child of the Train Station, a Giant of Modern Art: Egon Schiele between Tulln, Krems, Klosterneuburg, and Vienna; His Childhood, Networks, Symbolism, and Art of Expression," in *Egon Schiele: Almost a Lifetime*, ed. Christian Bauer, trans. Matthias Goldmann and Camilla R. Nielsen (Munich: Hirmer, 2015), 13–69, esp. 32–34.

26 Agnes Husslein-Arco and Alexander Klee, eds., *Sünde und Secession: Franz von Stuck in Wien / Sin and Secession: Franz von Stuck in Vienna*, trans. Rebecca Law, Lisa Rosenblatt, and Nick Somers, exh. cat. Lower Belvedere, Vienna (Munich: Hirmer, 2016).

27 *Offizieller Katalog der Internationalen Kunst-Ausstellung des Vereins bildender Künstler Münchens "Secession"* (Munich: Bruckmann, 1907), 30 (cat. nos. 155–58), esp. cat. no. 157; illustrated in the plate section.

28 Alexander Klee, "Franz von Stuck's 'mystical symbolism of primitive dimensions' and His Links with Vienna," in Husslein-Arco and Klee, *Sin and Secession* (see note 26), 33–49, esp. 46.

29 Robert Schmidt, "Die zweite Ausstellung der königlichen Akademie der Künste zu Berlin," *Die Kunst für Alle* 23, no. 8 (January 1908): 172; fig. on p. 179.

30 In connection with the mixing up of Christian symbols and nature, Pereña points to the tradition of Romanticism and its reception around 1900. See Pereña Sáez, *Egon Schiele* (see note 15), 138–52.

31 On this, see, among others, Matthias Haldemann, "Rhetorik der Fläche: Zeigen und Entziehen in Schieles Bildkunst," in Wipplinger, *Conference Volume on the First Egon Schiele Symposium* (see note 8), 46–57.

32 Kerstin Jesse, "Die W. W. Seide? Ist sie angekommen?" Egon Schiele und die Wiener Werkstätte, in *Egon Schiele: Expression and Lyric; Conference Volume on the Second Egon Schiele Symposium at the Leopold Museum*, ed. Verena Gamper and Hans-Peter Wipplinger (Vienna: Leopold Museum, 2018), 196–219. – Regarding further aspects of emphasis (contours) of those depicted mostly with lighter color: Astrid Kury, "Heiligenscheine eines elektrischen Jahrhundertendes sehen anders aus …" Okkultismus und die Kunst der Wiener Moderne, Wien 2000.

33 Alessandra Comini, *Egon Schiele's Portraits* (Berkeley: University of California Press, 1974), 54 and 206 n. 14.

34 Oskar Kokoschka, *Die träumenden Knaben* (1908; Vienna: Jugend und Volk, 1968).

35 In a photograph of the unfinished (and now lost) painting *Begegnung* (Encounter) of 1913, a landscape is recognizable in the background. See Kallir P259.

36 Pereña traces the reduction to geometric planes of color and forms in the figure and its surroundings that Schiele often employs as well as the aspect of fragmentation, and other aspects, to his "view of the subject as a compound of different substances that can be combined in different ways. Pereña Sáez, *Egon Schiele* (see note 15), 101, 102, and 110.

37 Otto Benesch, "Egon Schiele," in *Kollektiv-Ausstellung Egon Schiele* (see note 1), 8.

38 See Tobias G. Natter, ed., *Egon Schiele: The Complete Paintings, 1909–1918* (Cologne: Taschen, 2017), 479–80 (cat. no. 36), 495 (cat. no. 56), and 496 (cat. no. 57).

39 Kallir P175, P190, and P194.

40 Cf. *Stadt am blauen Fluss I* (City on the Blue River I), 1910. Kallir P183.

41 Cf. the trees in the background in Kallir P186 and P267.

42 Rudolf Leopold, *Egon Schiele: Paintings, Watercolours, Drawings*, trans. Alexander Lieven (London: Phaidon, 1973), 557. – Sandra Maria Dzialek, Egon Schieles Häuserlandschaften – ein materialtechnologischer Blick auf den Bestand der Gemälde des Leopold Museums, in *Egon Schiele: Milieus and Perspectives; Conference Volume on the Fourth Egon Schiele Symposium at the Leopold Museum*, ed. Verena Gamper and Hans-Peter Wipplinger (Vienna: Leopold Museum, 2022), 155–67.

43 Pereña Sáez, *Egon Schiele* (see note 15), 110.

44 See Natter, *Egon Schiele* (see note 38), 523–25 (cat. no. 110).

45 Egon Schiele to Carl Reininghaus, February 27, 1912, in *Egon Schiele: Poems and Letters, 1910–1912*, ed. Elisabeth Leopold, trans. Jeff Tapia (New York: Prestel, 2008), 101; cf. Egon Schiele to Carl Reininghaus, February 27, 1912 (based on content), Leopold Museum, Vienna; ESDA, ID no. 45.

46 Genesis 3:19, King James Version.

47 Arthur Roessler, *Erinnerungen an Egon Schiele*, 2nd ed. (Vienna: Wiener Volksbuchverlag, 1948), 60.

48 See Kallir P307, P309, P316, P317, P319, and P320.

49 See *Ferdinand Hodler und Wien*, exh. cat. (Vienna: Österreichische Galerie, Oberes Belvedere, 1992), passim and esp. 79–84; Jane Kallir, *Egon Schiele* (New York: Harry N. Abrams, 1994), 108.

50 Egon Schiele to Guido Arnot, with plan for the hanging, August 17, 1915, Tiroler Landesmuseum Ferdinandeum, Innsbruck; ESDA, ID no. 922.

51 *Katalog der Wiener Kunstschau in der Berliner Secession*, exh. cat. Berliner Secession (Berlin: Secessionshaus, 1916), 28 (cat. nos. 89–91).

52 On the right wall, among others: Gustav Klimt, *Tod und Leben* (Death and Life), 1910–15, and Oskar Kokoschka, *Bildnis Carl Moll* (Portrait of Carl Moll), 1913.

53 Leo Heller, "Aus Berlin," *Der Humorist* (January 20, 1916), 6.

54 See, among others, Comini, *Egon Schiele's Portraits* (see note 33), 138; Jane Kallir, "Coming of Age (1912–1915)," in *Self-Portraits and Portraits*, ed. Agnes Husslein-Arco and Jane Kallir, exh. cat. Belvedere, Vienna (Munich: Prestel, 2011), 127, 128; Natter, *Egon Schiele* (see note 38), 563 (cat. no. 180).

55 See Natter, *Egon Schiele* (see note 38), 562, 563 (cat. no. 179); Jane Kallir, *Egon Schiele: Drawings and Watercolours*, ed. Ivan Vartanian (New York: Thames & Hudson, 2003), 325–26.

56 Schiele portrayed himself countless times in his oeuvre. But that does not necessarily mean he was depicting his own personality. See Natter, *Egon Schiele* (see note 38), 562, 563 (cat. no. 179).

57 Cf. works by Franz von Zülow and Carl Krenek.

58 Egon Schiele to Anton Peschka, July 12, 1913, Leopold Museum, Vienna; ESDA, ID no. 133.

59 Hildegard Kretschmer, *Lexikon der Symbole und Attribute in der der Kunst*, 7th ed. (Stuttgart: Reclam, 2019), 63, 64.

60 Egon Schiele to Anton Peschka, draft letter, after May 23, 1911 (based on content), Albertina, Vienna; ESDA, ID no. 343.

61 See Kallir P278, P282, and P283.

62 See Kallir P179, P189, P236, P263–65, and P280.

63 Pereña Sáez, *Egon Schiele* (see note 15), 210–14.

64 Smith, *Between Ruin and Renewal* (see note 21), 56.

65 See Kallir P275, P304, and P306.

66 Gerd Pichler, "Der 'Tausendkünstler': Koloman Mosers malerisches Oeuvre," in the online *catalogue raisonné* of the Belvedere, Vienna: https://werkverzeichnisse.belvedere.at/online/text/355447/koloman-moser/chapter1 (accessed March 4, 2020).

67 See ibid. and the online *catalogue raisonné*: GE122, GE137, GE140, GE151, GE154, GE157, GE165, GE166, and GE182.

68 Egon Schiele to Oskar Reichel, January 31, 1911, in *Egon Schiele: Poems and Letters* (see note 45), 73; cf. Egon Schiele to Oskar Reichel, January 31, 1911, Leopold Museum, Vienna; ESDA, ID no. 113.

69 Pia Müller-Tamm, "Sehen zeigen, Sehen lassen: Blickinszenierung und Betrachteransprache in Schieles figürlichen Darstellungen," in *Egon Schiele: Inszenierung und Identität*, ed. Pia Müller-Tamm (Cologne: DuMont, 1995), 39.

70 Leopold Liegler, "Beitrag für das 'Erinnerungsbuch Egon Schiele,'" November 1943 (based on content), Albertina, Vienna; ESDA, ID no. 2565, 12.

71 Ibid., 16.

72 Egon Schiele, war diary, July 20, 1916, Albertina, Vienna; ESDA, ID no. 1148.

73 Cf. Otto Nirenstein, *Egon Schiele. Persönlichkeit und Werk* (Vienna: Zsolnay, 1930), 97; Otto Kallir, *Egon Schiele: Oeuvre-Katalog der Gemälde* (Vienna: Zsolnay, 1966), 422 (P214); Jane Kallir, *Egon Schiele: The Complete Works*, exp. ed. (New York: Harry N. Abrams, 1998), 334 (comments on P302). No source is mentioned in the literature.

74 Erhard Gorys, *Lexikon der Heiligen* (Munich: Deutscher Taschenbuch-Verlag, 1997), 108.

75 Ibid., 147–48.

76 Jane Kallir, *Egon Schiele* (see note 73), 334 (comments on P302).

77 Egon Schiele to Oskar Reichel, August 17, 1912, in *Egon Schiele: Poems and Letters* (see note 45), 101; cf. Egon Schiele to Oskar Reichel, August 17, 1912, private collection, Switzerland; ESDA, ID no. 503.

78 *Gemäldekataloge*, ed. Bayerische Staatsgemäldesammlungen, vol. VIII/1–3, *Deutsche Künstler von Marées bis Slevogt*, vol. 2, Jank–Runze, comp. Christian Lenz et al. (Munich: Hirmer, 2003), 305.

79 Friedrich Jansa, *Deutsche bildende Künstler in Wort und Bild* (Leipzig: Jansa, 1912), 69.

80 Kallir P218.

81 See anonymous, *Landscape with St. Hubert*, Flemish, ca. 1530, Bayerische Staatsgemäldesammlungen—Alte Pinakothek, Munich, inv. no. WAF 762. Joachim Patinir, *Jerome in the Landscape*, ca. 1512, Louvre, Paris, inv. no. R.F. 2429.

82 Klimt, too, rigorously eliminated people from his landscapes.

83 Anton Faistauer, *Neue Malerei in Österreich: Betrachtungen eines Malers* (Zurich: Amalthea, 1923), 20.

84 One exception: *Die Stadt am blauen Fluss II* (City on the Blue River II), 1911 (Kallir P212). At the bottom edge, laundry can be seen hanging on a line. Its colors reflect those of certain elements of the houses.

85 See Kallir P291, P293, P294, P295, and P311.

86 See Franz Smola, "Autumn Landscapes and Faded Towns," in the present catalogue.

87 From this time onward, people are occasionally seen in natural environments in his works on paper as well: Kallir, D2133, D2139, D2140, D2156, and D2160.

88 Kerstin Jesse to Jane Kallir, e-mail, July 9, 2019, message concerning an unknown painting that the present author discovered in a historical photograph. Kallir included the work in her *catalogue raisonné* as P313a; see Jane Kallir to Kerstin Jesse, e-mail, January 24, 2020.

89 See Kallir P293.

90 Hans and Heinrich Böhler, Ludwig Jungnickel, and Egon Schiele to Josef Hoffmann, postcard, November 14, 1914, Sammlung W. Kornfeld, Bern; ESDA, ID no. 2374, and Schiele-Jungnickel correspondence, ESDA, ID nos. 2238, 1028, 1159, 1174, 1199, 1265.

91 *Katalog der Wiener Kunstschau* (see note 51), 16 (cat. no. 42).

92 Natter, *Egon Schiele* (see note 33), 588–89 (cat. no. 217), esp. 589.

93 Anonymous, "Wiener Sezession 'Jung-Österreich,'" in *Sport und Salon* (March 22, 1913), 12.

AUSTRIA'S DILEMMA

WARTIME POLITICS AND PROPAGANDA IN SCHIELE'S LANDSCAPES

Kimberly A. Smith

1. Egon Schiele, *Four Trees*, 1917, oil on canvas. Belvedere, Vienna (Kallir P310). Formerly Belvedere, Vienna, this painting has been restituted to the legal heirs of Josef Morgenstern in 2020. Photo: Johannes Stoll/Belvedere, Vienna

Several years after the centenary of Egon Schiele's death, fascination with his life and work shows no signs of slowing down. On the contrary, the sheer output of books and essays, exhibitions and accompanying catalogues, popular articles and auction sales, demonstrates the continued relevance of this early twentieth-century modernist and the Viennese culture from which he emerged. The field of Schiele studies has benefited from recent texts that strengthen our understanding of this quintessentially Viennese modern art by shedding light on the cultural and ideological implications of Schiele's images. Yet even as this promising research emerges, the figural work dominates both scholarly and popular discussions of Schiele's significance, with isolated exceptions.[1] The imbalance misrepresents the centrality of the landscape in Schiele's oeuvre. From his earliest to his final years, sketching and painting landscapes formed a key part of Schiele's approach to studying and making modern art. The current catalogue and the exhibition it accompanies represent a welcome reminder of the vital role that both tree- and townscapes played in

Schiele's overall production. And, opportunely, it offers me a chance to revisit some of my earlier writing. In particular, I would like here to consider the political dimensions of Schiele's landscapes, which I have previously traced to their ability to concretize a materialist vision of the Austro-Hungarian Empire as a multi-ethnic community anchored in its land. This essay first returns to that argument and its genesis, before considering the landscapes' utility as political propaganda at a particularly acute moment in World War I.

A central premise of my work on Schiele's landscapes has been that these images of Austria's small towns, rolling fields, and slender trees together constituted not merely a paean to the charm of these vistas, but a sustained effort to imagine Austria as an authentic community bound by its ties to these natural phenomena.[2] The need for such visual enunciations of shared identity stemmed from Austria-Hungary's structural complexity as a diverse, multinational state. This inherent tension, what Ernst Gellner coined the "Habsburg Dilemma," became an increasingly vexing

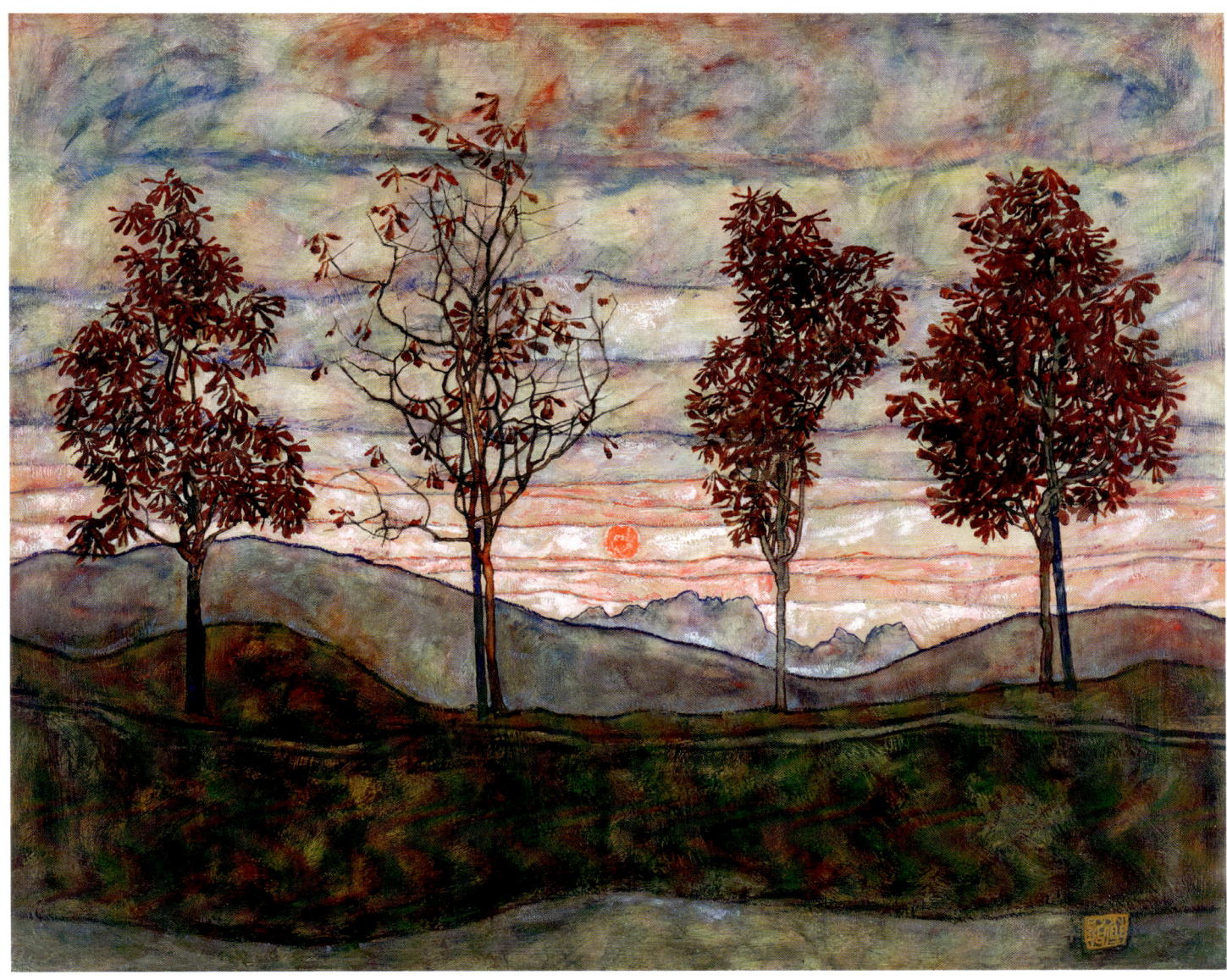

issue in the late years of the empire.[3] Before reviewing this relation between Schiele's landscapes and Austrian identity, it may be useful to outline the political dynamics at work in the Habsburg Empire.

As is well known, the Habsburg Empire charted an atypical course of state building in the modern period, brokering a dynastic model of multiethnic, imperial statehood in the era of the sovereign nation state. As a matter of political theory, any polity will need to find ties that bind, whether economic, linguistic, political, cultural, and/or symbolic. And any nation or state's solution to this

challenge will necessarily be shifting and incomplete, a project always in the making. Yet Austria found itself in particularly intricate circumstances since, unlike modern nation states like England, France, or Germany, its sense of unity was not to be located in a dominant shared language, ethnic heritage, or popular sovereignty. Instead, as a political entity, Austria's identity had historically been organized around the emperor himself, divinely positioned with the task of overseeing a complicated civil apparatus and multiple ethnolinguistic communities. Although the empire had moved toward constitutional principles and universal male suffrage in an effort to adapt to changing expectations, the "decline of Habsburg power … brought into sharp focus the contrast between the old legitimacy, which had once been based on divine ordination, and the new legitimacy, based on democratic assent in nation-states."[4]

Earlier generations of scholarship commonly identified these factors as the source of Austria's eventual undoing. Outflanked by modern nation states, its dynastic collection of historico-political entities was seen as unable to survive in the new era of national self-government. More recently, historians have contested the idea that Austria's imperial and complex organization predetermined the state's anachronistic decline. John Deak argues against the notion of the Habsburg Empire as a state condemned to failure, proposing that its extensive bureaucracy created spaces in which individuals continually negotiated the competing demands of diverse ethnic communities in a decentralized state.[5] While these multiethnic groups may have been creatively managed by the state's bureaucrats, other scholars counter that emergent nationalisms represented a barrier to fostering any cohesive sense of what it meant to be Austrian in the modern era. The diverse historico-political entities that made the Habsburg Empire geopolitically exceptional subjected it to proliferating internal fissures and competing nationalist claims which presented a real problem to shaping coherent statehood. John Connelly states that: "… the more representative Austria became, the greater its basic problem: every institution of representation became national and thus destabilizing."[6] Though nominally bound by loyalty to the emperor, the Austrian Empire lacked a supranational concept captivating enough to rival the growing demands for self-determination by its ethnically diverse groups. In his recent comprehensive study, Connelly explains the

dilemma of creating a unified and compelling state identity: "No larger sense of community connected the Habsburg nationalities …Whatever the monarchy was, it was not a cause and was unable to tap the wells of commitment that sustained nationalism or socialism. The monarchy was like a landscape or a mood, a pleasing backdrop one might feel nostalgia for once it was gone..."[7]

Connelly describes the monarchy as a "landscape" as a way of gesturing to its non-essential character, a charming but ultimately unimportant panorama. It also neatly leads us back to the role of Schiele's painted landscapes in late imperial Austria which hoped to be anything but ineffectual images resigned to the background. At this fraught political moment, as I have argued previously, Schiele's landscapes participated in a forging of communal identity that rested on several distinct but interrelated threads. First, Schiele grew up as the son of the station master in the village of Tulln, lived with his family in the railway station house, and enjoyed easy access to train passage. Perhaps due to these close connections to the railroad, he was an enthusiastic traveler from an early age. Yet aside from a handful of professional trips to Munich, over the course of his life, Schiele never left the confines of the Habsburg Empire and, more importantly, only made pictures of those sites he visited *within* the borders of the empire. Thus, from Krumau (Český Krumlov), in the largely Czech part of Bohemia, to Győr in the Hungarian part of Austria-Hungary, to the border town of Trieste, Schiele's land- and townscapes literally and exclusively visualize Austria's varied topographies.[8]

Second, with no signs of industrial encroachment, landscapes like *Four Trees* [Fig. 1] show a world untouched by recent technology, working factories, or modernizing economies.[9]

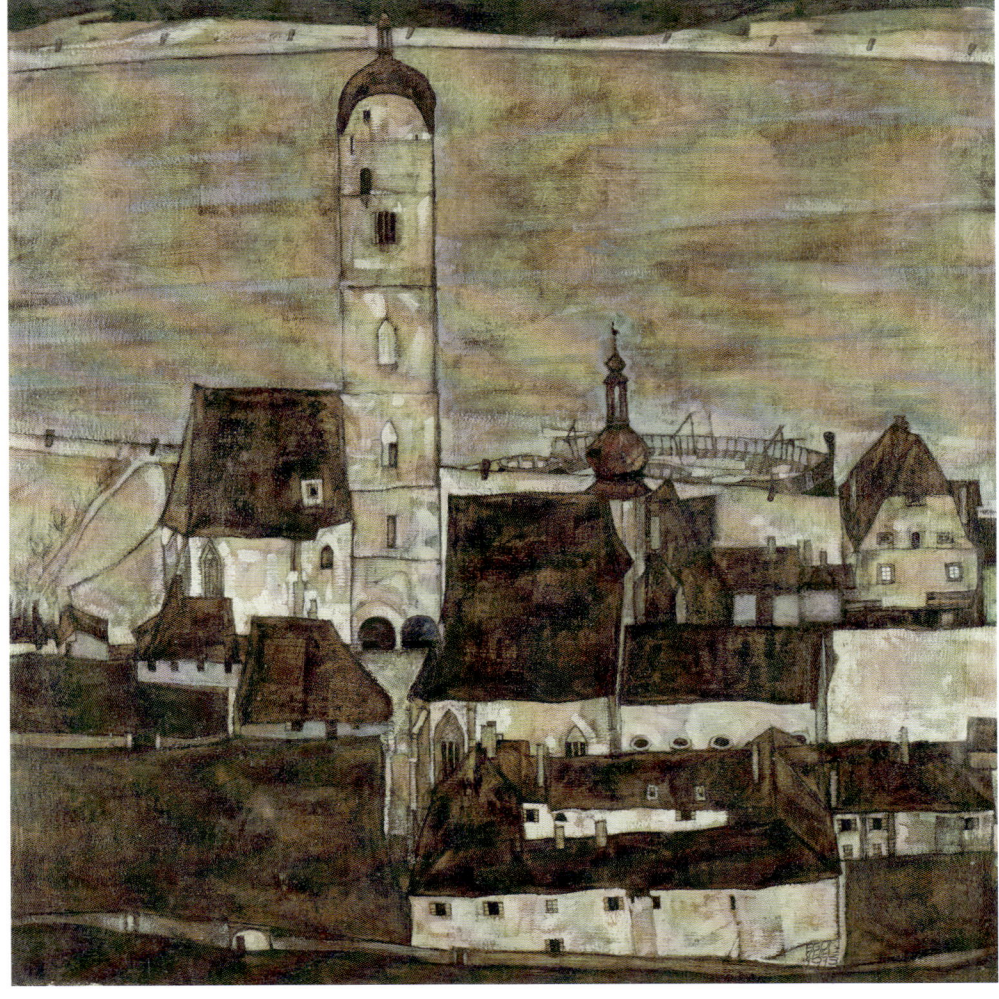

2. Egon Schiele, *Stein on the Danube, Seen from the Kreuzberg (Large)*, 1913, oil on canvas. Leopold Museum, Vienna (Kallir P269). Photo: Leopold Museum, Vienna

Indeed, even the railroad, such a central part of Schiele's own biography and the means by which he accessed these very landscapes, remains determinedly unseen. The images thus present an Austrian environment comprised of rural scenes firmly grounded in a pre-modern past. Importantly, it is not just their subject matter that ties these paintings to a pre-industrial history, and this sense of an environment untouched by contemporary realities is not restricted to the treescapes. The townscapes emphasize the gothic aspects of Austria's villages, and are marked by a formal rhetoric borrowed from that of medieval panel painting, stained glass windows, and slowly grown villages. Schiele's paintings of the town Stein [Fig. 2 and Cat. nos. 54–56], for example, compress pictorial space, stacking shapes to create a clustered design that evokes the compacted compositions of gothic art. Similarly, in images like *Town among Greenery (The Old City III)* [Cat. no. 68], recessive space is thwarted by clustering buildings in a colorful, cloisonnistic pattern. Both paintings echo the spatial strategies of gothic painting, which the Viennese art historian Max Dvořák defined as omitting "wherescever possible all spatial depth within the picture so that … the

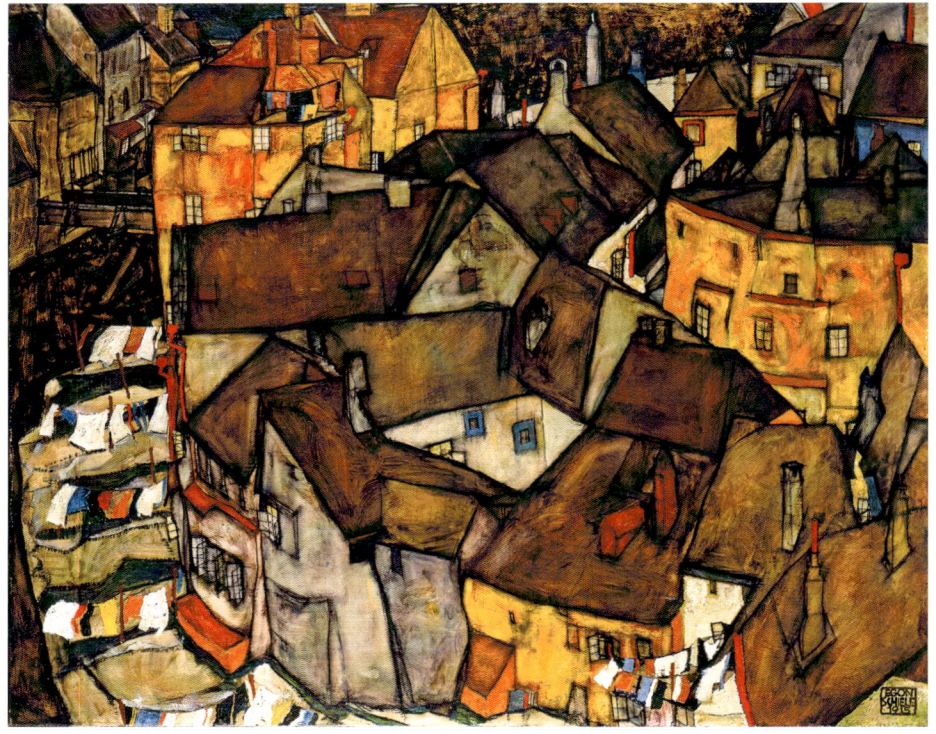

3. Egon Schiele, *Krumau Town Crescent I (The Small City V)*, 1915, oil on canvas. Israel Museum, Jerusalem (Kallir P291). Photo: HIP / Art Resource, NY

complex of buildings … seem to cling to one another."[10] In addition, prismatic coloration and layered pigment produces an effect akin to that of gothic stained glass windows. One contemporary, for example, wrote that in Schiele's images of Krumau "even the coloration rises out of a strong mesh in matte-shimmering, fading registers, or it forces its way as a flaming sheaf into the dark space."[11] And finally, paintings like *Krumau Town Crescent (The Small City V)* [Fig. no. 3] demonstrate Schiele's characteristically lively, tactile line. Defining surfaces that themselves seem to move and breathe, this distinctive line is also a "mark of the Gothic style, for urban historians conceived of the medieval town as a fundamentally organic entity, growing additionally over long periods, in contrast to modern methods of city planning."[12] Schiele's images thus act as pictorial arguments for a social identity based on the gothic principle of naturally occurring kinships. Defined by luminous hues

nestled in animate, linear structures, these clustered, cellular townscapes propose that Austria's fundamental character rests on an innately generated community rather than the orchestrated policies of modern society. As I wrote in 2004:

> *The paintings present themselves as material homologies, their organic form presuming a necessary resemblance to the towns they represent. In other words, both paintings and town offer themselves to the viewer as vital beings, autochthonic and authentic products of a natural order… Both painted work and built town are imagined as organisms, thus literalizing the natural ideal of the Gemeinschaft.*[13]

Third and, for the purposes of this essay, most significantly, I have argued that Schiele's interest in the work of cultural geographer Erwin Hanslik encourages a reading of his gothicized landscapes as images tuned to the contemporary challenges of articulating a workable Austrian identity.[14] In that sense, they are not only evocations of a general notion of organic community—that is, of *Gemeinschaft*—but of a specifically Austrian community whose political integrity stems from ineluctable geographic bonds. Again and again, Schiele's landscapes demonstrate the power of nature in forming social spaces. Articulated with Schiele's characteristically responsive line, and surrounded by a pulsating environment, buildings seem to grow spontaneously from their surroundings, sprouting like vital beings from that ground [Cat. no. 49]. Often, these structures appear compositionally overwhelmed by nature's forms, which are visualized as powerful and determining presences [Fig. 4]. As pictorial arguments for nature's ability to shape human history, the landscapes embody and imagine Austria as a naturally determined nation, mapping onto Hanslik's environmental theories of political and cultural identity. Before summarizing Hanslik's ideas, I would like briefly to situate myself in the research, as a means of pointing to the ways in which the scholarly conversation around both Schiele and Hanslik has evolved in the last generation.

I first developed my arguments about the relevance of Hanslik to Schiele's work in 1995 and 1996, while in Vienna conducting research for my dissertation on the landscapes. One of the most significant, published sources available at the time was Christian Nebehay's indispensable collection of Schiele's correspondence. That book also contains brief biographies of the individuals mentioned in these letters and, in a short profile, Hanslik is described as an assistant professor [Privatdozent] of anthropo-geography.[15] This detail piqued my interest. If Schiele had some connection to a university geographer, perhaps learning more about this individual could aid my understanding of the landscapes. However, the only references to Hanslik I could locate in the published literature were in Nebehay's book, and a footnote in the first edition of Jane Kallir's comprehensive Schiele catalogue raisonné.[16] Aside from these sources, Hanslik seemed to have been entirely forgotten.[17] A letter sent to the artist from Hanslik's secretary, and reprinted in Nebehay, suggested that Schiele had been asked to contribute illustrations to one of the author's books.[18] Nebehay wrote that these drawings had been completed but never found, and assumed the book had not been published.[19] Kallir surmised that Schiele seemed not to have produced the requested illustrations.[20] Schiele's correspondence contained other intriguing references to his connection with this mysterious geographer. For example, in a letter to his friend Anton Peschka, Schiele writes that Hanslik had loaned him some of his books and characterizes their content as significant.[21]

As I searched for more information during the fall of 1995, I found that the Österreichische Nationalbibliothek (Austrian National Library) held several books by Hanslik, which I set about reading in their entirety. At the time, the Austrian National Library's reading room was a dimly lit space, full as now with people bunked for hours at shared desks, silently engaged with their individual projects. I recall sitting in that room, working my way through Hanslik's original books, wondering if I would find anything useful. Scholars of history know that a great deal of research consists of following every possible lead, though many will end up going nowhere. Some aspects of the process take on the feel of a historical treasure hunt, tracking clues in the hopes of finding bits of information that might shed light on one's objects of study. As another day of library work unwound, I vividly remember turning a page, and seeing a drawing of heads that I recognized as being by Schiele's hand. And there, at the bottom right corner of the drawing was Schiele's distinctive, blocky signature [Cat. no. 69]. I could not have been more surprised. I had turned a page expecting to continue reading, only to be faced with the missing illustration.[22] Three rows of heads, shown in frontal, three-quarter, and profile positions, forming together a nine-figured grid. I recalled that the illustrations in the letter from Hanslik's secretary were described as "your drawings of the formation of the skull."[23] The drawing had indeed been contributed in time for the book's publication, and here it was: phrenological heads illustrating Hanslik's theory of human development, in which geographic circumstances determine both individual and collective intellectual, social, and emotional traits. I documented the drawing in my 1998 dissertation and, after all these years, still find it rather stunning that Schiele contributed to *Wesen der Menschheit* (The Essence of Humanity) with an illustration of environmentally-based skull phenotypes, and that he thought highly enough of Hanslik's ideas to create such a drawing. [24]

That Schiele actually followed through with the illustration provides potent evidence of Hanslik's relevance for Schiele's work, and the seriousness with which he engaged with the geographer's ideas. Because Hanslik's theories of nation formation hinge on people's unequivocal ties to the earth, they offer a compelling lens through which to interpret Schiele's landscapes, specifically the paintings' ability to evoke a unified Austria unburdened by modern and destabilizing nationalisms. Hanslik's writing essentially argued two points in various permutations across multiple books: nations are grounded in the land, from which their geopolitical authority springs; and Austria was uniquely situated to be the geographic, and therefore necessary, mediator between eastern and western Europe. An example of the first theory appears in *Wesen der Menschheit*: "The essence of history is never that which is political but rather that which happens between earth and human beings. The state results only from the societies of the earth."[25] In *Österreich: Erde und Geist* (Austria: Earth and Spirit), Hanslik describes the significance of this naturally deterministic approach to statehood for Austria:

> *If they are now parts of two humanities, and not just many different peoples, cooperating in Austria, then one can more easily have hope of solving the Austrian problem ... Austria is not a simple composition of individual peoples; rather, it has a higher meaning; it is the combination of two wings of humanity, the western and the eastern. As such, it not just possible but also necessary, above all for the whole world.*[26]

Indeed, he took this point further to insist that Austria was the quintessence of European identity as a whole, positioned as it was in the space between, making it not a liminal absence but precisely its opposite: the crucible presence of the European community. Schiele's landscapes can be better understood if we realize that Hanslik's theories resonated with him as a credible, indeed powerful idea of Austrian identity and importance. They were consistent with Schiele's belief in the *significance* of landscape, that there was something about the land, about place, that was individually and culturally constitutive. As I argued in *Between Ruin and Renewal*:

> *Hanslik's Institute and Schiele's landscapes signify similar conceptions of Austria as a nation united by the power of nature and tell us something about the world in which both men lived. The issue of national identity both animates the landscapes, and reveals their fictions. Drawing on the concept of environmental determinism, they represent Austria as a country defined by vital forces: nature's empire.*[27]

Hanslik's theories dovetailed with the images Schiele had been producing for years, with their politically nascent but persistent evocation of Austria as a country made inevitable by its environment.

I would like here to build on these arguments, by concentrating directly on the momentous consequences of World War I. Having previously established the landscapes' ability to represent a particular vision of Austria, a natural empire united internally and inexorably by its geographic environment, I want to look more closely at how Schiele and Hanslik's environmentally determined image of Austria could be marshalled for political ends specifically in the context of World War I. As

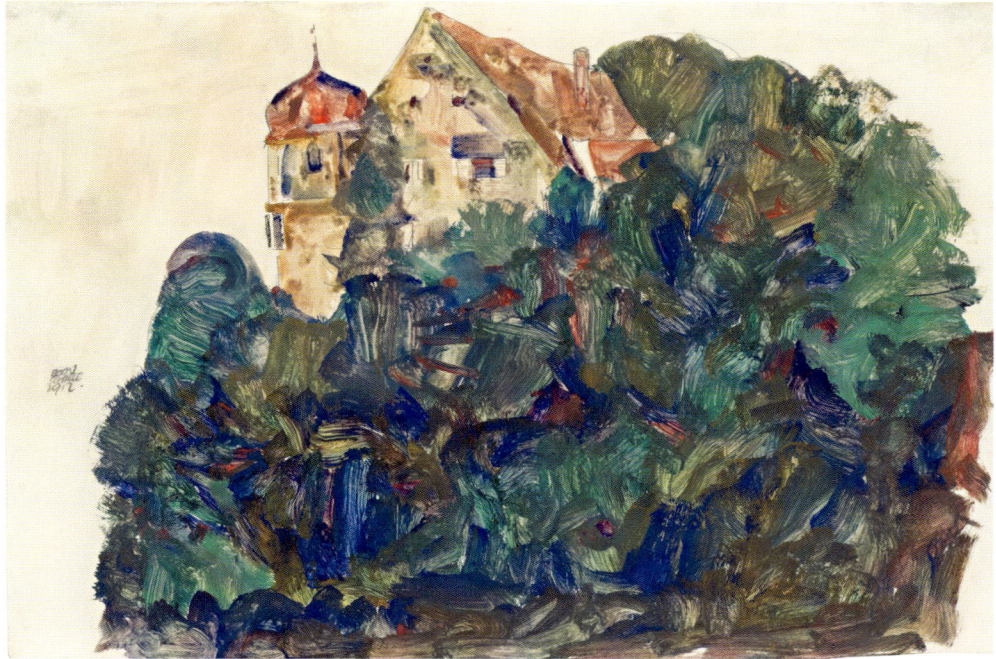

4. Egon Schiele, *Deuring Castle, Bregenz*, 1912, gouache, watercolor, and pencil. Leopold Museum, Vienna (Kallir D1216). Photo: Leopold Museum, Vienna

mentioned previously, when I first wrote about Hanslik's broad anthropogeographic vision of world history and its significance for Schiele's paintings, there was almost no secondary literature on Hanslik or the organization that he founded, the Institut für Kulturforschung (Institute for Cultural Research). Since then, a small but growing body of research on Hanslik has continued to improve our understanding of his place within Austrian and German geopolitical thinking.[28] Far from an isolated or marginal figure, Hanslik and his Institute were active participants in both academic and popular discussions about the politics of space in the late and post-war years. Hanslik's ideas elicited varying reactions from peers and the press, ranging from glowing to condemnatory. The work of the Institute provoked the ire of none other than Hermann Broch in a scathing critique published under a pseudonym, as Jennifer Jenkins has demonstrated in her fascinating study of this text.[29] Yet it is a sign of their active presence in contemporary discourse that Hanslik's theories elicited both

positive and negative responses.[30] Articulated through a steady presentation of maps, lectures, animated films and books, Hanslik's pseudoscientific mix of anthropological, developmental, and environmental theories had a demonstrable impact on the development of cultural geography.[31] Much of the reception of Hanslik's books and promotional activities took place in the context of World War I. Although Hanslik had been active as a professor and author as early as 1909, he founded the Institute for Cultural Research in 1915 in response to the war, which he invoked repeatedly as the reason for why its work was so necessary.[32] The degree to which Hanslik tapped into wartime anxiety about Austria's political future can be seen in a review published in the *Wiener Allgemeine Zeitung*:

> *The closing year brings a pronouncement in a book … This work, conceived by an individual spirit, means more than just a book. It is the expression of the confession, the conviction, the religion of a new*

5. Erwin Hanslik, "Aufriss Österreichs," illustration from *Österreich als Naturforderung* (Vienna: Institut für Kulturforschung, 1917), 31.

common ground that, invoked by Erwin Hanslik, already in the spring of 1915, during the bloodlust that made all voices drunk, began to build a site of the future.[33]

The effusive praise in this review seems prompted not simply by respect for the author's ideas, but a palpable sense of relief that someone had articulated a possible post-war path.

World War I made the challenges of a multinational empire, and its place within the broader European community, that much more severe. The Habsburg Dilemma and its problem of a shared national consciousness was certainly not specific to the war. As discussed, the erosion of a political principle that could justify the continued existence of the imperial, multinational state had been felt for some time. The internal pressures from that tension predated the war, but they were felt particularly intensely once citizens and soldiers were mobilized to fight for their country. In her excellent study of the everyday life of Austrians during the war, Maureen Healy writes: "During World

War I, the imprecise definition and fluctuating popular understanding of the state in Austria became an acute problem because millions of civilians were expected to sacrifice and 'hold out' for this state."[34] Moreover, as Deak and Jonathan Gumz have argued, the "First World War expanded the reach of emergency laws, once considered separate from the rule of law, and they became increasingly permanent conditions, warping and discrediting the constitutional state and its claims."[35] At the same time, the crushing destruction of war itself offered a potential path out of the logjam of an imperial identity at odds with modern constitutional democracy. Stefan Jonsson describes the paradox in his detailed study of Robert Musil's epic *The Man Without Qualities*: "The Austrian failure to solve the nationality problem signifies an inability to envision how a semifeudal empire could be transformed into a liberal capitalist society… Only a war or a revolution could break the double bind that blocked political progress in Austria-Hungary…"[36] Or, as succinctly stated by Deak, "War unmade the Habsburg state."[37] And here, Connelly seems to agree: "It [the monarchy] was something to kill for but not to die for, and the more dying it demanded, the more clearly its days were numbered."[38]

The pivotal year in the run up to the empire's un-making was 1917. Austrians were nearing the point of unremitting crisis as a result of a conflict that had lasted far longer than most anticipated, the death of the Emperor Franz Josef, and growing food shortages. Historian Jay Winter calls that year "the 'climacteric' of 1917," writing that this was "…the turning point, the moment that the political character of the war changed."[39] Winter argues that before 1917, the struggle was defined by an "imperial" war culture, focused on national solidarity and the fight for an existing social order, which co-existed after 1917 with a new and

2. AUFRISS ÖSTERREICHS.

▨ WESTEN
⊞ OSTEN
⌘ ORIENT
— WELTGESCHICHTLICH WIRK=
=SAME AUFRISSLINIEN ÖSTERREICHS.
KARST, KARPATHEN,
BALKAN, RHODOPE.

powerful culture of anxiety, a "revolutionary" battle culture that churned with resentment yet "also gestured toward positive transformations, in part to ensure that something good would come out of the immense suffering."[40] As the fighting ground on and the logic of empire faltered, if Austria were to have a legitimate future, its ethnically multiplicitous make-up would have to be reimagined as a coherent community apart from historical allegiance to the emperor. What vision of a postbellum Austrian state could have been feasibly imagined in 1917? Austria's citizens turned their thoughts to what might give meaning to the tragedy of total destruction and the weight of their sacrifices. After 1917, "the world could not go back... the events of 1917 made questions about the future urgent: What would a post-war world look like? How would the map of the world be redrawn? What ideas and ideologies would shape its contours?"[41]

As founder and director of the Institute for Cultural Research, Hanslik produced a variety of maps [Fig. 5] to answer precisely these questions. And it was in the crucial year of 1917 that, under the auspices of his Institute, Hanslik published in quick succession four separate volumes: *Die Menschheit in 30 Weltbildern*; *Österreich als Naturforderung* (Humanity in Thirty World Images: Austria as Requirement of Nature); *Österreich. Erde und Geist*; and of course, the book to which Schiele contributed his illustration, *Wesen der Menschheit*.[42] Again and again, in this series of closely timed publications, Hanslik posited an anthropogeographic ideology that proposed to define the emerging post-war era's geopolitical outlines, as visualized in multiple illustrative maps. In these texts, he argues forcefully that the future of Austria will be determined not by human but by environmental laws. As such, not only will this broad, multiethnic Austria continue, but Hanslik is emphatic that

a non-imperial yet expansive Austria would play a pivotal role after the combat, stemming from its position between the eastern and western parts of Europe.[43]

In this context, it becomes especially noteworthy how resolutely Schiele's landscapes visualize an Austria naturally united by organic and unchangeable ties to place. For a country reeling from economic hardship, military losses, and growing internal chaos, Schiele's land- and townscapes may have delivered a particularly resonant message. at precisely the moment that Austria and its fate seemed most at risk. In 1917, as the war dragged on and entered its final phrase, Schiele's landscapes had the potential to shape a compelling vision of Austria as a necessary and naturally sanctioned nation, just as the state limped traumatically into the battle's most catastrophic year. These images of a homeland rooted in its environment, and tied to Hanslik's argument for environmentally determined state authority, participated in a general effort to solidify national unity and public support for the conflict. From this perspective, the landscapes had the potential to function as effective wartime propaganda. Perhaps it is not surprising, then, that William Johnston has described Hanslik's *Österreich: Erde und Geist* as one of "the most striking propaganda works of the wartime period."[44] Johnston draws a distinction between Hanslik's visions of an emergent Austria and those of the writer Hugo von Hofmannsthal or other post-war political thinkers, and derides Hanslik's theories as "geopolitical megalomania." While critical, his characterization of Hanslik's brand of anthropogeography as propaganda nevertheless opens up a promising field of inquiry for the political role of landscape during World War I.

If Hanslik's notions of an environmentally determined Austria can be thought of as a form of propaganda, that is if they could be deployed rhetorically as ideological arguments meant to shape public opinion, how did they operate within the larger field of wartime propaganda? The concept and mobilization of propaganda during the struggle has been debated and studied from multiple angles. There are plentiful examples of images and text being used by both sides during the fighting to vilify and distort the enemy.[45] However, propaganda more broadly conceived can be defined as "a deliberate attempt to influence the opinions, beliefs and behaviors of particular groups in order to achieve political ends."[46] In this respect, propaganda operated as a vehicle for bolstering internal morale and actively shaping public perception by presenting a one-sided view of the issues. In the belligerent countries, mobilizing the home front became a priority, and propaganda represented an effective mechanism to meet this goal. World War I is often described in the literature as a "total war," in which residents at home as much as soldiers on the front were expected to contribute to the war effort.[47] Propaganda could sway citizens with emotional or cultural appeals that encouraged confidence in the legitimacy of the conflict.[48] As a recent history of propaganda during World War I points out, "fundamentally, propaganda is an attempt to persuade." In order to be persuasive, the author continues, propaganda "must work within a social context. … Propagandists will employ what Pierre Bourdieu, in another context, called cultural codes."[49]

If propaganda succeeds by deploying existing "cultural codes," both Schiele and Hanslik were experts at doing exactly this. They were adept at drawing on long traditions in intellectual and art history in which national identity is yoked to the environment, thus making the state's political existence seem as elemental and inescapable as nature itself. While Hanslik's expressive, literary flourishes and focus on the geographic exceptionalism of Austria were unique, the concepts of environmental determinism were already well represented in Austrian and German scholarship. Hanslik built on the theories of an earlier generation, including geographer Friedrich Ratzel and historian Karl Lamprecht.[50] In his analysis of how Hanslik's ideas influenced Schiele's late figural painting, Franz Smola describes Hanslik's ability to tap into pre-existing theories and make them relatable to the public: "Hanslik employs an easily understandable language, rolls over old stereotypes, and combines them with his own insights. His texts sound like speeches, oscillating between ecstatic euphoria and inflammatory, pamphlet-like declamation."[51] Similarly, Schiele was skilled at adapting existing visual vocabularies to new purposes. As discussed earlier, Schiele's landscapes savvily refer to medieval style and media, incorporating formal references that allude to a naturally occurring nation. In the history of landscape as a means of imagining community, one also thinks of Caspar David Friedrich and his political use of natural imagery in the face of the Napoleonic threat, or the Austrian painter Ferdinand Georg Waldmüller's regional landscapes.[52] Schiele's accomplishment was to modernize a central European art historical tradition of articulating shared politics through the symbols of landscape.

Research into how propaganda functioned during a time of total war suggests that it was not only dictated by imperial leadership, but evolved and was performed by local offices and citizens in the community. "Propaganda was not just a vertical process, but also a horizontal one, even to some extent a great upsurge from below, sustained by a huge number of individuals."[53] I suggest that Schiele and Hanslik were two of these individuals, both deeply concerned with fostering a sense of Austrian identity among its citizens, particularly as the first fully industrialized combat intensified and further destabilized an imperial structure already under pressure from its own internal conflicts. Hanslik's multiple publications with the Institute that he founded in 1915 clearly demonstrate his explicit interest in communicating a clear and persuasive theory for Austrian statehood and relevance. Schiele developed a commitment to promoting a cohesive sense of Austrian political and cultural identity that became particularly pronounced in the last years of the war. Conscripted in 1915 but declared unfit for active duty, he was given administrative duties and stationed in different locales outside of Vienna. He hoped for an assignment to the k.u.k. Kriegspressequartier (War Press Office), the branch responsible for coordinating press and propaganda during the war, including literary production, theater, film, painting, and photography.[54] At this stage, his interest in joining the War Press Office may have been due less to patriotic impulse than wanting artistic work away from the front.[55] In January 1917, Schiele returned to Vienna as a draftsman with the k.u.k. Konsumanstalt für die Gagisten der Armee im Felde (Imperial and Royal Depot for Officers on Active Service), and he was ultimately posted to the War Press Office in 1918 at the Vienna Army Museum.[56] Based on his correspondence, Schiele appears to have been somewhat ambivalent about the war in its early years but, by 1917, his letters demonstrate a more obviously patriotic tone. In addition, that year he developed the idea of a collective Kunsthalle, which would engage architects, art historians, artists, musicians, writers, and other members of Vienna's creative community. Schiele began actively laying the groundwork for the project and articulating its mission, which he described at length in a letter of March 1917, partially excerpted here:

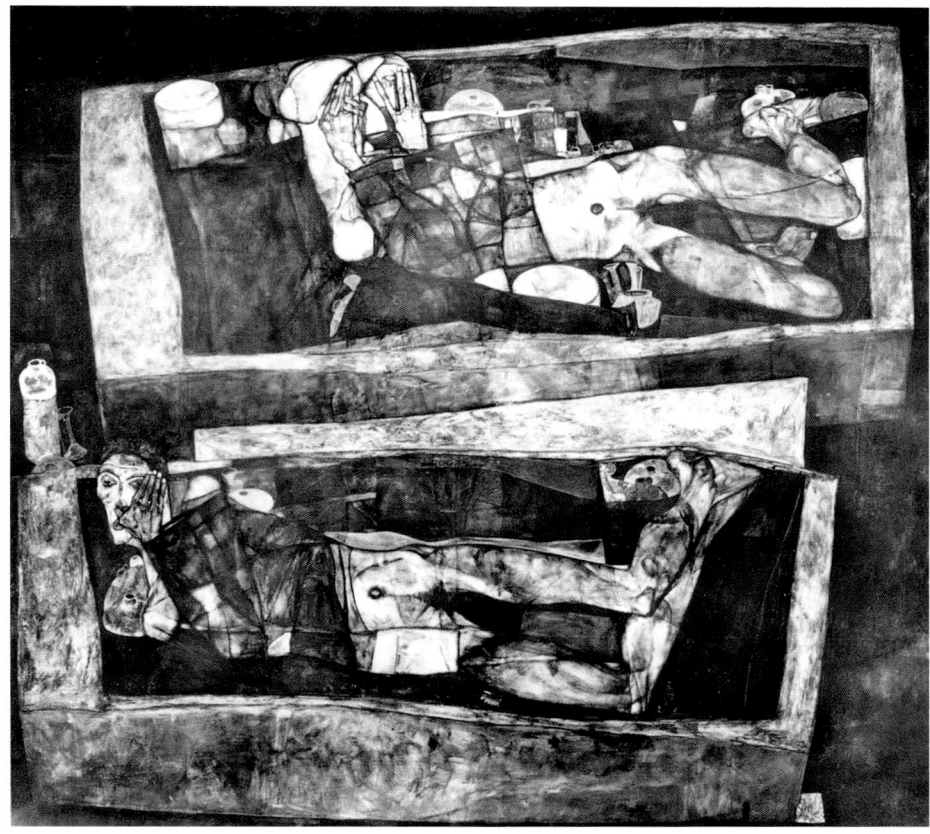

Since the bloody horror of the world war befell us, some have presumably already realized that art is more than a matter of bourgeois luxury. … [E]very intellectual person has the duty to preserve Austrian cultural heritage from decline and to help realize the plans of a younger generation that is beginning a new rebuilding and unconditionally wants to break with the damages of the past. … What we are undertaking is not the result of a passing whim; it is at once a moral and patriotic act. … [W]e want the talent to stop fleeing the country and that all those whom Austria has produced may create for Austria's honor.[57]

6. Egon Schiele, *Resurrection (Graves)*, 1913, oil on canvas. Whereabouts unknown (Kallir P251). Image courtesy Kallir Research Institute, New York

The ambitious venture was never realized, but Schiele's letter gives us insight into how art and politics came together for him in the late years of the war. As a fulcrum for nourishing Austria's creative talent, the Kunsthalle was conceived as a project in culture and nation rebuilding, a serious aesthetic and patriotic undertaking.

Propaganda during the conflict could swell from below, but of course, it was also a key component of official messaging from above. In 1917, Schiele and Hanslik each became involved with aspects of state-sponsored propaganda programs, both in and outside of Austria. In May of 1917, Schiele was tasked with selecting art for the summer "Kriegsausstellung" (War Exhibition) at the Prater. The first "War Exhibition" had been held in 1916 as a massive theme park dedicated to encouraging public enthusiasm for the war. In her study of the "War Exhibition," Healy writes: "A remarkable display of state-sponsored propaganda transmitted through channels of popular entertainment, the 'War Exhibition' reveals the complex, mutually dependent relationship of propaganda and entertainment during World War I."[58] With dozens of halls

and attractions, the presentation conveyed a "relentlessly optimistic, positive depiction of a losing war."[59] Like the first "War Exhibition," its second iteration in 1917 included various entertaining attractions intended "to whip up support for the war among the local population."[60] When Schiele took on the role of organizing the art hall for that year's version of the "War Exhibition," he was stepping into an existing model for uniting visual culture with state propaganda. Schiele submitted one of his own paintings to the effort, *Resurrection (Graves)*, which he bought back from the Galerie Hauer and retitled for the purposes of the show as *Heroes' Graves—Resurrection: Fragment for a Mausoleum* [Fig. 6].[61]

Heroes' Graves—Resurrection (now known simply as *Resurrection [Graves]*) was also exhibited in another government sponsored propaganda exhibition in September 1917: the "Österrikisk Konstutställning" (Austrian Art Exhibition) at the Liljevalchs Konsthall in Stockholm. In this case, the state's efforts at persuasion were directed externally to the neutral country of Sweden. The point of

7. Team installing the "Austrian Art Exhibition" assembled for a press conference at Stockholm's Liljevalchs Konsthall on September 4, 1917. From left: Anton Hanak, Erwin Hanslik, Josef Hoffmann, Ernst Wagner, Hans Boehler, and Anton Faistauer. Photograph by Erik Holmén published in Stockholm's *Hvar 8 Dag*, September 16, 1917. Image © Kungliga Biblioteket, Stockholm

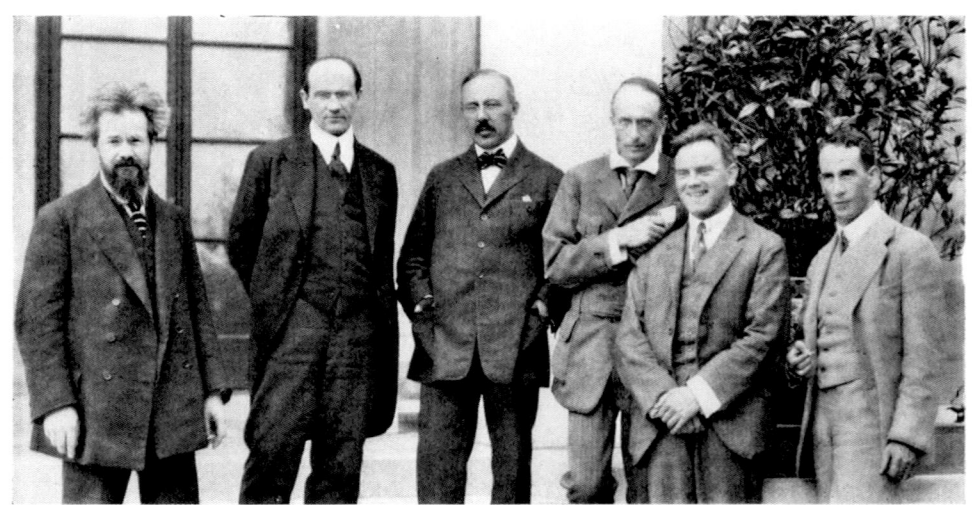

Foto Holmén, Stockholm.   Kliché: Kem. A.-B. Bendt Silfverspatre, Sthlm—Gbg

PORTRÄTTGRUPP TILL DEN ÖSTERRIKISKA UTSTÄLLNINGEN I STOCKHOLM.   *Fr. v.: professorerna Hanak, Hanslik och Hoffman samt målarne dr. Wagner, Boehler och Faistauer.*

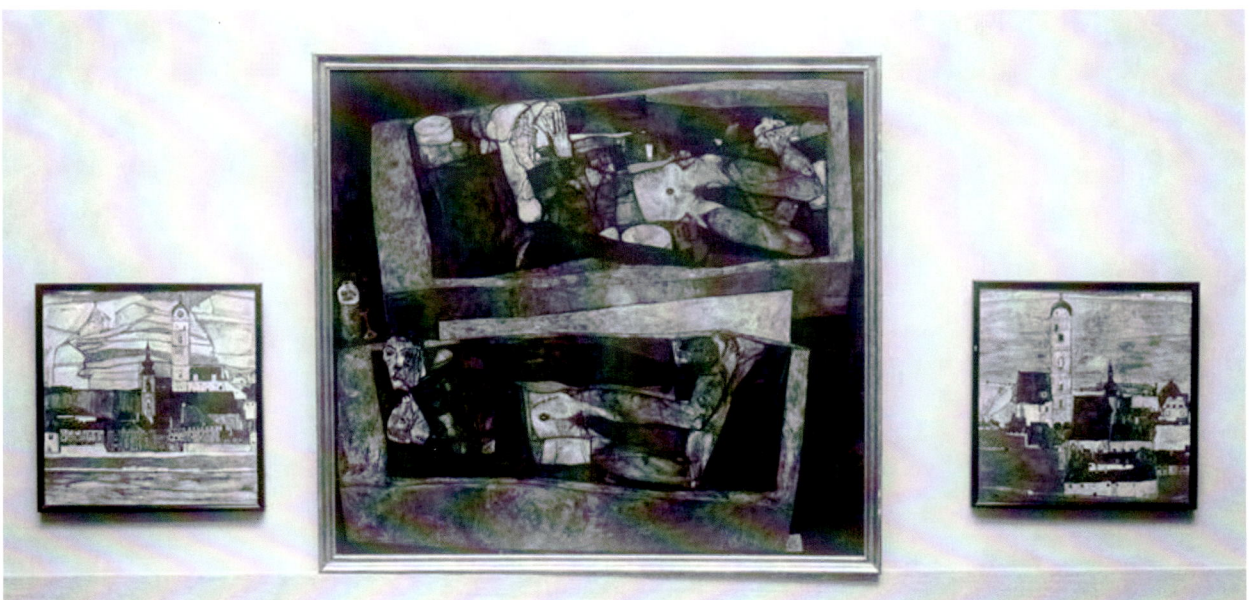

propaganda targeted at neutral countries, and at this moment in the conflict, differed somewhat from that of domestic messaging. Communicating a united image of the empire continued as a fundamental precept, but persuading Sweden that Austrian commerce and culture could function effectively was just as important. The role of neutral nations often hinged on embattled economic relations with the belligerent countries and, as the war moved into its final two years, the emphasis began to shift to how trade and finance might be restored in a post-war political economy.[62] The Central Powers and the Entente vied for the neutrals' resources and markets, "with a view to securing a strategic advantage, starving the enemy populace into submission or revolt, and securing a head start in the renewed economic competition which was to follow the conclusion of peace."[63]

Thus, the exhibition in Stockholm should be seen as part of this effort to secure the support of a neutral nation both during and, just as importantly, after the war. Sympathy for Austria's cultural and political position could

thus anticipate some kind of post-war peace, in which economic relations between the two countries would ideally be reestablished. Due to Elizabeth Clegg's pathbreaking research tracing a rather complicated set of organizational decisions, we have a much clearer picture of how the Stockholm exhibition was conceptualized and executed.[64] As Clegg points out, it is surprising that this exported "Austrian Art Exhibition" has not received more attention in the literature, as it was a massive event incorporating art, design, fashion, and music, undertaken at a particularly sensitive moment in the conflict. Her archival research reveals that the show was initially spearheaded by military authorities through the War Press Office, while at the same time, the Viennese Chamber of Commerce, with support from the Ministerium des Äussern (Ministry of Foreign Affairs), was also interested in staging a presence at Stockholm to benefit trade relations. Ultimately, the direction of the exhibition was granted to the Ministry of Foreign Affairs, which appointed modern architect and designer Josef Hoffmann to head up the enterprise.[65]

8. Installation view of the Egon Schiele room at the 1917 "Austrian Art Exhibition," held at Liljevalchs Konsthall and showing *Stein on the Danube, Seen from the South (Large)*, *Resurrection*, and *Stein on the Danube, Seen from the Kreuzberg (Large)*, modern print from original glass negative. Stadsmuseum, Stockholm

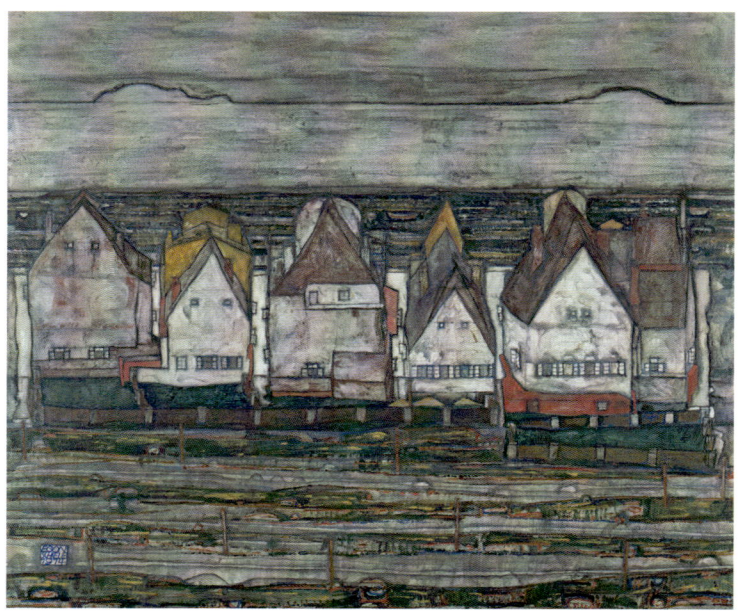

9. Egon Schiele, *Houses by the Sea (Row of Houses)*, 1914, oil on canvas. Leopold Museum, Vienna (Kallir P281). Photo: Leopold Museum, Vienna

efforts in art, design, fashion, and music, the text declares:

> *Under the undeniable reduction of relationships to neutral states and exchange with them which the war brought with it, as well as the countermeasures of the Entente, the central states must therefore produce promotions and propaganda of a suitable style, namely, with the most expedient support of its economy, while at the same time calling on private entrepreneurial spirit for support. For that reason, the expenditures for propaganda of this kind should by no means be seen as lost, useless, but rather as necessary and profitable.*[67]

These efforts are to be "decidedly in the interest of the politics of the Central Powers." In the section on art, the report emphasizes that the politics of these works cannot be overtly expressed, or the persuasive effect will be lost. For the exercise to be effective, it cannot be perceived as propaganda. Accordingly, the document notes: "Politics must absolutely not be allowed to come to the fore; rather, it is all about presenting Austria as a country of modern high culture that is still capable of achievement and that is doing outstanding work for peace even during the war."[68]

Though the planning and execution for the Stockholm exhibition had been transferred to civilian authorities, the undertaking continued to stem from propagandistic goals. The Chamber of Commerce had identified Stockholm as a worthwhile venture through its Komitee für österreichische Edelarbeit und Kunst (Committee for Austrian Luxury Handcraft and Art), a group established explicitly for the purposes of propaganda. Indeed, the founding statement of the committee was entitled "Die Schaffung eines Propaganda-Komitees für österreichische Edelarbeit und Kunst" (The Creation of a Propaganda Committee for Austrian Luxury Handcraft and Art).[66] Authored by Chamber Secretary Erich Pistor, and marked "confidential" by the Handels- und Gewerbekammer Wien (Vienna Chamber of Trade and Commerce), the document describes the importance of having a propaganda arm targeted to neutral countries, pointing out that England, France, and Germany already have well-financed and organized commercial propaganda teams to engage with neutral nations. Identifying

The exhibition in Stockholm was thus conceived as part of the Committee for Austrian Luxury Handcraft and Art's defined propaganda efforts, acting as what Clegg has described as a concerted "charm offensive."[69] I conclude this essay by considering the role of Schiele's paintings at the 1917 "Austrian Art Exhibition." Although Schiele could not travel to Stockholm due to his military posting, he participated in the "Austrian Art Exhibition" by submitting fifteen oil paintings and a number of drawings.[70] Schiele and Hanslik appear to have first come in contact around their activities in Stockholm. The letter from Hanslik's secretary to Schiele in September 1917 requests the artist's help providing materials for Stockholm, as well as the drawing for *Wesen der Menschheit* discussed earlier in this essay.[71] Hanslik had been named a member of the exhibition's delegation [Fig. 7], and its "ideological spokesman."[72] It is unclear how Hanslik was selected for this position, but he did have close connections with a number of artists and other cultural figures in Vienna, including the painter and art education reformer Franz Cižek, and Alfred Roller, director of Vienna's School of Applied Arts, who oversaw the production of the Institute's many illustrational maps.[73] Not only was Hanslik the public-facing figure for the Austrian Art Exhibition, but he also started a local office for Kulturforschung (Cultural Research) in Stockholm around the same time as the exhibition.[74] He saw Stockholm as the most promising location outside of Austria to advocate for his geographic theories of collective identity, which proposed a peace predicated on the irrelevance of conventional political constructs.[75] If group identity was tied to the land, and therefore could not be changed, in the end war was futile. And, as we know, by virtue of its unique topographical location, Austria occupied a pivotal, preordained place in Hanslik's telluric vision of political history. As the promotional voice of the exhibition, Hanslik gave the same type of presentations in Stockholm that he had been developing back home. According to Clegg, in his press appearances and public lectures, Hanslik "tirelessly urged that the exhibition be viewed as an encapsulation of the 'Austria' extolled in his own writings: an environmentally conditioned, slowly evolving, harmoniously multiethnic whole … threatened by the 'sickness' of separatist nationalism but truly a model for the peaceful future of humanity."[76] An initial press conference was followed by a

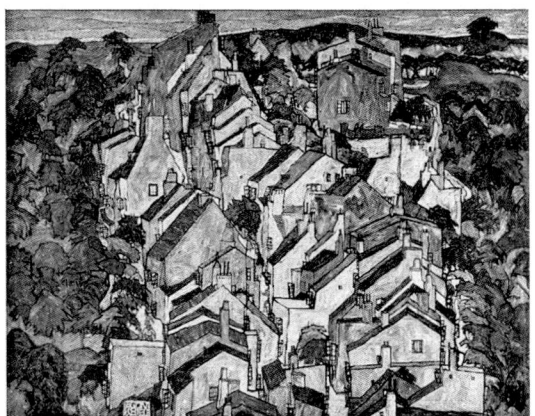

EGON SCHIELE   GAMMAL STAD

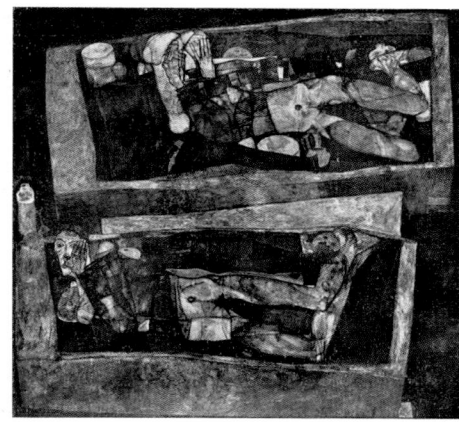

EGON SCHIELE   GRAVAR

well-attended slide lantern lecture in the Hall of Mirrors at Stockholm's Grand Hôtel, where Hanslik promoted his Austrianic vision of an environmentally determined geopolitics.[77]

And what was Schiele's role in the Swedish undertaking? Notably, eleven of the fifteen paintings by Schiele in the Stockholm show were landscapes [Figs. 8, 10].[78] These included the previously discussed works *Stein on the Danube, Seen from the Kreuzberg (Large)* [Fig. 2], *Stein on the Danube, Seen from the Kreuzberg (Small)* [Cat. no. 56], *Town among Greenery (The Old City III)* [Cat. no. 68], and

10. Reproduction of Egon Schiele's, *Gammal Stad* (*Town among Greenery [The Old City III]*), in the exhibition catalogue, *Österrikiska Konstutställningen, Ausst. Liljevalches Konsthall, September* (Stockholm: Liljevalchs Konsthall, 1917).

Sawmill [Cat. no. 49], as well as *Single Houses (Houses with Mountains)* [Cat. no. 29], and *Houses by the Sea (Row of Houses)* [Fig. 9].[79] *Town among Greenery (The Old City III)* was one of the two pieces by Schiele selected for reproduction in the exhibition catalogue.[80] I want to stress the significance of the intense focus on the landscapes for the exhibition at the Liljevalchs Konsthall [Fig. 8]. We have already established how seriously Schiele was invested in Hanslik's theories of national identity grounded in the environment, and that Hanslik's lectures and writings provided an intellectual framework for ideas of land-based identity that had long been present in Schiele's tree- and townscapes. Given the propaganda goals for the exhibition, the preponderance of landscapes suggests that they served the stated purposes of the "Austrian Art Exhibition" by solidifying cultural and commercial support for Austria. Remembering that Hanslik was the ideological spokesperson for this major "charm offensive," could portraits or allegories by Schiele have communicated these anthropogeographic principles as well? There is evidence that Schiele incorporated Hanslik's anthropogeographic theories into his figural works at this time, as Smola has convincingly demonstrated.[81] Indeed, one of these paintings that used typological formulas based on Hanslik's methods was included in the Stockholm show.[82] Yet it was Schiele's landscapes that were showcased and took pride of place at the 1917 "Austrian Art Exhibition." Hanslik's overarching principles were grounded in topographical geologies, illustrated with maps, and tied to a long intellectual tradition of environmental determinism. As demonstrated earlier in this essay, Schiele's landscapes had a particularly effective capacity to visualize and embody Hanslik's claims of Austrian geographic exceptionalism. And the Stockholm exhibition, a propaganda initiative sponsored by Austria's Ministerium and with Hanslik as its public spokesman, provided an opportunity to convey these ideas to an audience outside of Austria at a critical moment during the war.

What does this tell us about Austrian politics and art in the waning years of World War I? As the Habsburg Empire struggled to maintain integrity, create a cohesive sense of shared identity, and imagine its post-war prospects, in Stockholm, a land-based model of community offered an effective message of consolidated Austrian identity. Buttressed by Hanslik's vigorous and public assertions of an Austria formed by environmental conditions, Schiele's landscape paintings could act as visual enunciations of a geopolitical theory of nation formation. His images of organic towns and rural scenes functioned as embodied claims not only for a pluralistic and united Austria, but for its right to exist when the war concluded. If the Stockholm show was a propagandistic effort that began laying the groundwork for a future peace and trade relationship between the two states, then Schiele's landscapes and Hanslik's lectures proposed an environmentally based argument for a viable Austria in this scenario. They promised that Austria's collection of ethno-linguistically diverse groups would cohere because of geological rather than imperial principles, positing Austria as a natural nation and earth's laws as the permanent condition for a peaceful and post-war future. Stockholm represented an intensely concentrated moment of externally directed propaganda, in which Hanslik participated with words and Schiele with images. Of course, their vision of a pluralistic yet consolidated Austria ultimately could not be sustained, as we know. Yet in 1917, as the brutal realities of war encouraged its participants to imagine a future peace, Schiele's landscapes advocated hopefully for a vision of an Austria grounded in its environment, tied to its past, and persisting into the future.

1 For the exceptions, see Christian Bauer, "Places of Desire and Townscapes: Egon Schiele's Paintings of Krems and Stein" in *Egon Schiele: Almost a Lifetime*, ed. Christian Bauer (Munich: Hirmer Verlag, 2015), 82–91; Wolfgang Krug, "Landscapes on the Brink of War," in Rudolf Leopold, *Egon Schiele: Landscapes* (Munich and New York: Prestel Verlag, 2004); Helena Pereña Sáez, *Egon Schiele: Wahrnehmung, Identität und Weltbild* (Marburg: Tectum Verlag, 2010); Elisabeth von Samsonow, "Egon Schiele: Vitalist Deleuzian," in *Art History after Deleuze and Guattari*, ed. Sjoerd van Tuinen and Stephen Zepke (Leuven: Leuven University Press, 2017), 43–59; and Kimberly A. Smith, *Between Ruin and Renewal: Egon Schiele's Landscapes* (New Haven: Yale University Press, 2004).

2 Smith, "The Gothic Revisited: Nature and the Nation," in *Between Ruin and* Renewal (see note 1), 99–137; and Kimberly A. Smith, "Egon Schiele's Landscapes and the Allure of the Natural Nation," *Austrian History Yearbook* 33 (January 2002): 163–205. Benedict Anderson's concept of the "imagined community" has proven to be one of the most durable ways to theorize how large groups of people conceptualize themselves as having a shared national identity. See Anderson, *Imagined Communities: Reflections on the Origin and Spread of Nationalism* [1983] (London: Verso, 2016), 6.

3 Ernst Gellner, *Language and Solitude: Wittgenstein, Malinowski, and the Habsburg Dilemma* (Cambridge: Cambridge University Press, 1998).

4 Malcolm Spencer, "Modernity, Nationalism and the Austrian Crisis," in *Austrian Experiences of Modernity in the Writings of Musil, Roth, and Bachmann* (Rochester, NY: Camden House, 2008), 53.

5 John Deak, *Forging a Multinational State: State Making in Imperial Austria from the Enlightenment to the First World War* (Palo Alto, CA: Stanford University Press, 2015).

6 John Connelly, Review of *Forging a Multinational State: State Making in Imperial Austria from the Enlightenment to the First World War* by John Deak, *German Studies Review* 40, no. 3 (October 2017): 632.

7 John Connelly, *From Peoples into Nations: A History of Eastern Europe* (Princeton: Princeton University Press, 2020), 323.

8 Smith, *Between Ruin and Renewal* (see note 1), 134.

9 On the industrialization of Austria's economy, see David F. Good, *The Economic Rise of the Habsburg Empire, 1750–1914* (Berkeley: University of California Press, 1984).

10 Max Dvořák, *Idealism and Naturalism in Gothic Art* (1918), transl. Randolph J. Klawiter (Notre Dame, IN: University of Notre Dame Press, 1967), 161.

11 Max Eisler, "Egon Schiele in der Sezession," in *In Memorian Egon Schiele*, ed. Arthur Roessler (Vienna: Richard Lányi, 1921), 39.

12 Smith, *Between Ruin and Renewal* (see note 1), 88.

13 Ibid., 114.

14 Smith, "Egon Schiele's Landscapes" (see note 2), 178–199; Smith, *Between Ruin and Renewal* (see note 1), 122–132.

15 Christian Nebehay, *Egon Schiele, 1890–1918: Leben, Briefe, Gedichte* (Salzburg and Vienna: Residenz Verlag, 1979), 527.

16 Jane Kallir, *Egon Schiele: The Complete Works* (New York: Harry N. Abrams, 1990), 243, n. 27.

17 A third secondary source on Hanslik, of which I was not aware at the time, is Erich Zöllner, "Erwin Hanslik (1880–1940): Ein deutsch-polnischer Kulturhistoriker, Anthropogeograph und Publizist, Opfer der national-sozialistischen Euthanasieaktion," in *Bericht über den achtzehnten österreichischen Historikertag in Linz*, ed. Lorenz Mikoletzky (Vienna: Institut für Österreichische Geschichtsforschung, 1991), 114–115.

18 Letter from Erwin Hanslik's secretary to Egon Schiele, Sept. 4, 1917, reprinted in Nebehay, *Egon Schiele, 1890–1918* (see note 15), 432, no. 1299.

19 Nebehay, *Egon Schiele, 1890–1918* (see note 15), 432, no. 1299, n.1. "*Das Buch ist nicht erscheinen. Es wäre das einzige von Schiele illustrierte gewesen. Bisher hat sich auch keine seiner Zeichnungen dazu gefunden.*" Nebehay, 527–28, who also notes that Schiele listed several appointments with Hanslik in his 1918 datebook.

20 Kallir, *Egon Schiele: The Complete Works* (see note 16), 243, n. 27.

21 Letter from Schiele to Anton Peschka, Oct. 25, 1917, Albertina, Wien/A – Inv. Nr.: Egon Schiele Archiv ESA 268 r/v, reprinted in Nebehay, *Egon Schiele: 1890–1918* (see note 15), 431, no. 1291.

22 In Erwin Hanslik, *Wesen der Menschheit* (Vienna: Institut für Kulturforschung, 1917), n.p.

23 Nebehay, *Egon Schiele, 1890–1918* (see note 15), 432, no. 1299.

24 Kimberly Ann Smith, "Egon Schiele's Landscapes" (Ph.D. diss., Yale University, New Haven, CT, 1998), 166, UMI.

25 Hanslik, *Wesen der Menschheit* (see note 22), 62.

26 Hanslik, *Österreich: Erde und Geist* (Vienna: Institut für Kulturforschung, 1917), 62–63.

27 Smith, *Between Ruin and Renewal* (see note 1), 132.

28 For analyses of the connection between Schiele and Hanslik, see especially Kurt De Boodt and Paul Dujardin, "*Gesellschaft* or *Gemeinschaft*? Visions for Europe: Erwin Hanslik, Otto Neurath, and Richard von Coudenhove-Kalergi," in *Beyond Klimt: New Horizons in Central Europe*, exh. cat. Belvedere, Vienna, eds. Stella Rollig and Alexander Klee (Munich: Hirmer Verlag, 2018), 350–357, and Franz Smola, "Vom 'Menschen-

bewusstsein' zum neuen Menschenbild – Egon Schiele und der Anthropogeograph Erwin Hanslik," in *Die ästhetische Gnosis der Moderne*, eds. Leander Kaiser and Michael Ley (Vienna: Passagen Verlag, 2008), 123–175.

29 Jennifer Jenkins, "'Ein Fiasko des Geistes': Hermann Broch's Rediscovered Early Critique 'Ein offiziöser Geschaftlhuber der Kultur' (1918)," *Studia Austriaca* 26, (2018): 19–44. Jenkins reproduces Broch's text along with scholarly commentary in the same issue, 5–17.

30 Contemporary geographer Hugo Hassinger criticized Hanslik's definition of German-Slavic linguistic boundaries as "*ungeographisch*." See Petra Svatek, "Erwin Hanslik (1880–1940): Geopolitische Visionen eines Kartographen," in *16. Kartographiehistorisches Colloquium: Marbach am Neckar 2012*, eds. Markus Heinz und Armin Hüttermann (Bonn: Kirschbaum Verlag, 2016), 126.

31 Norman Henniges, "'Naturgesetze der Kultur': Die Wiener Geographen und die Ursprünge der 'Volks- und Kulturbodentheorie,'" *ACME: An International E-Journal for Critical Geographies* 14, no. 4 (2015): 1343. This influence would have dangerous connotations for subsequent theories of national determination based on the concept of *Grossraum* or "great space."

32 Smith, "Egon Schiele's Landscapes" (see note 2), 178.

33 Anon., "Menschheit," *Wiener Allgemeine Zeitung* 31 (December 1917): 4, as cited in Jenkins, "'Ein Fiasko des Geistes'" (see note 29), 30, n. 28.

34 Maureen Healy, *Vienna and the Fall of the Habsburg Empire: Total War and Everyday Life in World War I* (Cambridge: Cambridge University Press, 2004), 15.

35 John Deak and Jonathan E. Gumz, "How to Break a State: The Habsburg Monarchy's Internal War, 1914–1918," *American Historical Review* 122, no. 4 (October 2017), 1135.

36 Stefan Jonnson, *Robert Musil and the History of Modern Identity* (Durham, NC: Duke University Press, 2001), 27.

37 Deak, *Forging a Multinational State* (see note 5), 264.

38 Connelly, *From Peoples into Nations* (see note 7), 323.

39 Jay Winter, "War and Anxiety in 1917," in *The Myriad Legacies of 1917: A Year of War and Revolution*, ed. Maartje Abbenhuis, Neill Atkinson, Kingsley Baird, and Gail Romano (London: Palgrave Macmillan, 2018), 15.

40 Winter, "War and Anxiety in 1917" (see note 39), 16.

41 Maartje Abbenhuis, "Introduction: Death's Carnival: The Myriad Legacies of 1917," in *The Myriad Legacies of 1917: A Year of War and Revolution*, 3.

42 Erwin Hanslik, *Die Menschheit in 30 Weltbildern* (Vienna: Institut für Kulturforschung, 1917); *Österreich als Naturforderung* (Vienna: Institut für Kulturforschung, 1917); *Österreich: Erde und Geist*; and *Wesen der Menschheit*.

43 Hanslik, *Österreich: Erde und Geist* (see note 26), 16. See also Henniges, "'Naturgesetze der Kultur,'" (see note 31), 1333.

44 William M. Johnston, *Der österreichische Mensch: Kulturgeschichte der Eigenart Österreichs* (Vienna, Cologne, Graz: Böhlau Verlag, 2010), 142–43.

45 See Eberhard Demm, "Propaganda and Caricature in the First World War," *Journal of Contemporary History* 28, no. 1 (January 1993): 163–192; John Horne and Alan Kramer, "War Between Soldiers and Enemy Civilians, 1914–15," in *Great War, Total War: Combat and Mobilization on the Western Front, 1914–1918*, Publications of the German Historical Institute, eds. Roger Chickering and Stig Förster (Washington, D.C. and Cambridge: Cambridge University Press, 2000), 153–68.

46 Joachim Bürgschwentner, "War Relief, Patriotism and Art: The State-Run Production of Picture Postcards in Austria 1914–1918," *Austrian Studies* 21, Cultures at War: Austria-Hungary 1914–1918 (2013): 100.

47 The literature on World War I as a "total war" is too voluminous to list here, but for a useful set of essays, see Chickering and Förster, eds., *Great War, Total War: Combat and Mobilization on the Western Front, 1914–1918*.

48 David Welch, "Introduction," *Propaganda, Power and Persuasion: From World War I to Wikileaks*, ed. David Welch (London and New York: I.B. Tauris, 2014).

49 Troy R.E. Paddock, "Introduction," *World War I and Propaganda*, ed. Troy R.E. Paddock (Leiden and Boston: Brill, 2014), 13. See Pierre Bourdieu, *Distinction: A Social Critique of the Judgment of Taste*, trans. Richard Nice (Cambridge, MA: Harvard University Press, 1984).

50 Henniges, "'Naturgesetze der Kultur'" (see note 31), 1317–1331; Smith, "Egon Schiele's Landscapes" (see note 2), 168–173.

51 Smola, "Vom 'Menschenbewusstsein' zum neuen Menschenbild" (see note 28), 139. Moreover, Hanslik was not the only geographer during this period occupied with determining the true contours of *Mitteleuropa*, and thus spoke in a disciplinary language that would have been legible to his contemporaries. Svatek, "Erwin Hanslik" (see note 30), 123–25.

52 Eric Dorn Brose, "Patriotism, Nationalism, and the Liberation of Germany," *in German History 1789–1871: From the Holy Roman Empire to the Bismarckian Reich* (New York: Bergahn Books, 2013), 62–78; Mag. Elke Doppler-Wagner "Zur künstlerischen Rezeption Ferdinand Georg Waldmüllers," Dissertation, University of Vienna, 2007.

53 Stéphane Audion-Rouzeau and Annette-Becker, *14–18. Understanding the Great War*, trans. Catherine Temerson (New York: Hill and Wang, 2002), 109, cited in Paddock, "Introduction" (see note 49), 11.

54 For a comprehensive review of the work of the War Press Office, see Sema Colpan, Amália Kerekes, Siegfried Mattl, Magdolna Orosz, and Tatin Teller, eds., *Kulturmanöver: Das k.u.k. Kriegspressequartier und die Mobilisierung von Wort und Bild*, Budapester Studien zur Literaturwissenschaft 18 (Frankfurt: Peter Lang, 2015).

55 Sonja Niederacher, "Egon Schiele as an 'Office Soldier' during World War I," in *And Yet There was Art!: Austria 1914–1918*, exh. cat. Leopold Museum, eds. Peter Weinhäupl, Elisabeth Leopold, Ivan Ristic, and Stefan Kutzenberger (Vienna: Christian Brandstätter Verlag, 2014), 29.

56 Jill Lloyd, "Egon Schiele 1914–1918: The War Years," in *Egon Schiele: The Complete Paintings*, ed. Tobias G. Natter (Munich: Taschen, 2017), 304; Stephan Pumberger, "Storing and Administrating: Egon Schiele as Draftsman Behind the Frontlines," in *And Yet There was Art!: Austria 1914–1918*, 128–29.

57 Egon Schiele to Anton Peschka, March 3, 1917 in Nebehay, *Egon Schiele, 1890–1918* (see note 15), 417–18, no. 1182, reprinted from Arthur Roessler, *Briefe und Prosa von Egon Schiele* (Vienna 1921), 118–23.

58 Healy, *Vienna and the Fall of the Habsburg Empire* (see note 34), 88.

59 Ibid., 107.

60 Lloyd, "Egon Schiele 1914–1918" (see note 56), 304.

61 *Heldengräber-Auferstehung – Fragment für ein Mausoleum.* Egon Schiele to Anton Peschka, May 30, 1917, reprinted in Nebehay, *Egon Schiele, 1890–1918* (see note 15), 421, no. 1208.

62 Marc Frey, *The Neutrals and World War One* (Oslo: Institut for forsvarsstudier, 2000), 14.

63 Johan den Hertog and Samuël Kruizinga, eds., *Caught in the Middle: Neutrals, Neutrality and the First World War* (Amsterdam: Amsterdam University Press, 2011), 8.

64 Clegg's meticulous research into the exhibition's background is found in Elizabeth Clegg, "War and Peace at the Stockholm 'Austrian Art Exhibition' of 1917," *Burlington Magazine* 154, no. 1315 (October 2012): 676–688. See also Clegg, "An Interpretation of War: Austria-Hungary at the Front 1914–1918," in Weinhäupl, Leopold, Ristic, and Kutzenberger, eds., *And Yet There was Art!* (see note 55), 66–67.

65 Clegg, "War and Peace" (see note 64), 677–681.

66 "Die Schaffung eines Propaganda-Komittees für österreichische Edelarbeit und Kunst," Vienna, Österreichisches Staatsarchiv, Haus-, Hof- und Staatsarchiv, Ministerium des Äussern, Gesandtschaftsarchiv, Stockholm, Ausstellungen Box 112b, 1917.

67 Ibid., 2.

68 Ibid., 8.

69 Elizabeth Clegg, "Austria-Hungary's War: the 1914–1918 Centenary in Vienna," *The Burlington Magazine* 156, no. 1338 (September 2014): 601.

70 Schiele's paintings are listed in the exhibition catalogue as nos. 203–217, and the drawings are collected under no. 218. See *Österrikiska Konstutställningen: Ausst. Liljevalches Konsthall, September* (Stockholm: Liljevalchs Konsthall, 1917), Albertina K.S.B–6196 A.K. Stockholm 1917. On not traveling to Stockholm, see

Egon Schiele, letter to Anton Peschka, September 4, 1917, reprinted in Nebehay, *Egon Schiele, 1890–1918* (see note 15), 427, no. 1261.

71 Letter from Erwin Hanslik's secretary to Egon Schiele, Sept. 4, 1917, reprinted in Nebehay, *Egon Schiele, 1890–1918* (see note 15), 432, no. 1299.

72 Elizabeth Clegg, "'Austrian Art' on the Move: The Cultural Politics of International Exhibiting 1900–1918," in *Gustav Klimt: Painting, Design and Modern Life*, exh. cat., eds. Tobias G. Natter and Christoph Grunenberg (London: Tate Publishing, 2008), 56.

73 Smith, "Egon Schiele's Landscapes" (see note 2), 182; Smola, "Vom 'Menschenbewusstsein' zum neuen Menschenbild" (see note 28), 126.

74 Smola, "Vom 'Menschenbewusstsein' zum neuen Menschenbild" (see note 28), 126.

75 See Hanslik's article the following year, "Weltaufruf zur geistigen Abrüstung," *Der Anbruch: Flugblätter aus der Zeit* 1, no. 2 (January 1918): 1.

76 Clegg, "'Austrian Art' on the Move" (see note 72), 56.

77 Clegg, "War and Peace" (see note 64), 685. Clegg notes that reviews of Hanslik's presentation were mixed, with some quite enthusiastic and others skeptical of the speaker's insistence that Austria should be considered the crucible of a peaceful post-war Europe.

78 *Österrikiska Konstutställningen: Ausst. Liljevalches Konsthall, September*, nos. 203–217. For a reconstructed list of works by Schiele and other major artists in the Stockholm exhibition, see the appendix to Clegg, "War and Peace" (see note 64), 688.

79 The identity of two landscapes in the exhibition are not clear: catalogue no. 206 *Ensamma hus*, and catalogue no. 215 *Stein Donau*. In "War and Peace at the Stockholm 'Austrian Art Exhibition' of 1917," Clegg posits that no. 215 is actually *Houses by the River II (The Old City II)* [Kallir P279, Natter 154], misidentified as an image of Stein. However, in *Egon Schiele: The Complete Paintings*, Natter argues that no. 215 was a painting of Stein which has since been lost, to which he gives the title *Stein on the Danube in the Late Evening Sun* based on a letter to Carl Reininghaus in 1913 [Natter 141].

80 The other is *Resurrection (Graves)* (*Auferstehung [Gräber]*). *Österrikiska Konstutställningen, Ausst. Liljevalches Konsthall, September*, no. 205. A handwritten list of works intended for the show suggests that Schiele had a role in selecting which works would be chosen for the Stockholm venue. In Otto Kallir, *Egon Schiele* (Vienna: Paul Zsolnay Verlag, 1966), reproduced in *Wiener Kunst Auktionen/The Vienna Art Auctions*, 6 June 1998 (Vienna: Wiener Kunst Auktionen, 1998), no. 85.

81 Smola, "Vom 'Menschenbewusstsein' zum neuen Menschenbild" (see note 28), 141–146.

82 Egon Schiele, *Girl (The Virgin)* [*Mädchen (Die Jungfrau)*], 1917, oil on canvas. *Österrikiska Konstutställningen, Ausst. Liljevalches Konsthall, September*, no. 208.

"NATURE IS TO BLAME FOR EVERYTHING"

ON THE IMAGE OF NATURE IN SCHIELE'S LETTERS AND POEMS

Verena Gamper

1. Egon Schiele, *Red Foxglove*, 1910, watercolor, black chalk, white heightening on packing paper. The Albertina Museum, Vienna. Permanent loan Nebehay (Kallir D749)

"Nature is to blame for everything"[1]—so Egon Schiele concludes a letter from March 1909 in which the then-eighteen-year-old communicated his views of life to his legal guardian and uncle, Leopold Czihaczek. In a few words, he reveals what we, from today's perspective, see as the core of the young Schiele's understanding of nature: nature as a powerful authority that determines human actions; nature as the authority that bears responsibility, which is to be measured by ideas of ethical and moral values; nature as a divine authority with all-embracing influence and responsibility for guilt.

Depictions of nature—understood to mean depictions of plants or habitats—are a constant in Schiele's oeuvre, with varying meaning and weighting. But nature also plays an important role in his written statements as well, especially—as in his artistic oeuvre—from 1910 to 1913. There are numerous substantive analyses of Schiele's writings, which focus on the complex of works written in the summer of 1910 that includes a series of Expressionist poems and drafts of poems. Several of these poems were published during the artist's lifetime by Franz Pfemfert in his journal *Die Aktion*;[2] posthumously, his mentor for many years, Arthur

Roessler, ensured the fame of this group of works.[3] After Johannes Käfer left behind the brief sketch "Egon Schiele als Dichter" (Egon Schiele as Poet) in the *Erinnerungsbuch Egon Schiele* (Memorial Book for Egon Schiele) in 1946,[4] Horst Denkler made the first literary study of his poetic oeuvre in 1969,[5] before an intense analysis of the artist's Expressionist lyrical poetry began in 1990.[6] Nature plays the main role in most of these "*Wortbilder*" (word images). Restricting such study to these texts would, however, leave out the substantial body of Schiele's autograph manuscripts of nearly 1,500 letters, postcards, and notes,[7] which offer an uncommonly well contoured image of Schiele as a person, his ideas and themes, his networks and conflicts, and his ability to modulate language and his highly differentiated modes of expression. Whereas the poems and their powerful imagery were written within a very short time span, the surviving writings extend across the greatest possible period[8] and have thus far been incorporated into the analysis of his poetic work only on a case-by-case basis. There is also the advantage that in his letters Schiele never pursued an artistic ambition, so their language has a functional character.[9] He expresses there in clear words what often remains hermetic in his poetic texts

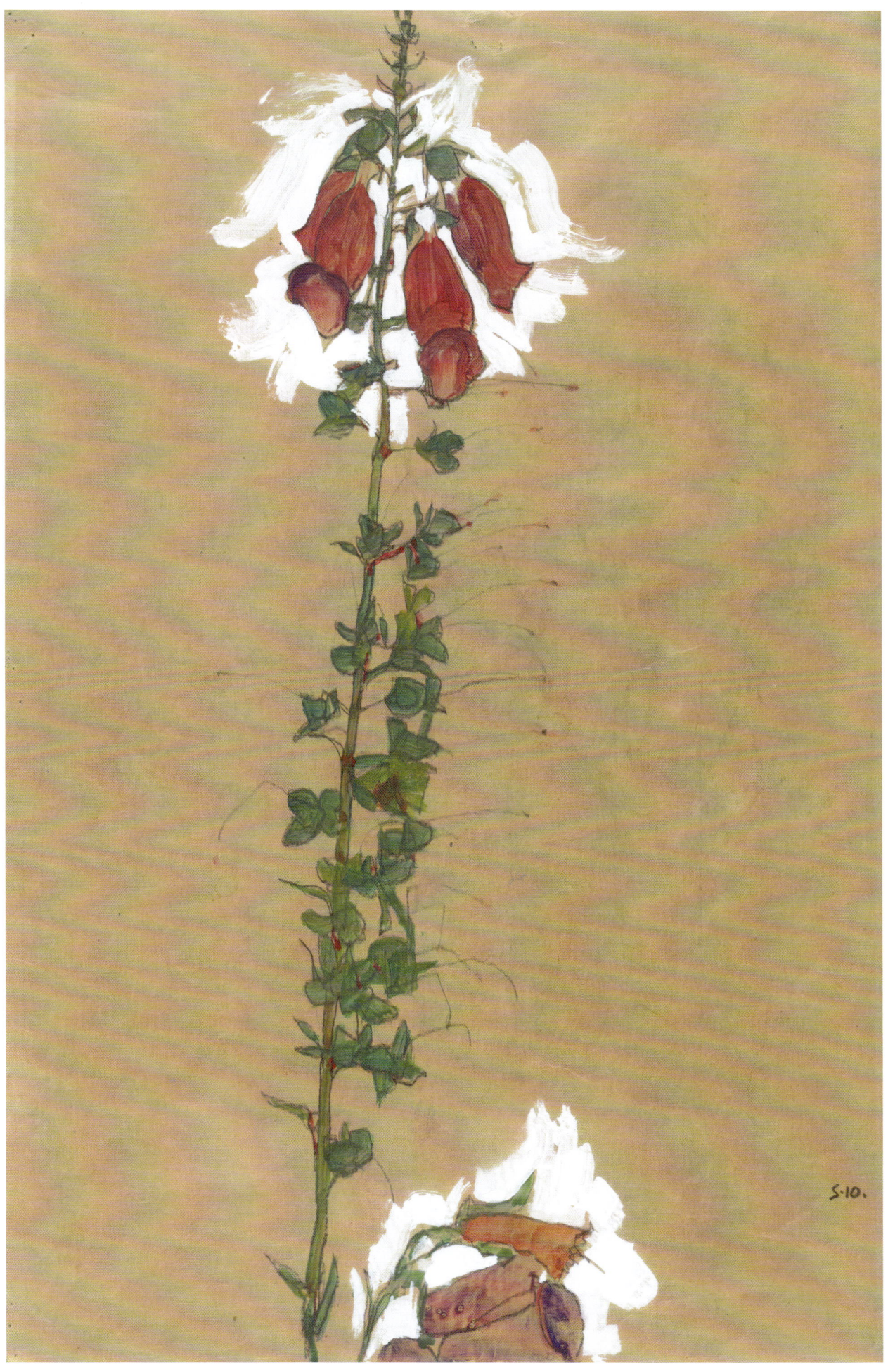

due to their aestheticizing of the word image. The focus of this study will thus be the question of how Schiele expressed his understanding of nature, also outside of the aestheticizing system of poetry.

To begin these studies I cite the letter mentioned at the beginning that Schiele wrote to Czihaczek in March 1909—that is, while still studying at the academy.[10] The "views of life" he announced there turn out to be his way of presenting himself to his guardian, who was critical of his lifestyle. The personified allegory "Mother Nature" plays an important role. Patience is presented as a foolish virtue—"To endure for the sake of endurance is a bleak madness; common patience is usually emotionlessness, inertia, and cowardice"—by which one could probably attain some cultural achievements, since one "levels mountains, sets limits on the sea; and makes walls and cities of stones," but "he who overcomes himself is braver than the one who overcomes the strongest walls," since "courage is the first virtue that is manifest to the Son of Nature." Dependence is seen as corrupting and damaging to the soul; independence, by contrast, "is a great fortune, twice as estimable for people of spirit, who like to be autonomous." Schiele is attempting here not just to question conventional norms of behavior but rather to attack them head on. He justifies this with the observation that "every individual has to fight his way through himself and enjoy to the full that to which nature bore him." It does not lie within the individual's latitude for action to decide on his development; he must rather resign himself to what nature has given him, since "Mother Nature watches the human species, as in the animal kingdom." In a cheeky escalation, Schiele concludes the letter, which amounts to a frontal attack on his uncle's model for life, with subtle threats: "That is not what I think, it is more what I feel, but I am

not the one who has written this, I am not to blame. One urge here is a constantly growing one that supports me in what I have expressed. Nature is to blame for everything."[11] Nature is portrayed as the scriptwriter and director of life; it also bears responsibility for the behavior of human beings. The life view promised at the beginning of the letter turns out to be a (self-) explanation of the human disposition of the eighteen-year-old, his *nature*. Moreover, the letter reveals that he understands nature not simply as the totality of all organic and inorganic phenomena, which exist without human assistance, but also in the sense of essence and character, as an anthropological and ethical category. In that respect, Schiele's concept of nature is based on the pre-Socratic concept of the *physis*.[12]

A few months after that letter, Schiele encouraged an unknown addressee to reflect on the "diverse problems of nature," on "its origin and purpose."[13] The exclusivity with which the turn to and sensation of nature is a theme in his letter permits us to infer how important that theme was to Schiele at the time. The initial call to get to the bottom of nature rationally is supplemented and purely quantitatively outdone by the recommendation of sensory perception: "Enjoy the wealth of colors in the morning and evening and dream of the great starry sea at night." The experience of nature is not yet described here in an synesthetic intertwining of sensory impressions, as it will be in Schiele's poems of 1910; it does, however, definitely occur via several sense organs: he speaks of sounds, meadows, birds, colors, forests, and storms, which could be perceived visually, auditorily, and emotionally. In addition to the victory of the senses over reason postulated here, Schiele also wrote about "divine nature,"[14] which brings to mind Friedrich Hölderlin's image of nature as the starting and ending point of human existence.

In Hölderlin's religiously tinged utopia, nature is not presumed to be redeemed by human dominion; rather, by spreading its dominion to humanity it is intended to "turn it into the true organism."[15] Humanity can only achieve perfection when "divine Nature, that can be written in no book, will dwell in the hearts of the community."[16]

In these early letters composed during the phase of discord with and departure from the academy, Schiele was already formulating central topoi of his understanding of nature as it would be expressed later: the human being as part of nature, nature's power over the human being, the primacy of the sensory-emotional perception of nature, and its connection to God.

A brief look at Schiele's artistic production in this period demonstrates the role that depictions of nature played in it. In the summer of 1909 at the "Internationale Kunstschau Wien" (International Art Show Vienna),[17] he participated with four figure paintings, but shortly thereafter at the first show of the Neukunstgruppe in December 1909 in Vienna and in February 1910 in Prague,[18] he presented two plant portraits alongside self-portraits and other figure paintings. I chose the term "plant portraits" deliberately, because they are not landscapes but depictions of plants that bear a resemblance to portraits.[19] Their proximity to the figure paintings in the exhibition is revealing and enables us to observe the strategy of anthropomorphizing that Schiele applied to the flowers and trees he undertook from the beginning of his career as an artist; it is one that he would maintain over the years. First, there is the portrait-like isolation of the plant, signalling it worthiness as a subject. Schiele did not differentiate between the human and the plant portrait, neither the format, the proportion, nor the design of pictorial space per-

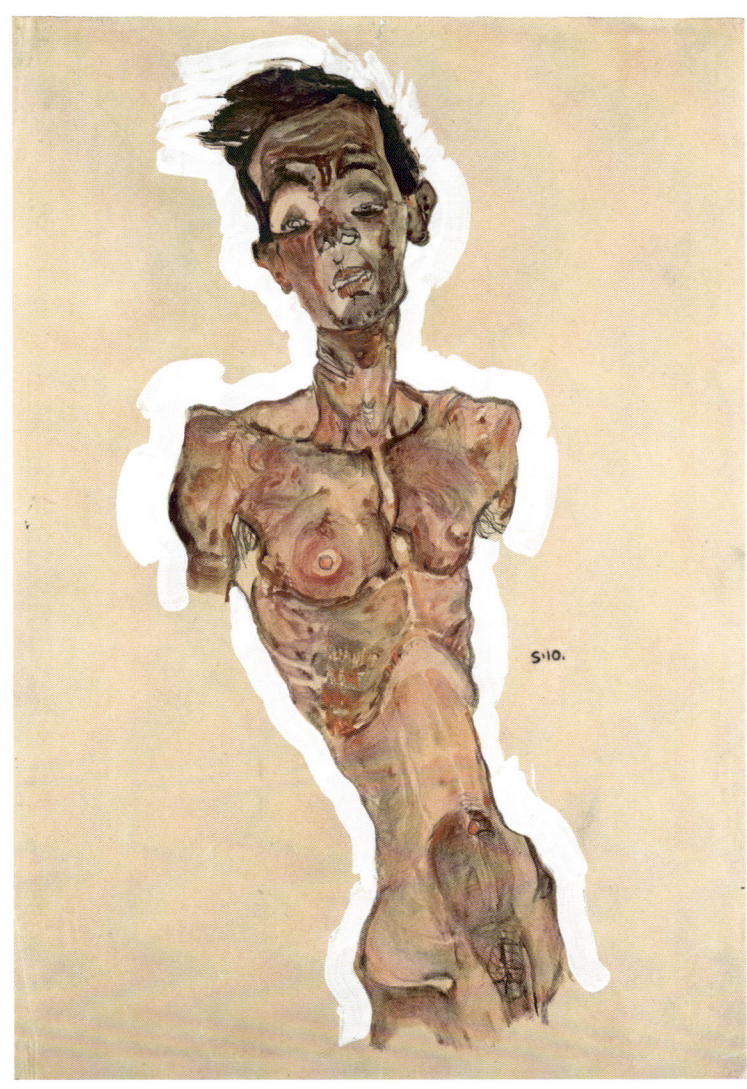

mits any inferences about the subject holding different value. Instead he used the occasion of his first autonomous public appearance in Vienna and Prague for a programmatic declaration of faith in the equality of human and plant. Schiele continued such equalizing in the watercolors he painted in 1910 in which he put a white, aura-like contour around the subject, regardless of whether it was a human or a plant body. *Roter Fingerhut* (Red Foxglove) [Fig. 1] and the exposed figure in *Selbstakt* (Nude Self-Portrait) [Fig. 2] meet not in the

2. Egon Schiele, *Nude Self-Portrait*, 1910, pencil, black chalk, gouache, and white heightening on packing paper. Leopold Museum, Vienna (Kallir D708). Photo: Leopold Museum, Vienna

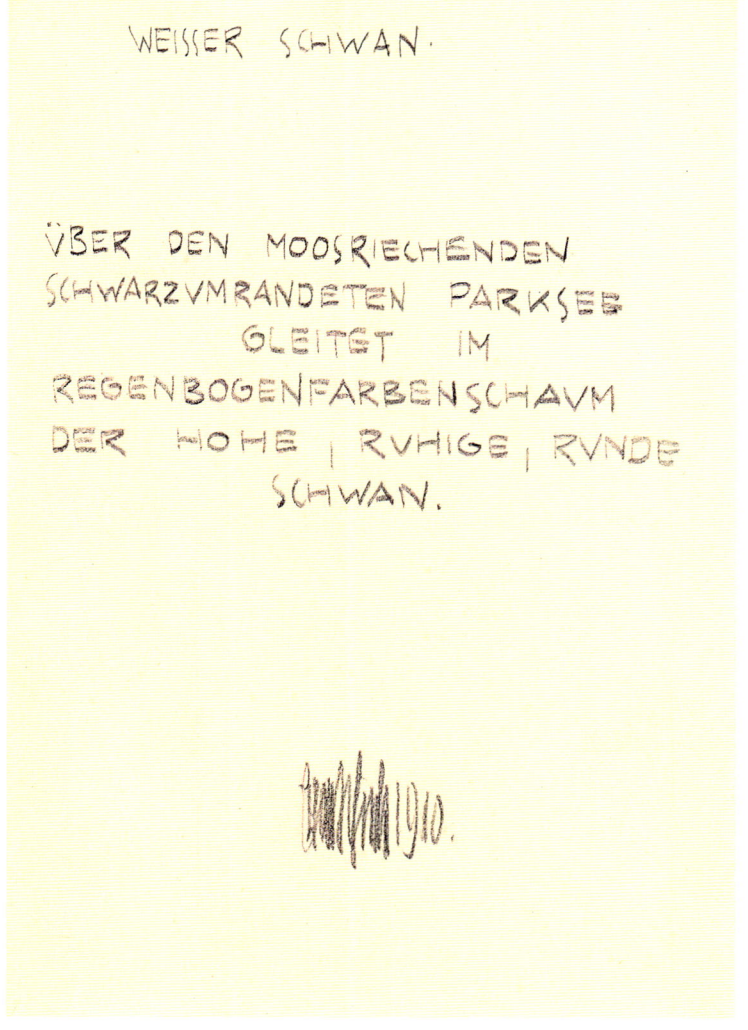

WEISSER SCHWAN.

VBER DEN MOOSRIECHENDEN
SCHWARZVMRANDETEN PARKSEE
GLEITET IM
REGENBOGENFARBENSCHAVM
DER HOHE, RVHIGE, RVNDE
SCHWAN.

3. Egon Schiele, "*Weisser Schwan*" (White Swan), 1910. Leopold Museum, Vienna (Egor Schiele Autograph Database, hereafter ESDA, ID no. 3). Photo: Leopold Museum, Vienna

Secessionist manner of vegetal stylization; instead, the plant is presented in its physical—one almost wants to say spiritual—state and thus subjectivized.[20]

In the summer of 1910, he produced the aforementioned group of poems and draft poems, most of which are executed calligraphically, almost like calligrams. Self-observation and the perception of nature are closely linked in them: even in those poems not explicitly constructed as self-portraits, the sensory impressions are formulated from the perspective of the first-person narrator. A distanced registration of events like that found in the poem "*Weisser Schwan*" (White Swan)—"Over the moss-scented black-bordered park lake glides amidst the rainbow-hued spume the high, calm, round Swan"—represents the exception [Fig. 3].[21] These poetic pieces are marked by an engagement with Symbolist lyric poetry, above all that of Arthur Rimbaud.[22] In the poems that foreground impressions of nature, Schiele unfurls an antinaturalistic bouquet of word pictures characterized by dissonant sensory impressions, synesthesia, and onomatopoeia. There are frequent alliterations, such as "*zirpten zittrige Vögel*" (quivery birds chirping) in the poem "*Landstrasse*" (Country Road), "*glitzrigglänzenden Gläser glänzen*" (glistening-gleaming glasses gleam) in the poem "*Zwei Chleriker*" (Two Clerics), and "*Baue Berg, bringe bald boshafte Büsche*" (Build mountain, soon bring malicious bushes) in the poem "Anarchist." The artist appears to be trying to play as comprehensively as possible on the keyboard of the senses: no sense organ escapes these lyrical stimuli. These poetic texts are connected to a stay in his mother's native city, Krumau (Český Krumlov, Czech Republic), which was the center of his life from May 1910 to August 1911—with extended interludes elsewhere. He may have encountered Rimbaud's poetry through fellow artist Erwin Dominik Osen or the high school student Willy Lidl.[23] Krumau, portrayed by Schiele as an antimodern city on the Moldau (now Vltava) River with its crooked streets and cramped together buildings, is reflected in the "wet roads"[24] and the "black-bordered park lake,"[25] or more specifically in formulations such as "The raised city was cold in the water before me" [Fig. 4].[26] The "orangegraygreen grass field"[27] and the "wrinkled earth,"[28] in turn, are traces of the rural milieu that Schiele had sought out as contrast to Vienna, of which he had grown tired.[29]

Before Schiele left Vienna for Krumau, he wrote a letter to Anton Peschka in which he brought into play nature as a place of refuge and creation, which has been frequently cited with respect to his tense relationship to the city and his comparatively glorifying image of the rural: "I wish to leave Vienna, very soon. How ugly it is here. Everybody is envious of me and deceitful; former colleagues look at me with dissembling eyes, in Vienna there is only shadow, the city is black, everything is done by recipe. I want to be alone."[30] After this angrily sulking overture, the way out of the unloved urban, which he sometimes equates with the artistic milieu opens up for him: "I wish to visit the Bohemian forest." Powerful imagery follows, wallowing in and wandering through nature: he wants to see "crashing trees," hear "shaking leaves," smell "warm marsh marigolds," "kiss the earth," and "be able to watch the breathing earth glimmering."[31] This letter, whose synesthetic word pictures already point to the poems that will be written soon after it, expresses a yearning for nature of a neo-Romantic character typical of the era.

Schiele never summed up the anthropomorphizing of nature, the breaking down of the boundaries between creatures—and between these creatures and God—more precisely in words than in a prose poem of 1910 in which he noted "the similarity between plants and animals and between animals and man, and the similarity of man and God."[32] Yet elsewhere he also writes of "anthropoid flowers,"[33] and in the off-cited letter to Oskar Reichel of September 1911, he sketches the following image of "divine nature": "the true great Mother of all, similar to everyone, yet isolated, who wants and was, is and will be the will, always from these, our infinite means, which can create the most multifarious people, animals, plants, creatures in general, as soon as

this physics is there, as soon as the universal will of the world exists."[34] And in the summer of 1913, Schiele reported to Franz Hauer: "For the most part, I am now observing the physical movement of mountains, water, trees, and flowers. Everywhere one is reminded of similar movements in the human body, of similar stirrings of joy and suffering in plants."[35] These statements testify to the animistic view of nature held by the artist, who considered not only animate but also inanimate nature "all-ensouled" and thus related it analogously to the human being.

4. Egon Schiele, "*Nasser Abend*" (Wet Evening), 1910. Leopold Museum, Vienna (ESDA, ID no. 137). Photo: Leopold Museum, Vienna

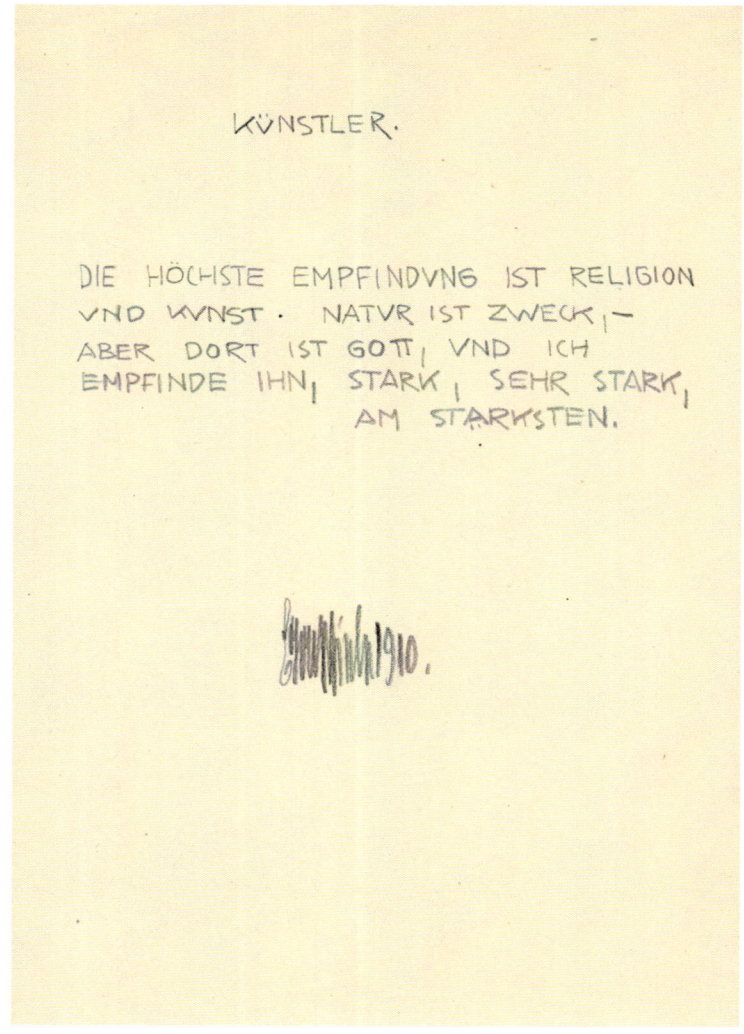

KÜNSTLER.

DIE HÖCHSTE EMPFINDVNG IST RELIGION
VND KVNST. NATVR IST ZWECK, —
ABER DORT IST GOTT, VND ICH
EMPFINDE IHN, STARK, SEHR STARK,
AM STARKSTEN.

5. Egon Schiele, "*Künstler*" (Artist), 1910. The Albertina Museum, Vienna (ESDA, ID no. 1933)

ceded in his antidualist model. Around 1900, this theory met with a great response, since it brought into play an alternative to the increasingly accelerating industrialized world and to the positivist and capitalist modern era. The latter was counteracted by monism in Haeckel's formulation as an attempt to reconcile religion and science.[37] With reference to Schiele, it should be noted that his ideas of unity were not nostalgically and reactionarily aimed at a "reenchantment of the world,"[38] but should rather be understood in the context of his reflection on the individual and the search for identity.

In *Abstraktion und Einfühlung* (translated as *Abstraction and Empathy*), published in 1908, which Schiele is said to have owned from 1910,[39] Wilhelm Worringer wrote of that rare and fortunate state of equipoise "in which man and world were fused into one."[40] Worringer believed that this state had been achieved by religions which start from the principle of immanence, "which, wearing the various colors of polytheism, pantheism or monism, regard the divine as being contained in the world and identical with it. At bottom, indeed, this conception of divine immanence is nothing other than a total anthropomorphisation [sic] of the world. The unity of God and world is only another name for the unity of man and world."[41]

Monism turns out to have been an important reference for Schiele's worldview in this context, as formulated in his artistic and literary works. The form of monism theorized by Ernst Haeckel was especially popular among artists and writers around 1900. In his book *Die Welträthsel* (translated as *The Riddle of the Universe*), Haeckel had promoted the unity of all beings, based on a concept of the monistic substance, which considers the material and spiritual world unseparable.[36] This was causally connected to the identification of nature with God, whose transcendence could not be con-

Schiele had already written about divine nature in an early letter to an unknown woman[42] and also in the letter to Peschka in which, full of yearning for rural Krumau as salvation from the hardships of urban Vienna, he spoke of the "divine breath" in nature.[43] Schiele summed it up, in harmony with monist ideas of unity, in his passionate poem "*Künstler*" (Artist): "The highest sentiment is religion and art. Nature is purpose, but God is there, and I sense him powerfully, very powerfully, most powerfully" [Fig. 5].[44] Schiele was placing art and religion on a level with the highest sentiment and defining nature as the place where he can sense God. Nature as a revelation of God will remain a topos for Schiele, as proved by the advice he proffered to his friend Erich Lederer in 1914: "You have to go into the countryside in all sorts of weather in order to reach the core of the divine drive in it."[45]

Experiencing God by experiencing nature was also the central theme of a passage in an autograph manuscript by Schiele that was discovered only recently. It is dated July 17, 1911, but not addressed, which gives it a programmatic, almost manifesto-like character [Fig. 6].[46] In it Schiele expresses himself on the elite approach to art:

> The work of art cannot be seen; one can only look into it; and few have the talent for that, I thank God. The crowd is, of course, no criterion for the work of art, because it is a crowd; the great one is always singular. A divine human being always leads the crowd! The true work of art is the revelation of a special nature of the artist; the object is unimportant; he is immortal.[47]

After distinguishing in this way between the common crowd and the individual "divine human being," he continued: "But parks are not works of art for the public: it is too raw to sense the divine in everyone; that is why it needs churches to be able to imagine a God, since meanwhile he breathes much more clearly in a field."[48] This brief passage is uncommonly dense with statements relevant to Schiele's understanding of nature and art. There is, first the *looking into* a work of art as opposed to pure *seeing*—a widespread topos of his day;[49] this is followed by his characterization of the perception of art as elite and the observation that he is chosen for it. Schiele pursued a strategy of separating the individual from the crowd, which has pejorative associations,

6. Egon Schiele to an unknown person, July 17, 1911. Private Collection (ESDA, ID no. 2764)

TANNENWALD.

JCH KEHRE EIN IN DEN ROTSCHWARZEN
DOM DES DICHTEN TANNENWALDES,
DER OHNE LARMEN LEBT VND
MIMISCH SICH ANSCHAVT,
DIE AVGENSTAMME DIE DICHT
SICH GREIFEN VND DIE SICHTBARE
NASSE LVFT AVSATMEN. —
WIE WOHL ! — ALLES IST
LEBEND TOT.

7. Egon Schiele, "*Tannenwald*" (Fir Woods), 1910 Leopold Museum, Vienna (ESDA, ID no. 1). Photo: Leopold Museum, Vienna

those he dismissed elsewhere as "soldiers, civil servants, teachers, redundant ones, craftsmen, clerics, levelers, nationalists, patriots, calculators, the people with class, the people with numbers in their heads."[50] This should be seen against the biographical backdrop: this letter was written three weeks before Schiele was forced to leave Krumau.[51] His unconventional lifestyle had displeased the neighbors, and he felt obliged to depart this former place of yearning in favor of its pendant in Lower Austria: Neulengbach. It seems reasonable to assume that Schiele's pamphlet was written in the face of the uncomprehending crowd in the context of its criticism of him. With regard to the experience of nature and God, particular attention should be paid to his remark that "parks are not works of art for the public" because "it is too raw to sense the divine in everyone." Schiele thus attributes to the crowd, on the one hand, an inability to perceive the work of art and associates this, on the other hand, with its inability to sense God in nature. Whereas the crowd needs churches "in order to be able to imagine a God," the graced individual recognized God in nature. Finally, these statements unite in a programmatic equation: the work of art is the revelation of the artist; nature is the revelation of God; but the common crowd cannot *look into* either one.

Schiele had already formulated a veritable dovetailing of divine and natural space in the poem "*Tannenwald*" (Fir Woods) [Fig. 7], in which he sketched the image of the "reddish-black cathedral of the dense fir woods."[52] A look at his painted oeuvre shows that a fusion of nature with religious symbols is not only encountered in Schiele's writings but also occurs repeatedly in Schiele's visual world; for example, in the trees that become crosses in *Kalvarienberg* (Calvary) [see ill. on p. 55] or the devotional trees as symbols of popular religion in *Waldandacht II* (Shrines in the Forest II) [see ill. on p. 17]. Such fusing of natural and divine spaces represents a fundamental difference between the neo-Romantic landscape and its historical current of reference. Whereas in the former the coming together of nature and God is always based on a referential structure, in Schiele's monist manner the "the sensory and the supersensory coincide and are one."[53]

In a prose poem from 1910, Schiele memorably formulated the emotional aptitude of the chosen that he recognized in artists and their connection to nature and God:

> Who is it among the spiritually gifted who sees nature as a problem of the sacred arts? Would they imagine it is the result of human handiwork? An artist above all is one of great spiritual gifts, who expresses views of thinkable phenomena in nature. May they be researchers whom nature approaches and shows herself to them to convey it to the surrounding world. Artists easily feel the great tremulous light, the warmth, the breathing of living things the coming and waning. They intuit the similarity between plants and animals and between animals and man, and the similarity of man and God. They are not scholars devouring books out of ambition—they are themselves. Religion, for them, is a degree of feeling. They will never indulge in superficial gestures or enter chapels to listen, they'll never feel devotion there. No, outside in the raging autumn storm or high upon cliffs where rare flowers are for them they can sense God. [...] They are chosen ones, fruits of Mother Earth.[54]

In this image, artists function as translators of nature, since with their gift for emotion they have access to everything living and understanding of their unity with God. Artists are seers, knowers, recognizers: "I see myself evaporate and breathe out more and more powerfully; the vibrations of my astral light become quicker, more immediate, simpler, and like a great recognition of the world."[55] In a letter to Josef Hoffmann [Cat. no. 20] written a year earlier, Schiele revealed himself as someone who could communicate with organic and inorganic nature: "I can speak with all living creatures, even with plants and stones; speak, speak directly into their face, into their essence. Every tree has its face; I

recognize its kind of eyes, its kind of arms, its components, its organism. I want to be addressed by everything!"[56] In February 1913, he expressed something very similar when he wrote: "I know that among a thousand there is but one who lives with love of people, animals, plants, & things, who recognizes the organism of all things, who sees in the soul life of plants and in their visage the living breath of their face."[57] All of these remarks have in common not only the idea of the unity of all beings but also that Schiele declares that access to God is only possible for the chosen and therefore is not a learnable ability. All the statements in which he announced his aversion to all book knowledge should be understood in that context: "Where the 'Ex libris' begin, the lively begins—where the 'students' begin, the lively dead"[58] or "There are thousands of scholars, of whom ten are visionaries, and among a thousand scholars, one genius, one inventor, one creator."[59] By contrast, he describes himself repeatedly as having "become knowing"[60] or, in the famous letter to Hermann Engel: "The revelation of a certain being; it can be a poet, an artist, a man of knowledge, a spiritist."[61] In an autograph from July 1911, he summed it up: "I consider knowledge and science to be fundamentally different things."[62] The passages that directly preceded and follow this sentence are of special interest here: "That the brain is not the most natural thing that is known is something every philistine knows, everything starts out from it, even the creation of a work of art.—The hand and the eye are keys that open." Or: "So let it be said: that the artist is the only one who is the ruler, the dominator, of 100, 1000, and 10,000, that he only creates for himself, because it is the same as breathing."[63]

The artist as "*Empfindungsmensch*" (person of sentiment) is a topos that s fundamental to the dominant view, already published during

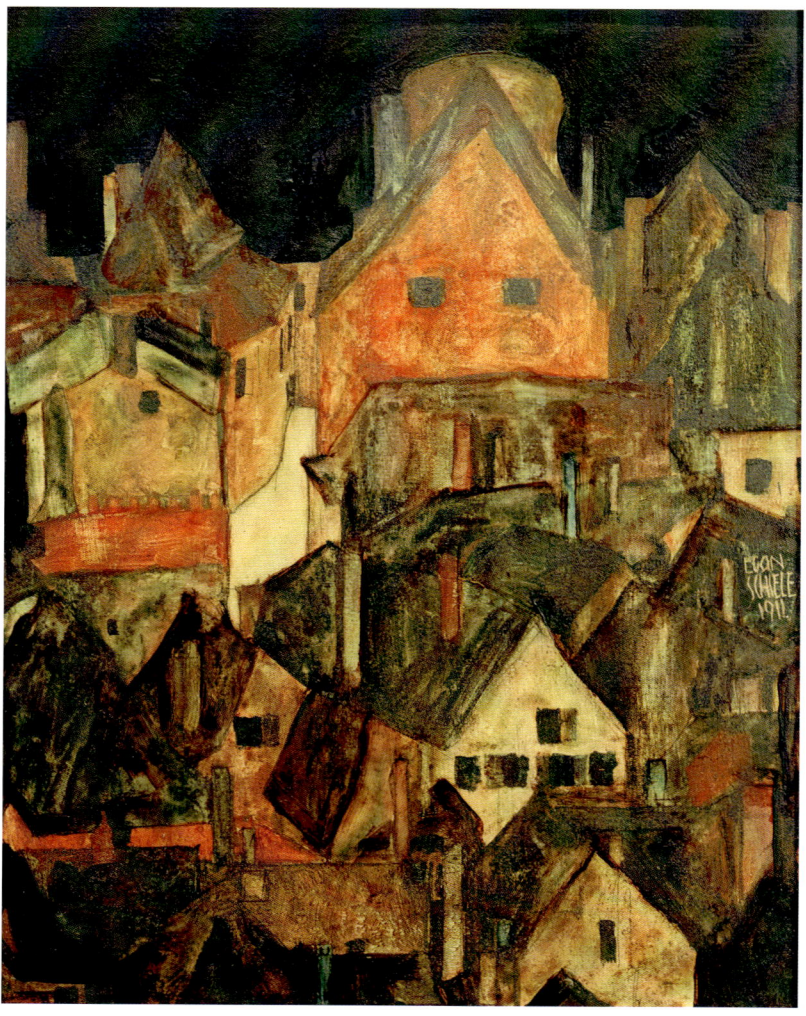

by positioning personal expression and spiritual intensity against the imitation of nature and reason as artistic volitions indebted to different motives. Schiele's art embodies in an almost textbook fashion the Gothic as a specific fusion of emotional expression and mystical qualities, of spiritual passion and melancholy gravity. His townscapes above all are distinctive for this: in them he depicted striking medieval urban structures [Fig. 8]. Krumau on the Vltava River and Stein on the Danube are towns in accordance with his taste, in which the purifying and reforming energies of the modern era had left hardly any traces at all. The Gothic quality of these towns lies in their organic structure: they are living organisms that have grown over centuries, in which the streets can be read as veins and the buildings as cells.[67] When Schiele emphasized this Gothic quality in his townscapes, he was formulating a criticism of the positivist worldview that tried to explain everything that exists rationally and scientifically. This critique is all the more powerful when he does not render any "pure landscapes"[68] but rather cultured nature, a world in which the spheres of nature and culture are portrayed not as antagonistic but rather interlocked as accomplices.[69]

The letter with no addressee of the summer of 1911 is also interesting with reference to the type of nature discussed in it, since Schiele does not mention any "natural" landscapes, such as forests or mountains, as places to experience God but rather parks and fields—decidedly humanmade nature. Schiele's neo-Romantic image of nature is thus not "chaste" nature; rather, he depicts landscapes in which the natural and the artificial are peaceably united. Already in his early work, Schiele painted not pristine nature but rather gardens in front of houses, villages amid fields, boulevards, and waysides [Fig. 9].[70] The trees later presented in a portraitlike manner are also

8. Egon Schiele, *Krumau at Night (Dead City II)*, 1911, oil, gouache, and pencil on wood. Private Collection, Vienna (Kallir P209). Photo: akg-images

his lifetime, of Schiele as a "neo-Gothic."[64] In general, the "Gothic" quality in Expressionism is identified with a decidedly antinaturalistic style and an intense spirituality. Its most influential theorists in that context is Worringer with his 1911 text *Formprobleme der Gotik* (translated as *Form in Gothic*).[65] Worringer did not explicitly make a connection between the Gothic and Expressionism, but he described the "Gothic" as an anticlassical stance that was not tied to any time and could be manifested at any time. In his dissertation *Abstraction and Empathy*,[66] Worringer provided the Expressionist movement with theoretical tools

artificial in their isolation and feature lime-covered trunks or domesticizing stakes [see ills. on pp. 11, 15, 26, 39, and 51].[71] Nevertheless, he was far from disturbing his paintings with the aesthetic collisions that his specific habitat in Vienna and Lower Austria had experienced as a result of the reforming energies of the nineteenth century; he depicted no smoldering smokestacks and factories but rather bucolic villages in gentle landscapes of fields, with churches and wayside shrines—an image of an ideal coexistence of man and nature under the sign of God, as if it had dropped out of time. *Rabenlandschaft* (*Landschaft mit Raben*) (Landscape with Ravens) of 1911 formulates most impressively, in visual terms, the primacy of nature that incorporates every being into a cyclical movement of birth and death [see ill. on p. 16]. Schiele revealed in a letter of May 14, 1912, to his future brother-in-law Peschka his taste for nature between the poles of the sublime and the authentic and his ideal of a landscape in which the cultural traces of human beings should be subordinated to the aesthetic parameters of nature:

> *The Semmering Pass does not please me; it looks kitschy there. The mountains are small and cracked and brusque, and the train track and the street are playfully glued on in some places—in short, the landscape looks as if it had been cut out of a paper model booklet and pasted up. The mountains are like the dairies one can purchase; by contrast, the peaks around them are taller, but the core is tiny, also the many romantic-kitschy-steep new alpine huts and modern villas and hotels. Quite inorganic. When you get to Styria, however, it is better. There it is damp-green foggy and the tall roofs of the torn-apart stone buildings are outstandingly suited to the mountains; the buildings are laid out almost like the mountains.*[72]

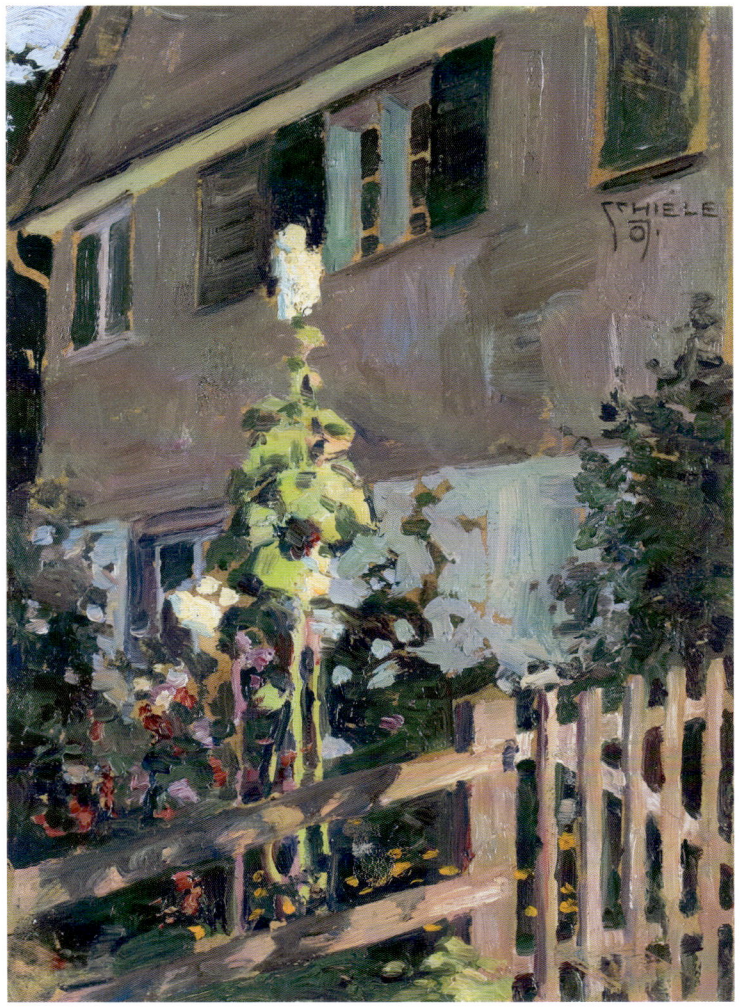

He compared the Semmering Pass, which had been developed as a local recreation area for Vienna's bourgeoisie to spend their leisure time, to bucolic, rural Styria, only to finally dismiss a chic spa town in Carinthia as "raped nature": Pörtschach is said to be "very elegant, first-class spa town. establishments, hotel, pension, villa, spa, baths, boathouses, steamship, promenade, entertainment, park, raped nature."[73]

The key word "inorganic" arises in this letter to Peschka in connection with the architecture in the Semmering Pass; Schiele had used the

9. Egon Schiele, *House with Blooming Mallows, Bregenz*, 1907, oil on cardboard. Private Collection, Courtesy Leopold Fine Arts, Vienna (Kallir P56)

term previously in a negative characterization of Vienna.[74] In September 1911, by contrast, the very positively connoted "organic" initially occurred in his letters. The nature of his break with his uncle Czihaczek had been, according to Schiele, "completely organic" and prepared.[75] In reference to the painting *Die Eremiten* (The Hermits) [see ill. on p. 59], he said of the two figures that they grew up "alone in it [the world], came organically from the ground."[76] The image of the organic as that which follows the laws of nature, that which develops not violently but naturally, so to speak, is connected to the "cycle of existence,"[77] as he expressed it in letters to his mother: "Living and dying are beautiful. I look forward to both! As long as there are elements, bodies will also meet up!"[78] Two years earlier, Schiele had formulated it as an aphorism: "As long as there are elements, complete death will not be possible."[79] Worringer used the terms "organic" and "inorganic" for his definition of the two aesthetics of the work of art that he viewed as antipodal: indebted to the urge to empathy or the urge to abstraction, respectively.[80] He described the process of anthropomorphizing as a process of empathy: "a transference of man's own organic vitality onto all objects of the phenomenal world."[81] The organic thus embraces not only living nature but all beings—a concept that coincided with Schiele's use of the term. In the letter to Reichel cited above, Schiele wrote of the "ephemerality of the material in the sense of an existence" and noted: "a certain birth and death, coming; living, which should be understood to mean unceasing disintegration, which is, however, halted by organic means in order to live, indeed, can largely be reversed, so that with these means there can be no complete death."[82] Finally, Schiele postulated the inseparability of life and death in an unbeatably memorable formulation: "My essence, my—putrescence."[83]

In conclusion, and recapitulating my observations thus far, it can be said that in addition to Schiele's poetic texts, which have already been the subject of detailed studies, his surviving correspondence with his family, collectors, and colleagues and his diary entries represent rich sources for a variety of questions about his understanding of art. This is also true of Schiele's image of nature, which could be illustrated by analyzing selected writings. The latter date primarily from the years 1910 to 1913, although nature would remain a theme repeated in his letters and notes even in the following years. Whereas his early statements on nature revealed his neo-Romantic, monistic concept of the world as well as his ideas on the relationship of nature and art, his writing on nature after 1914 was increasingly prosaic. After a phase of allegorizing nature, after emphasizing its animistic all-ensouled character and the pantheistic image of God's identity with all beings, in his war diary, for example, Schiele expressed by contrast an almost sober image of nature. The diary reads in part like a hiker's record: Schiele spent every free moment in open nature, far from the events of the war, which are mentioned only in passing or, with few exceptions, as the cause for a loss of freedom that was relevant to Schiele and an abstaining from art that he found difficult to bear. Some summaries of his days are limited to noting experiences of nature, which represented for Schiele, a break from everyday life and thus a symbol of freedom—the thing that he regarded as most worth striving for, and not just since the war began. In the spring of 1916, Schiele was stationed in Mühling and had been judged fit only for office duty. For lack of other means, he painted his impressions of nature in words in his diary, so to speak: "The meadows were lushly sown with flowers; we saw a fiery-red sun, with dark, violet conifers and deciduous trees before it, and violet-transparent clouds

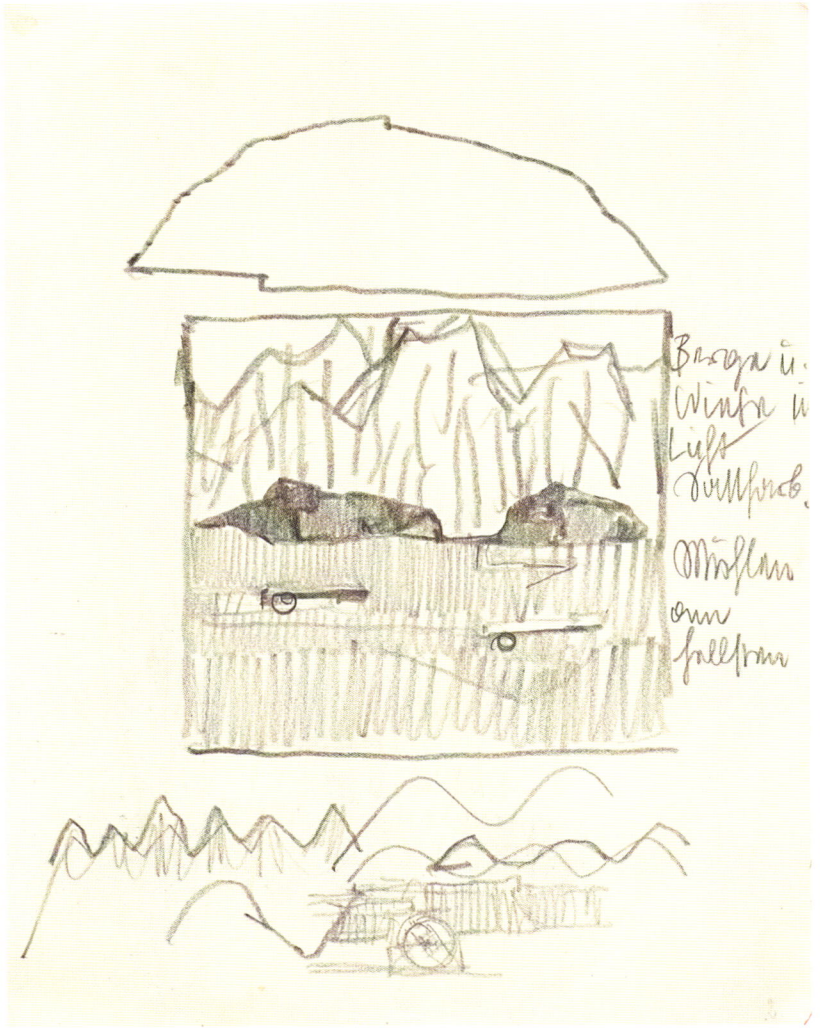

above it";[84] "white houses on which the most powerful sunlight shined—the sky was a deep, dark violet against the horizon. The mountain ridges […] were sketched in the purest oxide paints sharply against the sky;"[85] or "the mountains in front were lit in red, at first—the sky behind them dark greenish-blue—on the opposite side—the sky brightly sunny—transparent green—The sky above us yellow, churned up by flying clouds.—Suddenly, one saw from the mountain a madder pink, almost unlimited sheen."[86] These sketches of a landscape with their precise indications of color,

evoke the compositional sketches into which Schiele breathed chromatic life by means of added written indications of color [Fig. 10]. Although they have a brilliant visual power, these observations are limited to impressions. They are far removed from the word arrangements that stimulated all the senses that he had previously composed as poems as in letters from those years in which he had formulated complex statements relevant to his personal philosophy of art and nature.

Translated from the German by Steven Lindberg

1 Egon Schiele to Leopold Czihaczek, March 5, 1909, whereabouts unknown; Egon Schiele Autograph Database (http://www.schiele-dokumentation.at, hereafter ESDA), ID no. 222.

2 See *Die Aktion: Wochenschrift für Politik, Literatur, Kunst*, published in Berlin-Wilmersdorf by Franz Pfemfert: vol. 4, no. 11 (March 14, 1914): cols. 135–36; vol. 4, no. 15 (April 11, 1914): cols. 323–24; vol. 4, no. 20 (May 16, 1914): col. 428; vol. 5, nos. 3–4 (January 16, 1915): cols. 37–38; vol. 5, nos. 31–32 (August 7, 1915): col. 398.

3 Arthur Roessler, ed., *Briefe und Prosa von Egon Schiele* (Vienna: Richard Lányi, 1921).

4 Johannes Käfer, "Egon Schiele als Dichter," December 1946, entry in the *Erinnerungsbuch Egon Schiele*, based on an idea from Max Wagner, Albertina, Vienna, inv. no. ESA 508, 45r–47v; ESDA, ID no. 2567.

5 Horst Denkler, "Malerei mit Wörtern: Zu Egon Schieles poetischen Schriften," in Renate von Heydebrand and Klaus Günther Just, eds., *Wissenschaft als Dialog: Studien zur Literatur und Kunst seit der Jahrhundertwende* (Stuttgart: Metzler, 1969), 271–88.

6 Ursula Storch, "'Eure Sprache,—Eure Zeichen, —Eure Macht': Zu Egon Schieles literarischer Begabung," in *Egon Schiele: Frühe Reife, Ewige Kindheit*, ed. Hans Bisanz, exh. cat. Historisches Museum der Stadt Wien, May 10–September 2, 1990 (Vienna: Eigenverlag der Museen der Stadt Wien, 1990), 18–24; Ursula Storch: "'… I believe that every artist must be a poet': Text and Language in the Case of Egon Schiele," in Tobias G. Natter, ed., *Egon Schiele: The Complete Paintings, 1909–1918* (Cologne: Taschen, 2017), 424–41; Jacques Le Rider, "Ästhetische Identität soll dem Nichtidentischen beistehen, das der Identitätszwang in der Realität unterdrückt': Überlegungen zu Egon Schiele," in Alice Bolterauer and Dietmar Goltschnigg, eds., *Moderne Identitäten* (Vienna: Passagen, 1999), 155–92; Eva Werth, *"Illumination mutuelle": Des rapports entre littérature et peinture chez Egon Schiele (1890–1918)*, Paris 2006 (Diss.); Eva Werth, "Stilistische Aspekte im Werk Egon Schieles," in Johann Thomas Ambrózy, Carla Carmona Escalera, and Eva Werth, eds., *Egon Schiele Jahrbuch*, vol. 1, Vienna 2011, 131–83; Eva Werth, "Egon Schiele und die Lyrik" in Verena Gamper and Hans-Peter Wipplinger, eds., *Egon Schiele: Expression and Lyric; Conference Volume on the Second Egon Schiele Symposium at the Leopold Museum* (Vienna: Leopold Museum, 2018), 74–95; Helena Pereña Sáez, *Egon Schiele, Wahrnehmung, Identität und Weltbild* (Marburg: Tectum, 2010); Elisabeth Leopold and Sandra Tretter, "Painting with Words: Notes on Egon Schiele's Pictorial and Literary Works," in *Egon Schiele: Poems and Letters, 1910–1912*, ed. Elisabeth Leopold, trans. Jeff Tapia (New York: Prestel, 2008), 8–11; Sandra Tretter, "'Ich bin Mensch, ich liebe den Tod und liebe das Leben': Egon Schieles 'Wortbilder' des Jahres 1910," in Elisabeth Leopold and Diethard Leopold, eds., *Egon Schiele: Melancholie und Provokation*, exh. cat. Leopold Museum, Vienna (Vienna: Brandstätter, 2011), 78–93; Norbert Christian Wolf, "Wortbild—Bildwort: Egon Schiele und *Die Aktion*," in Gamper and Wipplinger eds., *Egon Schiele: Expression and Lyric* (see note 6), 170–93.

7 In 1979, Christian M. Nebehay published in chronological order all of the known autograph manuscripts in Nebehay, *Egon Schiele, 1890–1918: Leben, Briefe, Gedichte* (Salzburg: Residenz, 1979). Since 2011, all available autographs from and to Schiele and from his milieu have been collected, with texts and images, in the Egon Schiele Datenbank der Autografen (Egon Schiele Autograph Database, ESDA), which is maintained by the Leopold Museum: www.schiele-dokumentation.at.

8 The oldest surviving autograph by Schiele dates from 1898, ESDA, ID no. 179.

9 Schiele was a master at modulating his style of language according to the recipient of his message. This expedient opportunism left its mark not only in the tone struck in his letters but also in the aesthetic formulation of his handwriting. But the calligraphy in his correspondence never reached the degree of artificiality found in his lyric poetry.

10 Egon Schiele to Leopold Czihaczek, March 5, 1909, whereabouts unknown; ESDA, ID no. 222.

11 Ibid.

12 Only from the fifth century BC onward, did the term *physis* refer to nature as the totality of all things that resulted without human activity. Cf. Thomas Buchheim, s.v. "physis," in Christoph Horn and Christof Rapp, eds., *Wörterbuch der antiken Philosophie* (Munich: C. H. Beck, 2002), 345–51.

13 Egon Schiele to an unknown woman, July 6, 1909, Gustav Klimt | Wien 1900 Private Foundation; ESDA, ID no. 225.

14 Ibid.

15 Ludwig Strauss, "Zu Leben und Werk Hölderlins," in idem, *Gesammelte Werke in vier Bänden*, ed. Tuvia Rübner, vol. 2, *Schriften zur Dichtung* (Göttingen: Wallstein, 2000), 250.

16 Friedrich Hölderlin, *Hyperion; or, The Hermit in Greece*, trans. Willard R. Trask, adapted by David Schwarz, in Hölderlin, *Hyperion and Selected Poems*, ed. Eric L. Santner (New York: Continuum, 1990), 1–133, esp. 96.

17 "Internationale Kunstschau Wien 1909," April 22–July 1, 1909.

18 "Neukunst," Kunstsalon Pisko, Vienna, December 1, 1909–end of December 1909; "Neukunst," Klub deutscher Künstlerinnen, Prague, February 1–17, 1910.

19 The two works in question are, first, the painting *Herbstbaum mit Fuchsien* (Autumn Tree with Fuchsias) (Kallir P158), and, second, the painting listed in the Pisko catalogue as "*Spätsommer, dekoratives Bild*" (Late Summer, Decorative Painting), which based on the price list in the Prague catalogue, where this exhibit is listed as "*Sonnenblume*" (Sunflower), can be identified as the *Sonnenblume II* (Kallir P159) now in the collection of the Wien Museum. On this, see Verena Gamper, "'Die Ausstellung ist heute unentbehrlich.' Schiele und das Medium Ausstellung," in Verena Gamper and Hans-Peter Wipplinger, eds., *Egon Schiele: Dialogue and Staging. Conference Volume on the Third Egon Schiele Symposium at the Leopold Museum* (Vienna: Leopold Museum, 2022), 74–97.

20 This group also includes all the depictions of isolated trees produced in the years that followed alongside his figure paintings and townscapes, such as *Herbstbäume* (Autumn Trees) (Kallir P218) or *Ein Baum im Spätherbst* (A Tree in Late Autumn) (Kallir P222) of 1911 or *Herbstsonne I* (*Sonnenaufgang*) (Autumn Sun I [Sunrise]) (Kallir P236) and *Herbstbaum in bewegter Luft (Winterbaum)* (Autumn Tree in Turbulent Air [Winter Tree]) (Kallir P239) of 1912. If 1910 represents the anthropomorphizing of plants, 1911 can be characterized *à l'envers*: when human figures are depicted, they are "naturalized," fused into a continuum visually using the painting technique, so that it is hardly possible to distinguish between the figure and its surroundings, between human being and nature. Examples of this include *Prozession* (Procession) (Kallir P198) and *Jesuiten* (Jesuits) (Kallir P197).

21 Egon Schiele, "White Swan," (1910), in *Egon Schiele: Poems and Letters* (see note 6), 45; cf. Egon Schiele, "*Weisser Schwan*," Leopold Museum, Vienna, inv. no. 7442; ESDA, ID no. 3.

22 It has been documented that Schiele owned a German translation of Rimbaud's poems by K. L. Ammer published in 1907: *Arthur Rimbaud: Leben und Dichtung*, trans. K. L. Ammer, with an introduction by Stefan Zweig (Leipzig: Insel, 1907). According to Alessandra Comini, eyewitnesses confirmed Schiele intently studied Rimbaud; see Comini, *Egon Schiele's Portraits* (Berkeley: University of California Press, 1990; orig. pub. 1974), 47 n. 67, 204.

23 On the question whether Schiele came into contact with Rimbaud's poetry through Erwin Dominik Osen or Willy Lidl, see Eva Werth, "Egon Schiele und die Lyrik," in Gamper and Wipplinger eds., *Egon Schiele: Expression and Lyric* (see note 6), 74–95.

24 Egon Schiele, "Country Road" (1910), in *Egon Schiele: Poems and Letters* (see note 6), 25; cf. Egon Schiele, "*Landstrasse*," Leopold Museum, Vienna, inv. no. 4494; ESDA, ID no. 138.

25 Egon Schiele, "White Swan" (1910), in *Egon Schiele: Poems and Letters* (see note 6), 45; cf. Egon Schiele, "*Weisser Schwan*," Leopold Museum, Vienna, inv. no. 7442; ESDA, ID no. 3.

26 Egon Schiele, "Wet Evening" (1910), in *Egon Schiele: Poems and Letters* (see note 6), 29; cf. Egon Schiele, "*Nasser Abend*," Leopold Museum, Vienna, inv. no. 4493; ESDA, ID no. 137.

27 Egon Schiele, "Two Clerics" (1910), in *Egon Schiele: Poems and Letters* (see note 6), 49; cf. Egon Schiele, "*Zwei Chleriker*," Leopold Museum, Vienna, inv. no. 4496; ESDA, ID no. 140.

28 Egon Schiele, "Field of Corn Ears" (1910), in idem, *I, Eternal Child: Paintings and Poems*, trans. Anselm Hollo (New York: Grove Press, 1985), 44; cf. Egon Schiele, "*Ährenfeld*," 1910, whereabouts unknown; ESDA, ID no. 296.

29 Egon Schiele to Anton Peschka, prior to May 12, 1910, in *Egon Schiele: Poems and Letters* (see note 6), 13–15; cf. Egon Schiele to Anton Peschka, prior to May 12, 1910, Leopold Museum, Vienna, inv. no. 7568; ESDA, ID no. 33.

30 Egon Schiele to Anton Peschka, prior to May 12, 1910 (see note 29), 13.

31 Ibid., 13–14.

32 Egon Schiele, "Who of the ones given life and senses" (1910), in *I, Eternal Child* (see note 28), 12–14, esp. 12; cf. Egon Schiele, "*Wer von lebend Primbegabten*," whereabouts unknown; ESDA, ID no. 297.

33 Egon Schiele to Anton Peschka, after May 23, 1911, Albertina, Vienna, inv. no. ESA 447; ESDA, ID no. 343.

34 Egon Schiele to Oskar Reichel, September 1911, whereabouts unknown; ESDA, ID no. 388.

35 Egon Schiele to Franz Hauer, August 25, 1913, Albertina, Vienna, inv. no. ESA 107 c; ESDA, ID no. 674.

36 Ernst Haeckel, *Die Welträthsel: Gemeinverständliche Studien über monistische Philosophie* (Bonn: Strauss, 1899); translated by Joseph McCabe as *The Riddle of the Universe at the Close of the Nineteenth Century* (New York: Harper, 1900).

37 Haeckel, *The Riddle of the Universe* (see note 36); idem, *Die Welträthsel* (see note 36), 333–36.

38 Pereña Sáez, *Egon Schiele* (see note 6), 256.

39 On this, see Hans Bisanz, "Egon Schiele: Kunst und Gedankenwelt," in Serge Sabarsky, ed., *Egon Schiele: Zeichnungen und Aquarelle aus den Beständen des Historischen Museums der Stadt Wien und aus amerikanischem Privatbesitz*, exh. cat. Historisches Museum der Stadt Wien, Vienna (Vienna: Eigenverlag der Museen der Stadt Wien, 1981), 10–15, esp. 11.

40 Wilhelm Worringer, *Abstraction and Empathy: A Contribution to the Psychology of Style*, Michael

Bullock (New York: International Universities Press, 1963), 128; idem, *Abstraktion und Einfühlung: Ein Beitrag zur Stilpsychologie* (Munich: Piper, 1921), 169.

41 Worringer, *Abstraction and Empathy* (see note 40), 128; idem, *Abstraktion und Einfühlung* (see note 40), 169.

42 See Egon Schiele to an unknown woman, July 6, 1909 (see note 13).

43 Egon Schiele to Anton Peschka, prior to May 12, 1910 (see note 29).

44 Egon Schiele, "*Künstler*," 1910, Albertina, Vienna, inv. no. 39881; ESDA, ID no. 1933. The identical wording is also part of the poem "*Skizze zu einem Selbstbildnis*" (Sketch for a Self-Portrait), 1910, whereabouts unknown; ESDA, ID no. 291. Finally, these phrases, in slightly transformed and generalized form, form the conclusion of the version of the Neukunst manifesto published in Pfemfert's journal *Die Aktion* in 1914, ESDA, ID no. 772: "The supreme sensation is religion and art. Nature is purpose. But God is there. And the artist must feel him, powerfully, most powerfully."

45 Egon Schiele to Erich Lederer, October 3, 1914, Gustav Klimt | Wien 1900 Private Foundation, Vienna; ESDA, ID no. 2692.

46 Egon Schiele to an unknown person, July 17, 1911, private collection; ESDA, ID no. 2764.

47 Ibid. On the theosophical theory, the idea of the chosen, sensitively perceiving human being, and their influence on Egon Schiele, see Astrid Kury, "*Heiligenscheine eines elektrischen Jahrhundertendes sehen anders aus …*": *Okkultismus und die Kunst der Wiener Moderne* (Vienna: Passagen, 2000), 195–218.

48 Ibid.

49 On this, see Pereña Sáez, *Egon Schiele* (see note 6), 205–10.

50 Egon Schiele to Arthur Roessler, January 6, 1911, in *I, Eternal Child* (see note 28), (translation modified), 8; cf. Egon Schiele to Arthur Roessler, January 6, 1911, Wienbibliothek im Rathaus, Vienna, inv. no. H.I.N. 180641; ESDA, ID no. 300.

51 On this, see his own statements, for example, in Egon Schiele to Karl Ernst Osthaus, October 10, 1911, in *Egon Schiele: Poems and Letters* (see note 6), 91; cf. Egon Schiele to Karl Ernst Osthaus, October 10, 1911, Leopold Museum, Vienna, inv. no. 5370; ESDA, ID no. 168.

52 Egon Schiele, "Fir Woods" (1910), in *Egon Schiele: Poems and Letters* (see note 6), 37; cf. Egon Schiele, "*Tannenwald*," Leopold Museum, Vienna, inv. no. 7368; ESDA, ID no. 1.

53 See Helena Pereña, "Nature, Religion, and Art," trans. Christopher Jenkin-Jones, in Helmut Friedel and Helena Pereña, eds., *Egon Schiele: "Das unrettbare*

Ich": Werke aus der Albertina (Cologne: Wienand, 2011), 110–26, esp. 112.

54 Schiele, "Who of the ones given life and senses" (see note 32), (translation modified), 12–13.

55 Egon Schiele to Oskar Reichel, September 1911 (see note 34). For a detailed analysis of Schiele's knowledge of occult views, see Kury, "*Heiligenscheine eines elektrischen Jahrhundertendes sehen anders aus …*" (see note 47) 195–218.

56 Egon Schiele to Josef Hoffmann, September 20, 1910, permanent loan from the Nebehay family to the Landesgalerie Niederösterreich, Krems; ESDA, ID no. 2762.

57 Egon Schiele to Carl Reininghaus, February 13, 1913, Leopold Museum, Vienna, inv. no. 7563; ESDA, ID no. 55.

58 Egon Schiele to Arthur Roessler, January 6, 1911, in *I, Eternal Child* (see note 28), 8; cf. Egon Schiele to Arthur Roessler, January 6, 1911, Wienblibliothek im Rathaus, Vienna, inv. no. H.I.N. 180641; ESDA, ID no. 300.

59 Egon Schiele to Anton Peschka, May 1911, Albertina, Vienna, inv. no. ESA 583; ESDA, ID no. 344.

60 Egon Schiele to Oskar Reichel, June 20, 1911, in *Egon Schiele: Poems and Letters* (see note 6), 81; cf. Egon Schiele to Oskar Reichel, June 20, 1911, Leopold Museum, Vienna, inv. no. 7559; ESDA, ID no. 134, and Egon Schiele to Oskar Reichel, September 1911 (see note 34).

61 Egon Schiele to Hermann Engel, September 1911, in *Egon Schiele: Poems and Letters* (see note 6), 87; cf. Egon Schiele to Hermann Engel, September 1911, Leopold Museum, Vienna, inv. no. 4497; ESDA, ID no. 141.

62 Egon Schiele to an unknown person, July 17, 1911, Private Collection; ESDA, ID no. 2764. In later letters, too, he wrote dismissively of "those who are supposed to live through books" as opposed to those "who exist through themselves. […] Few see the sun, and all the others need to have read novels and novellas to realize finally that there is a light." Diary entry by Egon Schiele, August 18, 1912, Leopold Museum, Vienna, inv. no. 4498; ESDA, ID no. 142. Schiele also wrote dismissively of someone "who vegetates in a structure of books"; Egon Schiele to Carl Reininghaus, February 13, 1913, Leopold Museum, Vienna, inv. no. 7563; ESDA, ID no. 55.

63 Egon Schiele to an unknown person, July 17, 1911, Private Collection; ESDA, ID no. 2764. This statement recalls the letter from the summer of 1909 in which he recommended to an unknown addressee that she reflect on the problems of nature and then proposed to her a number of modes of sense perception in order

to do so; Egon Schiele to an unknown woman, July 6, 1909 (see note 13).

64 After Roessler first characterized Schiele as a "neo-Gothic" in an essay in *Bildende Künstler: Monatsschrift für Künstler und Kunstfreunde* in 1911, the term became a commonplace when characterizing his artistic volition or personality.

65 Wilhelm Worringer, *Formprobleme der Gotik* (Munich: Piper, 1911); idem, *Form in Gothic*, trans. Herbert Read (London: Putnam, 1927).

66 According to Hans Bisanz, Egon Schiele received an edition of Worringer's *Abstraktion und Einfühlung* from his supporter Arthur Roessler in 1910; see Bisanz, "Egon Schiele: Kunst und Gedankenwelt" (see note 39), 11.

67 On the image of Gothic towns, see the discussion in Kimberly A. Smith: *Between Ruin and Renewal. Egon Schiele's Landscapes* (New Haven and London: Yale University Press, 2004), 65–97.

68 Arthur Roessler wrote to Egon Schiele about a "pure landscape" in contrast to a view of Krumau. Arthur Roessler to Egon Schiele, postcard, prior to August 1911, Albertina, Vienna, inv. no. ESA 569v; ESDA, ID no. 2572.

69 The following remark confirms the relative fusion of the categories "townscape" and "landscape" in Schiele's work: "I am sending you today three townscapes painted on wood, which I find much more colorful and preferable to all the other landscapes." Egon Schiele to Arthur Roessler, July 13, 1911, Wienbibliothek im Rathaus, Vienna, inv. no. H.I.N. 180654; ESDA, ID no. 360.

70 Schiele wrote about sublime nature in the form of mountains repeatedly in his letter: "yearning for mountain chains." It seems all the more astonishing that apart from the small-format painting *Berg am Fluss* (Mountain by the River) no other work is known in which he painted that subject without any other elements—and one can scarcely speak of sublimity in the case of *Berg am Fluss*. In 1913 he wrote to Reininghaus of his "desire [...] to paint mountain chains." Egon Schiele to Carl Reininghaus, March 29, 1913, Leopold Museum, Vienna, inv. no. 7799; ESDA, ID no. 36.

71 See, for example, *Herbstbäume* (Autumn Trees), 1911, Private Collection, Austria (Kallir P218); *Herbstsonne I (Sonnenaufgang)* (Autumn Sun I [Sunrise]), 1912, Private Collection, USA, Courtesy Galerie St. Etienne, New York (Kallir P236); and *Herbstbaum in bewegter Luft (Winterbaum)* (Autumn Tree in Turbulent Air [Winter Tree]), 1912, Leopold Museum, Vienna, inv. no. 449 (Kallir P239).

72 Egon Schiele to Anton Peschka, May 14, 1912, whereabouts unknown; ESDA, ID no. 471.

73 Ibid.

74 "Vienna, however, is inorganic for me, so I am finally in dramatic surroundings, — by Neulengbach." Egon Schiele to Karl Ernst Osthaus, October 10, 1911, in *Egon Schiele: Poems and Letters* (see note 6), 91; cf. Egon Schiele to Karl Ernst Osthaus, October 10, 1911, Leopold Museum, Vienna, inv. no. 5370; ESDA, ID no. 168.

75 Egon Schiele to Leopold Czihaczek, September 1, 1911, Leopold Museum, Vienna, inv. no. 5650; ESDA, ID no. 375.

76 Egon Schiele to Carl Reininghaus, February 27, 1912, in *Egon Schiele: Poems and Letters* (see note 6), 101; cf. Egon Schiele to Carl Reininghaus, February 27, 1912, Leopold Museum, Vienna, inv. no. 7452; ESDA, ID no. 45.

77 The "cycle of existence" is a reference to the wedding of his sister Gertrude and Anton Peschka. Egon Schiele to Marie Schiele, November 23, 1914, whereabouts unknown; ESDA, ID no. 814.

78 This statement coincides with the dispute over the funding of the tombstone for the late Adolf Schiele. Egon Schiele to Marie Schiele, July 15, 1913, Leopold Museum, Vienna, inv. no. 7562; ESDA, ID no. 131.

79 Egon Schiele to Leopold Czihaczek, September 1, 1911, Leopold Museum, Vienna, inv. no. 5650; ESDA, ID no. 375.

80 Worringer, *Abstraction and Empathy* (see note 40), 60–61; Worringer, *Abstraktion und Einfühlung* (see note 40), 4.

81 Worringer, *Abstraction and Empathy* (see note 40), 128; Worringer, *Abstraktion und Einfühlung* (see note 40), 170.

82 Egon Schiele to Oskar Reichel, September 1911 (see note 34).

83 Ibid. Schiele pursued a different thrust—namely, that of the artist made immortal by his art—when he wrote his mother that he "will be the fruit that after her decay will be left behind as an eternal creature." Egon Schiele to Marie Schiele, March 31, 1913, Albertina, Vienna, inv. no. ESA 216b; ESDA, ID no. 593.

84 Egon Schiele, war diary, May 10, 1916, Albertina, Vienna, inv. no. ESA 321; ESDA, ID no. 1049.

85 Egon Schiele, war diary, March 18, 1916, Albertina, Vienna, inv. no. ESA 321; ESDA, ID no. 978.

86 Egon Schiele, war diary, June 14, 1916, Albertina, Vienna, inv. no. ESA 321; ESDA, ID no. 1094.

PLATES

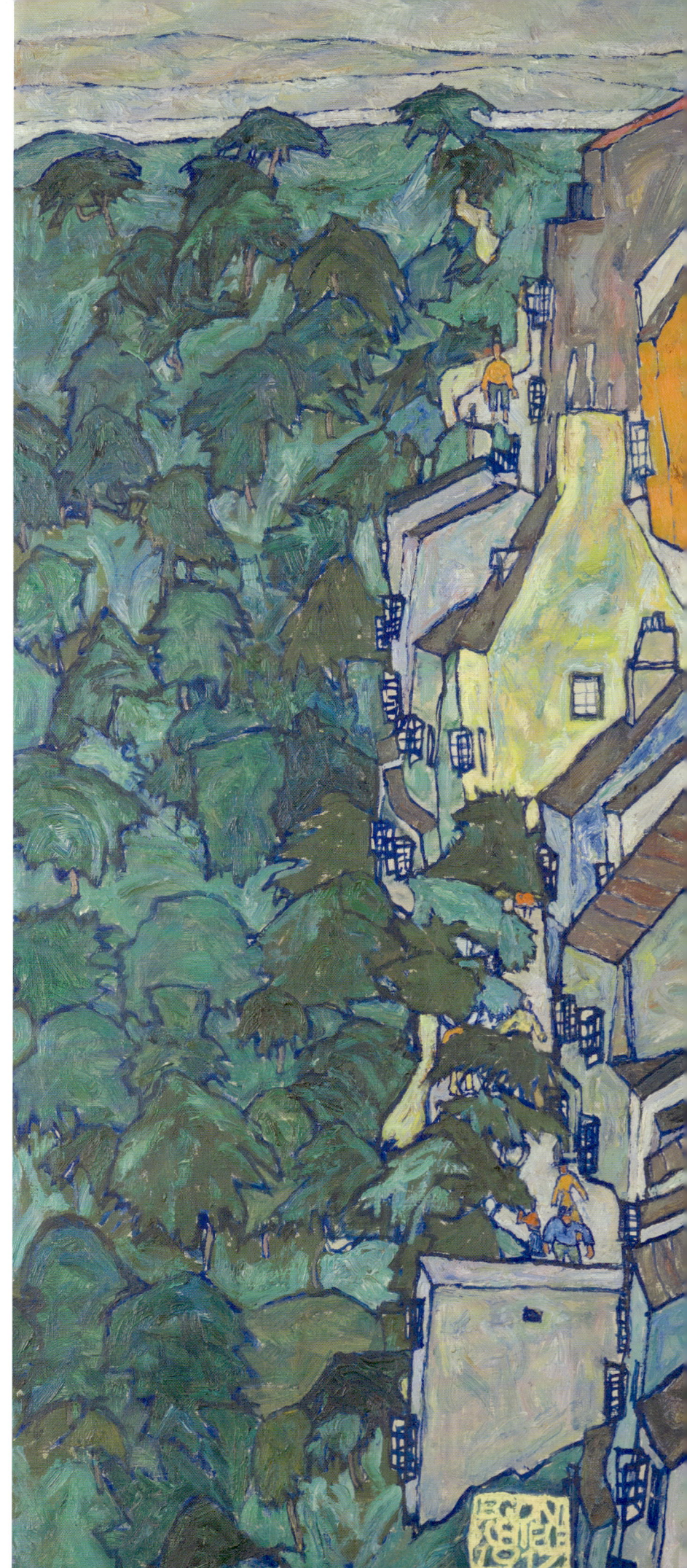

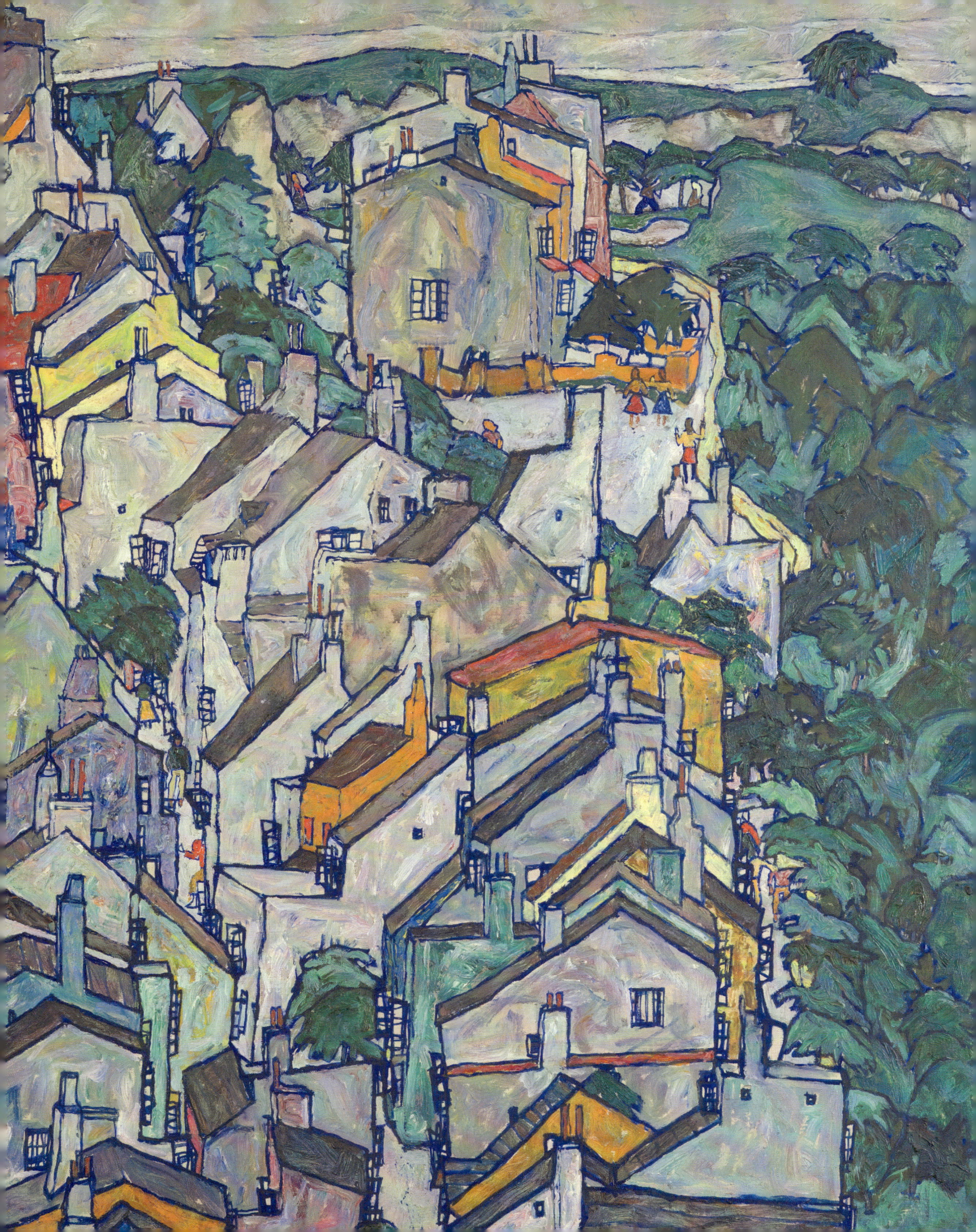

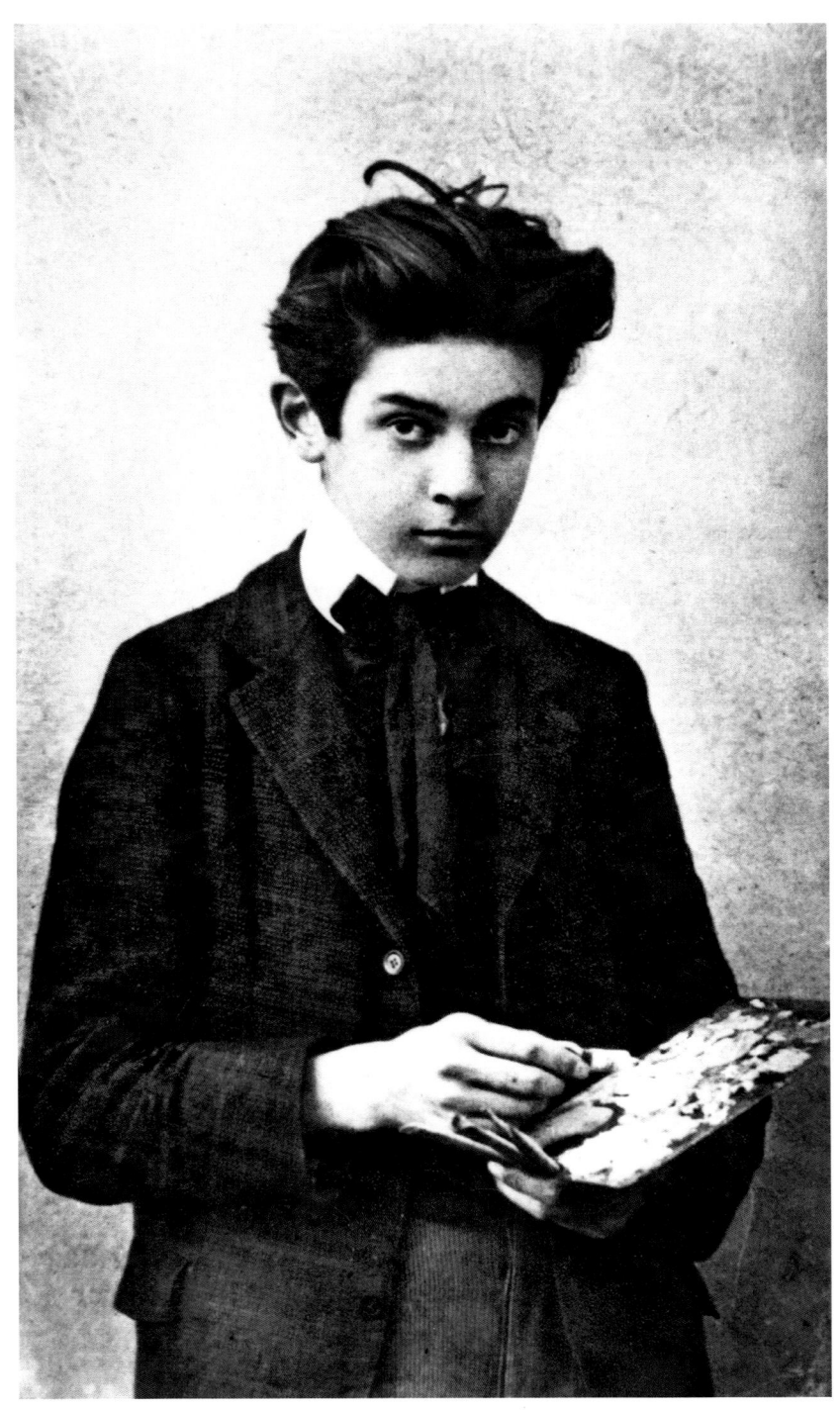

1. EGON SCHIELE WITH PALETTE AS A FIRST-YEAR STUDENT AT VIENNA'S ACADEMY OF FINE ARTS, SEPTEMBER 1906

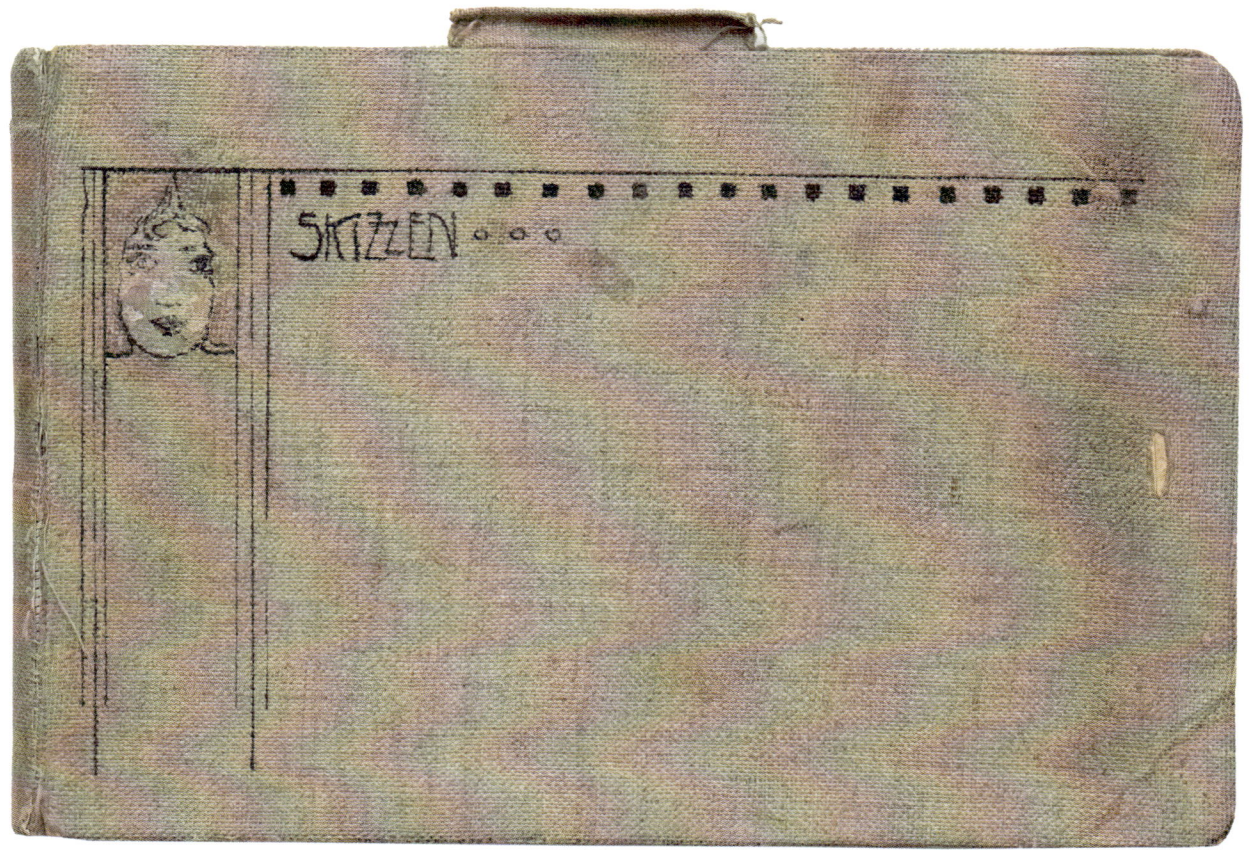

2. SKETCHBOOK, 1906

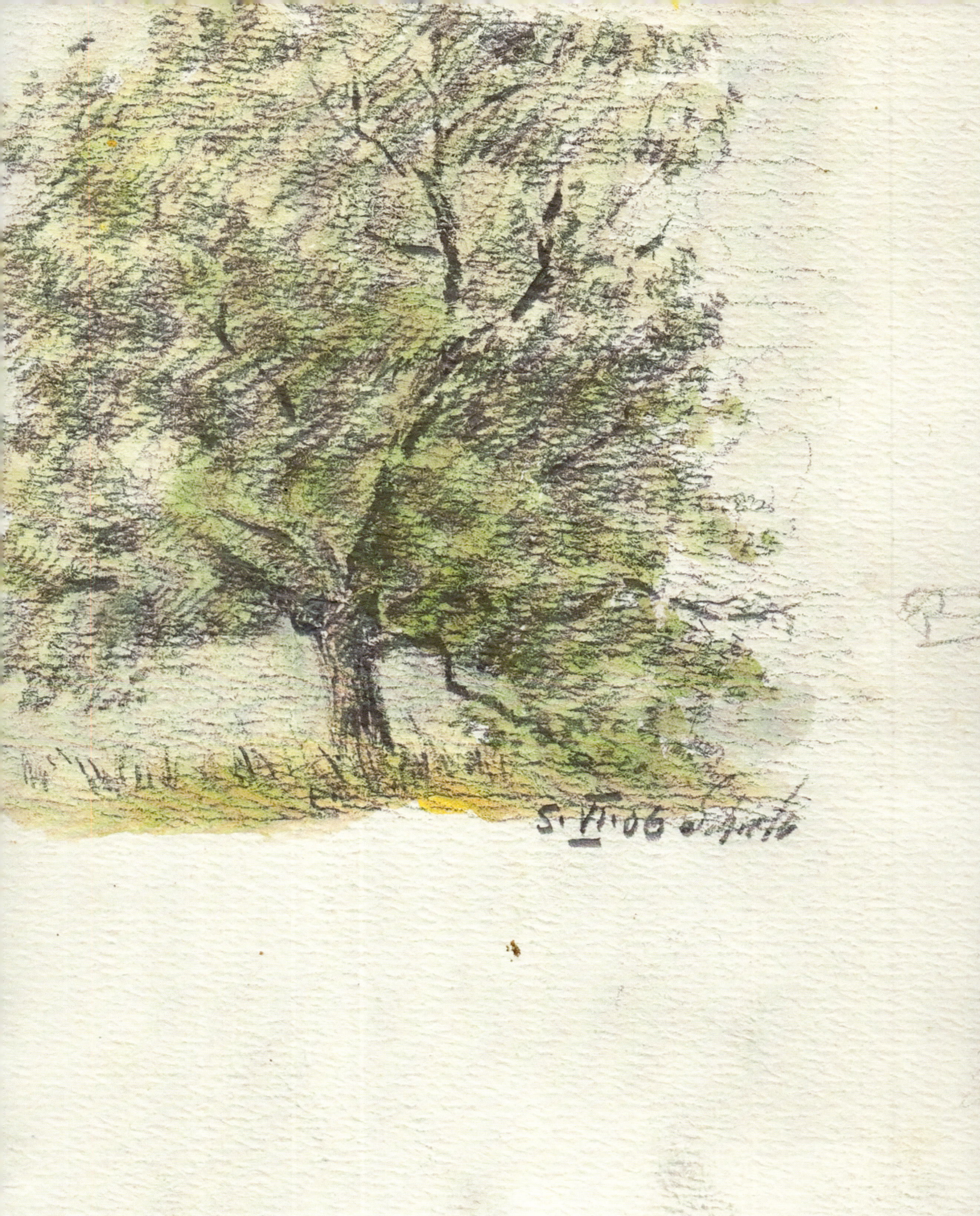

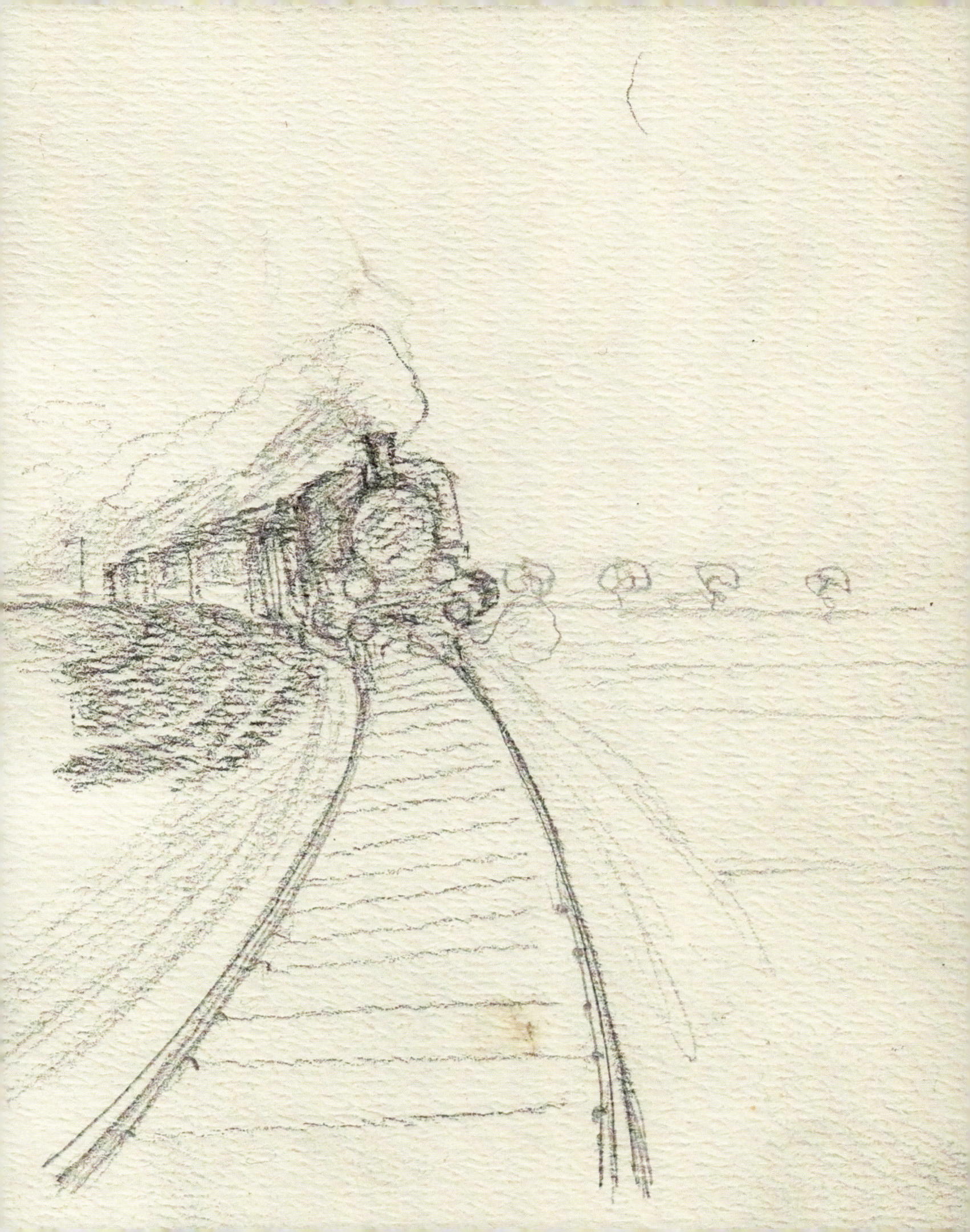

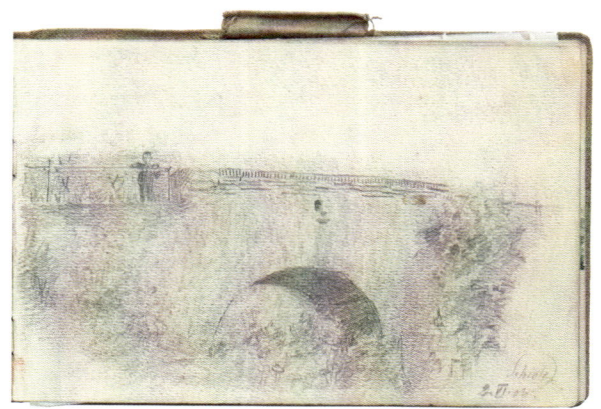
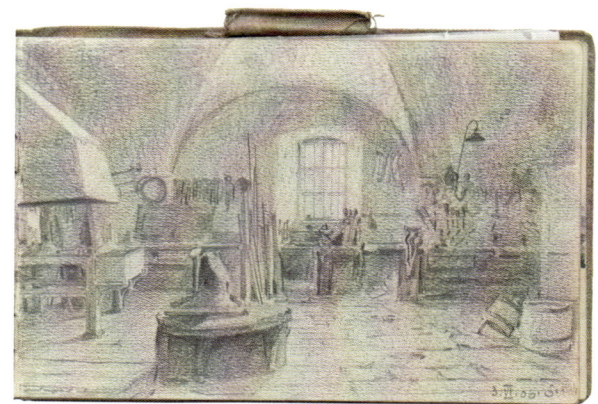
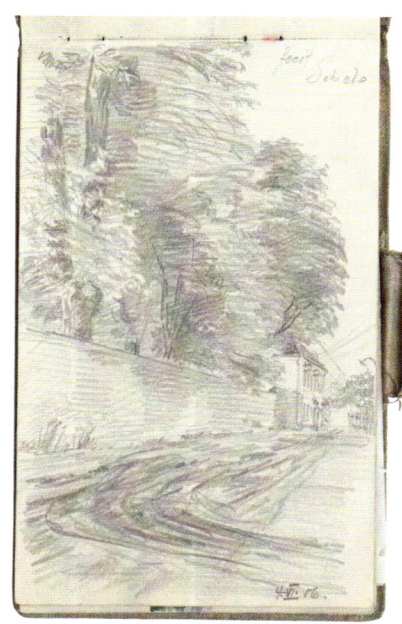
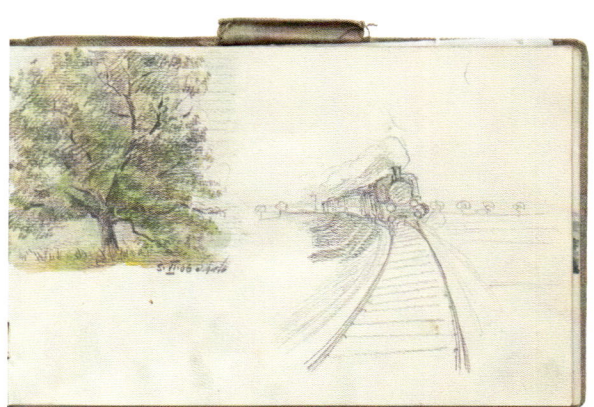
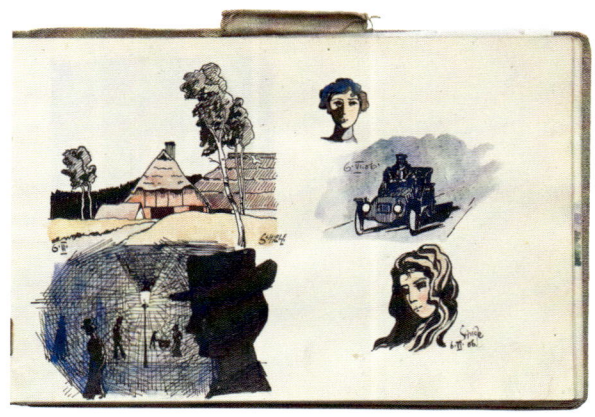
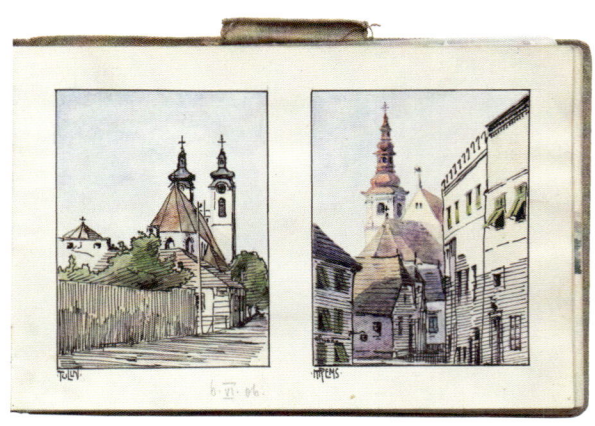

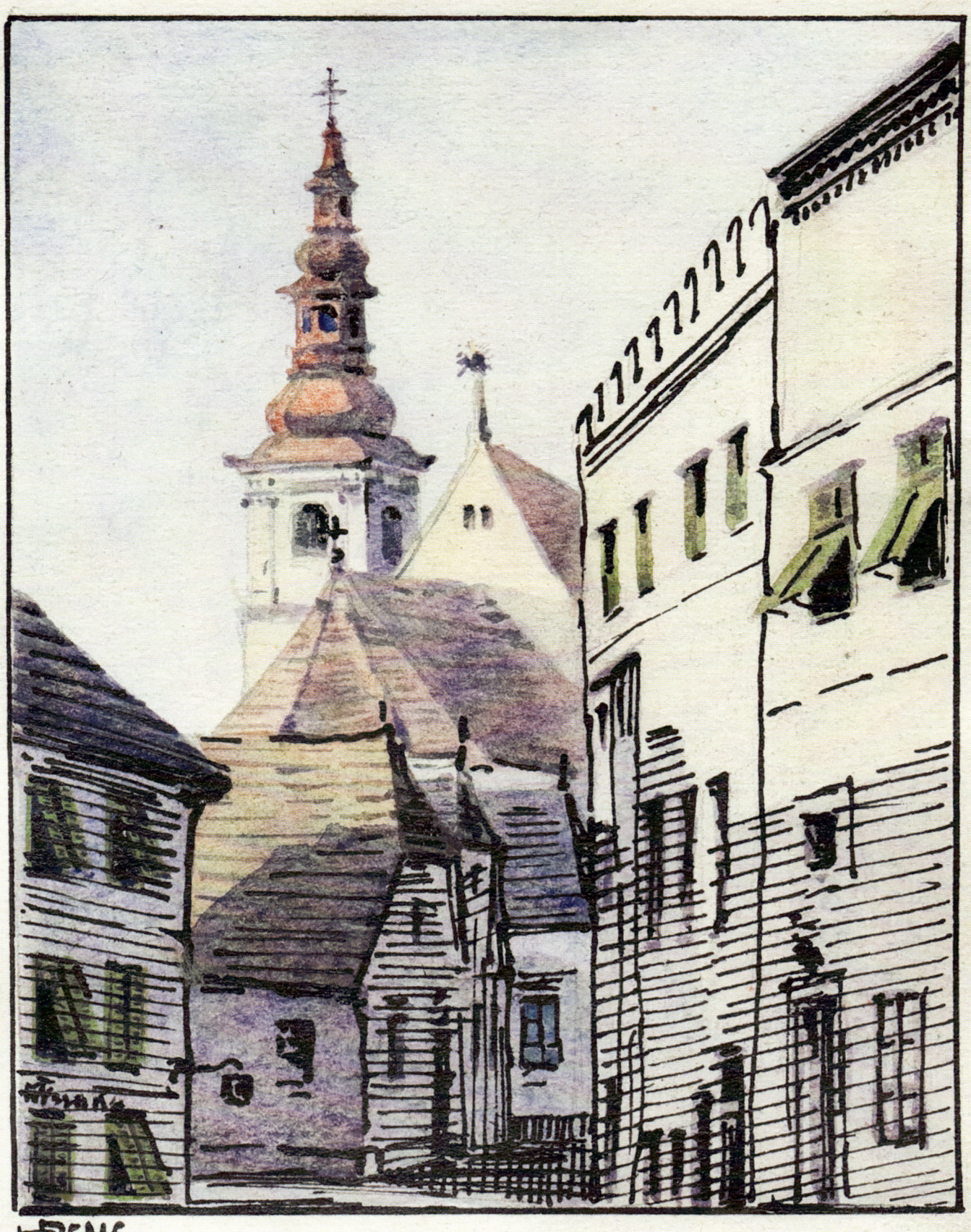

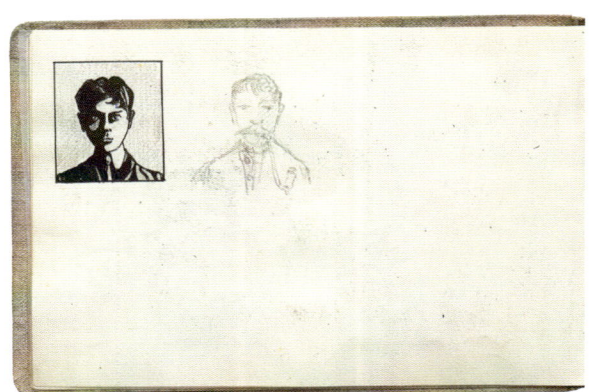

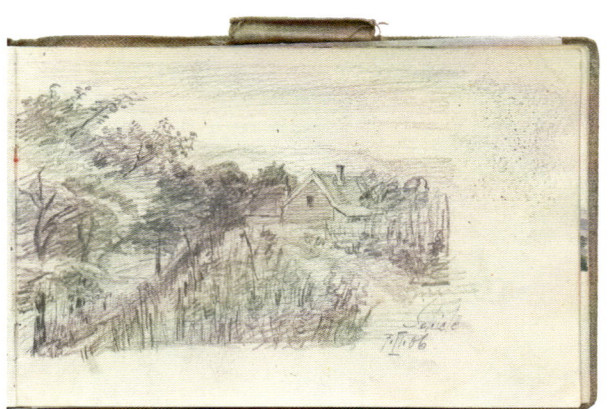

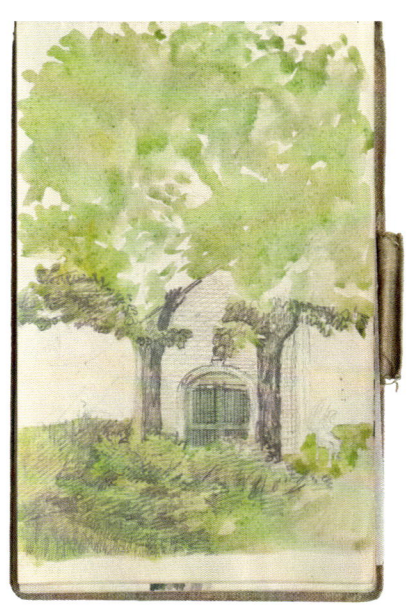

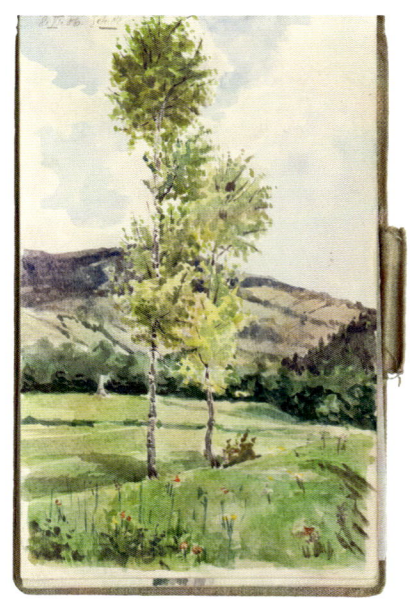

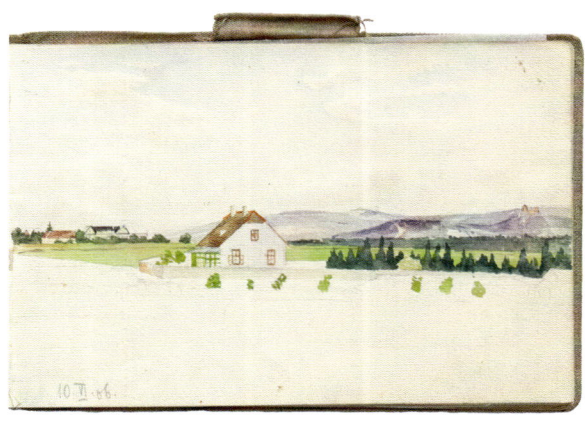

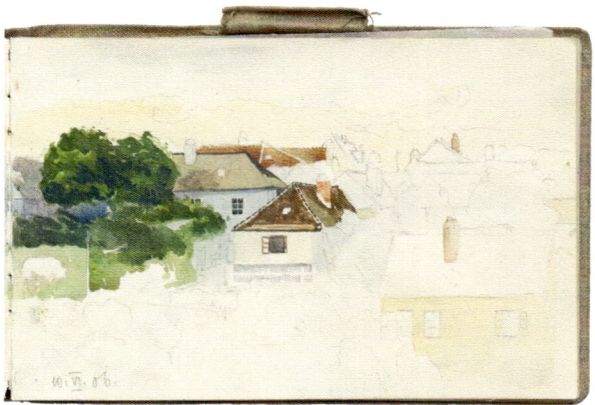

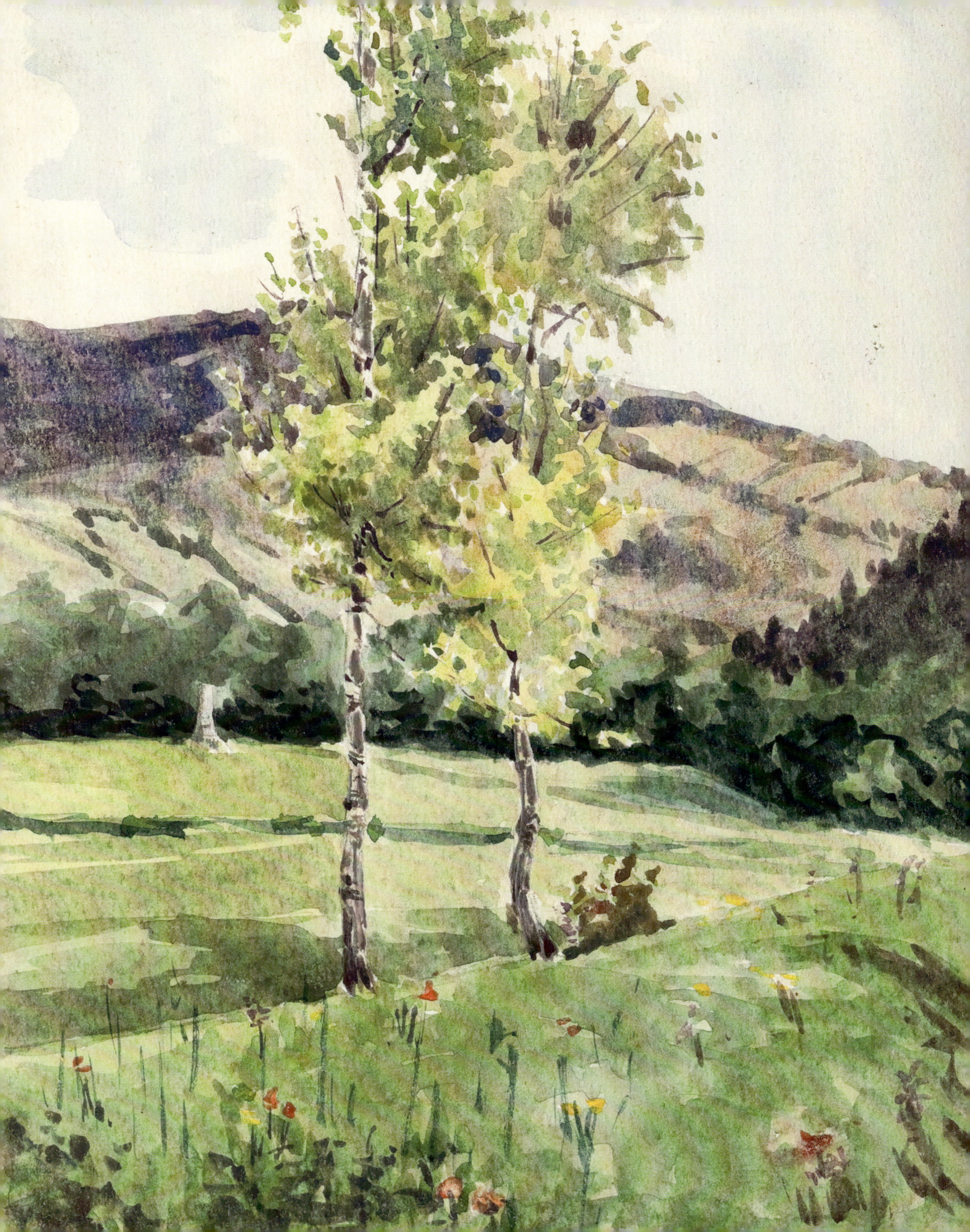

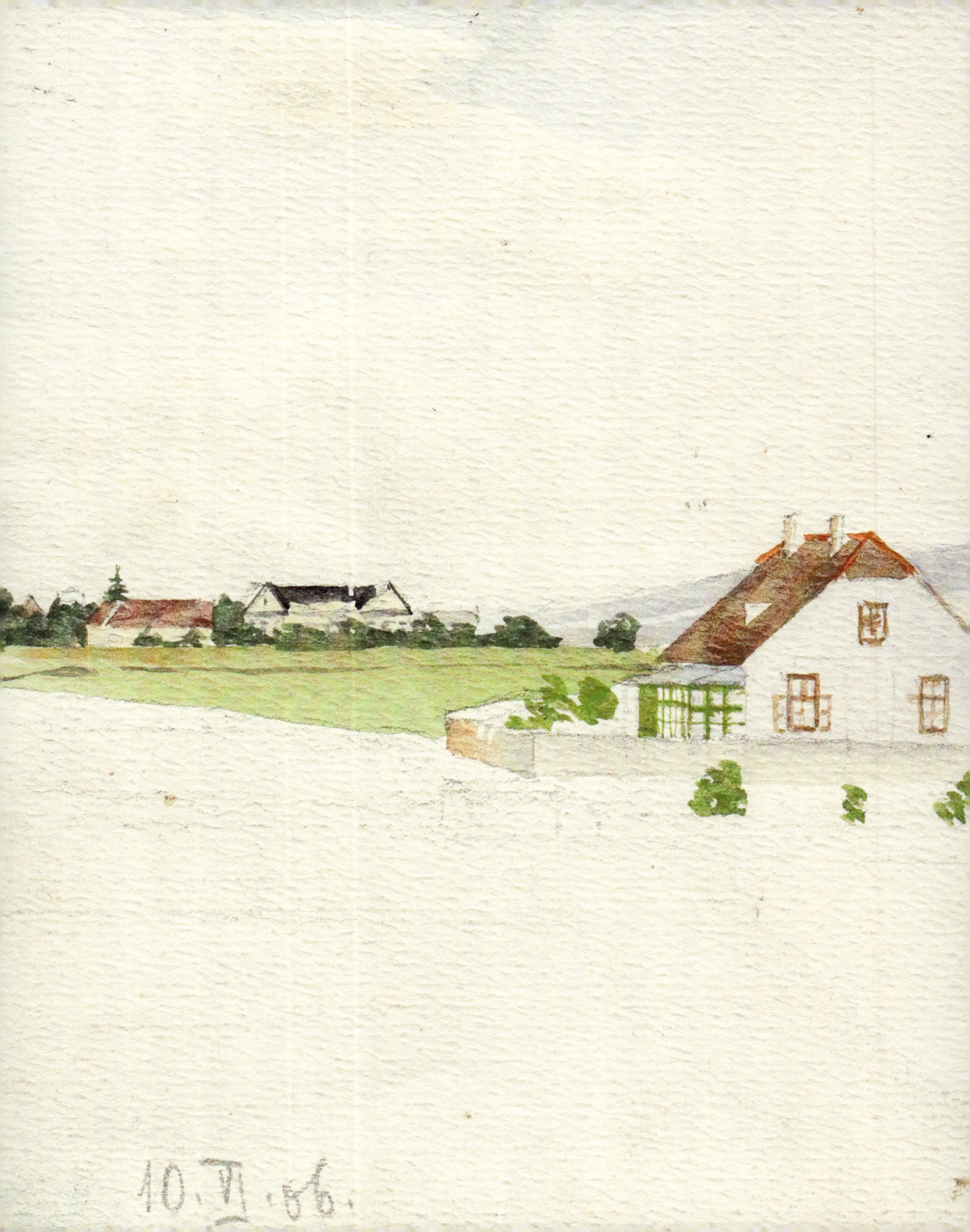

10. VI. 86.

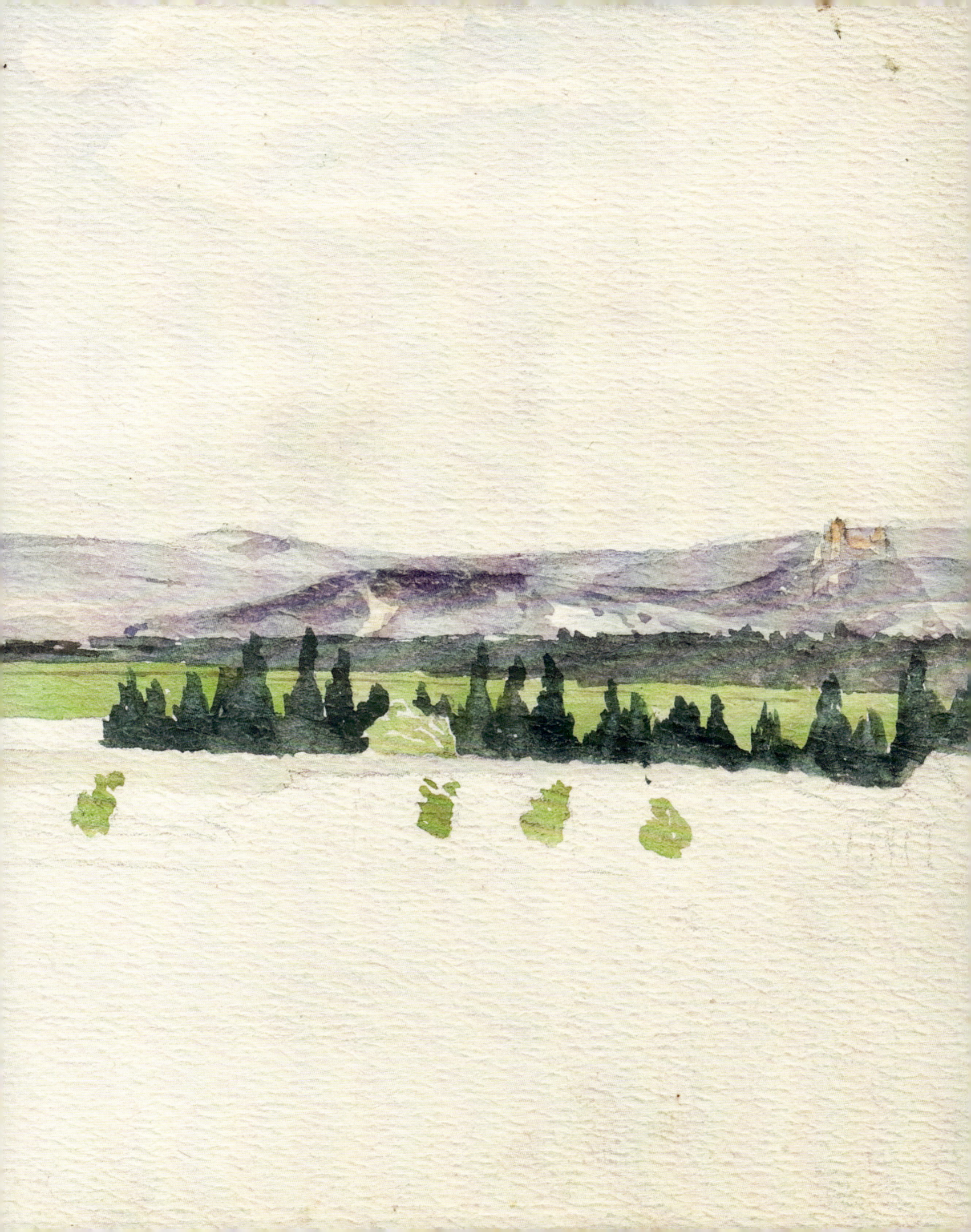

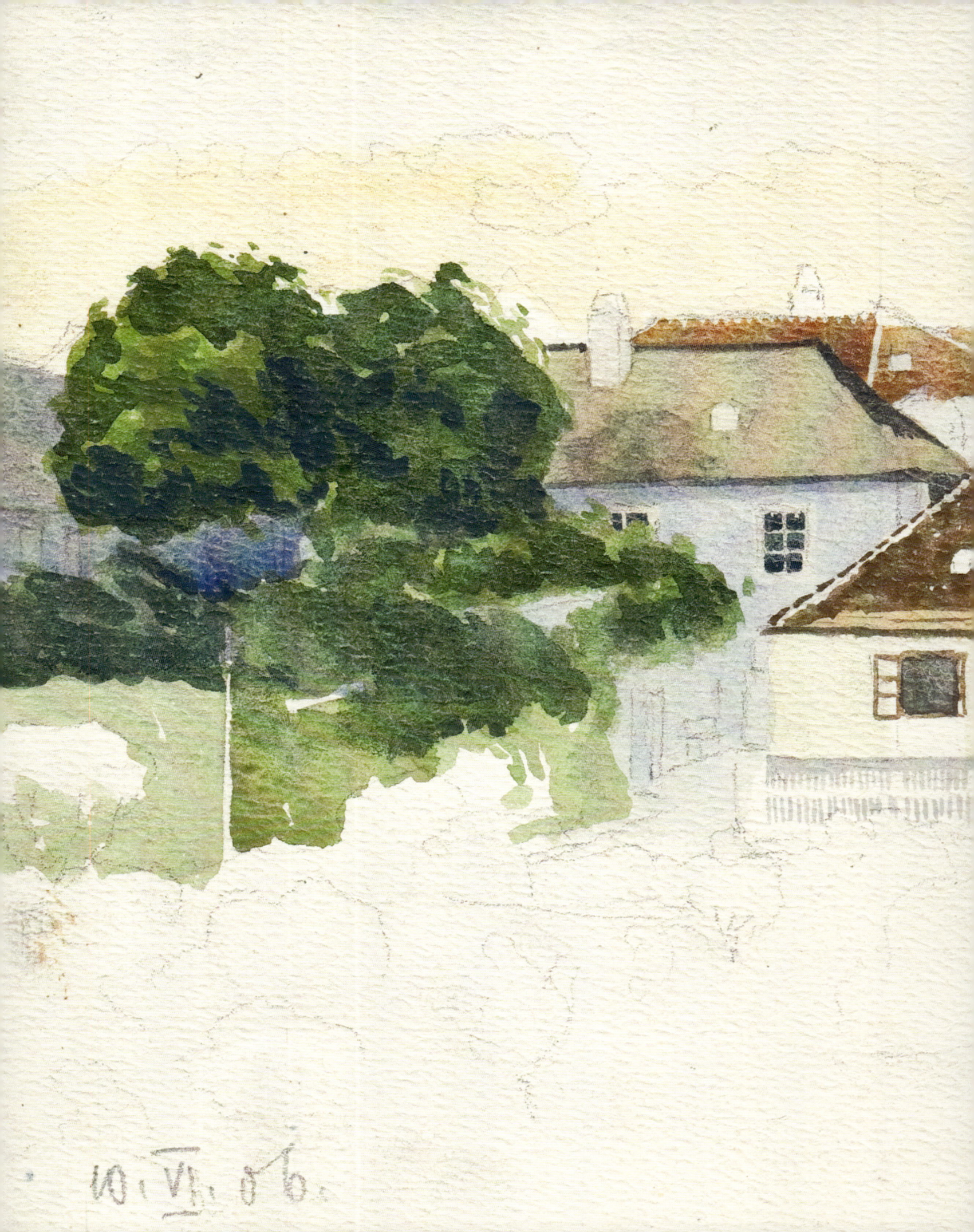

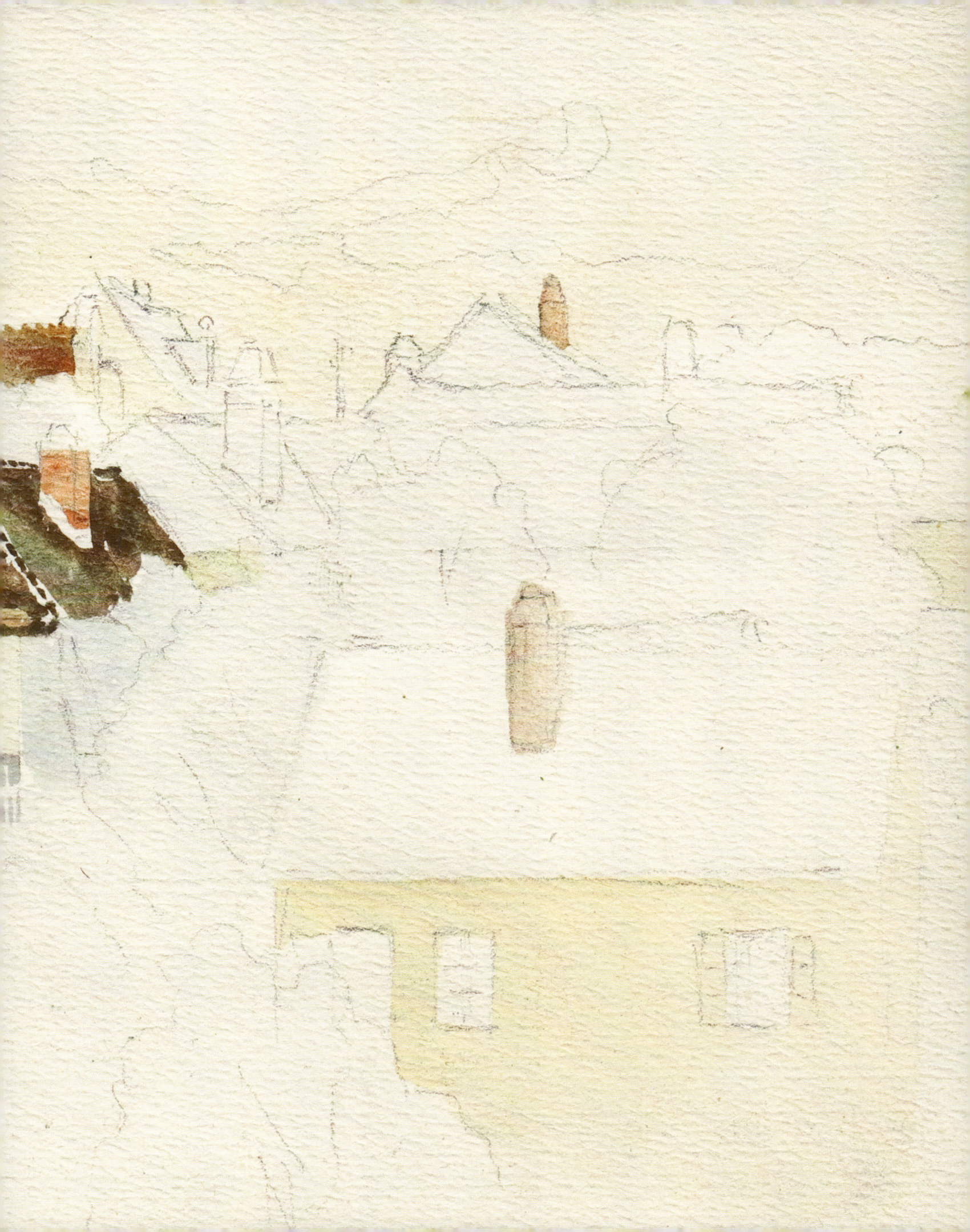

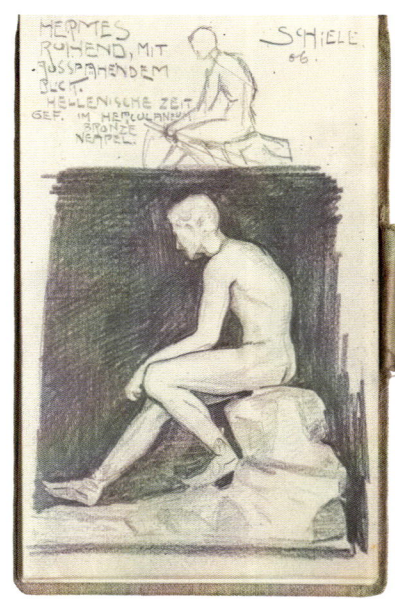

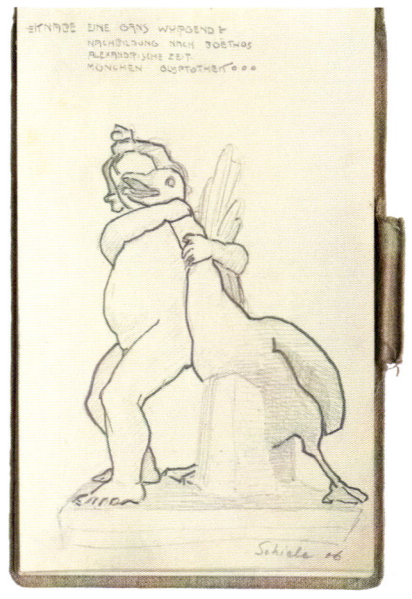

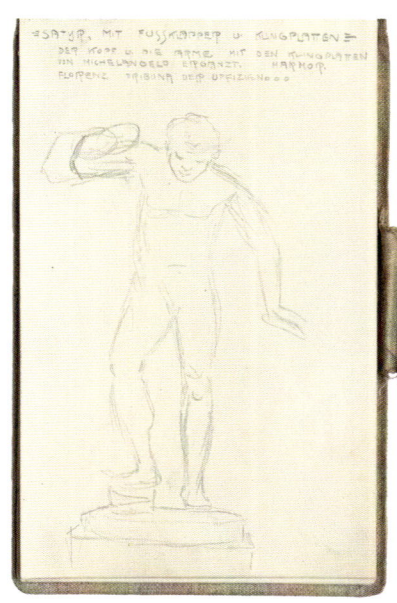

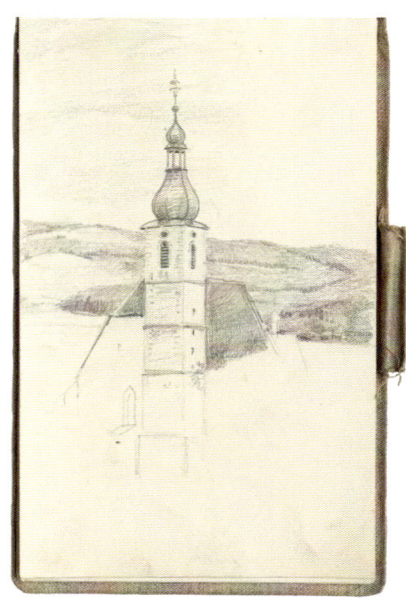

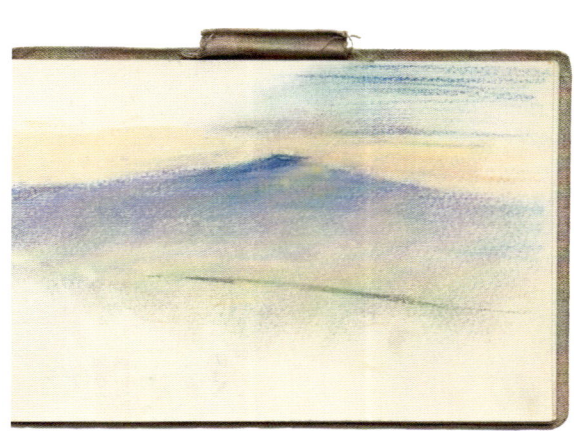

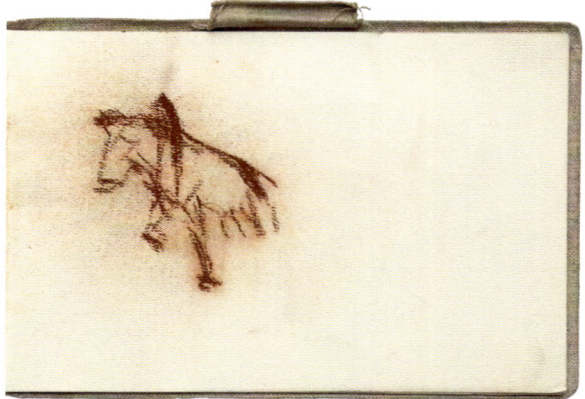

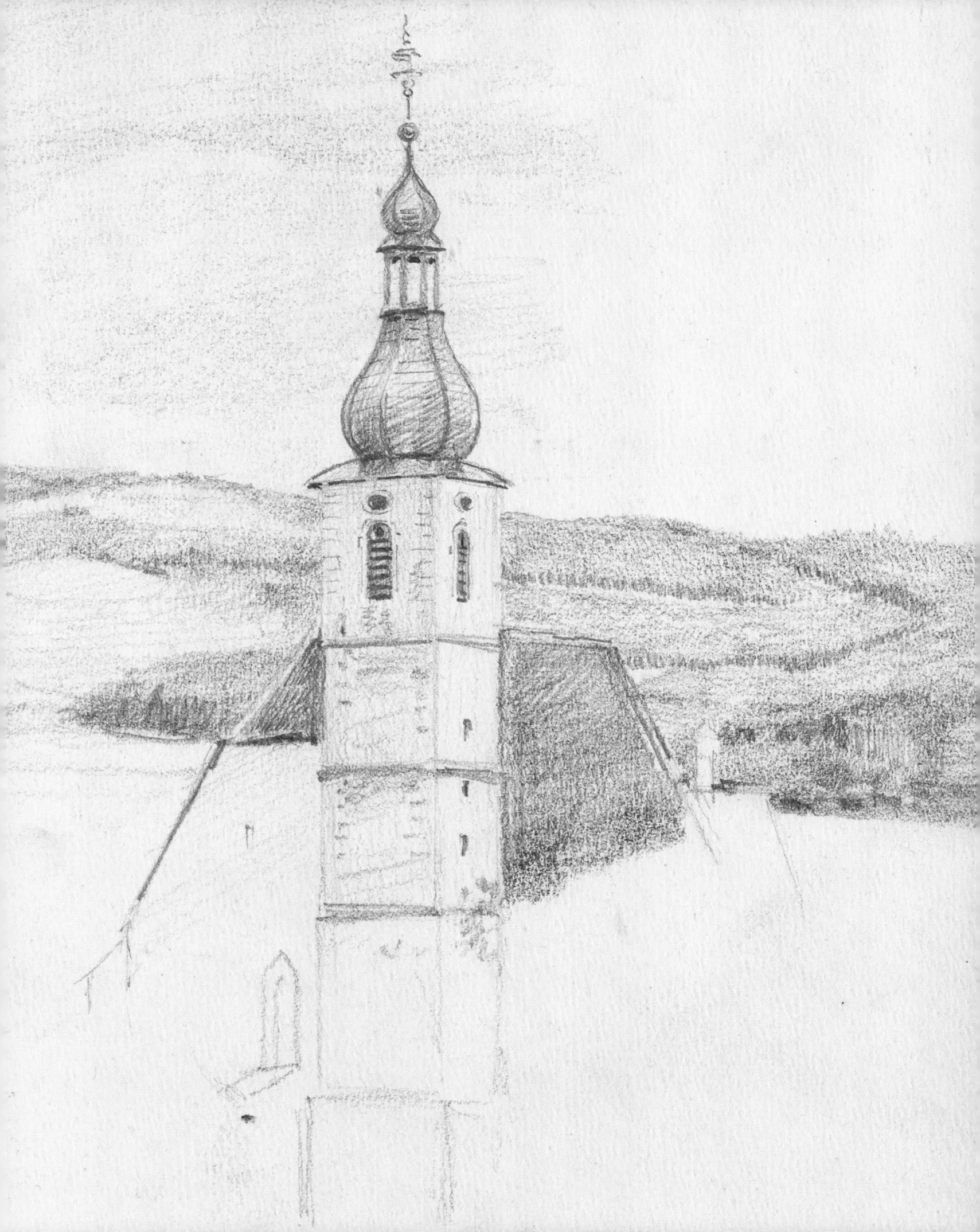

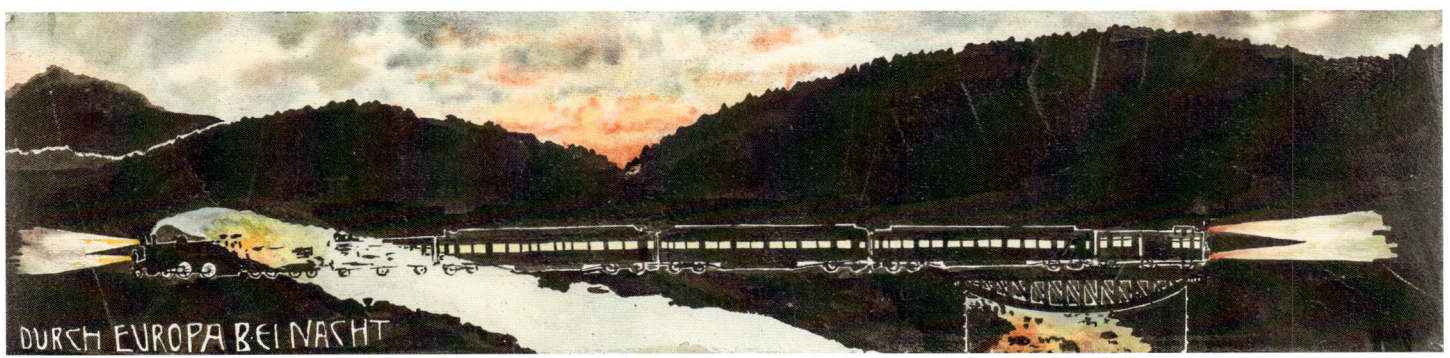

3. THROUGH EUROPE BY NIGHT, CA. 1906

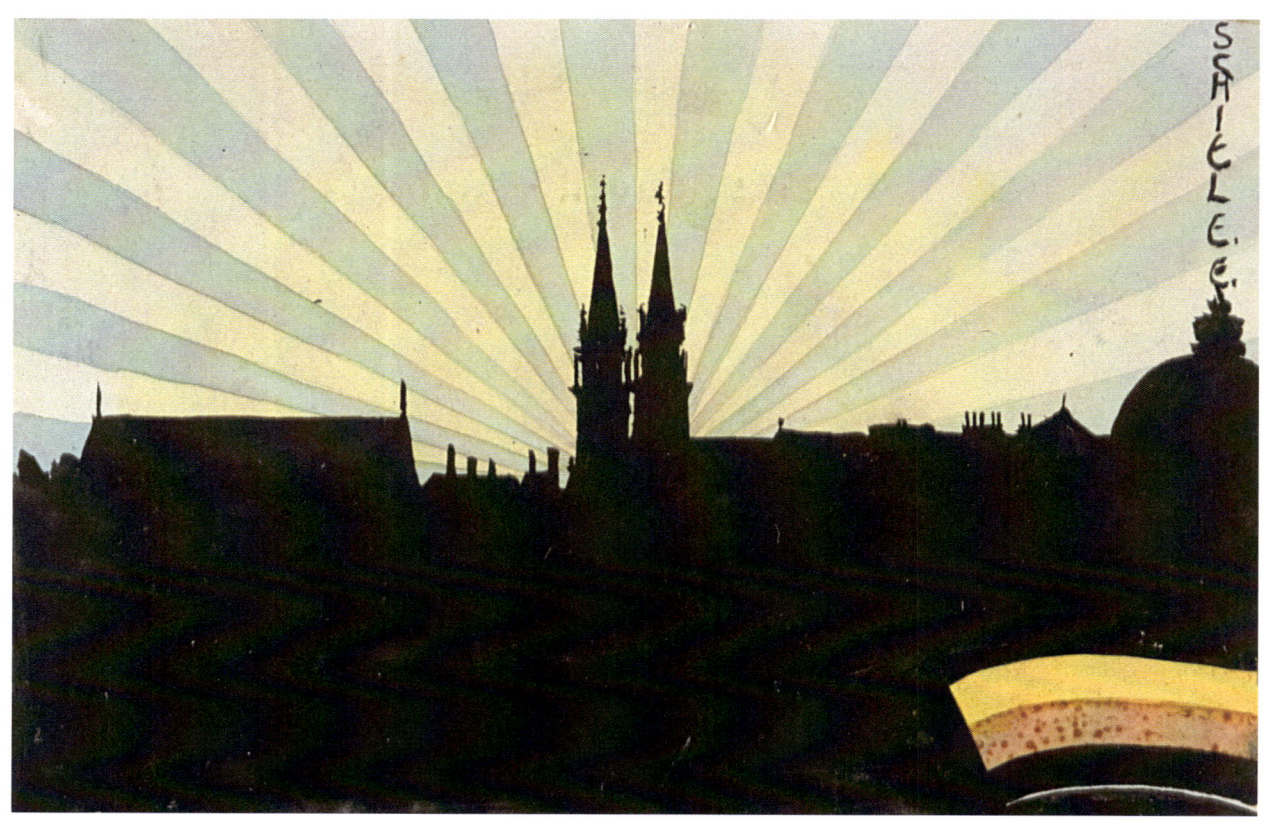

4. SILHOUETTE OF KLOSTERNEUBURG, CA. 1906

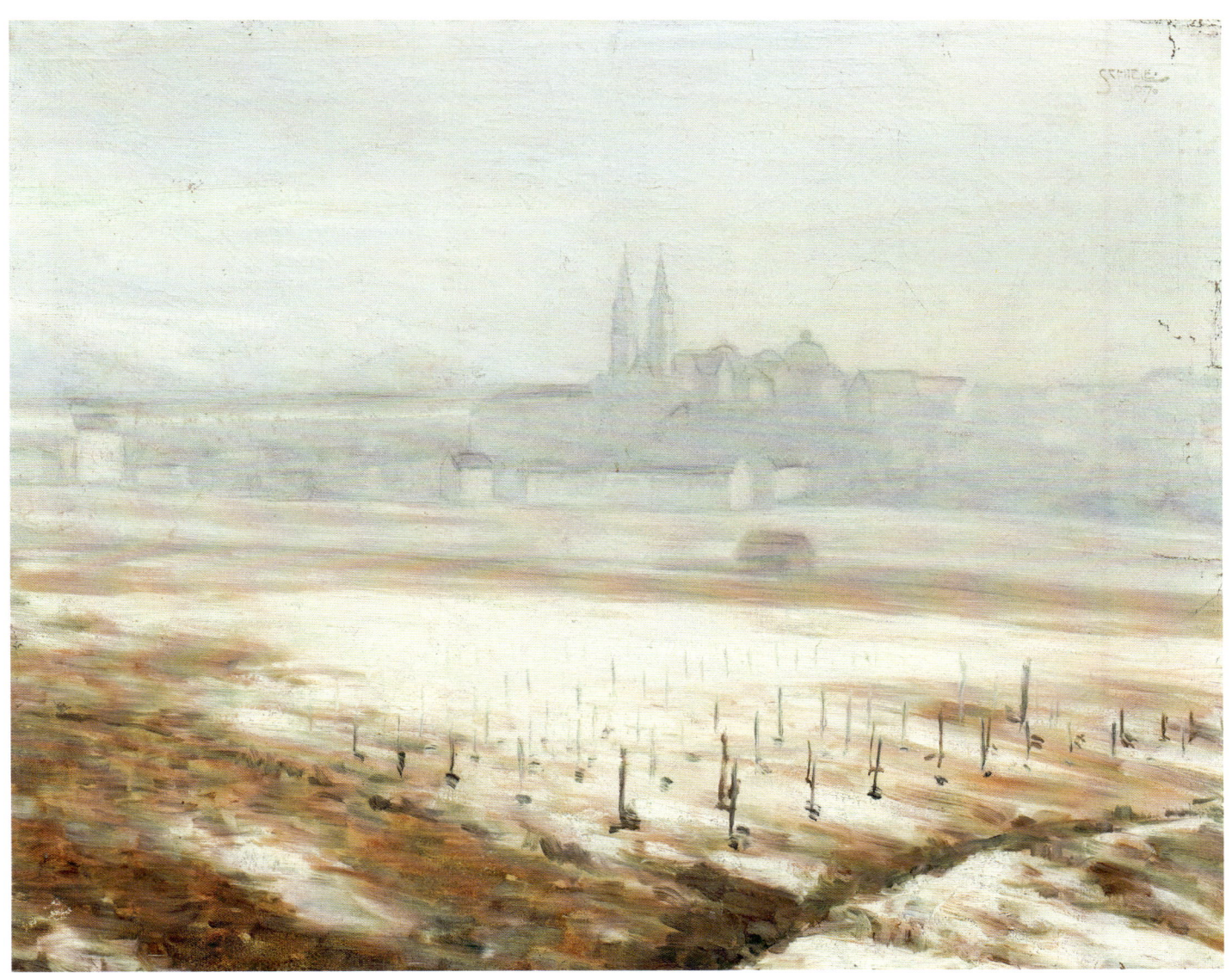

5. KLOSTERNEUBURG IN FOG, 1907

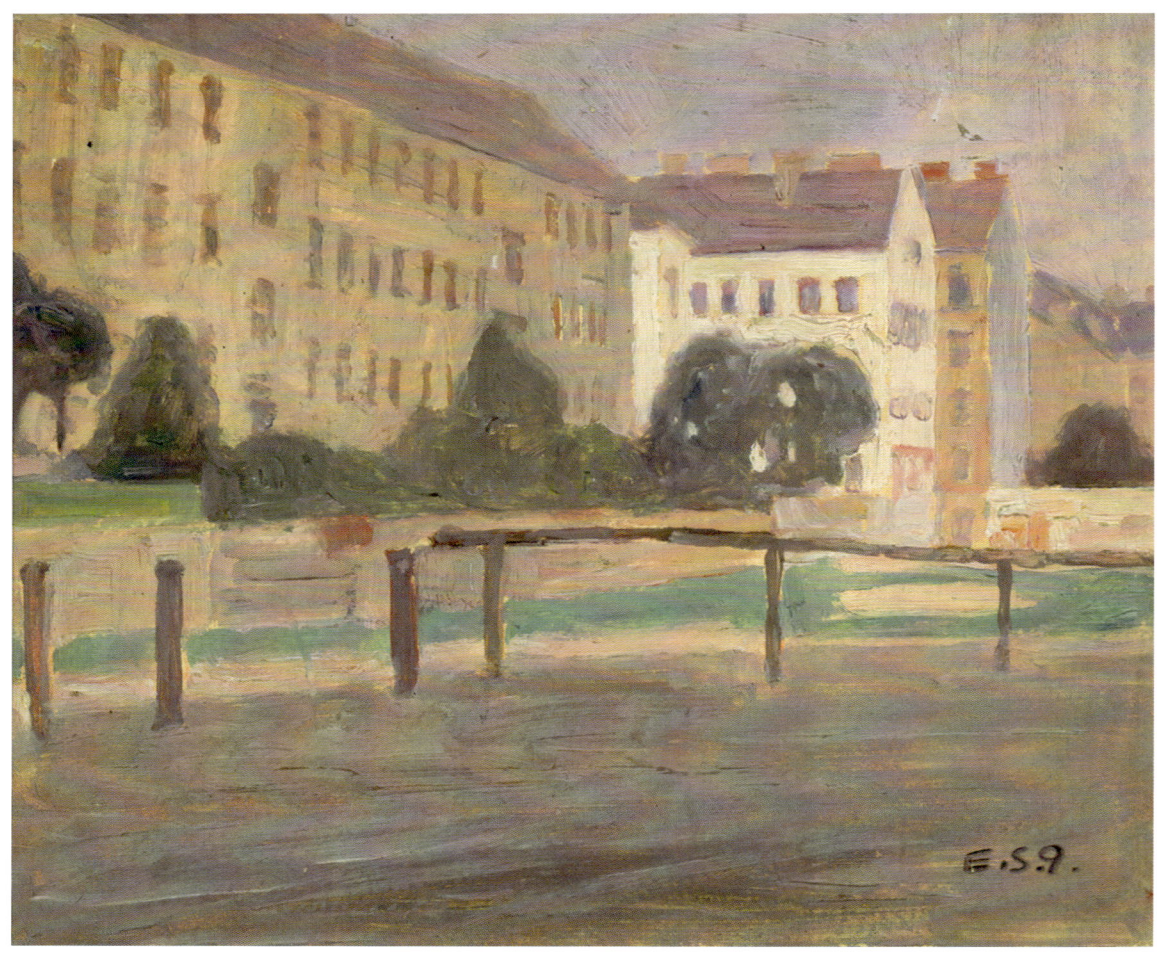

6. HOUSES IN THE SUBURBS, 1907

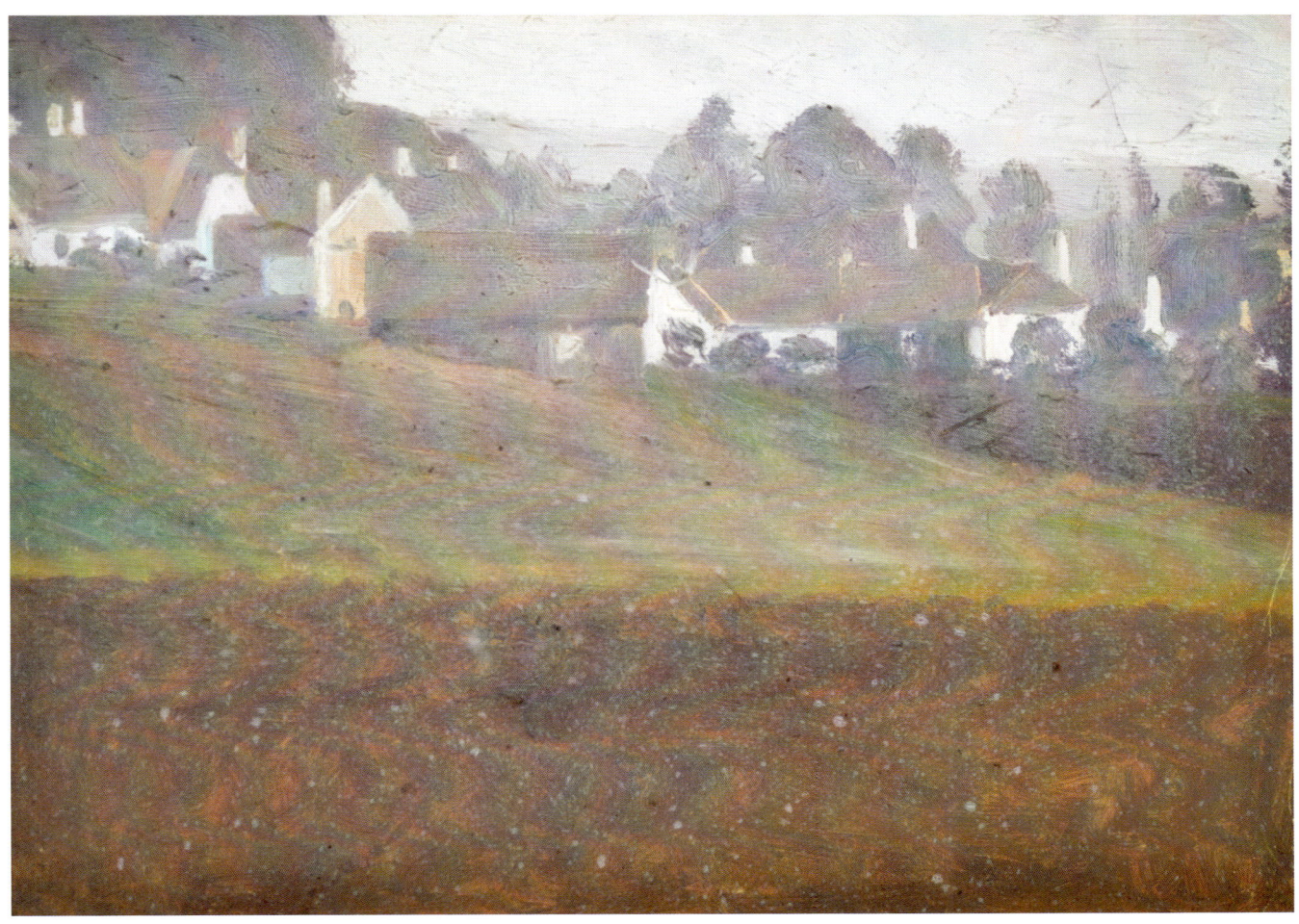

7. MEADOW WITH VILLAGE IN BACKGROUND I, 1907

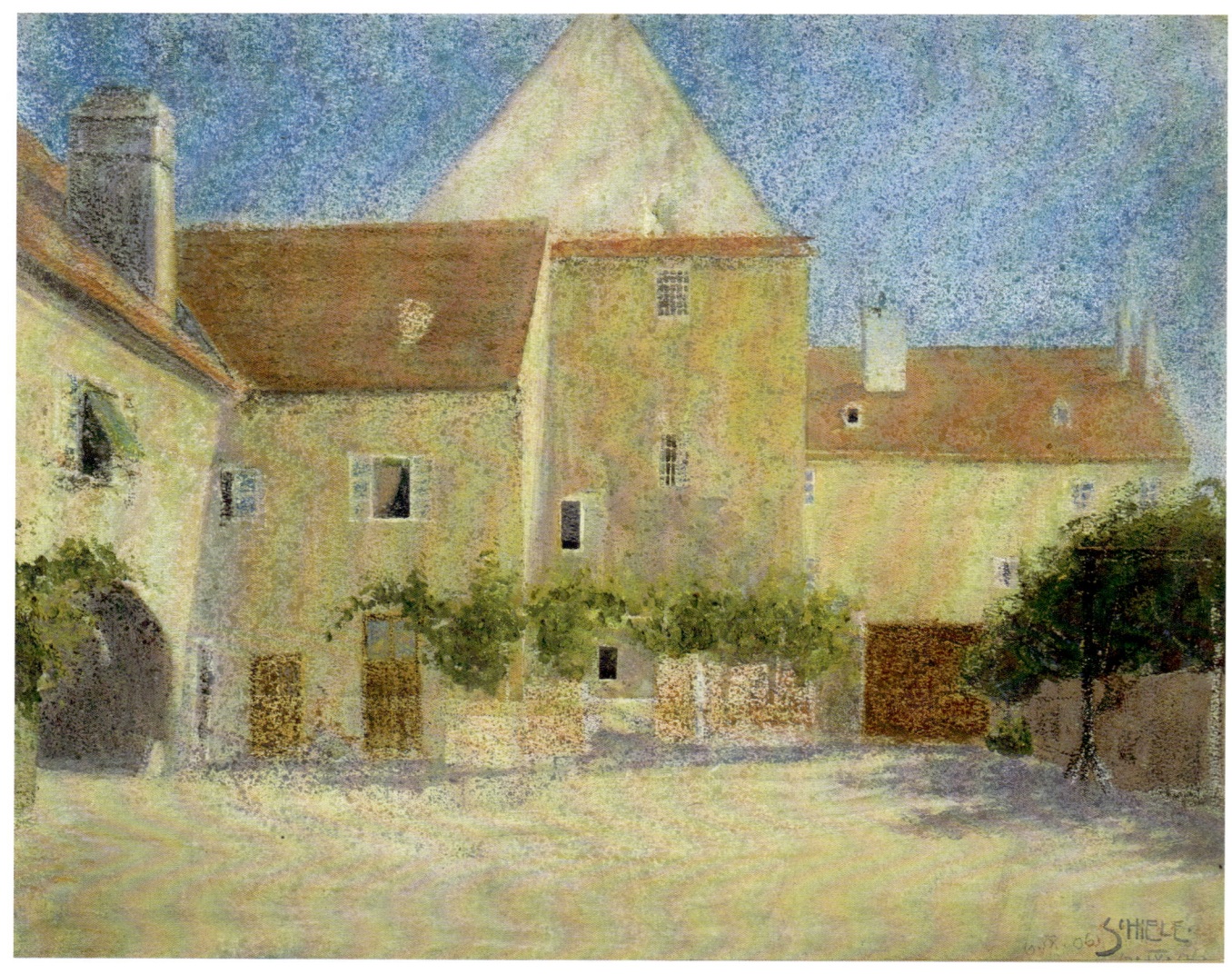

8. THE BLACKSMITH'S COURTYARD IN KLOSTERNEUBURG, 1906

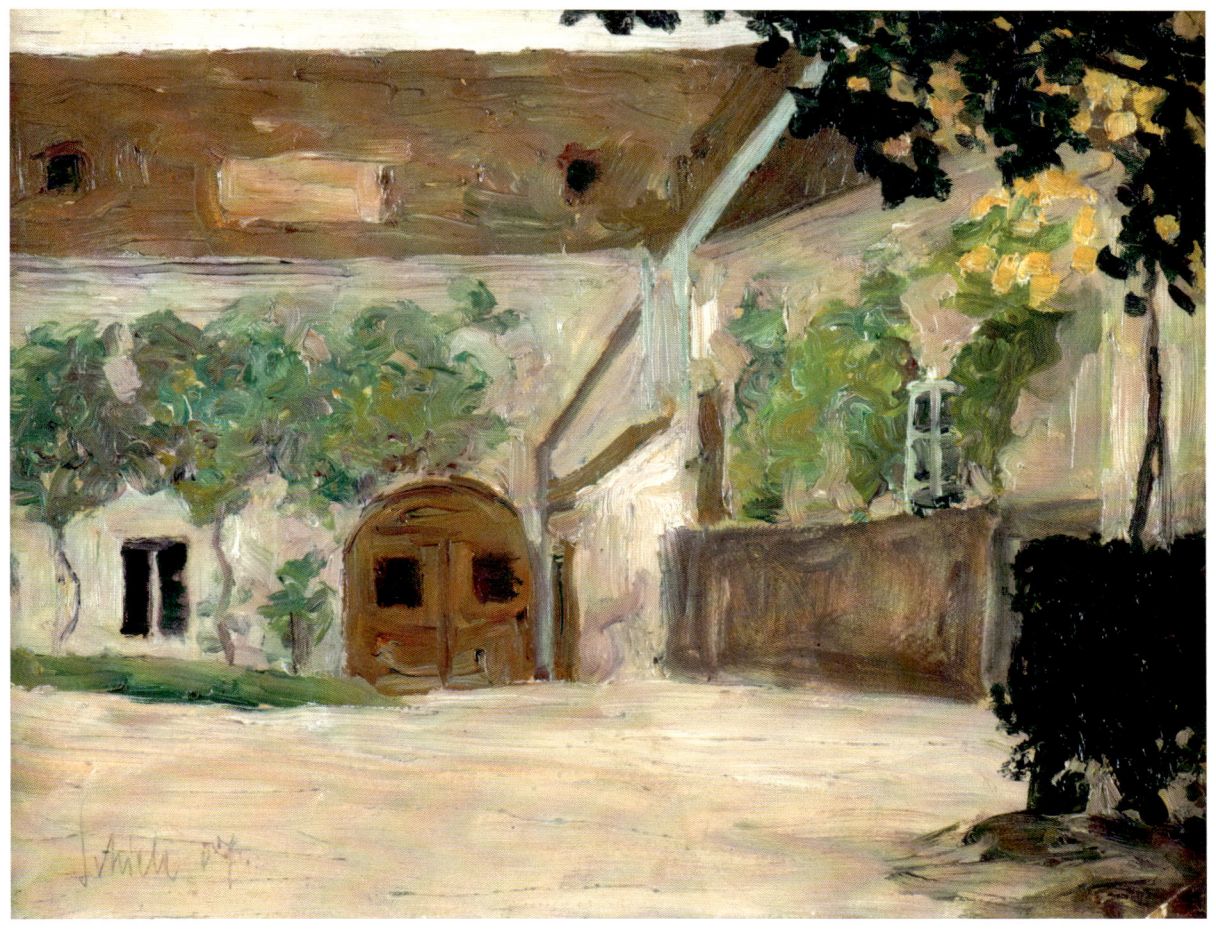

9. COURTYARD OF THE ABBEY CARPENTRY SHOP, KLOSTERNEUBURG, 1907

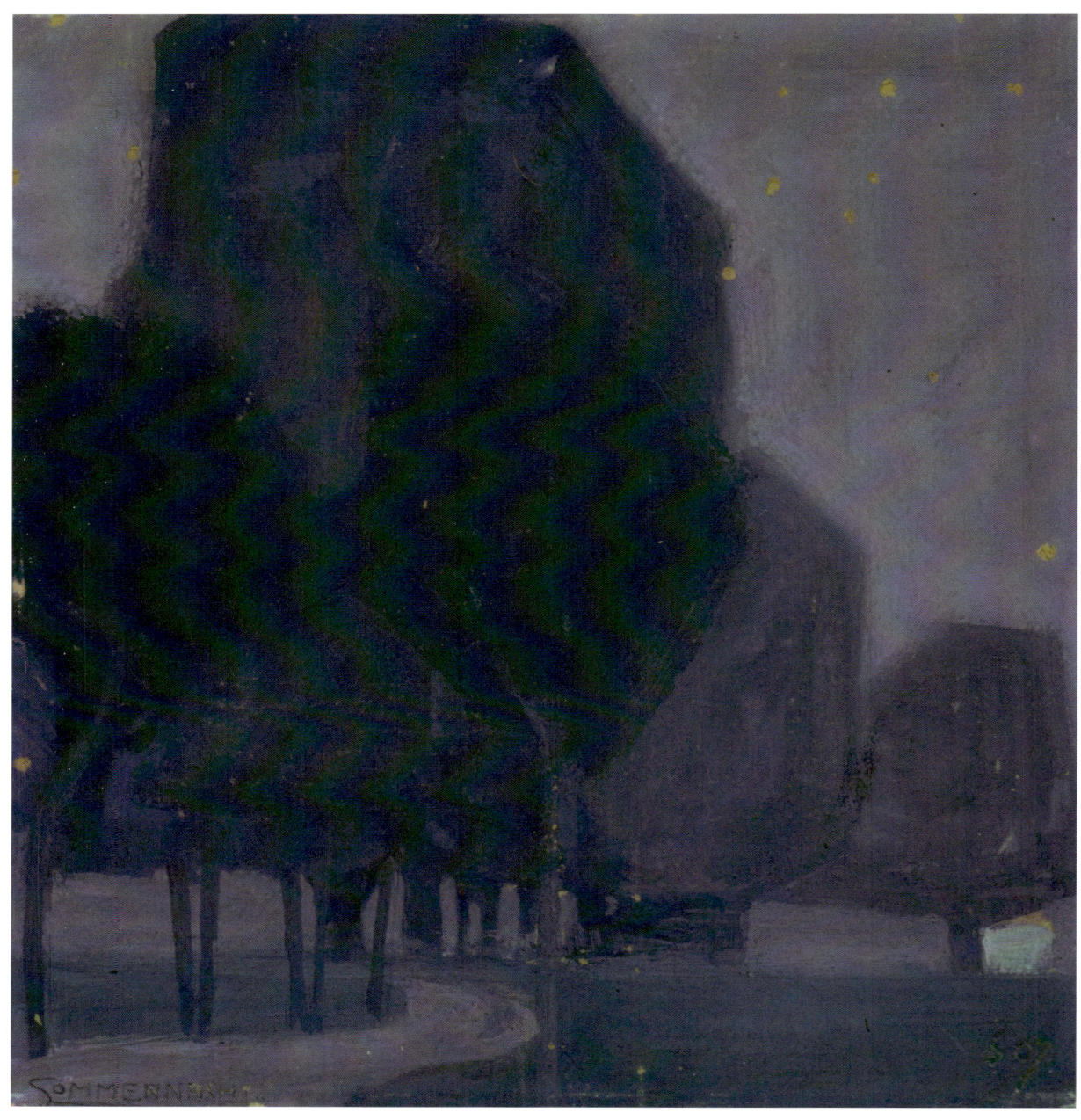

10. SUMMER NIGHT, 1907

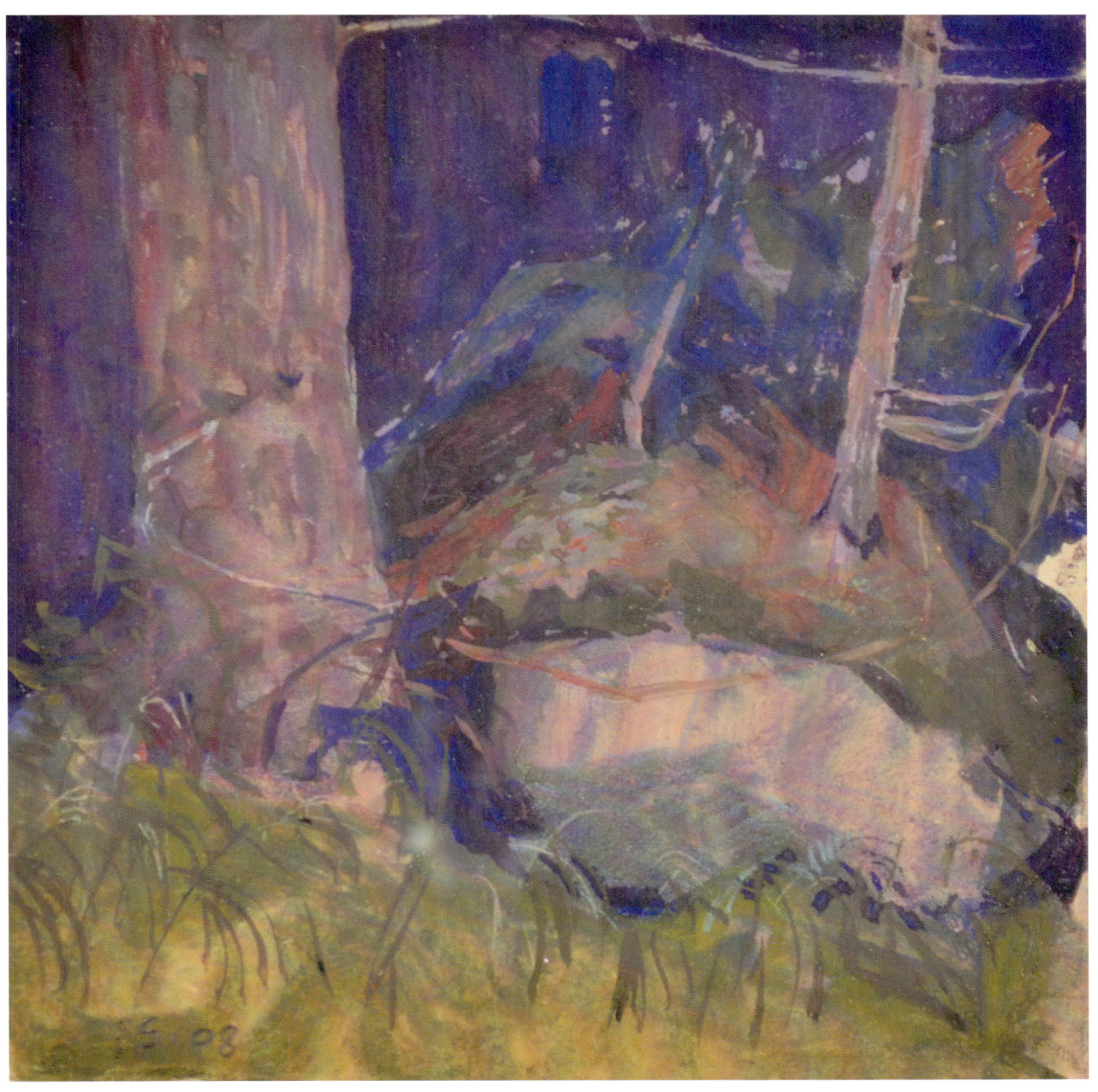

11. FOREST, HIRSCHBERGEN, 1908

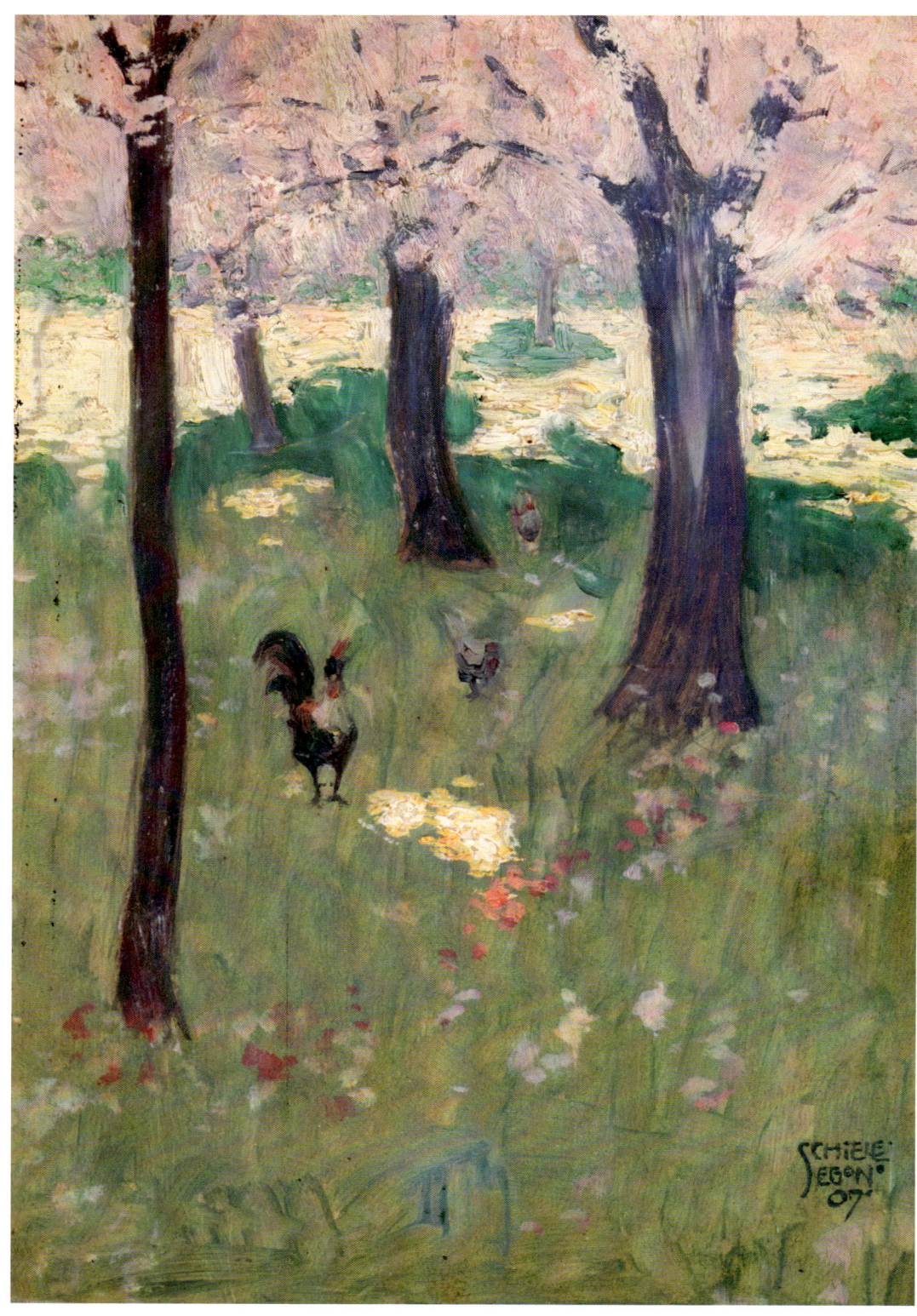

12. ORCHARD IN SPRING, 1907

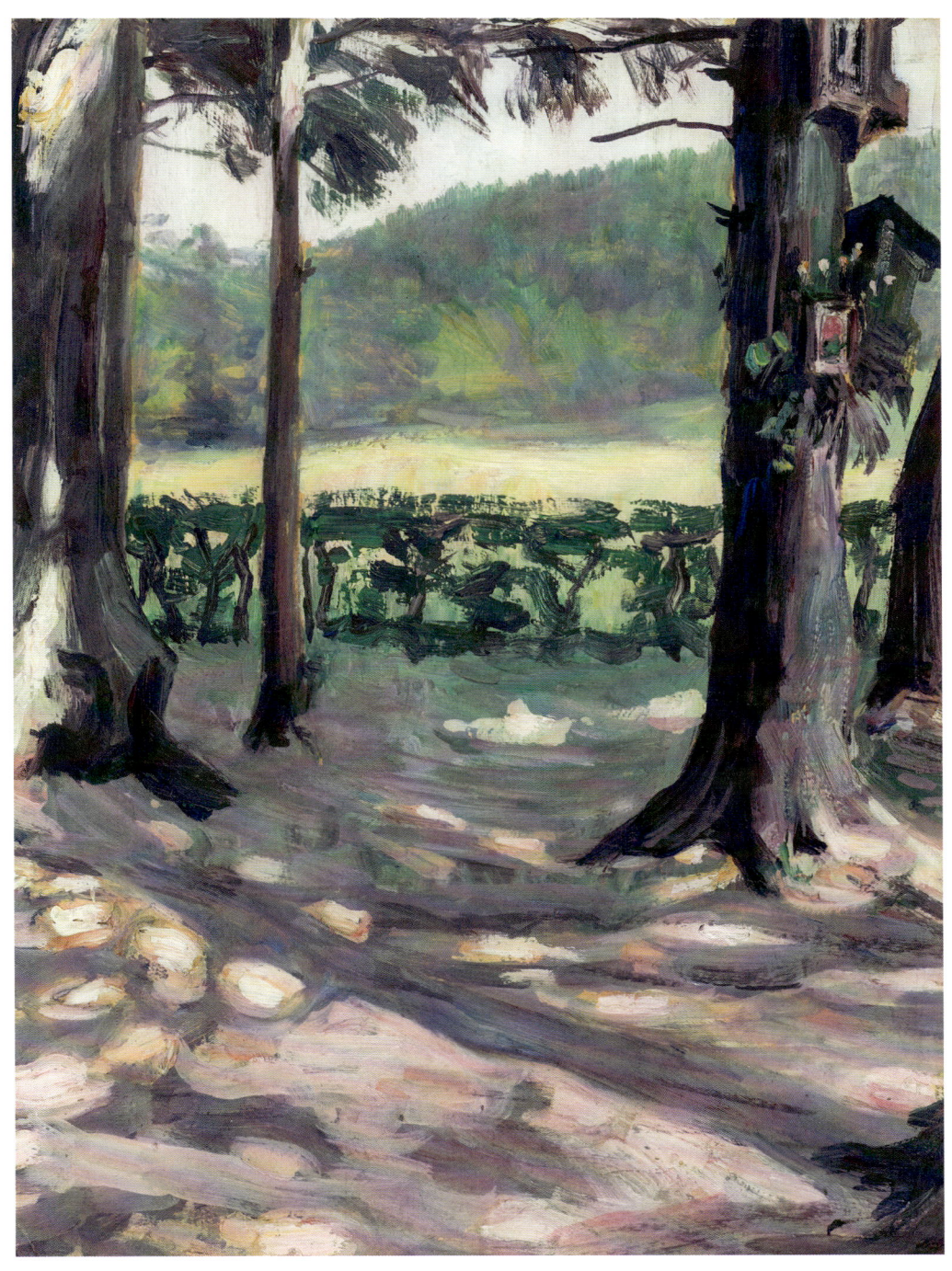

13. SHRINES IN THE FOREST I, 1907

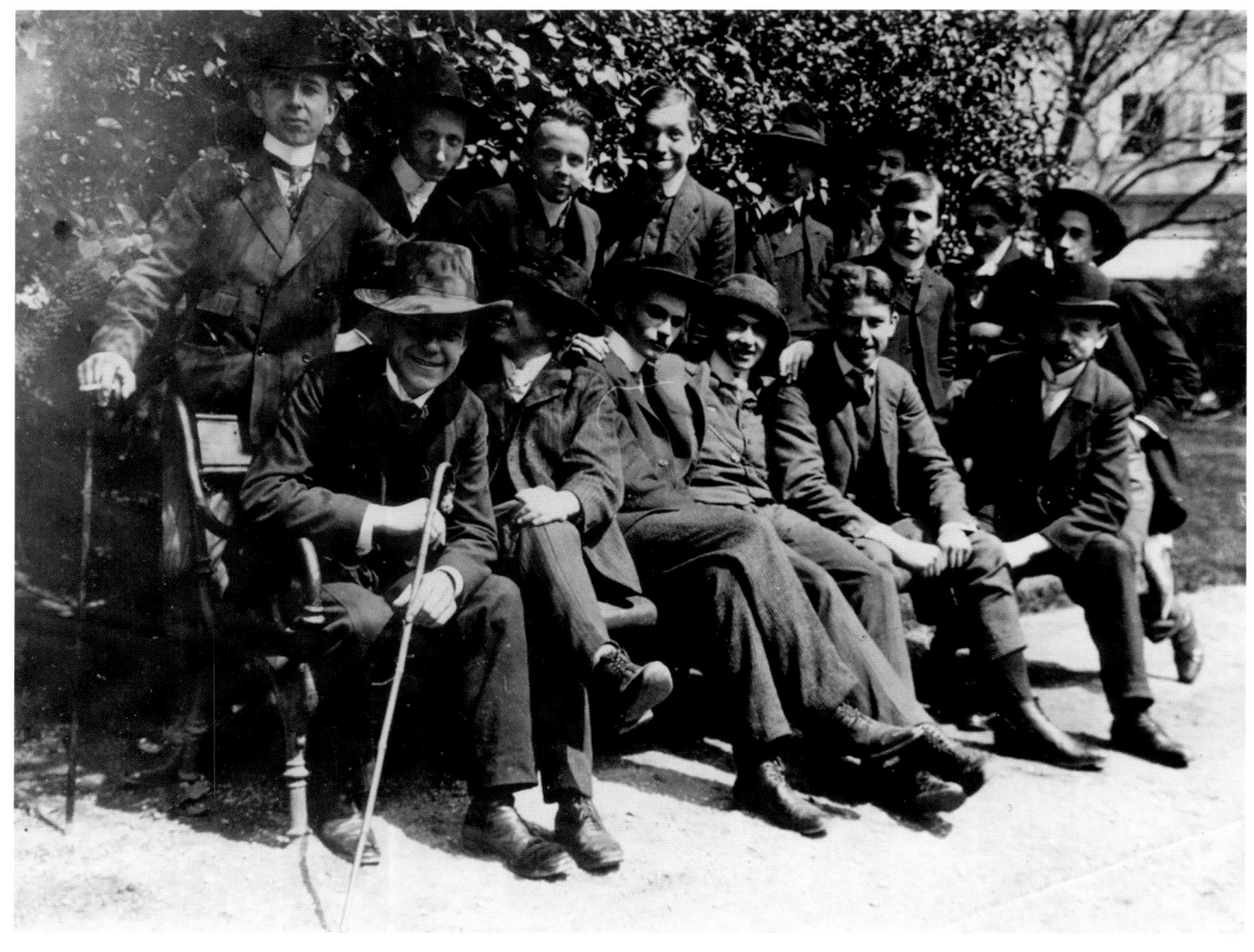

**14. STUDENTS FROM VIENNA'S ACADEMY OF FINE ARTS AT THE SCHILLERPLATZ, JUNE 1907.
SECOND ROW, FROM RIGHT: ANTON FAISTAUER AND EGON SCHIELE**

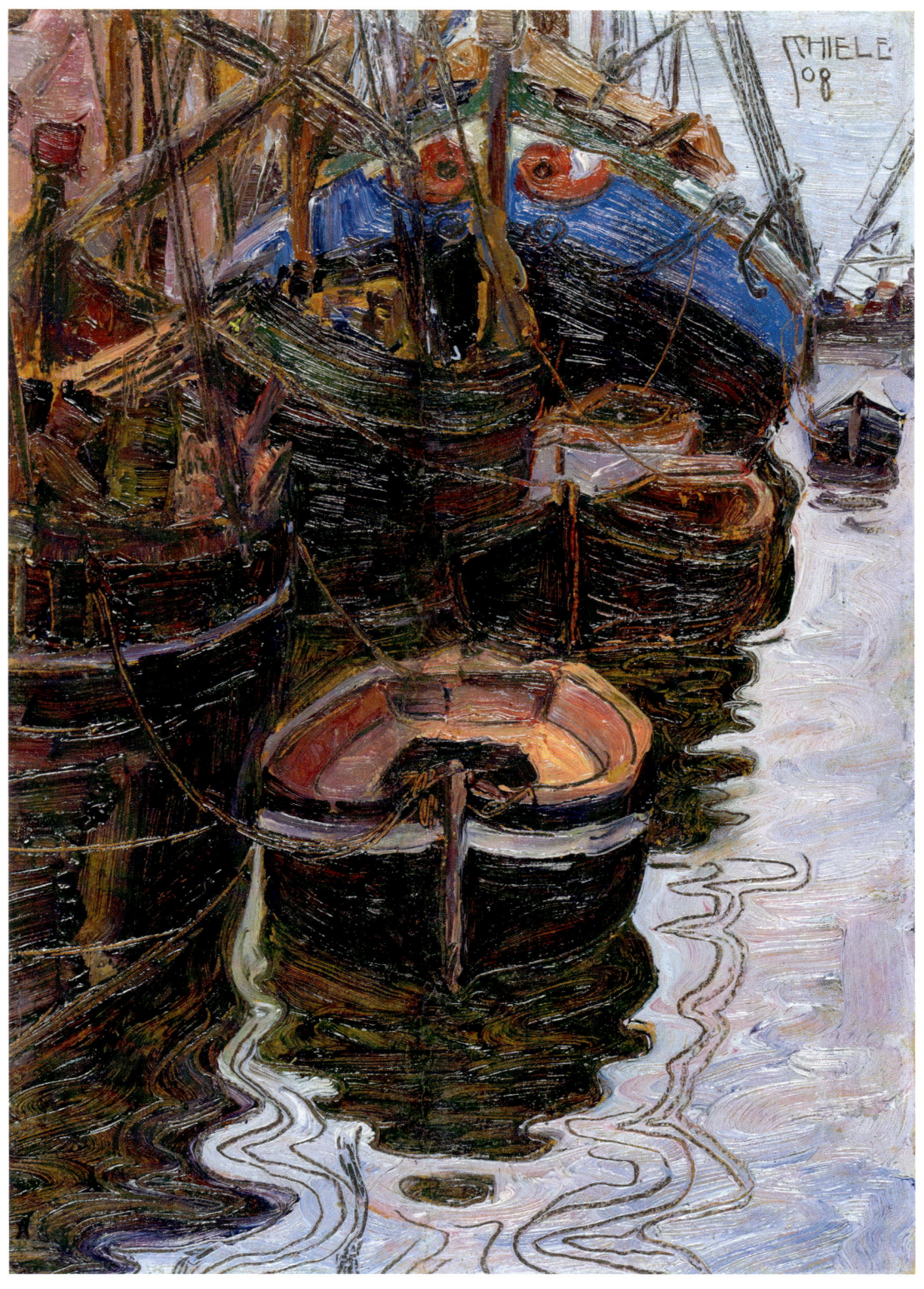

15. BOATS IN THE HARBOR (TRIESTE), 1908

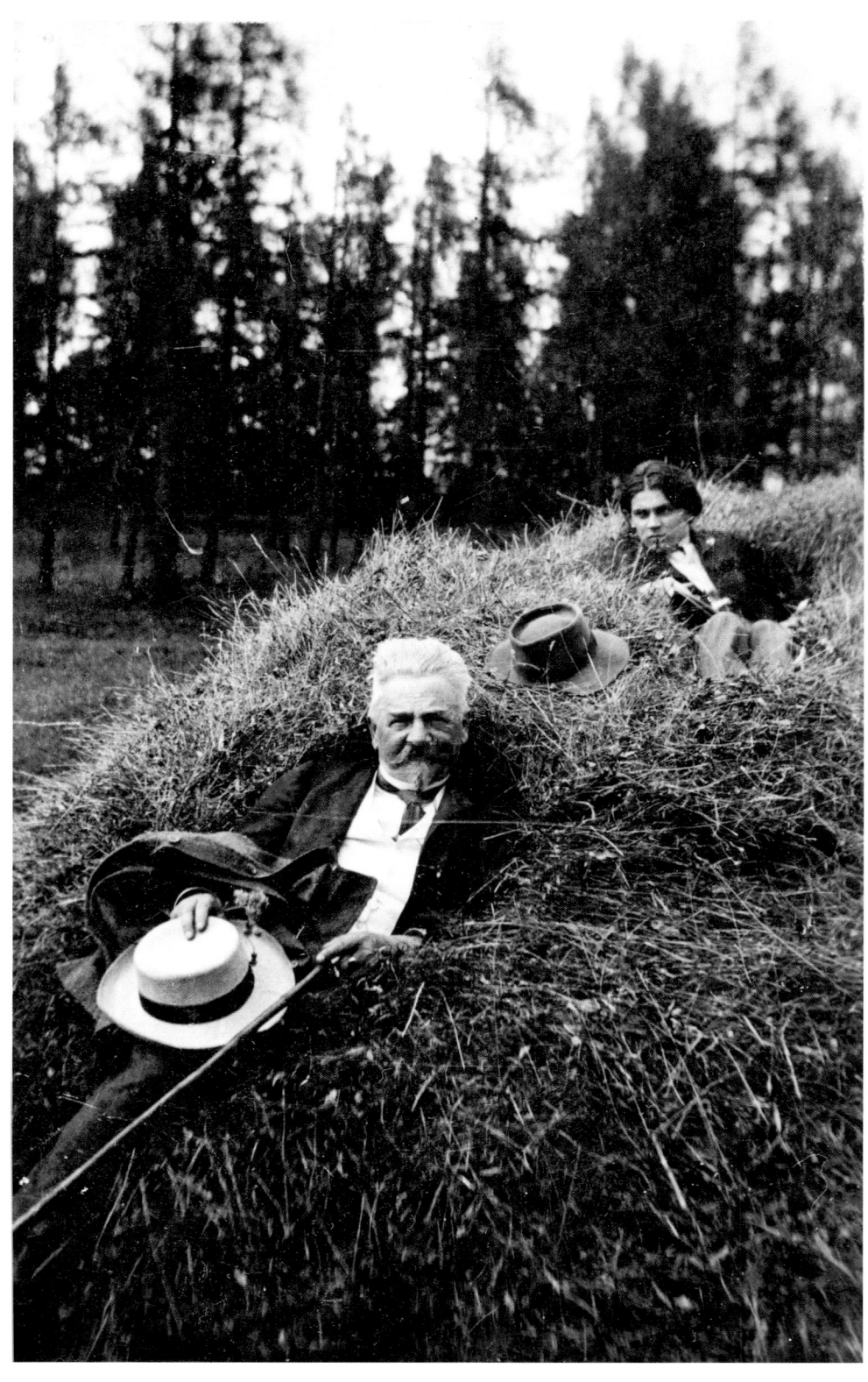

16. EGON SCHIELE IN A HAYSTACK WITH HIS UNCLE LEOPOLD CZIHACZEK, WHILE HIKING FROM NEULENGBACH TO HEGERBERG MOUNTAIN NEAR BÖHEIMKIRCHEN, JULY 15, 1908

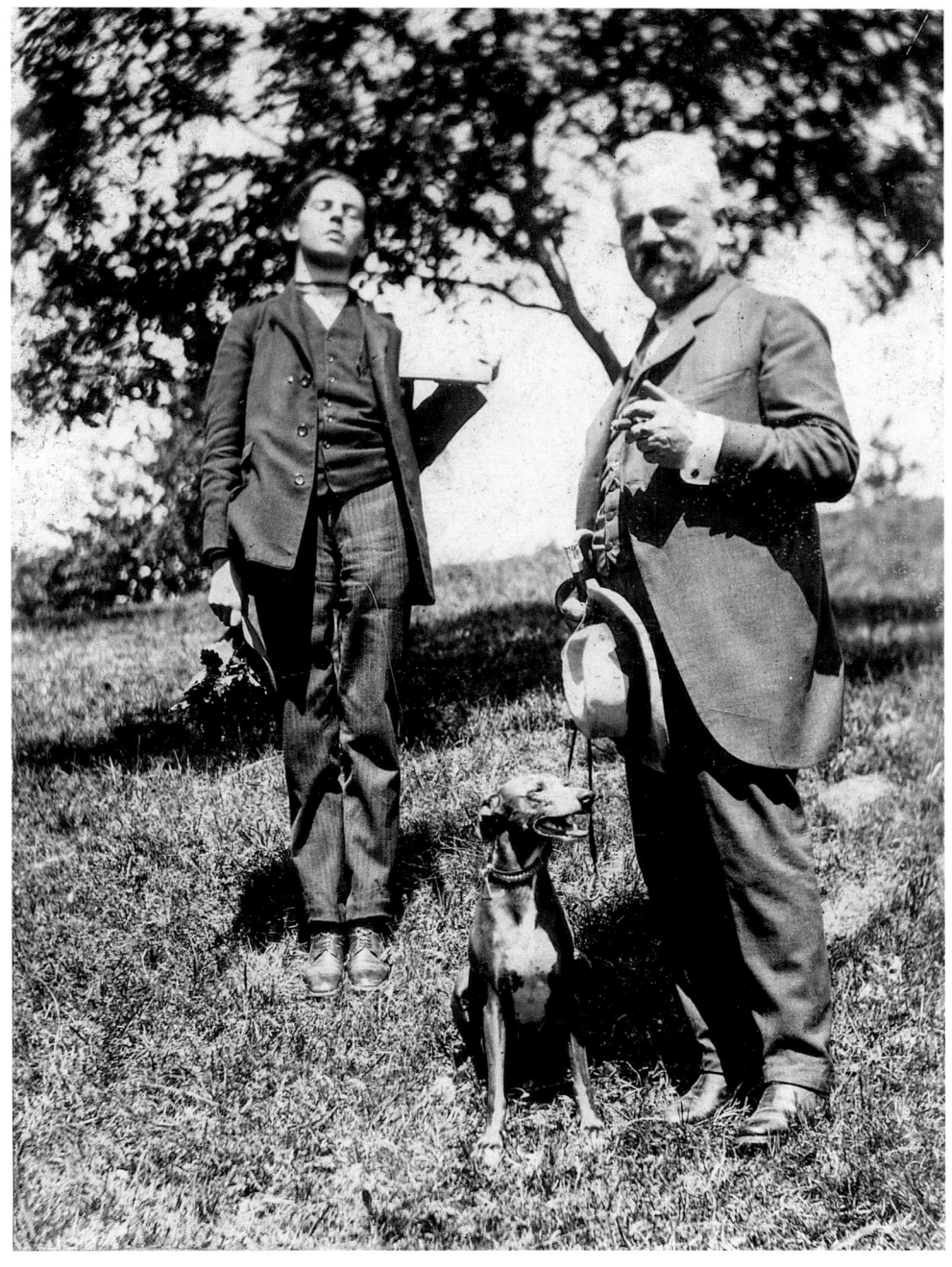

17. EGON SCHIELE WITH HIS UNCLE LEOPOLD CZIHACZEK AND HIS DOG MIRO (MURL) HIKING FROM THE VILLA WUNDSAM IN NEULENGBACH TO THE BUCHBERG MOUNTAIN, JULY 11, 1908

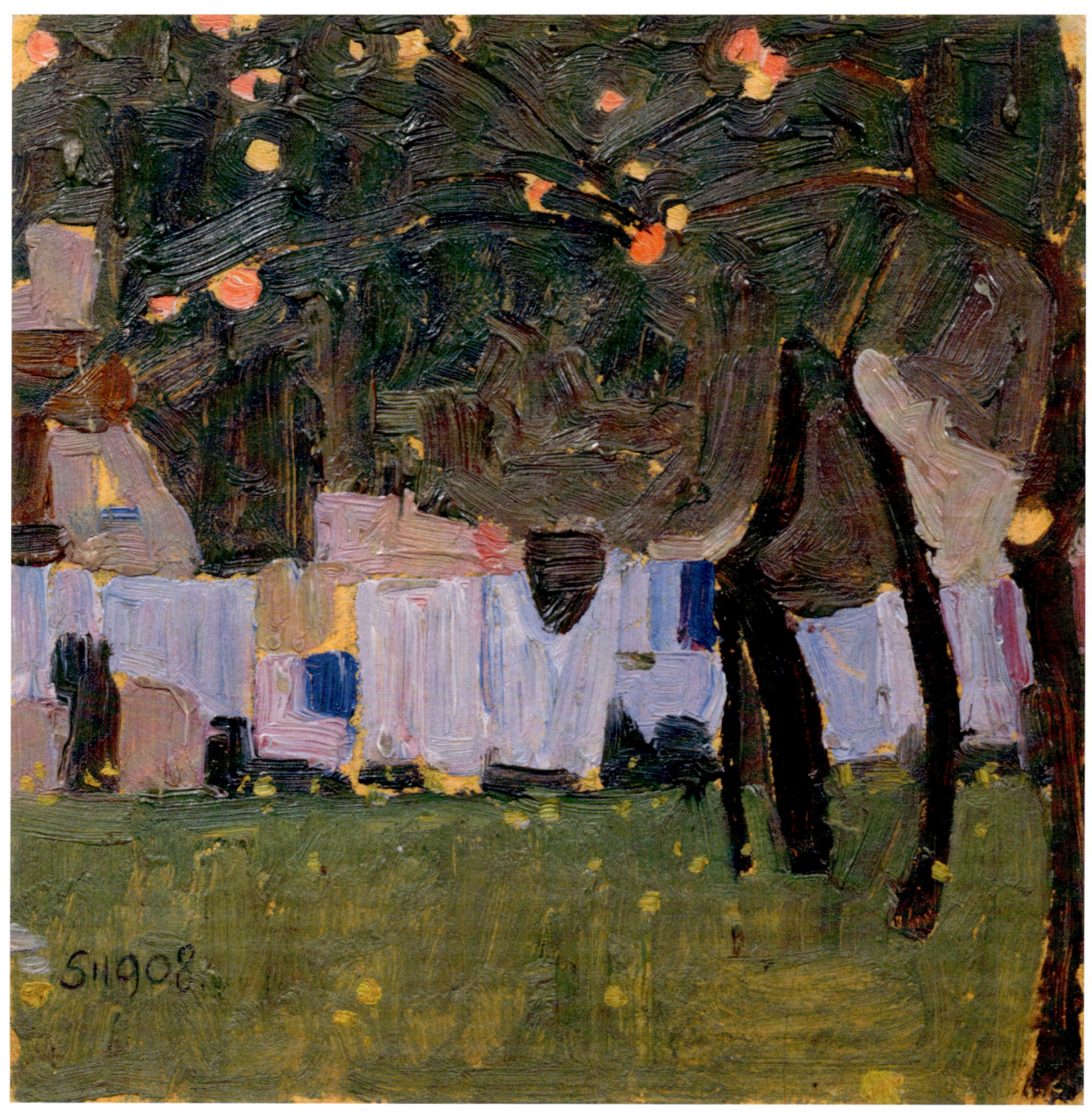

18. DRYING LAUNDRY, 1908

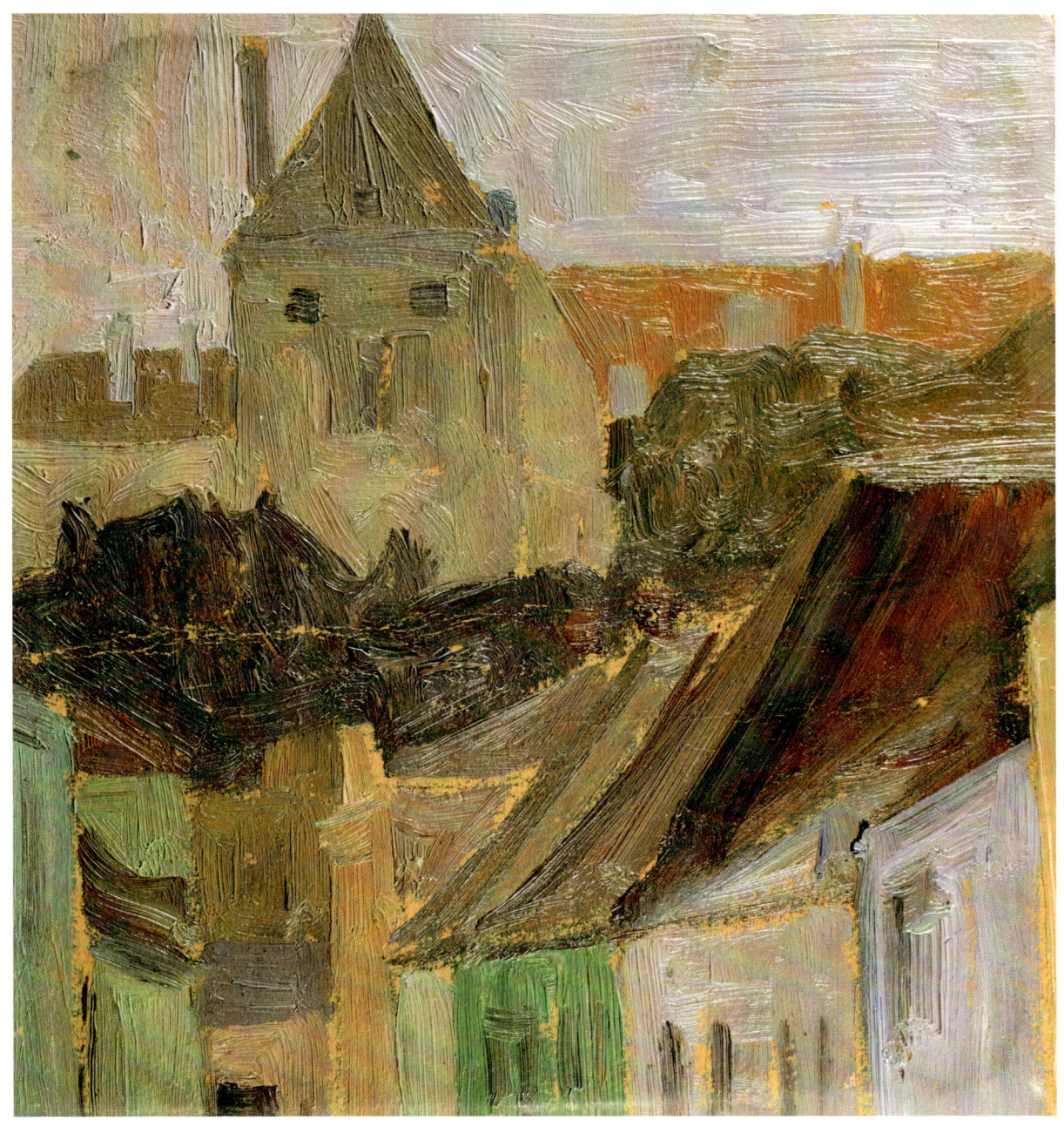

19. STUDY OF HOUSES (HOFKIRCHNERGASSE, KLOSTERNEUBURG), 1908

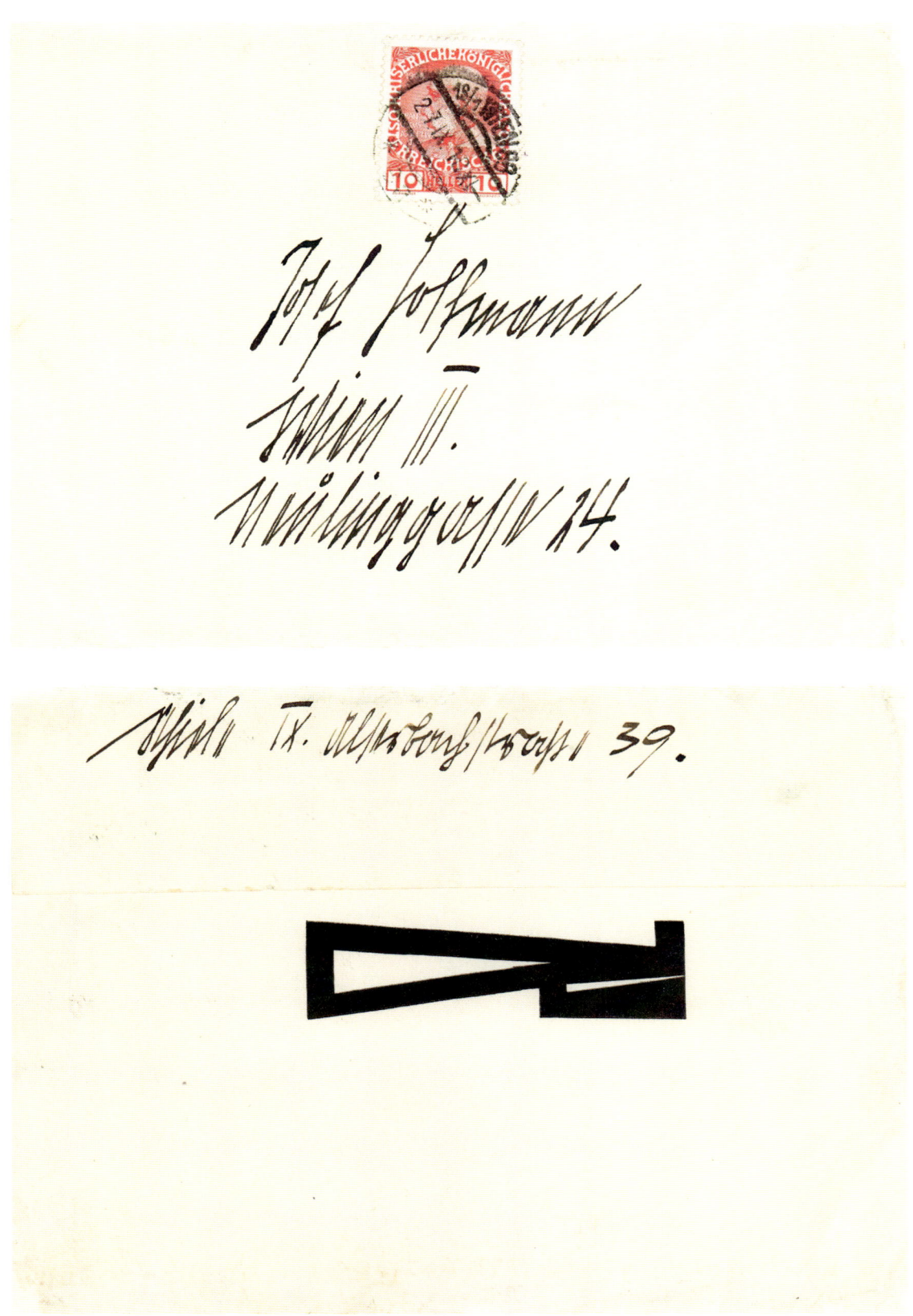

20. LETTER TO JOSEF HOFFMANN, SEPTEMBER 20, 1910

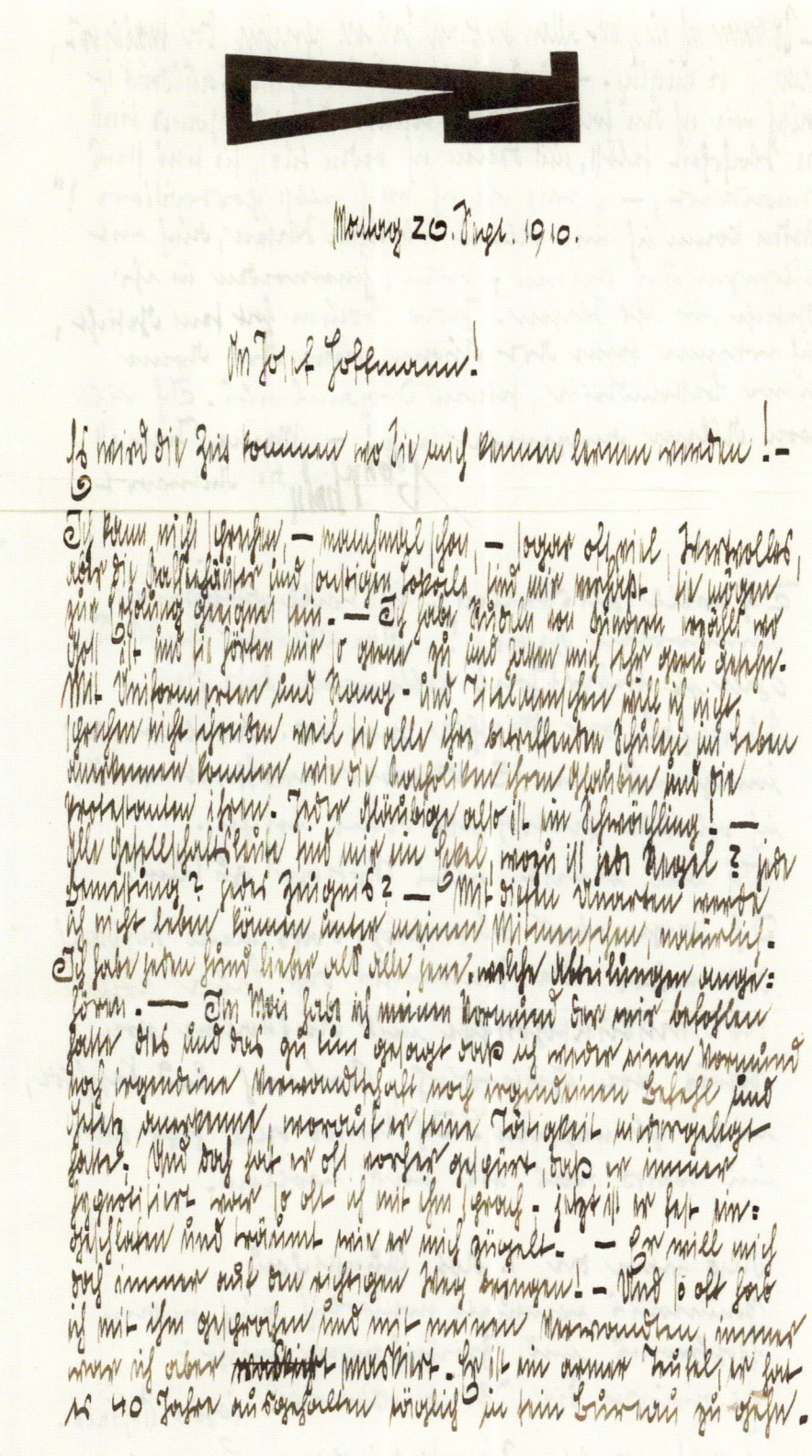

Montag 20. Sept. 1910.

An Josef Hoffmann!
Es wird die Zeit kommen wo Sie mich kennen lernen werden! –
Ich kann nicht sprechen, – manchmal schon, – sogar oft viel
Wertvolles, aber die Kaffeehäuser und sonstigen Lokale sind
mir verhaßt, sie mögen zur Erholung geeignet sein. – Ich habe
Rudeln von Kindern erzählt wo Gott ist und sie hörten mir so
gerne zu und hatten mich sehr gern gesehn. Mit Uniformierten
und Rang- und Titelmenschen will ich nicht sprechen nicht
schreiben weil sie alle ihre betreffenden Schulen im Leben
anerkennen konnten wie die Katholiken ihren Glauben und die
Protestanten ihren. Jeder Gläubige also ist ein Schwächling! –
Alle Gesellschaftsleute sind mir ein Ekel, wozu ist jede Regel?
Jede Bemessung? Jedes Zeugnis? – Mit diesen Unarten werde
ich nicht leben können unter meinen Mitmenschen, natürlich.
Ich habe jeden Hund lieber als alle jene, welche Abteilungen
angehören. – Im Mai habe ich meinen Vormund der mir befohlen
hatte dies und das zu tun gesagt daß ich weder einen Vormund
noch irgendeine Verwandtschaft noch irgendeinen Befehl und
Gesetz anerkenne, worauf er seine Tätigkeit niedergelegt hatte;
Und doch hat er oft vorher gespürt, daß er immer hypnotisiert
war so oft ich mit ihm sprach; jetzt ist er fest eingeschlafen und
träumt wie er mich zügelt. – Er will mich doch immer auf den
richtigen Weg bringen! – Und so oft hab ich mit ihm gesprochen
und mit meinen Verwandten, immer war ich aber maskiert. Er ist
ein armer Teufel, er hat es 40 Jahre ausgehalten täglich in sein
Bureau zu gehn.

■

Monday, Sept. 20, 1910.

To Josef Hoffmann!
A time will come when you will get to know me!—
I cannot speak—sometimes I can—often something worthwhile,
even, but the coffeehouses and other such places are odious
to me; they may be suitable for relaxation.—I have told packs
of children where God is, and they enjoyed listening to me so
much and liked seeing me very much. I don't want to speak or
write to people in uniform and those of rank and title, because
they were able to unquestioningly accept all of their respective
schools in life like the Catholics their faith and the Protestants
theirs. Every believer is thus a weakling!—All society people are
disgusting to me; what is each rule for? Every measurement?
Every certificate?—With such behavior, I will not be able to live
among my fellow humans, of course. I like any dog more than
all those who belong to some department.—In May I told my
legal guardian, who would order me to do this and that, that I
do not recognize any guardian nor any kind of relatives nor any
kind of order or law, upon which he resigned from this post; but
even before that he often sensed that he was always hypnotized
whenever I spoke with him; now he has fallen soundly asleep
and is dreaming of how he can rein me in.—He always wants to
get me on the right path!—And I have spoken with him and with
my relatives so often, but I was always masked. Poor devil—how
has he endured going to his office every day for forty years!

– So kann ich auch mit allen andern Leuten sprechen, doch maskiert, dann ist es möglich. – Und wie vieler Leute Gesichtsausdruck ist falsch wie ich den falschen haben kann. Aber die Hände sind die Wahrheit selbst, mit denen ich reden tue, sie sind stets demaskiert, – ‚wie oft ich mich selbst porträtiere!' Reden kann ich mit allen lebenden Wesen, auch mit Pflanzen und Steinen; reden, hineinreden in ihr Gesicht, in ihr Wesen. Jeder Baum hat sein Gesicht, ich erkenne seine Art Augen, seine Art Arme seine Bestandteile, seinen Organismus. Ich will von Allem angeredet sein! – Meine Tat ist die Antwort.
Egon Schiele

Ich will ausstellen, ich will größere Antworten geben! Im Oktober in Wien. Geht es lieber H. Josef Hoffmann daß die Kunstschau bei Miethke am 10. Oktober oder längstens am 15. Oktober eröffnet wird? Ich glaube fertig ist alles leicht. Ich bin bereit alles Nötige zu tun. Ich sage aber aufrichtig, daß mein Wunsch der wäre, die Panneaus der Leute von der Neukunstgruppe mit Ausnahme von Paris von Gütersloh, Kalvach und Peschka nicht zu nehmen. Ich kenne alle sehr gut und weiß was sie nur wollen.

Also wäre die I. Abt. Kunstschau Panneaus eventuell natürlich auch anderes Figurales und Zeichnungen, nicht? Es grüßt Sie Ihr dankbarer Egon Schiele.

Bitte! Verkaufen Sie mir bei Gelegenheit wieder einmal etwas ich möchte ausziehn und mich rühren können.

■

–I can speak with everyone else this way as well, but only masked, then it is possible.—And how many people have a false facial expression, just as mine can be false. But truth is in the hands with which I speak; they are always unmasked—"how often I portray myself!" I can speak with all living creatures, even with plants and stones; speak, speak into their face, into their essence. Every tree has its face; I recognize its kind of eyes, its kind of arms, its components, its organism. I want to be addressed by everything!–My act is the answer.
Egon Schiele

I want to exhibit. I want to give greater answers! In October in Vienna. Would it be possible, dear Herr Josef Hoffmann, for the Kunstschau at Miethke to open on October 10 or on October 15 at the latest? I think that everything will easily be ready. I am prepared to do everything necessary. But I tell you sincerely that my wish would be not to accept paintings from the people of the Neukunstgruppe with the exception of Paris von Gütersloh, Kalvach, and Peschka. I know them all very well and know just what they want.

So, section I of the Kunstschau would show paintings, possibly of course other things as well, figural works and drawings, right?
Greetings from your grateful Egon Schiele.

Please! Sell something for me again if you have the opportunity. I want to move out and have some room to move.

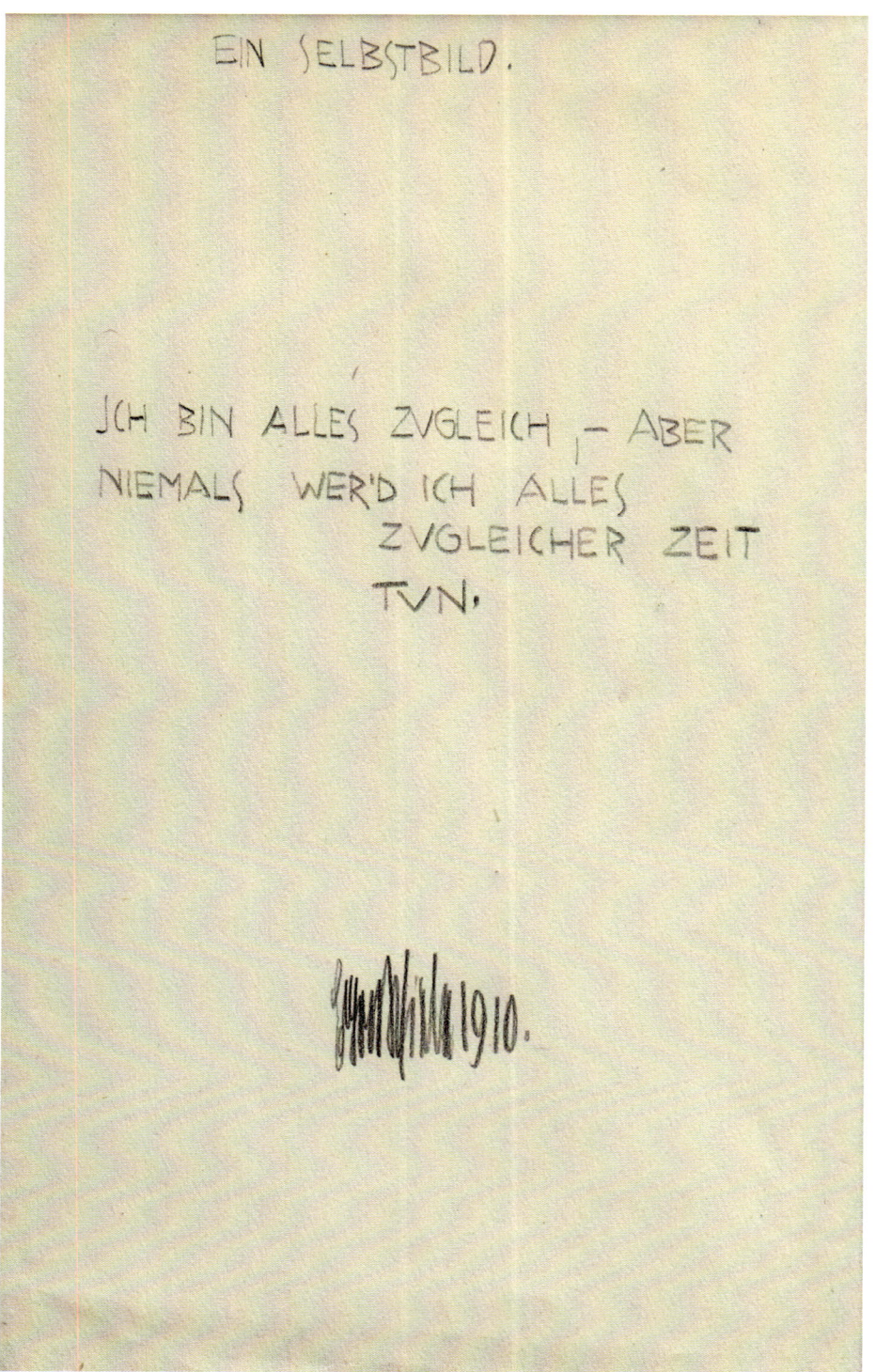

EIN SELBSTBILD.

ICH BIN ALLES ZUGLEICH, – ABER
NIEMALS WER'D ICH ALLES
ZUGLEICHER ZEIT
TUN.

Egon Schiele 1910.

■

A Self-Portrait

*I am everything at once—but
I will never do everything
at the same
time.*

Egon Schiele, May 1910

21. A SELF-PORTRAIT, 1910

GEWITTERANZUG.

SCHWARZE TRAUERWETTERWOLKEN ROLLTEN
ALLÜBERALL HOCH; WARNENDE WASSERWÄLDER,
        RAUNIGE HÜTTEN UND
        BRUMMBÄUME;
ICH GING GEGEN DEN SCHWARZEN BACH,
VÖGEL, GLEICH WIE FAHLE BLÄTTER
                        IM WIND.

Egon Schiele 1910.

■

Storm Brewing

Black mourning-weather clouds rolled
everywhere up high. Warning alluvial forests,
        desolate huts, and
        booming trees.
I walked toward the black stream.
Birds, just like pale leaves
                in the wind.

Egon Schiele, 1910

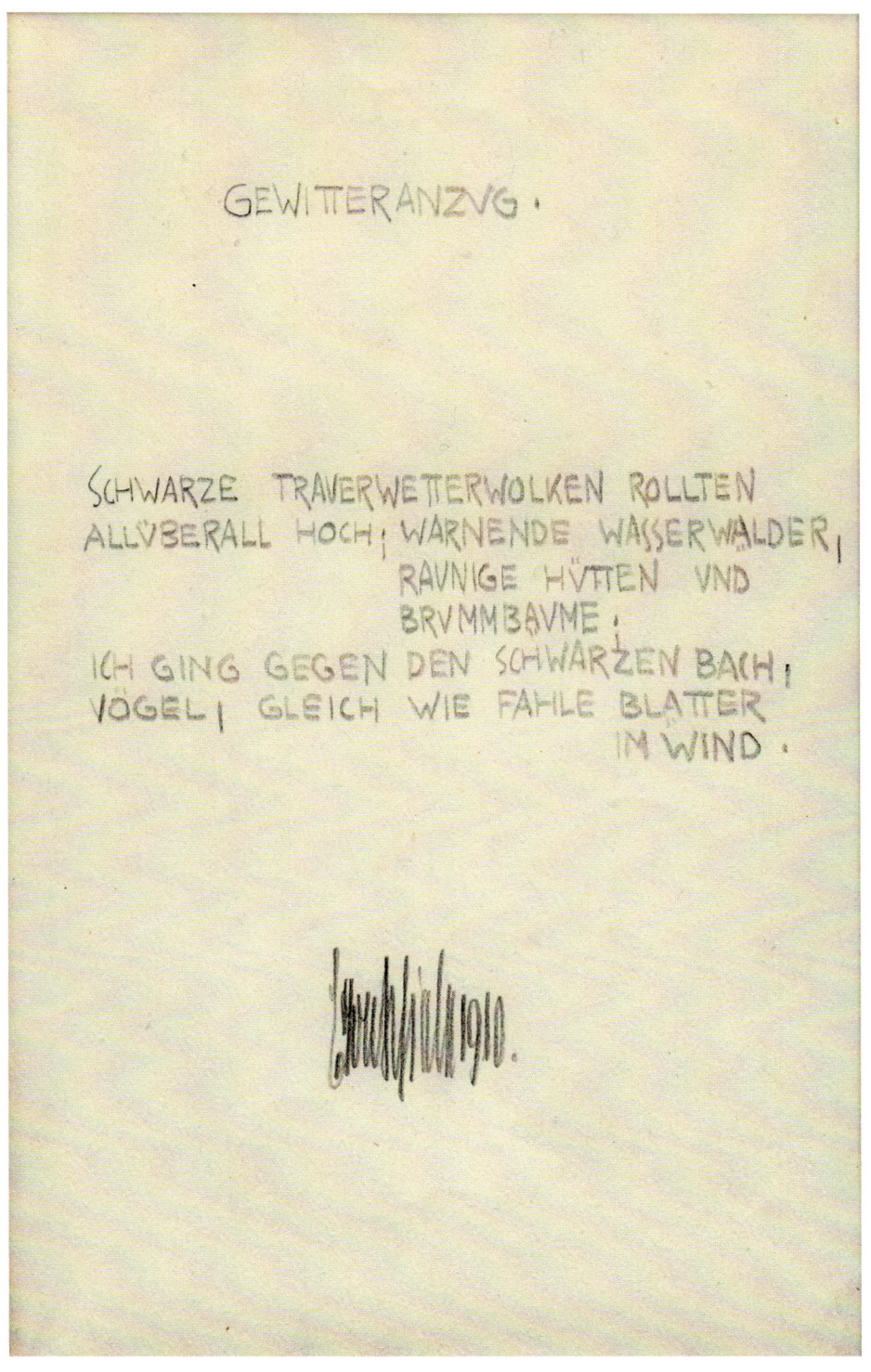

22. THUNDERSTORM, 1910

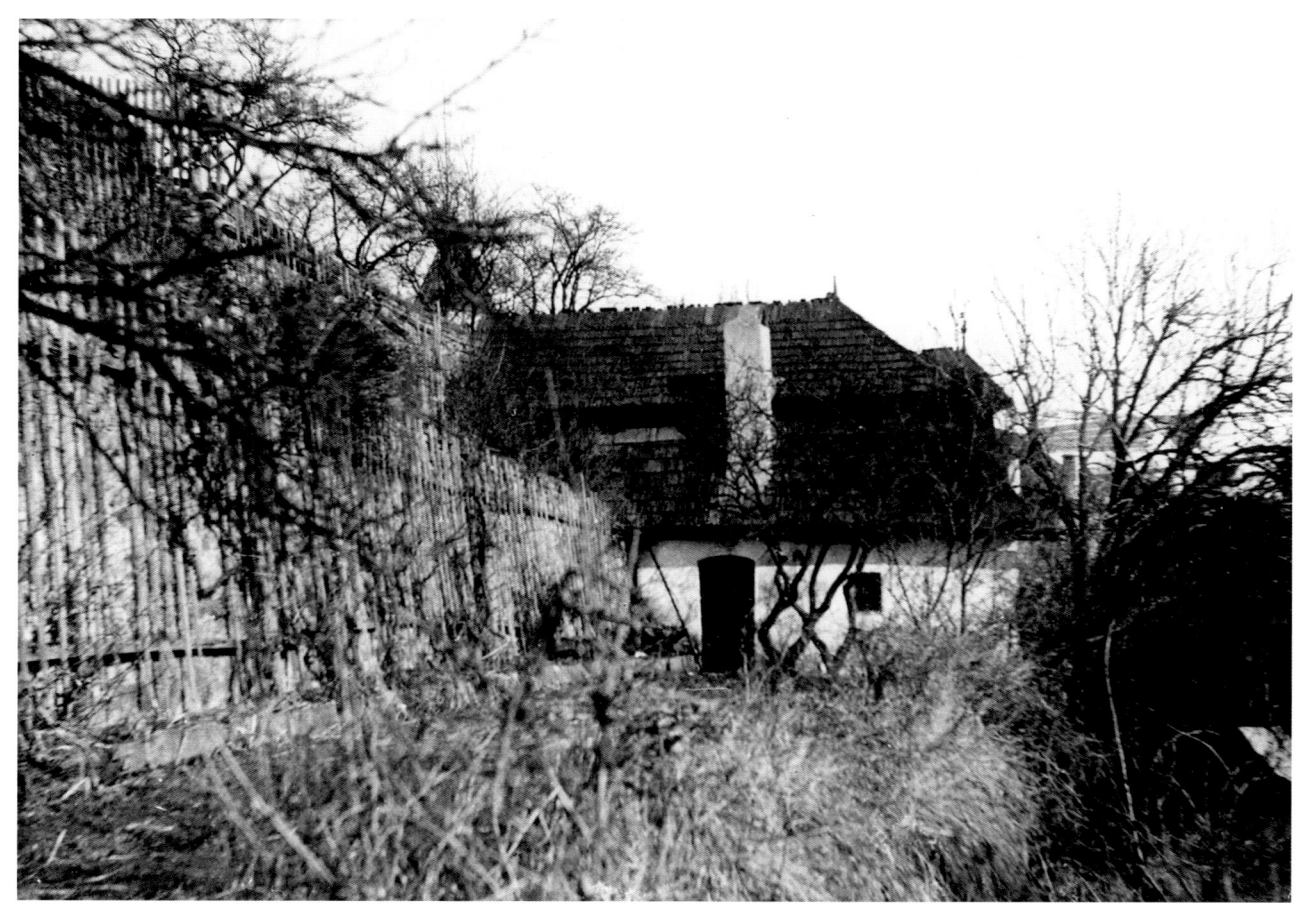

23. EGON SCHIELE'S GARDEN HOUSE IN KRUMAU, 1911

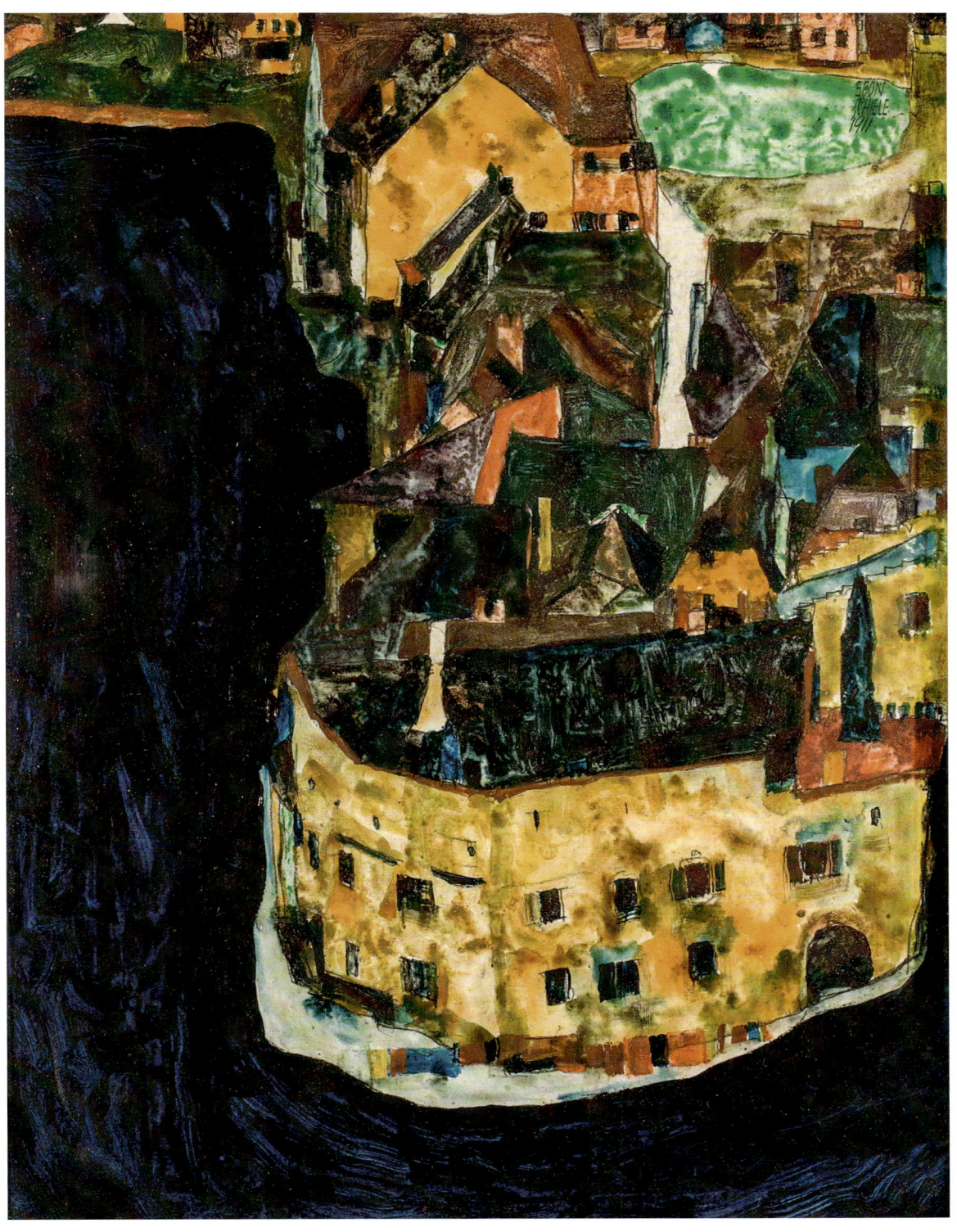

24. CITY ON THE BLUE RIVER II, 1911

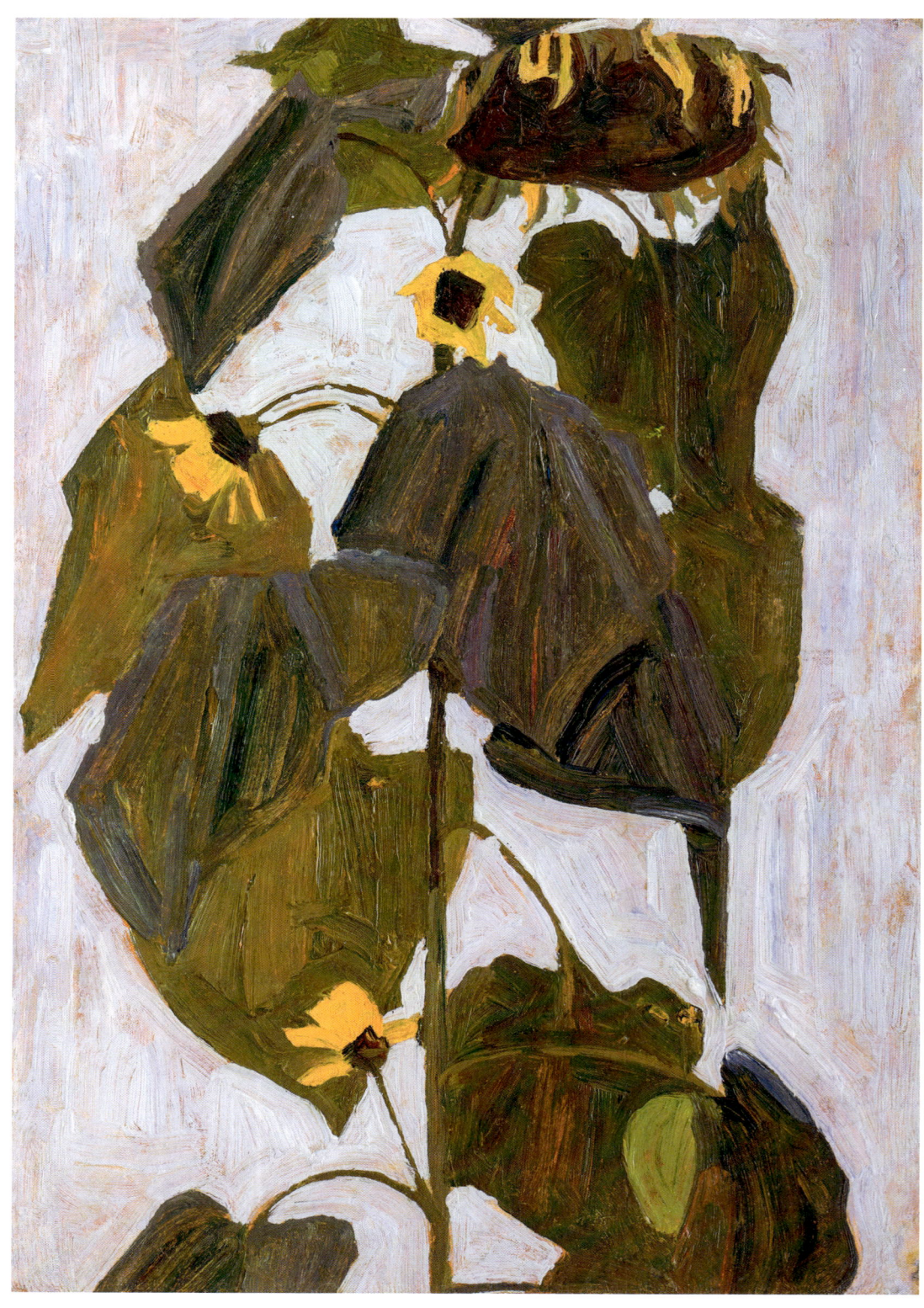

25. SUNFLOWER I, 1908

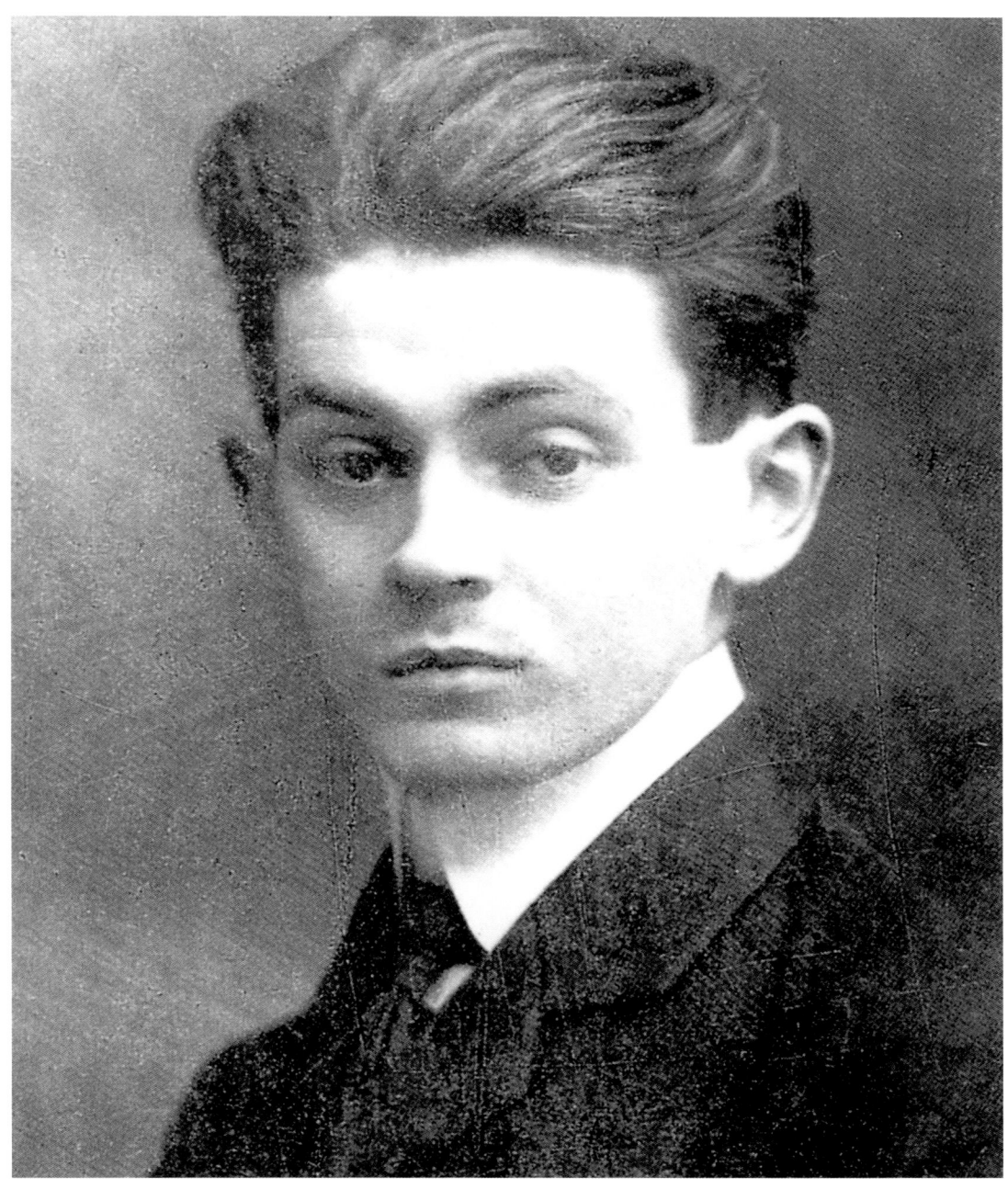

26. EGON SCHIELE, 1909

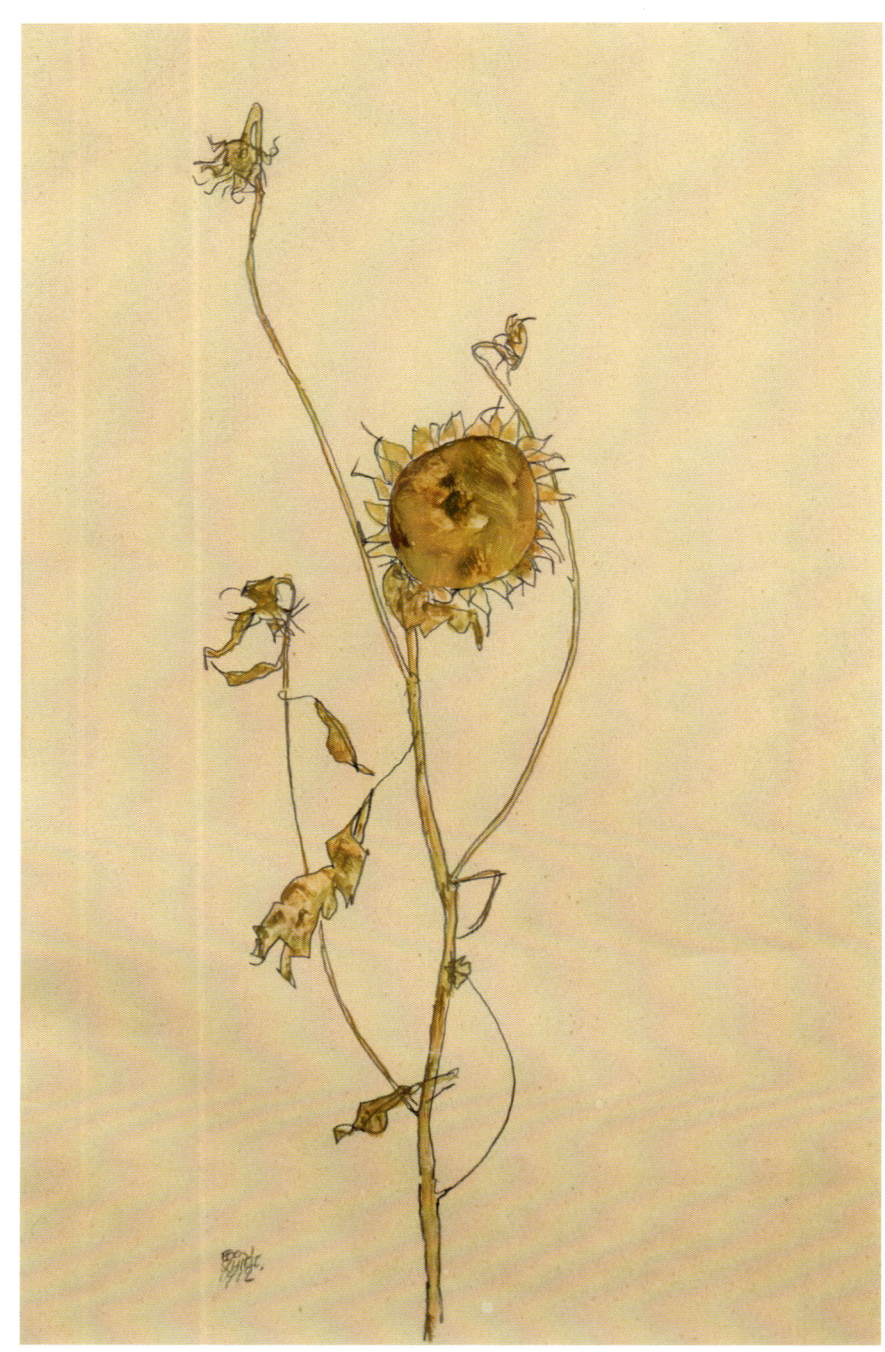

27. WILTED SUNFLOWER, 1912

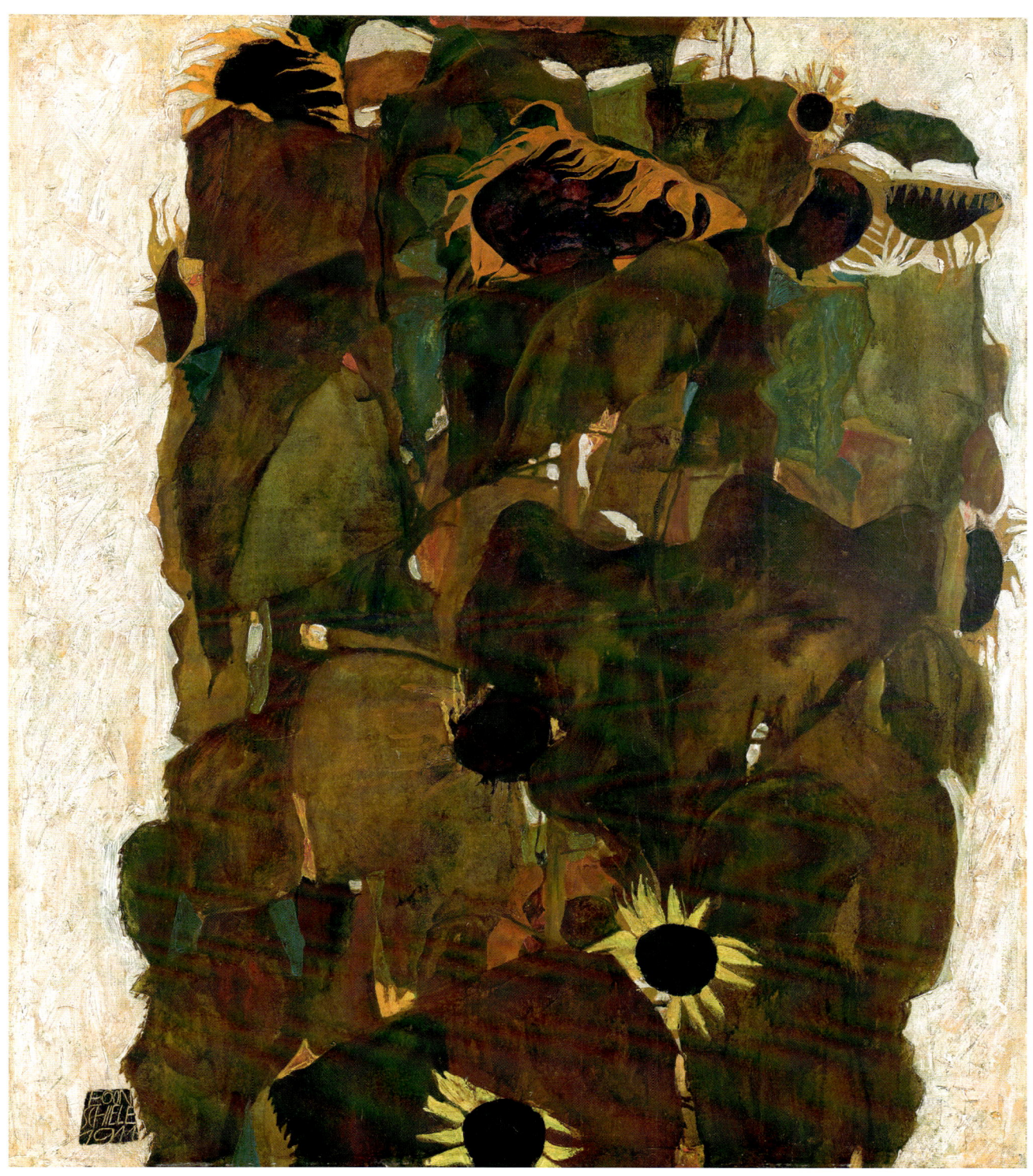

28. SUNFLOWERS, 1911

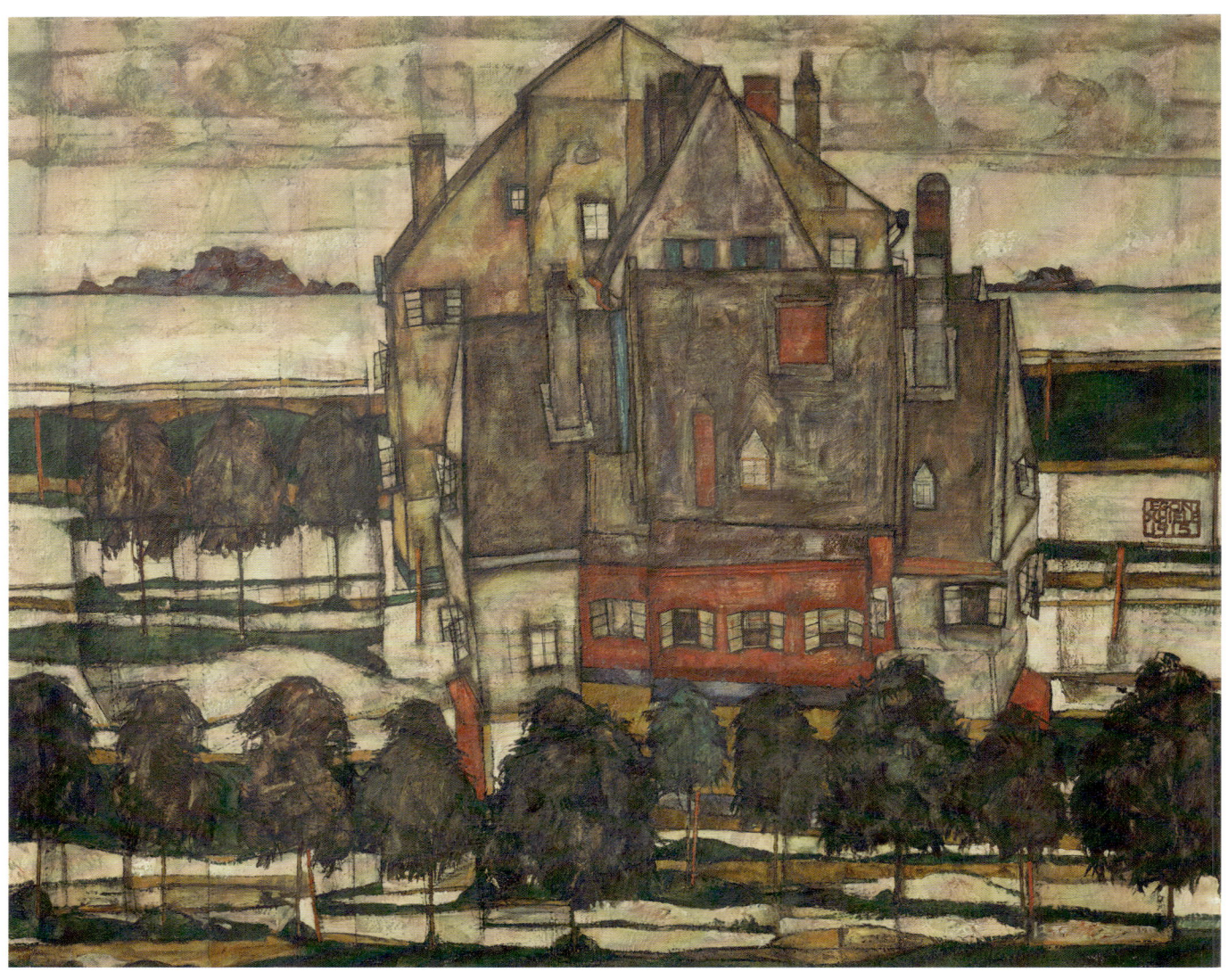

29. SINGLE HOUSES (HOUSES WITH MOUNTAINS), 1915

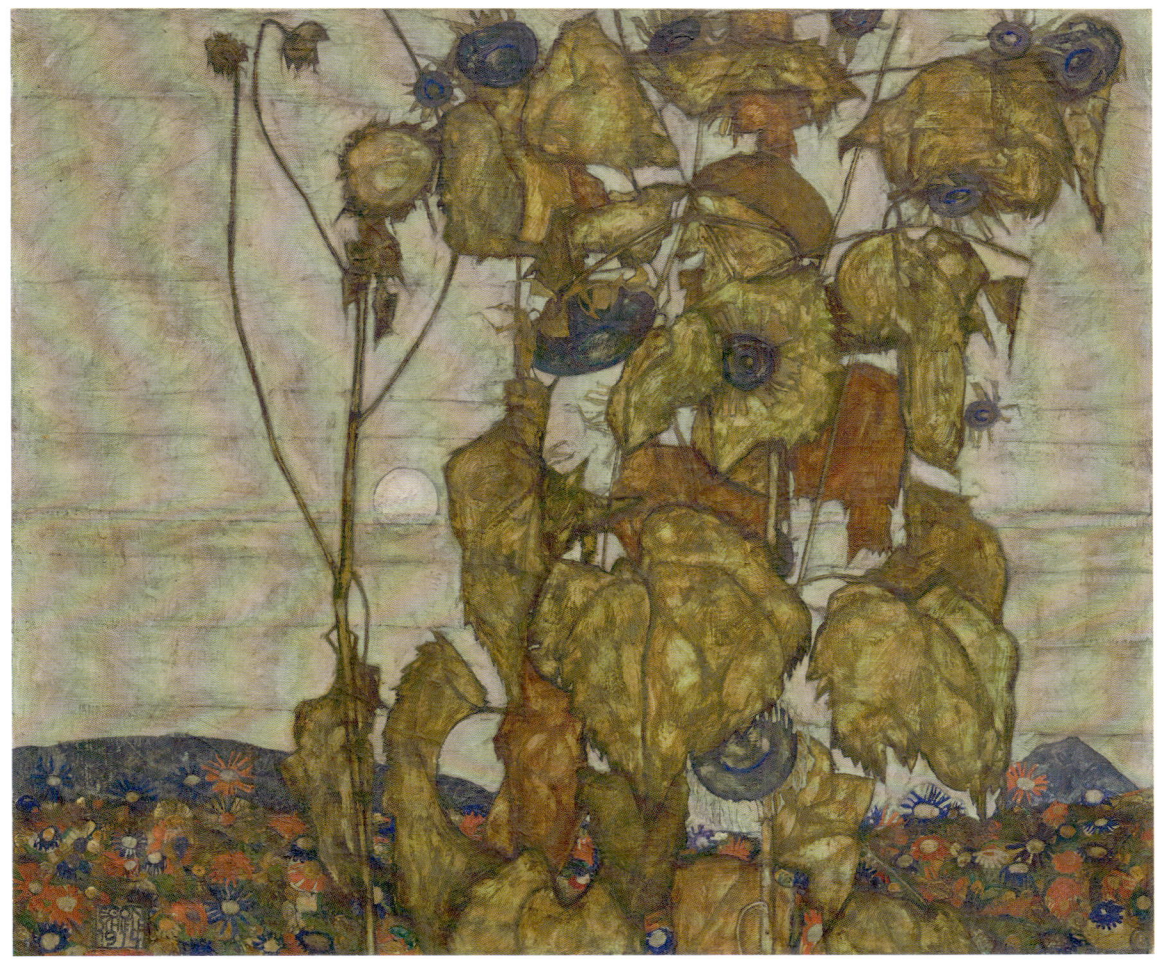

30. WILTED SUNFLOWERS (AUTUMN SUN II), 1914

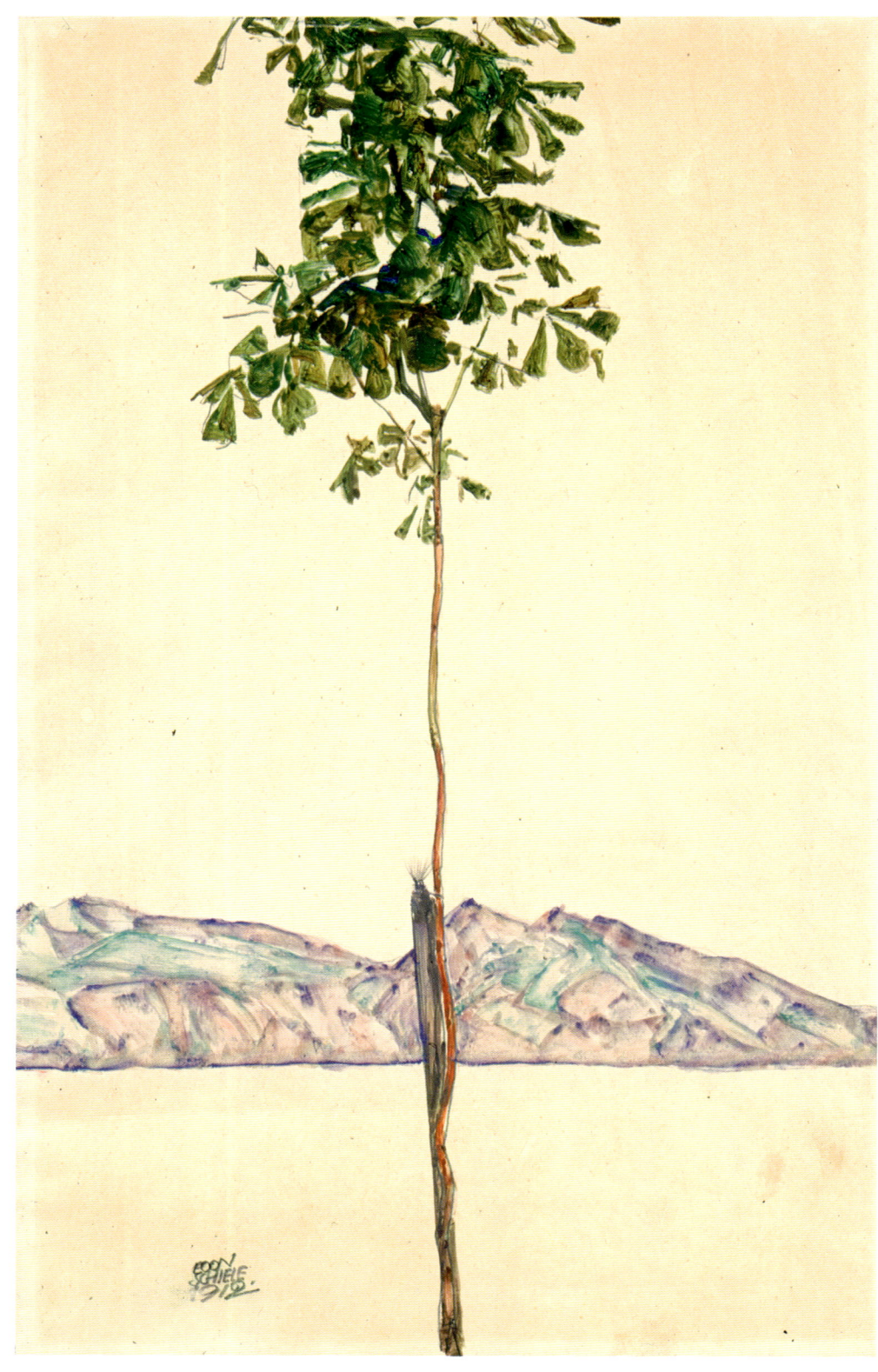

31. LITTLE TREE (CHESTNUT TREE AT LAKE CONSTANCE), 1912

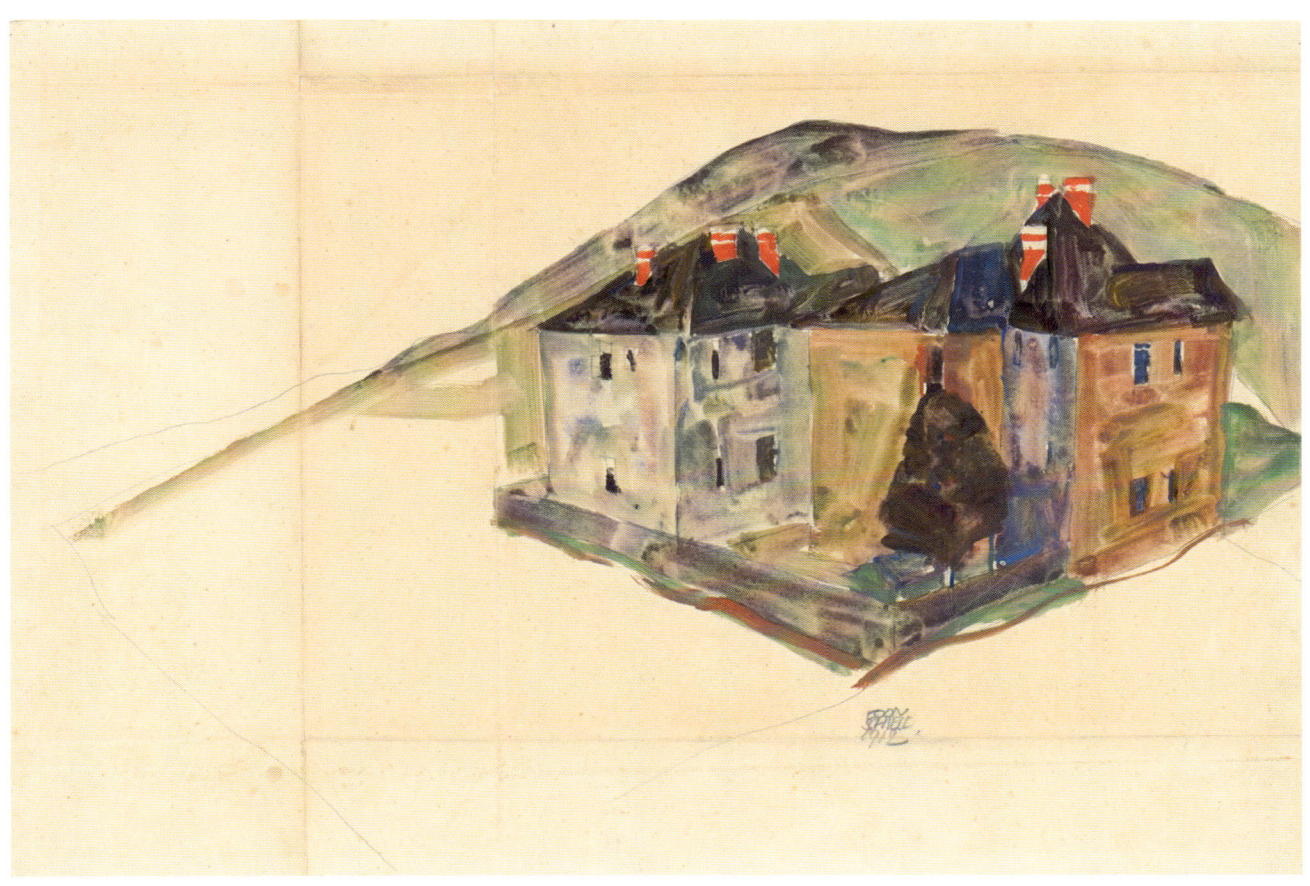

32. GROUP OF HOUSES ON A MOUNTAIN, 1912

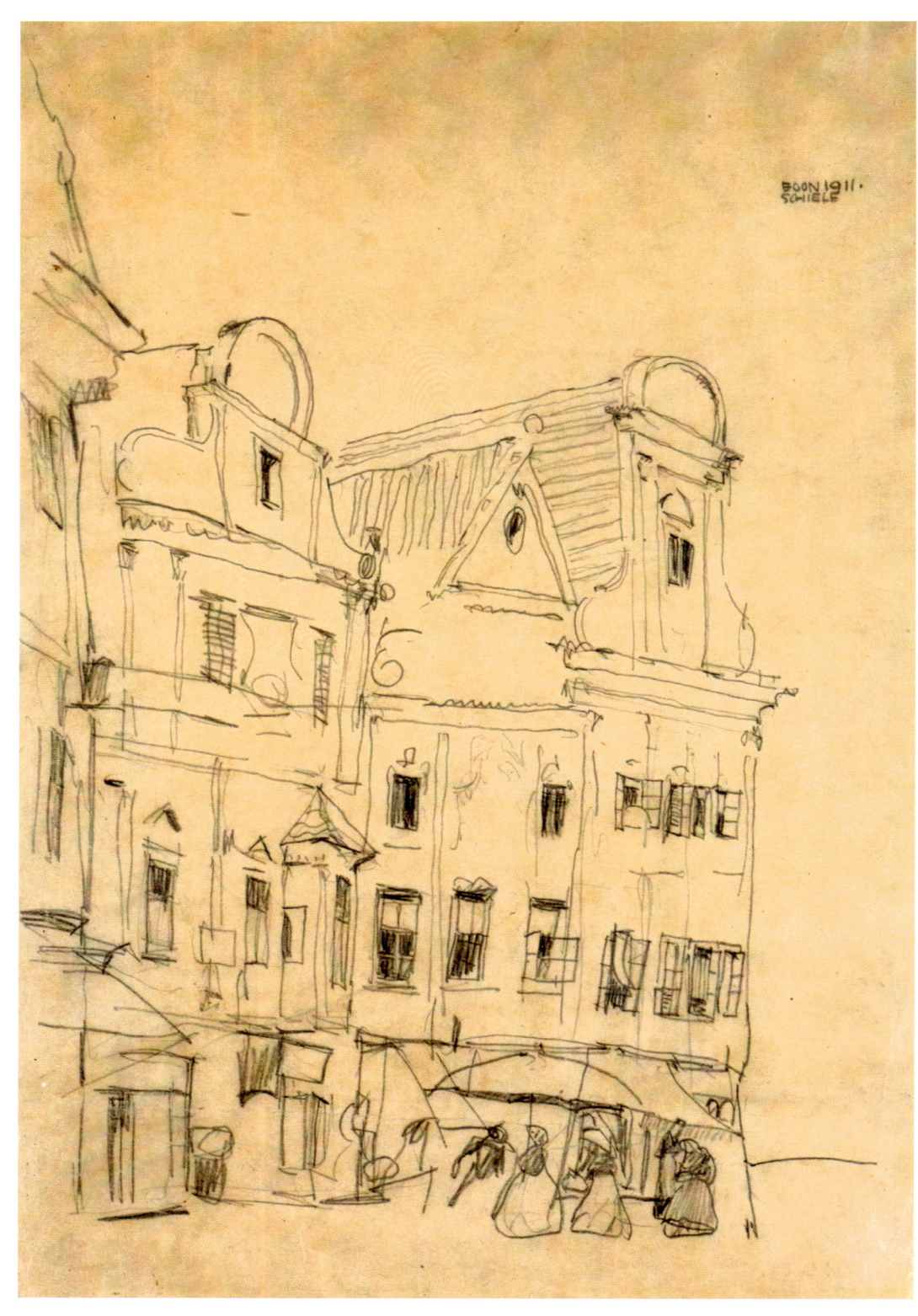

33. CITY HOUSES (KRUMAU RINGPLATZ), 1911

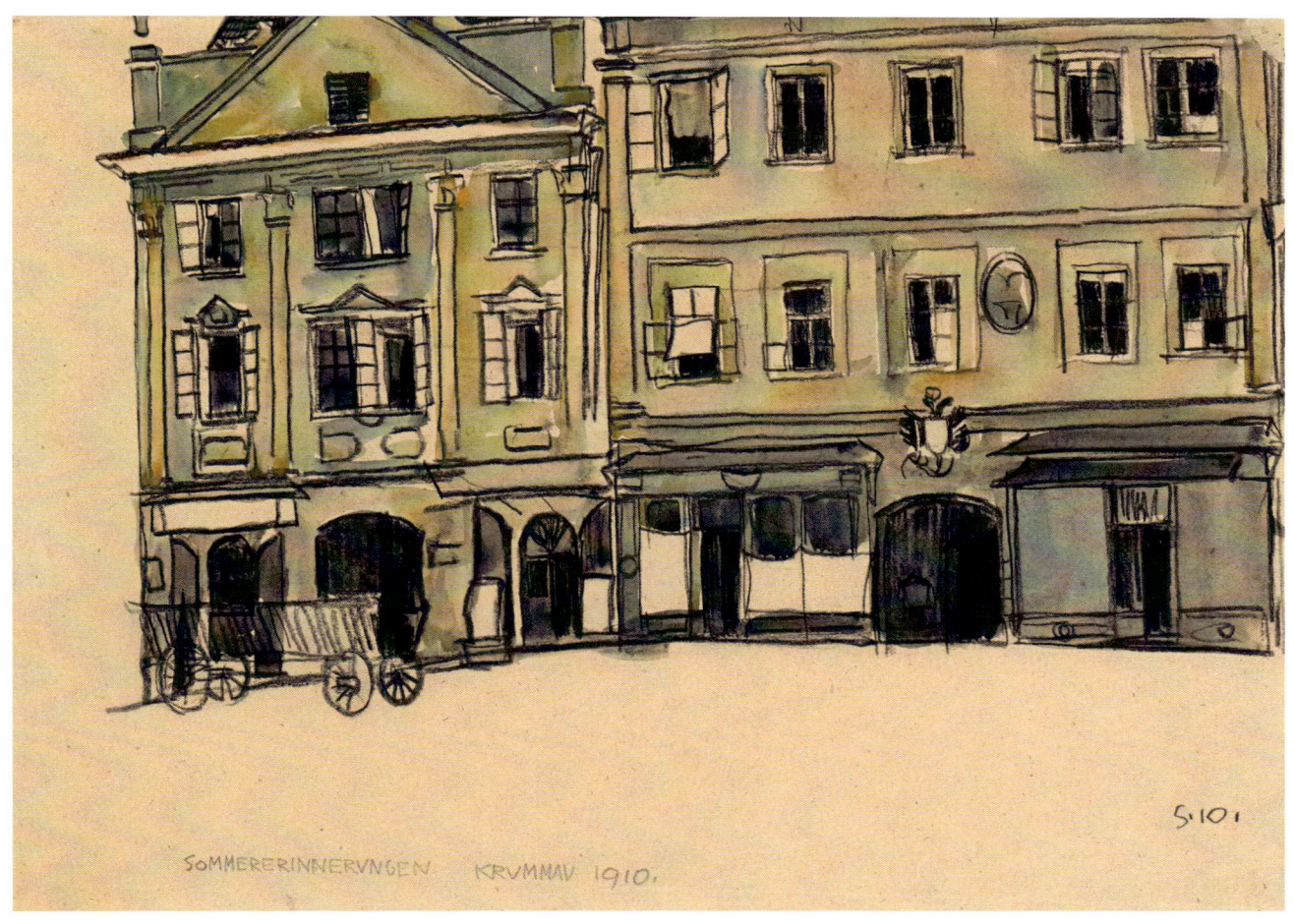

SoMMERERINNERVNGEN KRVMMAV 1910.

5.10.

34. RINGPLATZ, KRUMAU, 1910

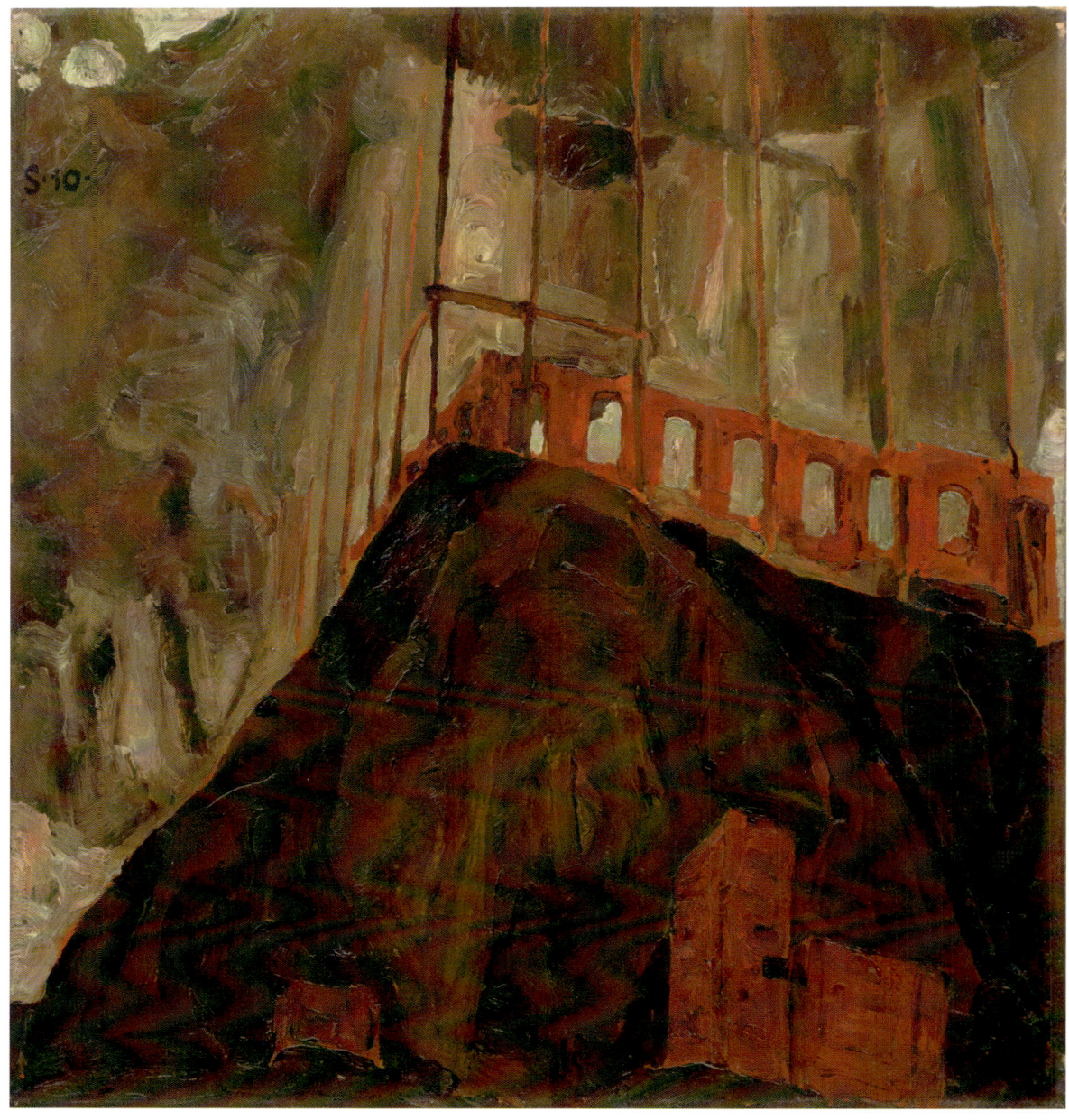

35. RED EARTH, 1910

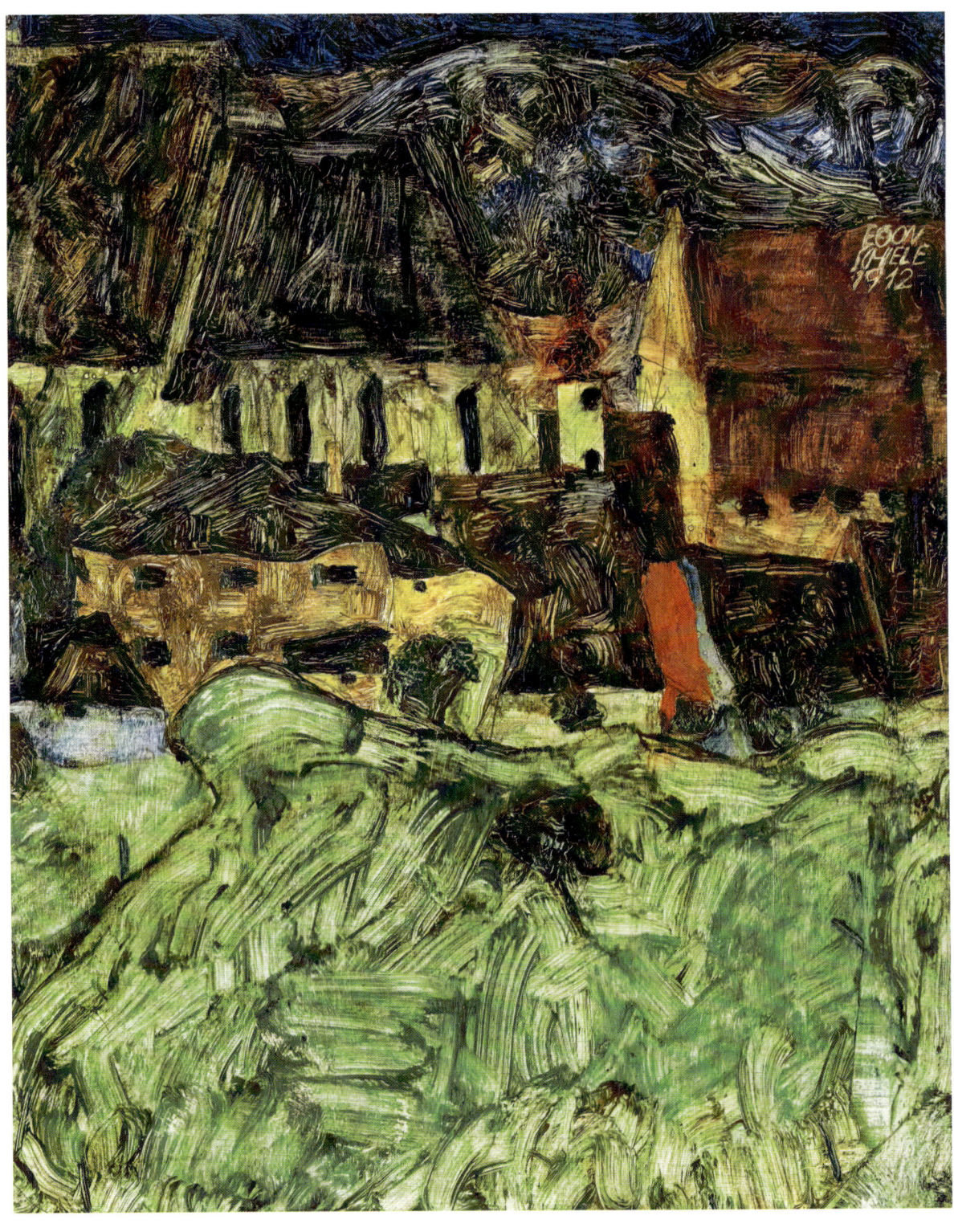

36. KRUMAU TOWNSCAPE (ST. VITUS'S CHURCH WITH HOUSES) (MEADOW, CHURCH, AND HOUSES), 1912

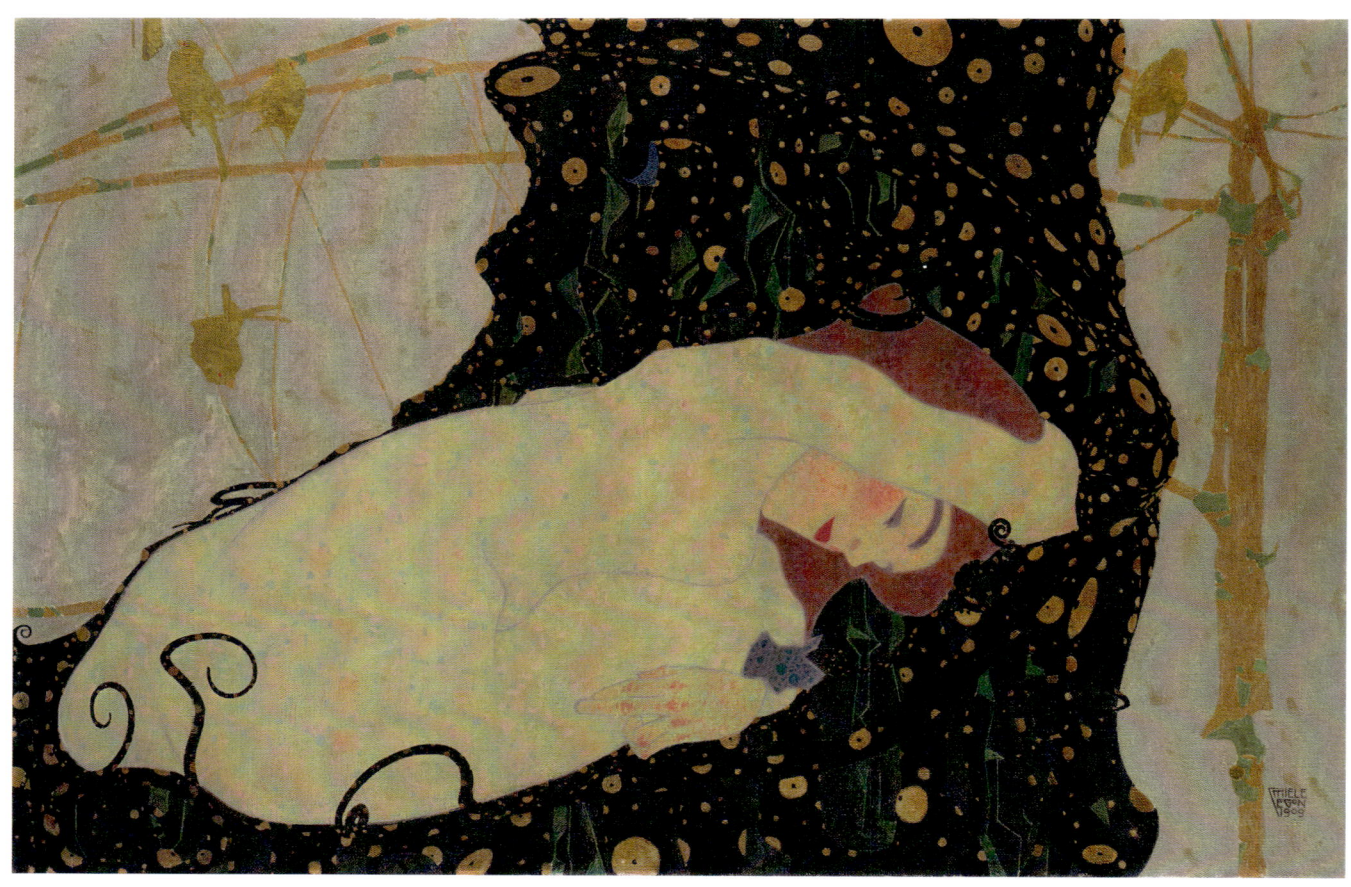

37. CURRENT OF YOUTH (DANAË), 1909

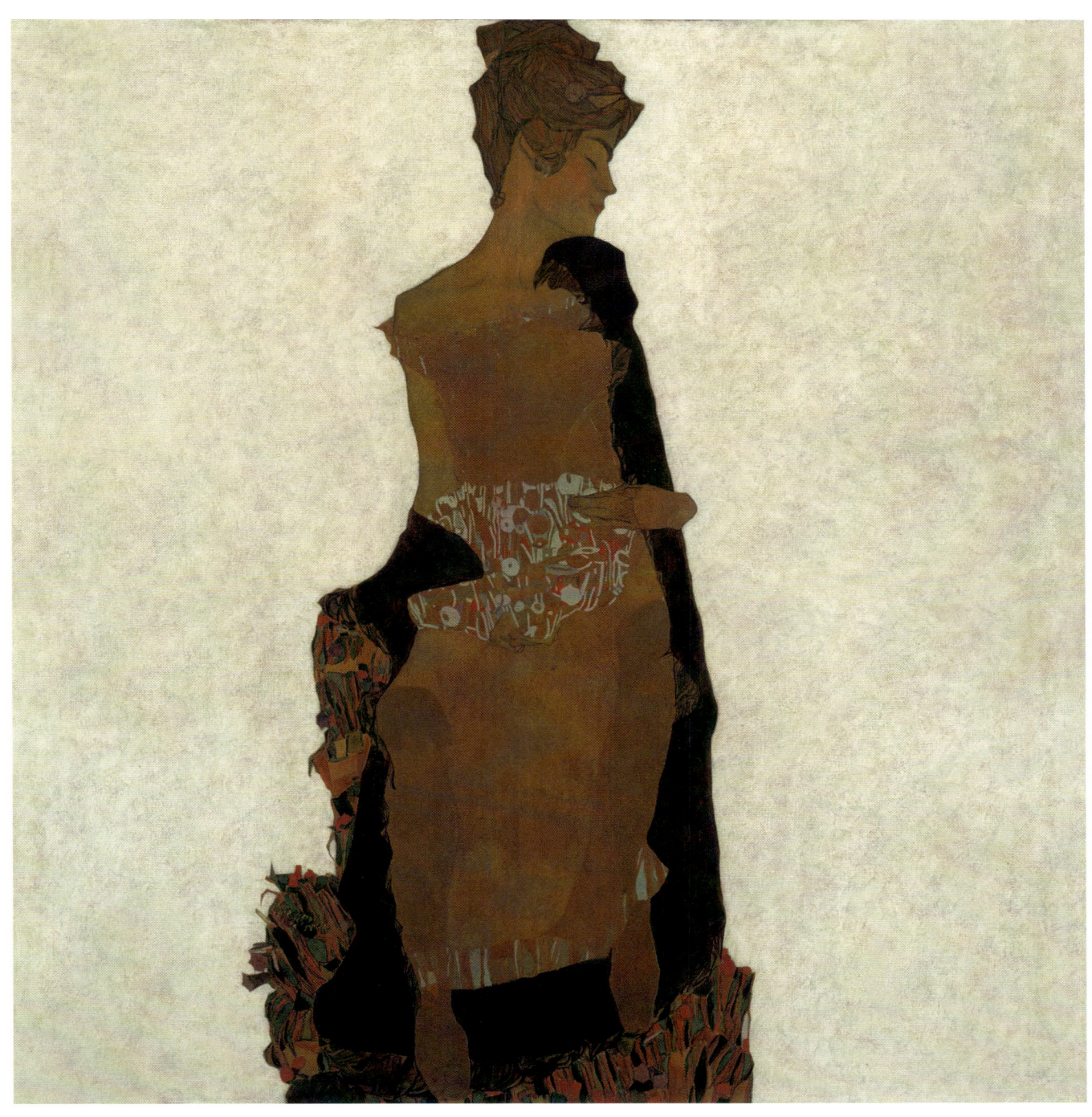

38. PORTRAIT OF GERTI SCHIELE, 1909

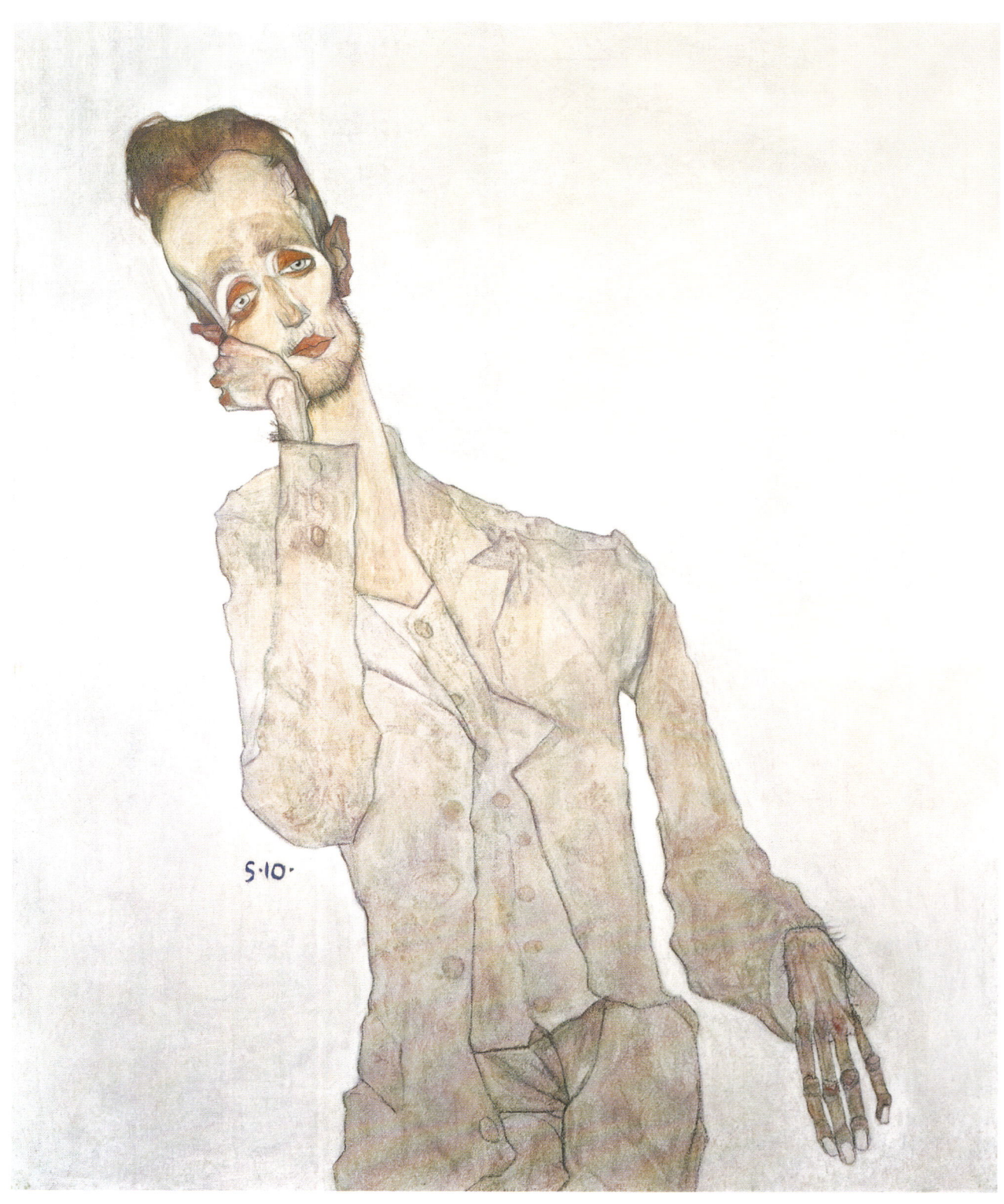

39. PORTRAIT OF THE PAINTER KARL ZAKOVŠEK, 1910

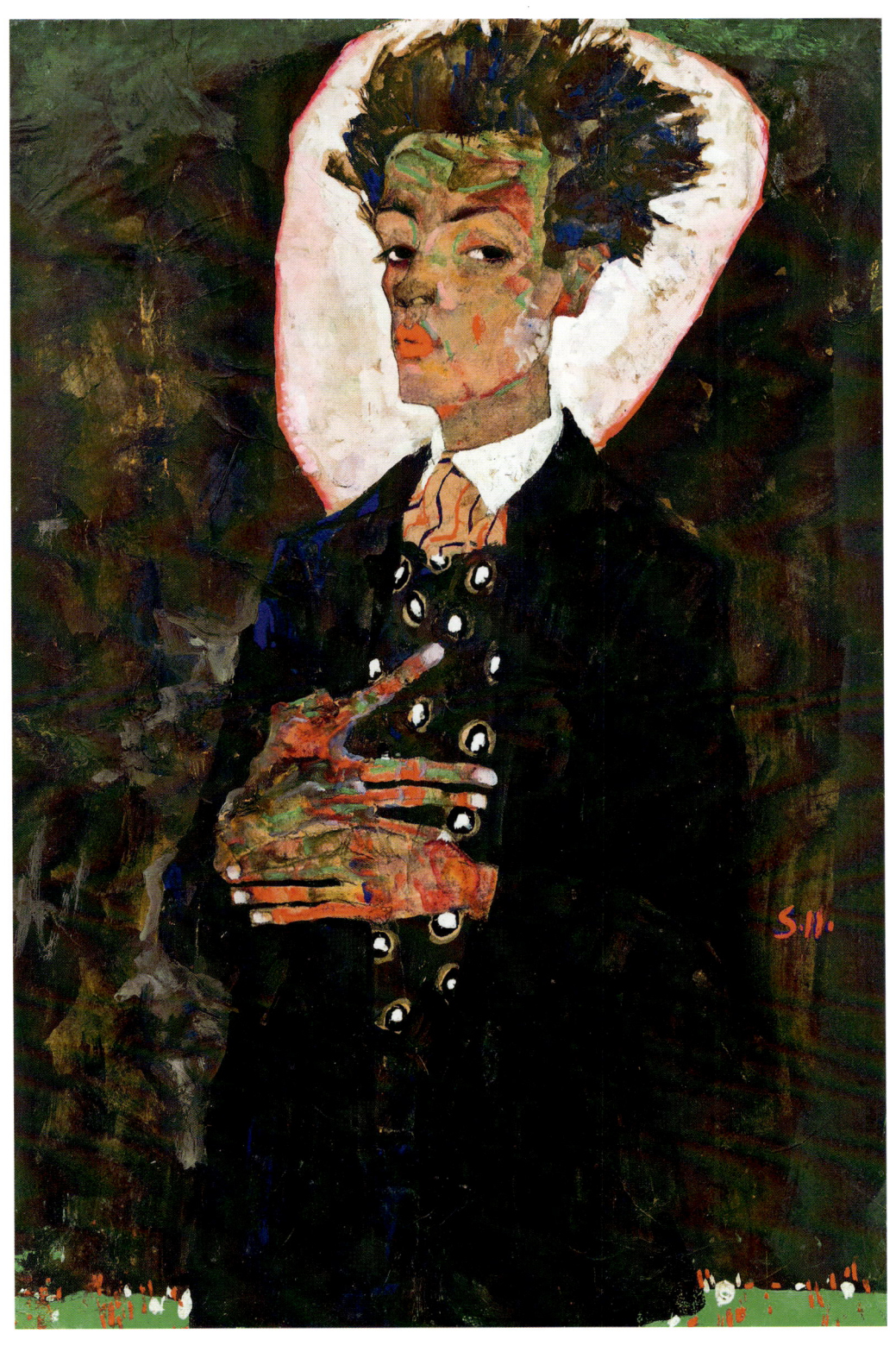

40. SELF-PORTRAIT WITH PEACOCK WAISTCOAT, STANDING, 1911

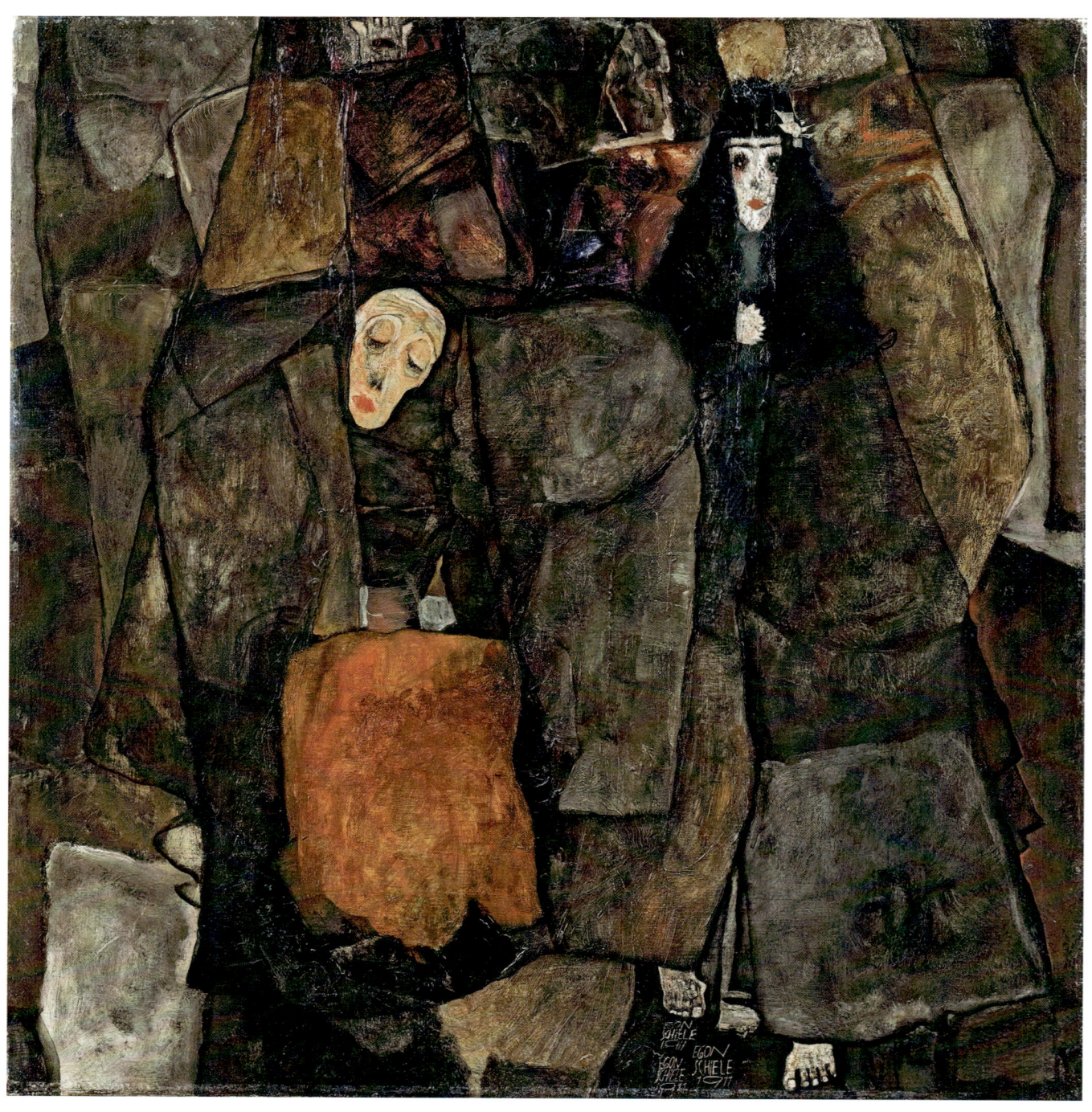

41. PROCESSION, 1911

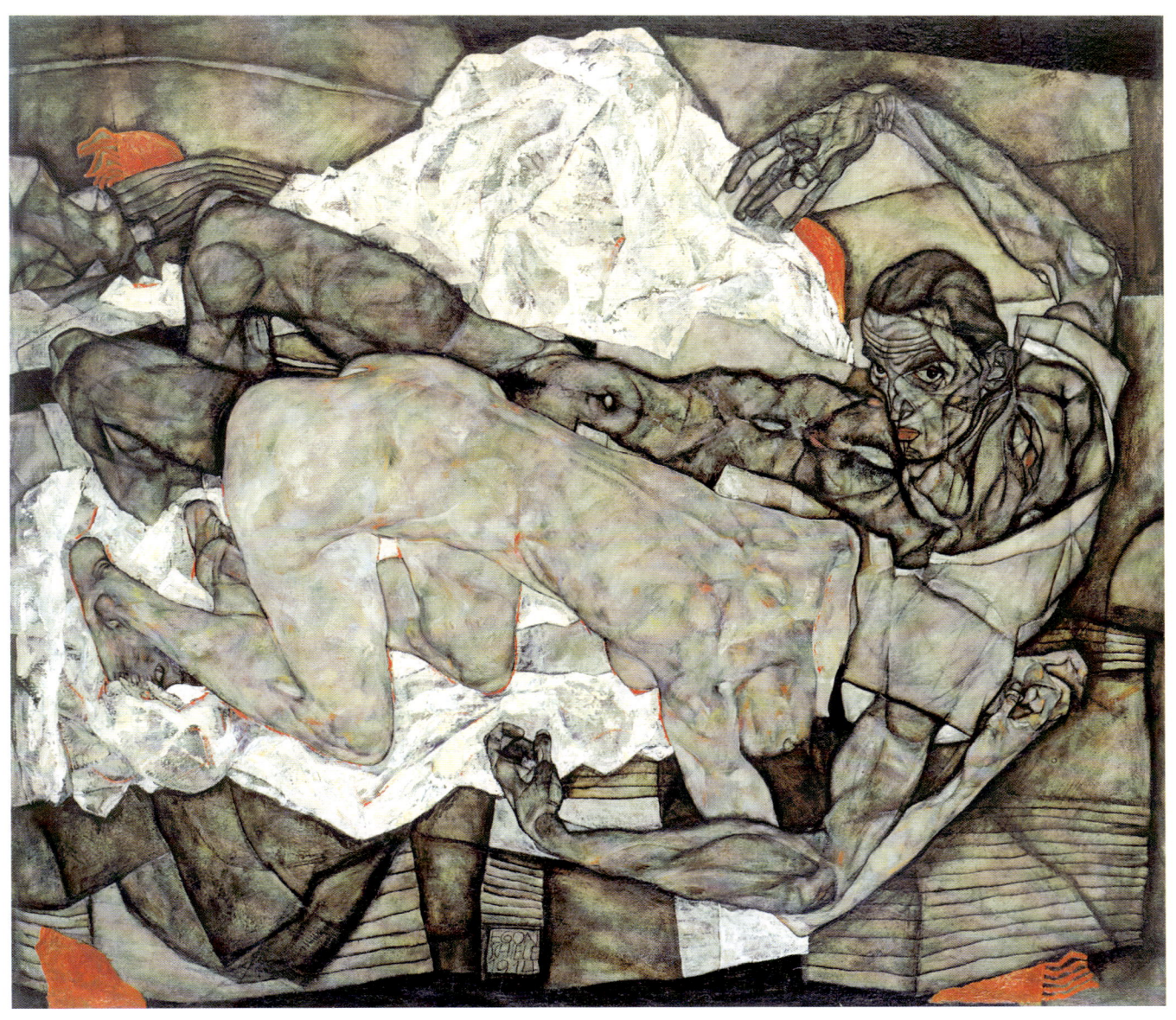

42. MAN AND WOMAN I (LOVERS I), 1914

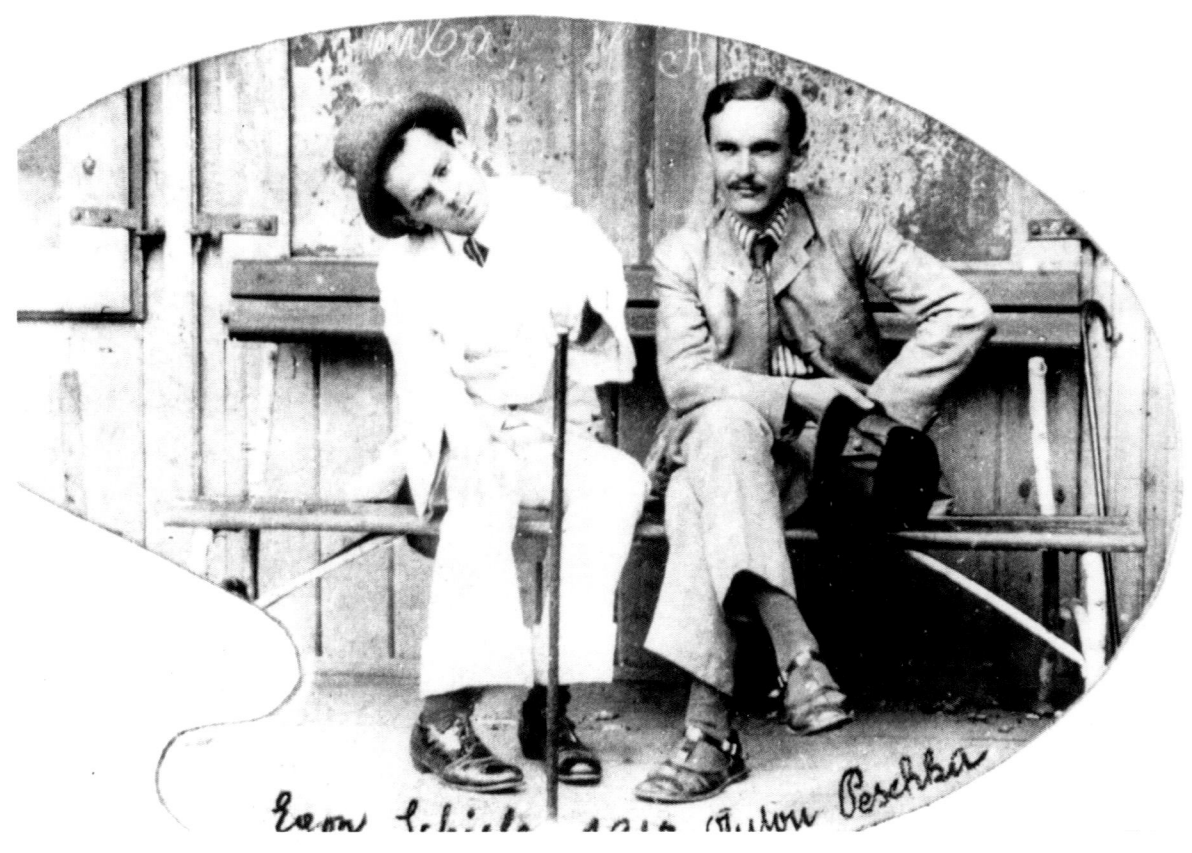

43. EGON SCHIELE AND ANTON PESCHKA IN KRUMAU, 1910

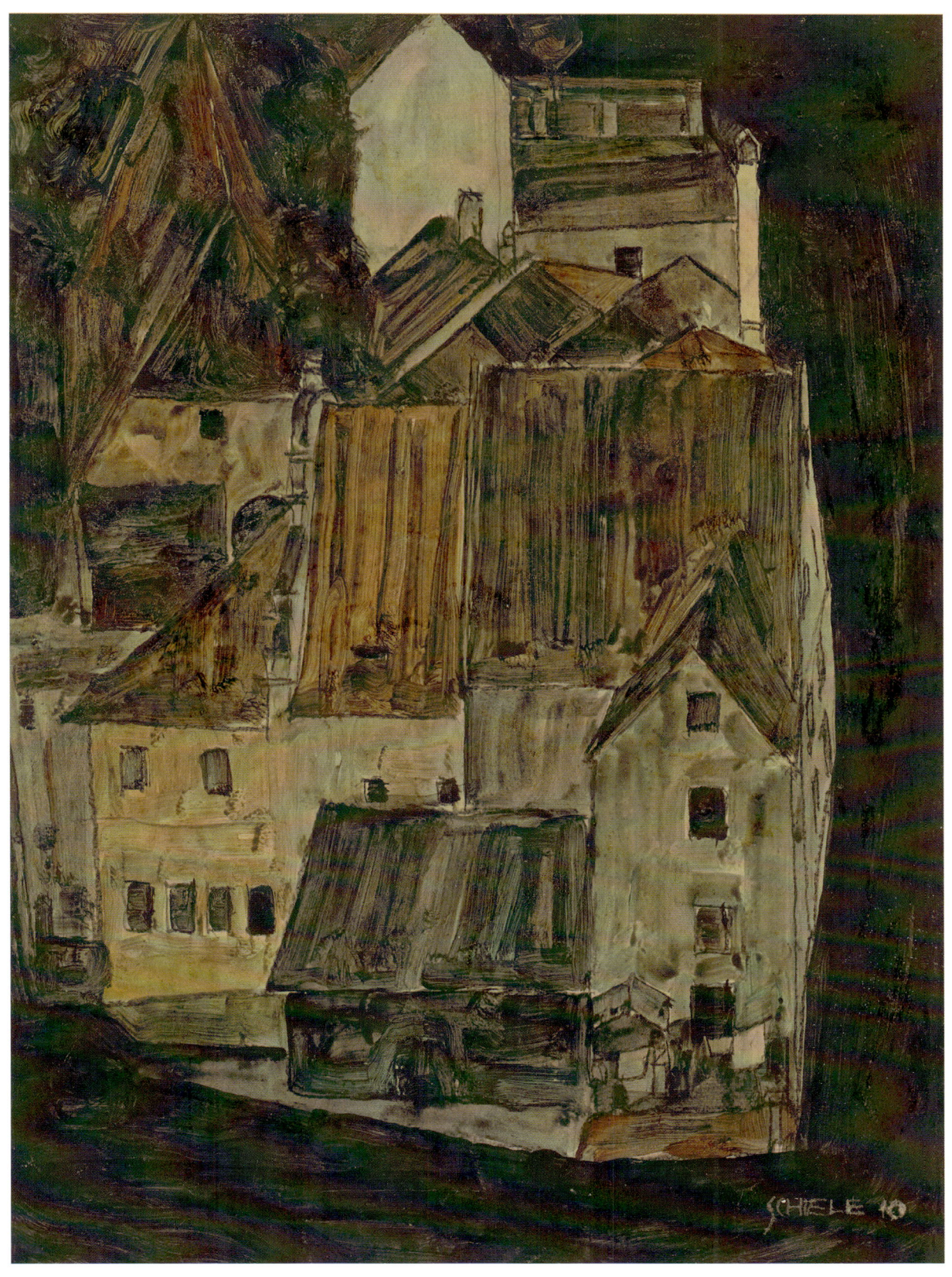

44. CITY ON THE BLUE RIVER I (DEAD CITY I)

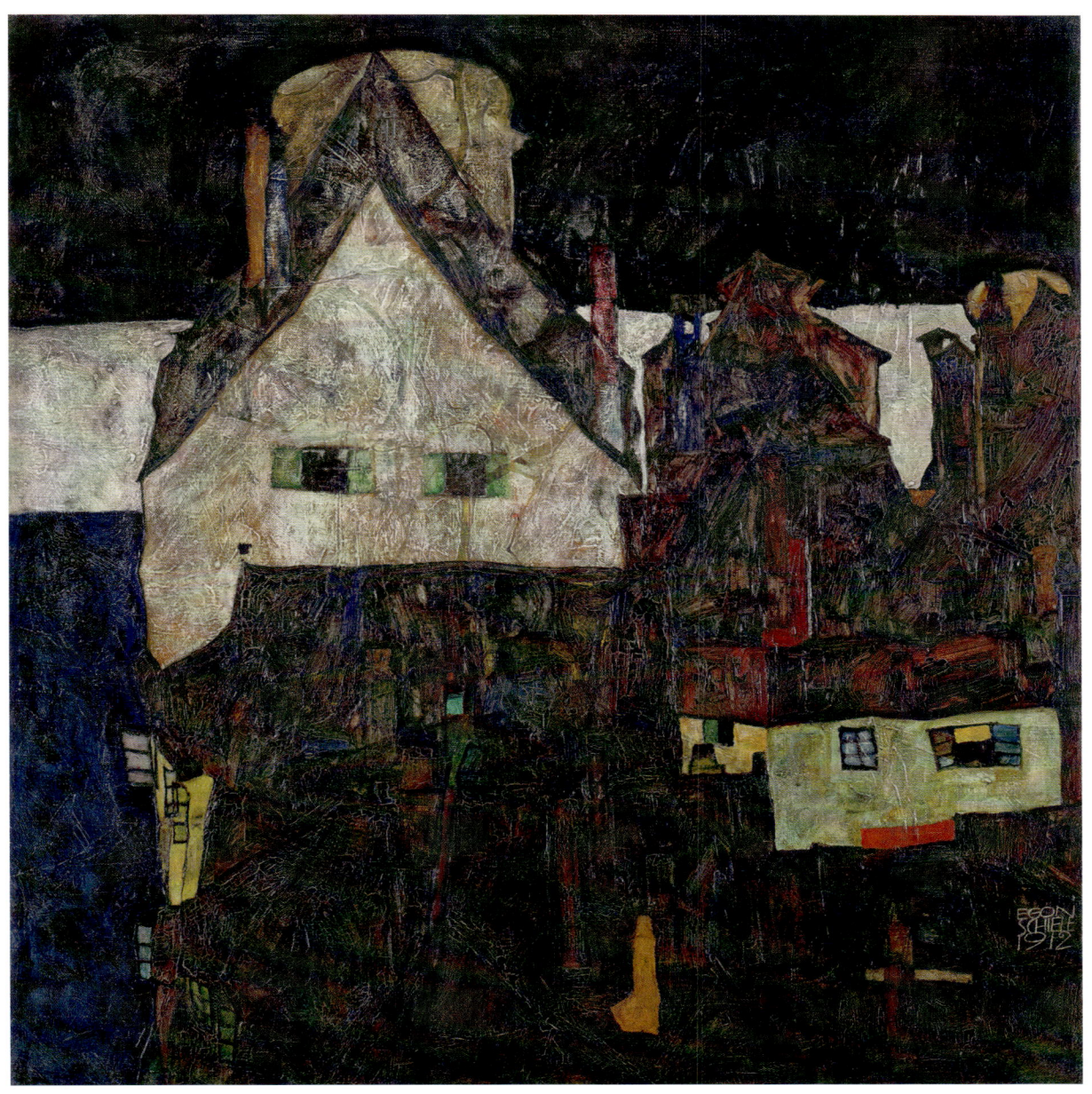

45. THE SMALL CITY I (DEAD CITY VI), 1912

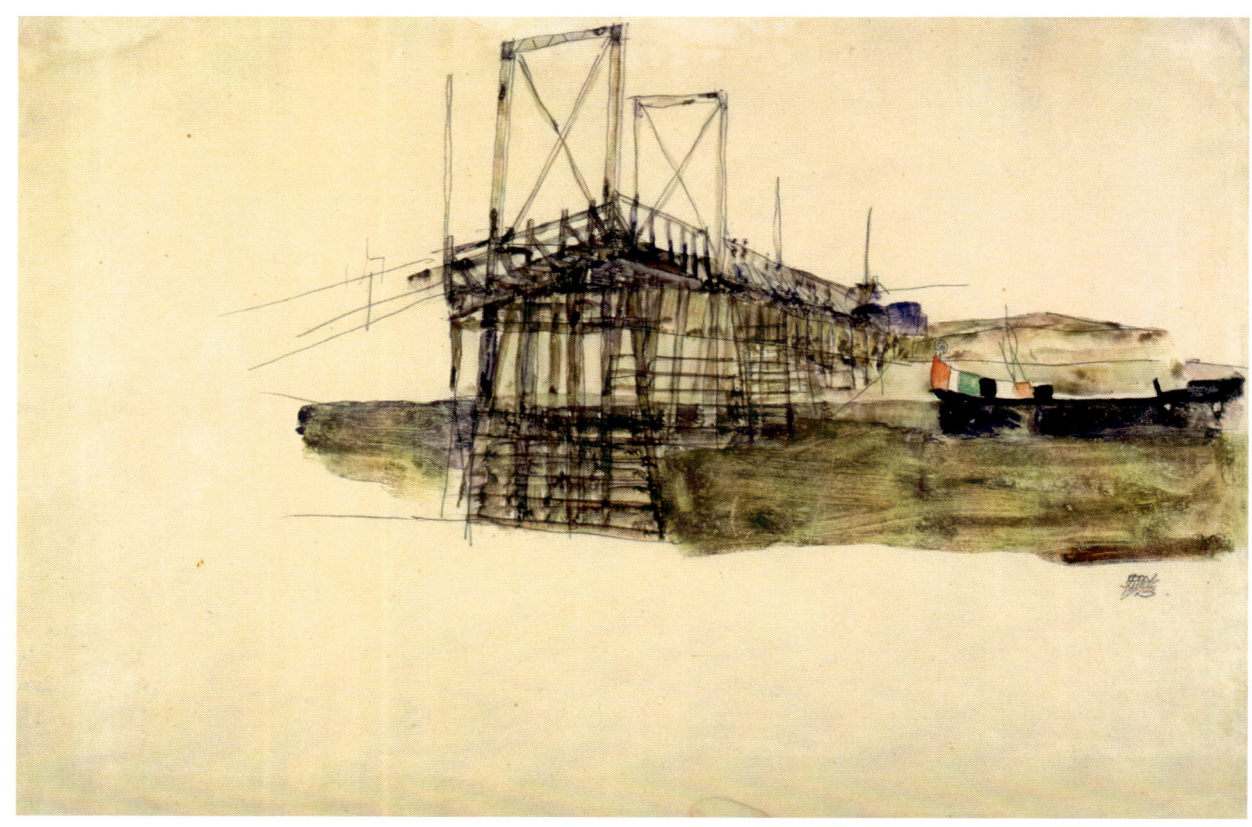

46. THE BRIDGE, 1913

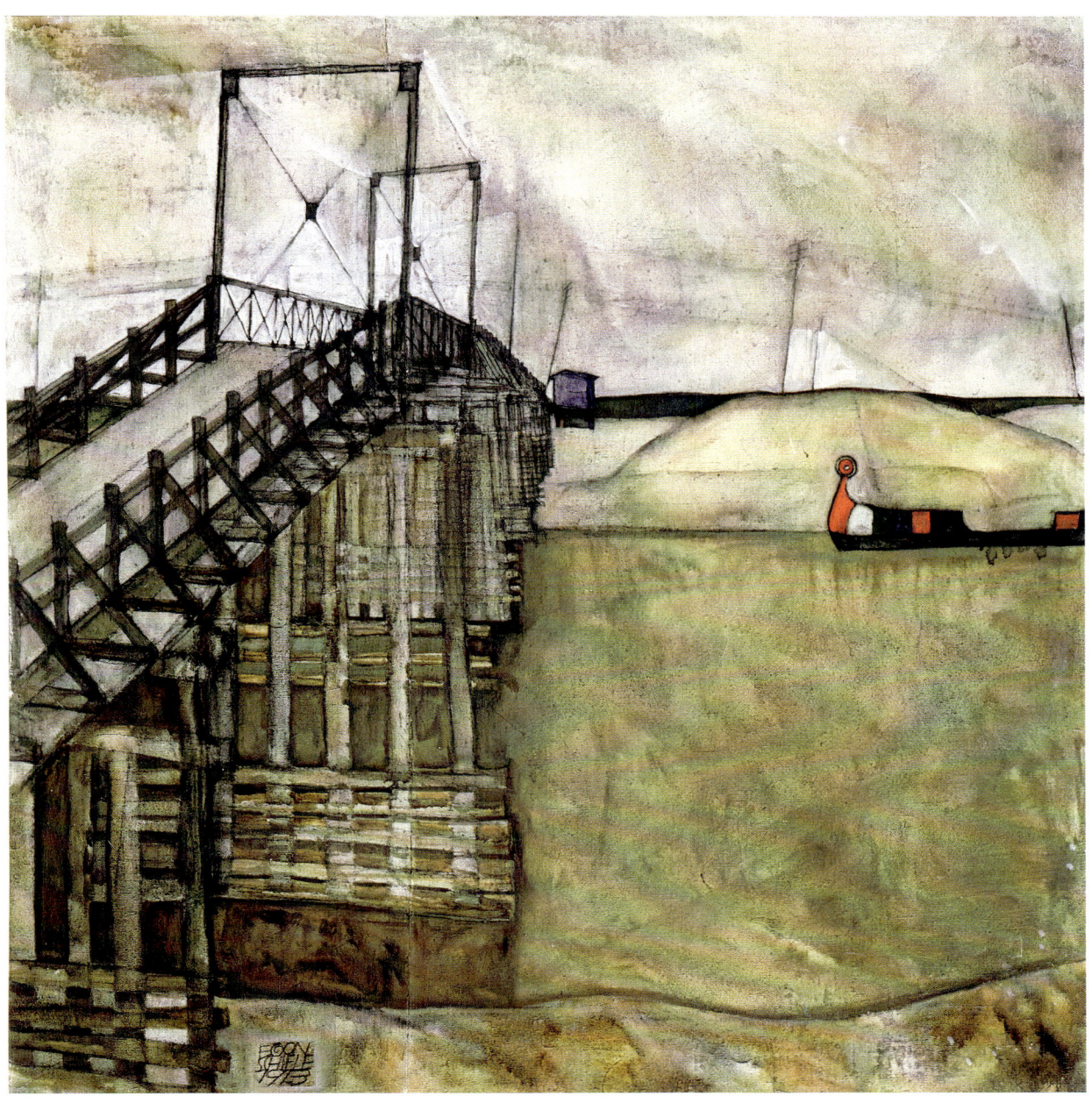

47. THE BRIDGE, 1913

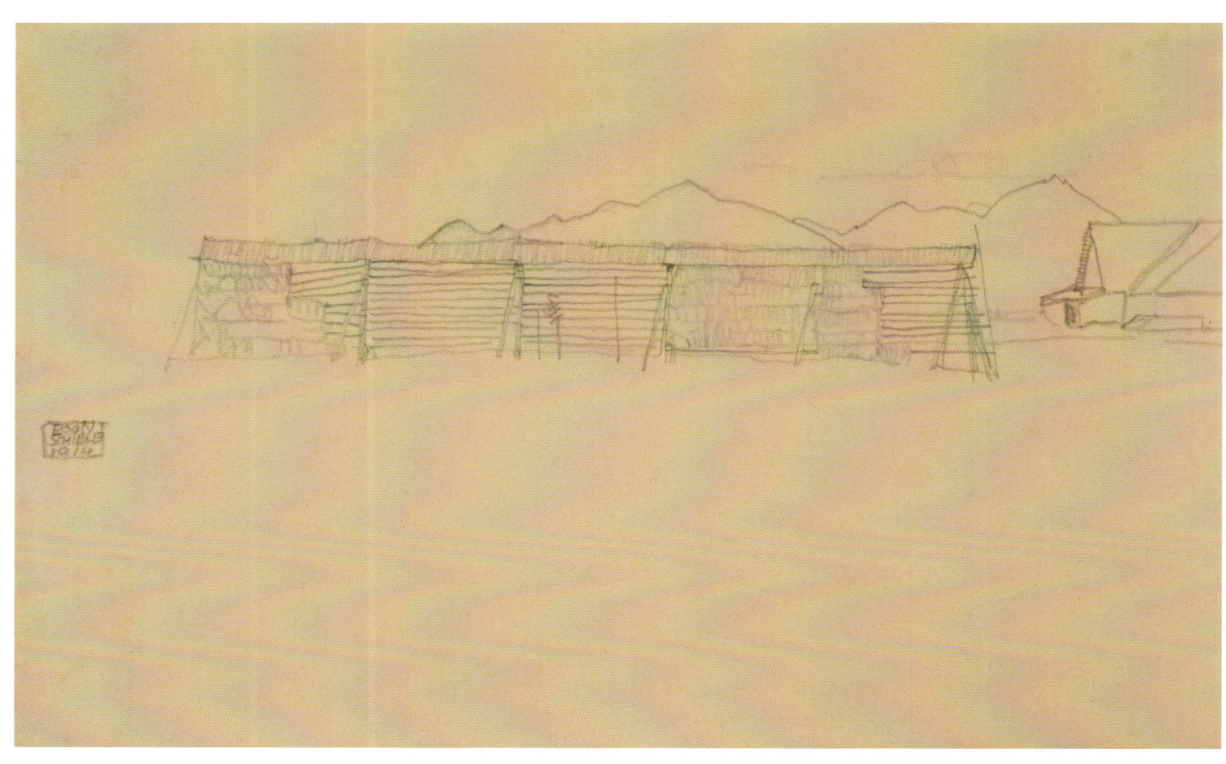

48. HAY RACKS, 1914

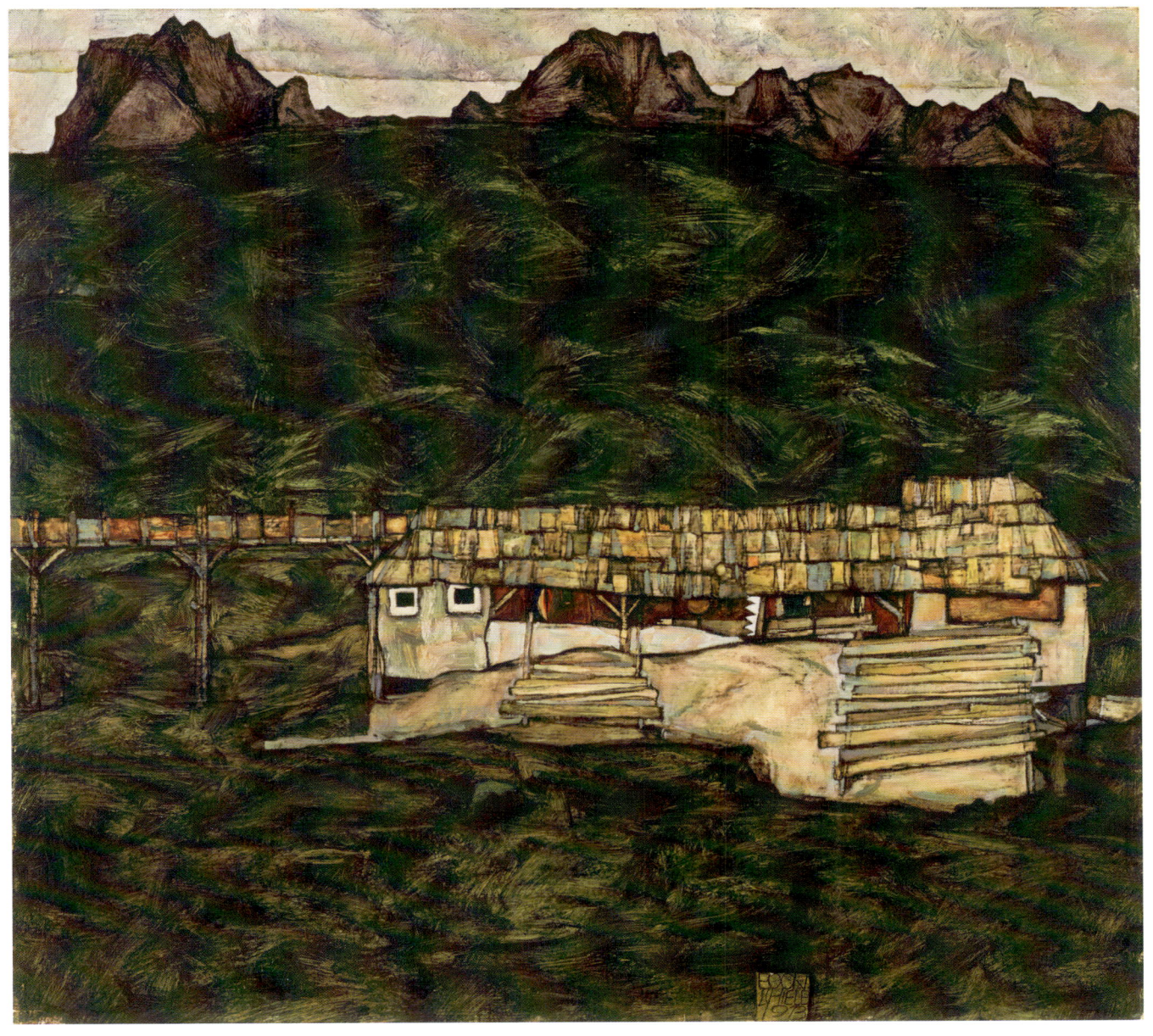

49. SAWMILL, 1913

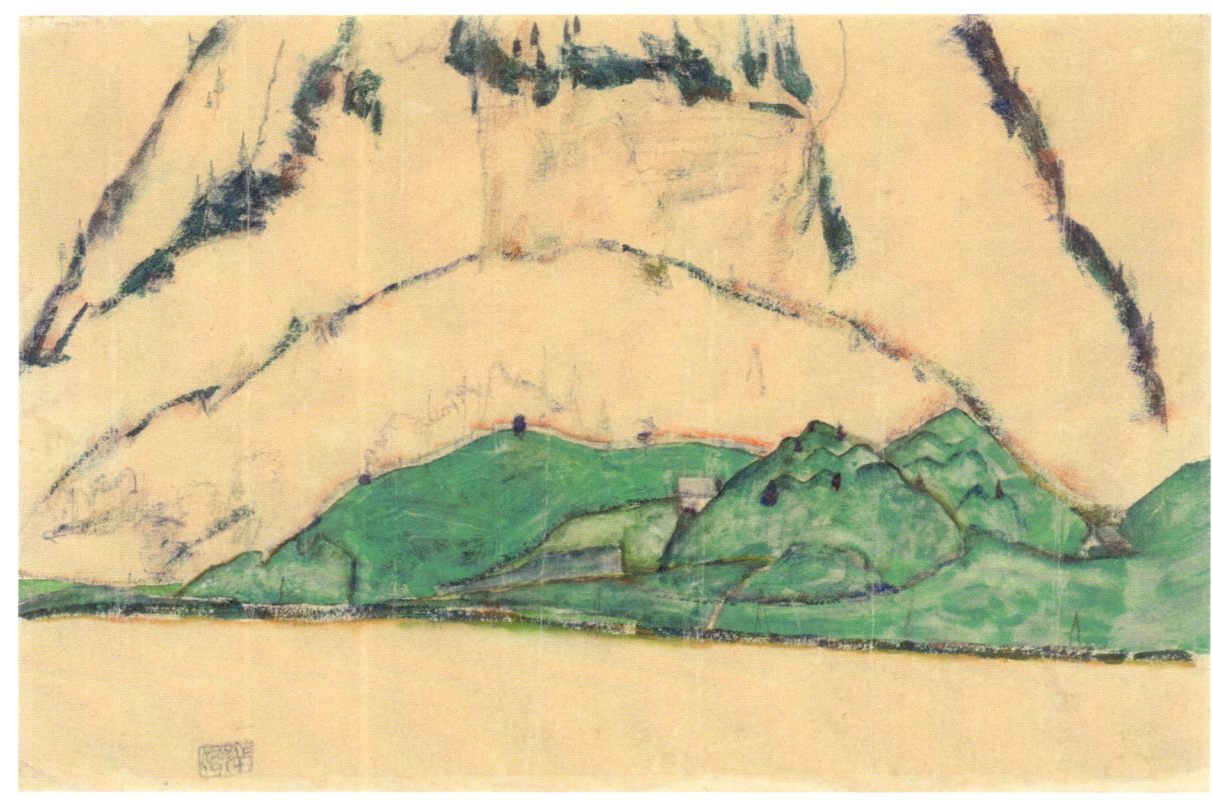

50. CARINTHIAN LANDSCAPE, 1914

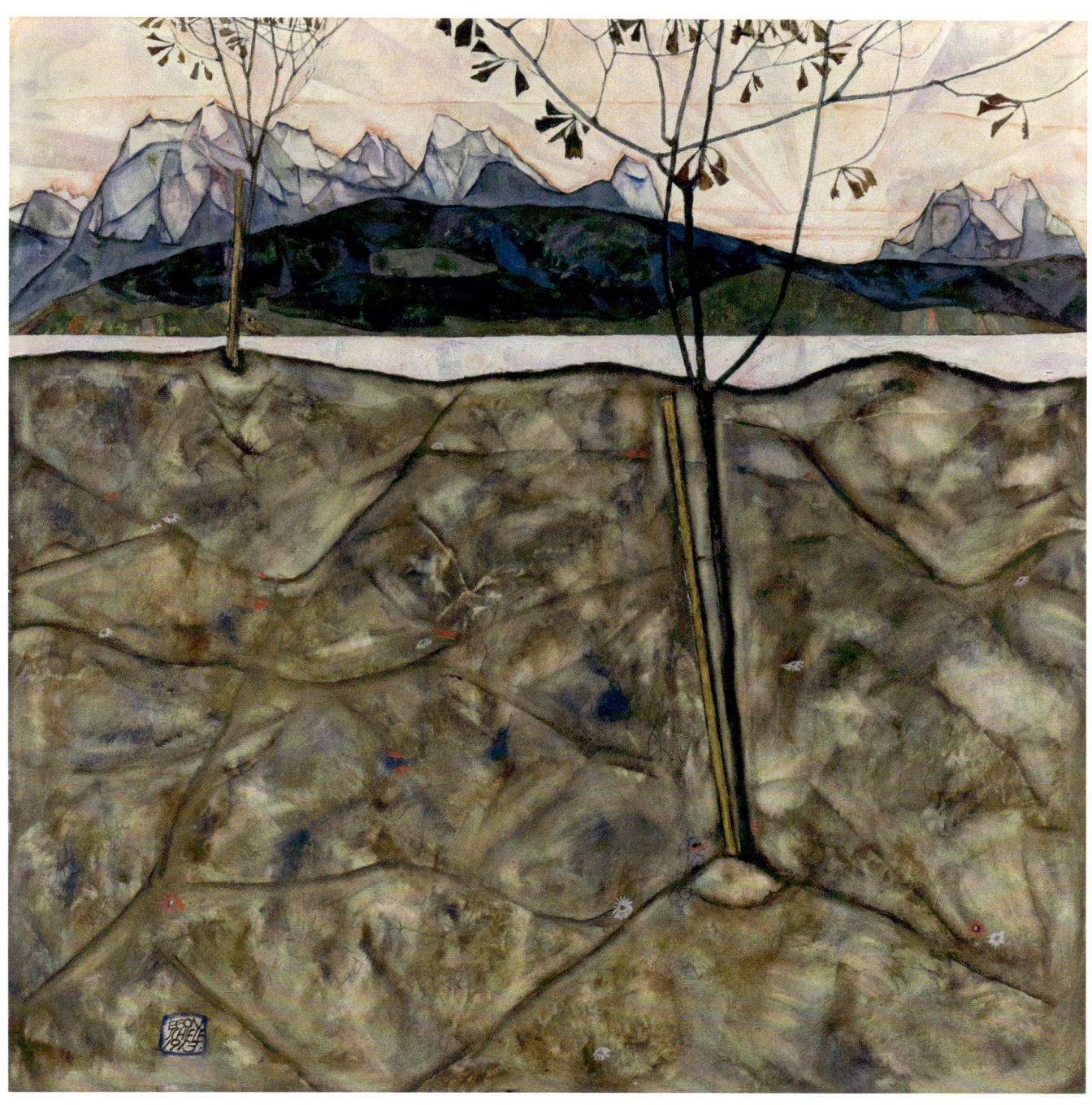

51. RIVER LANDSCAPE WITH TWO TREES, 1913

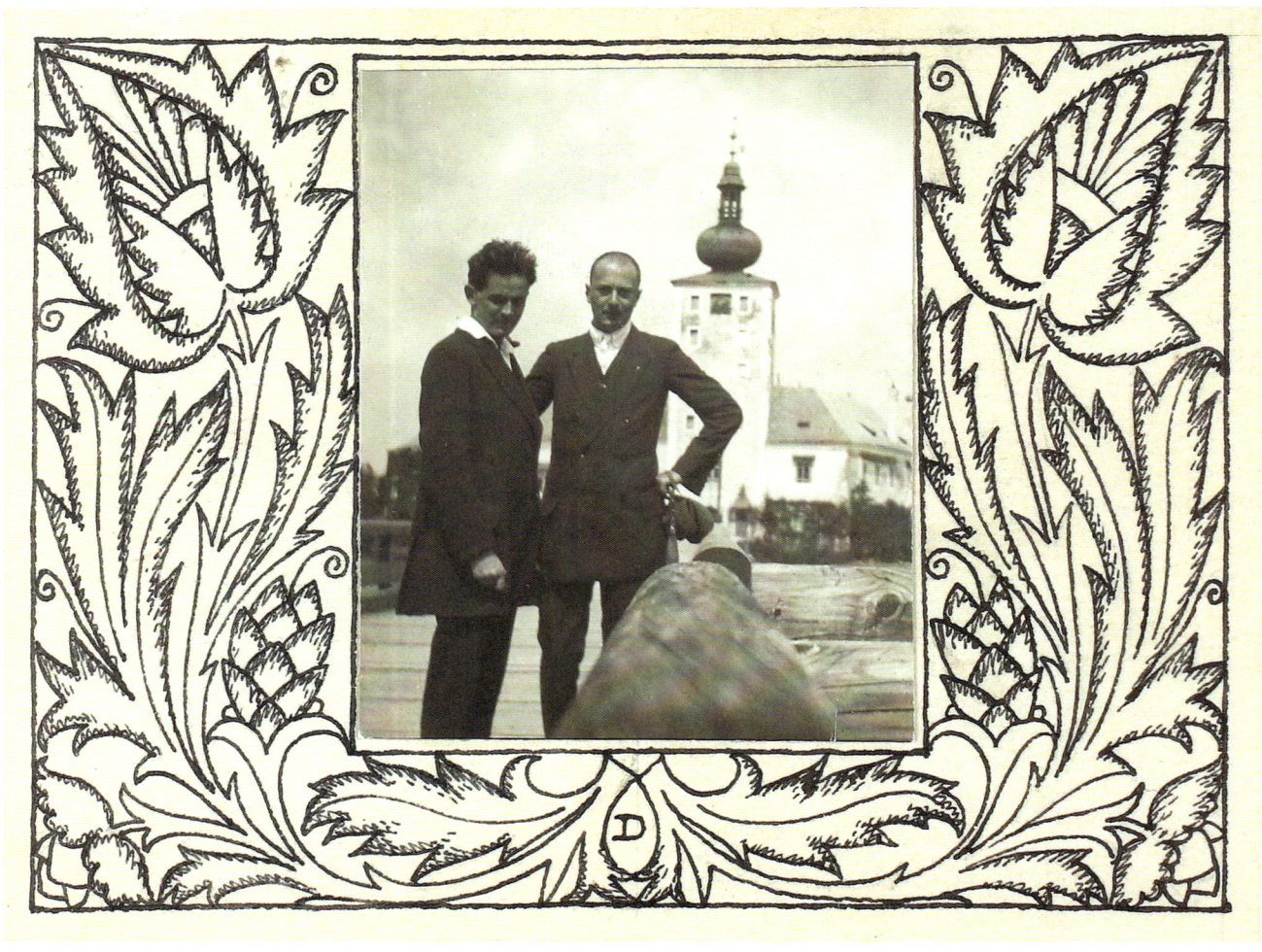

52. EGON SCHIELE AND ARTHUR ROESSLER IN FRONT OF ORTH CASTLE IN GMUNDEN ON LAKE TRAUN, SALZKAMMERGUT, 1913, WITH A DECORATIVE BORDER BY JÓZSEF DIVÉKY

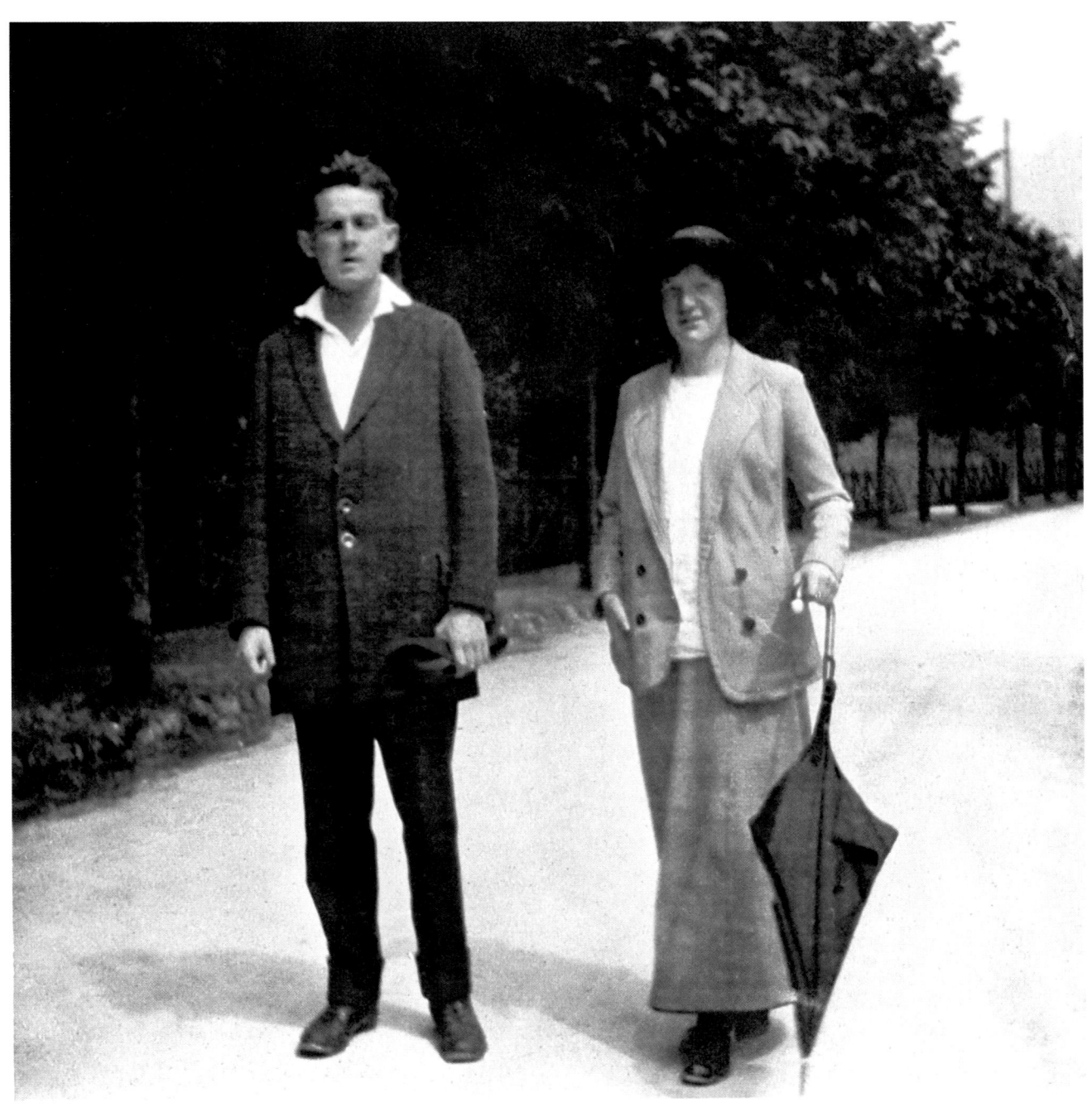

53. EGON SCHIELE AND WALBURGA (WALLY) NEUZIL ON LAKE TRAUN, 1913

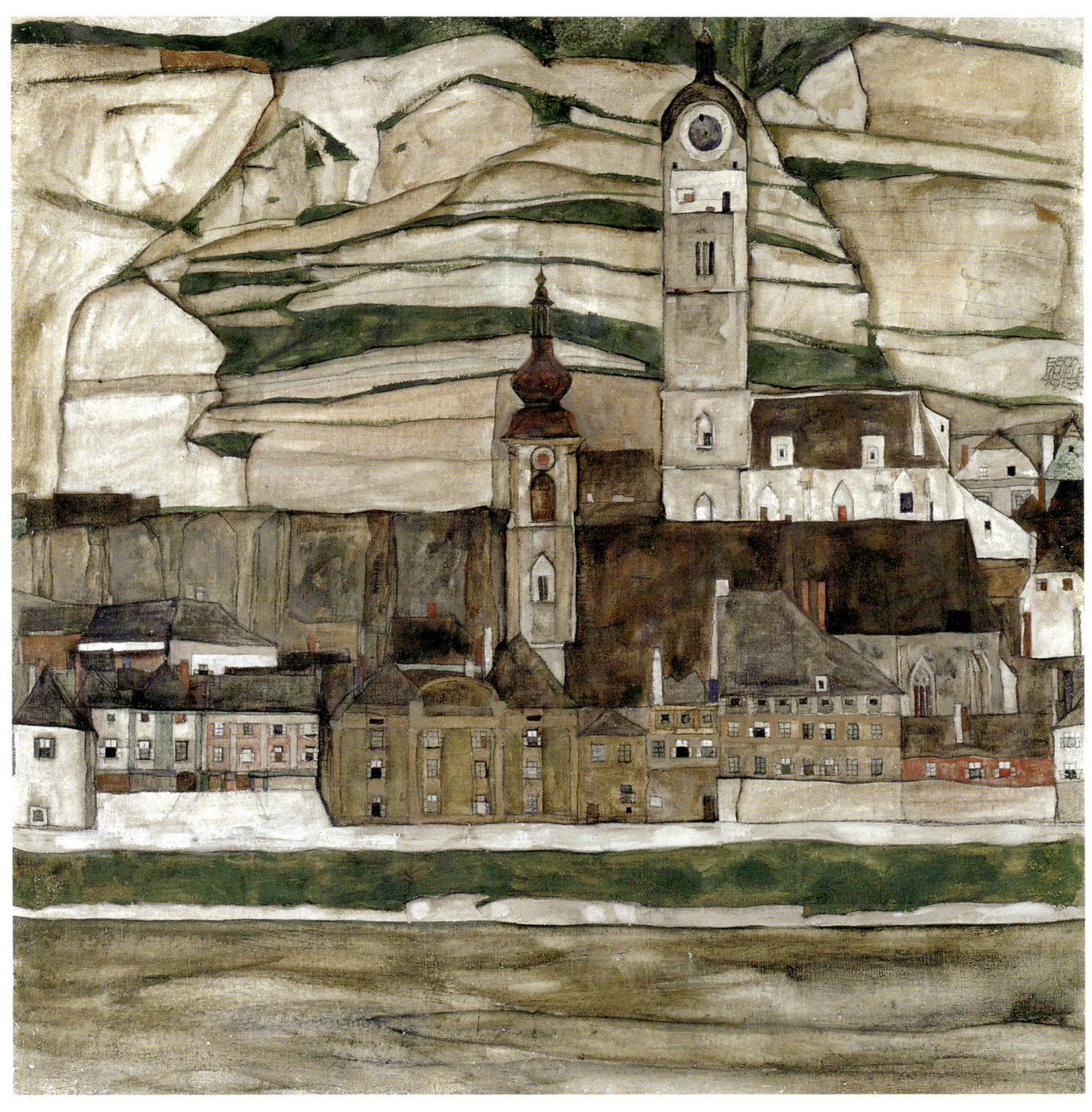

54. STEIN ON THE DANUBE, SEEN FROM THE SOUTH (LARGE), 1913

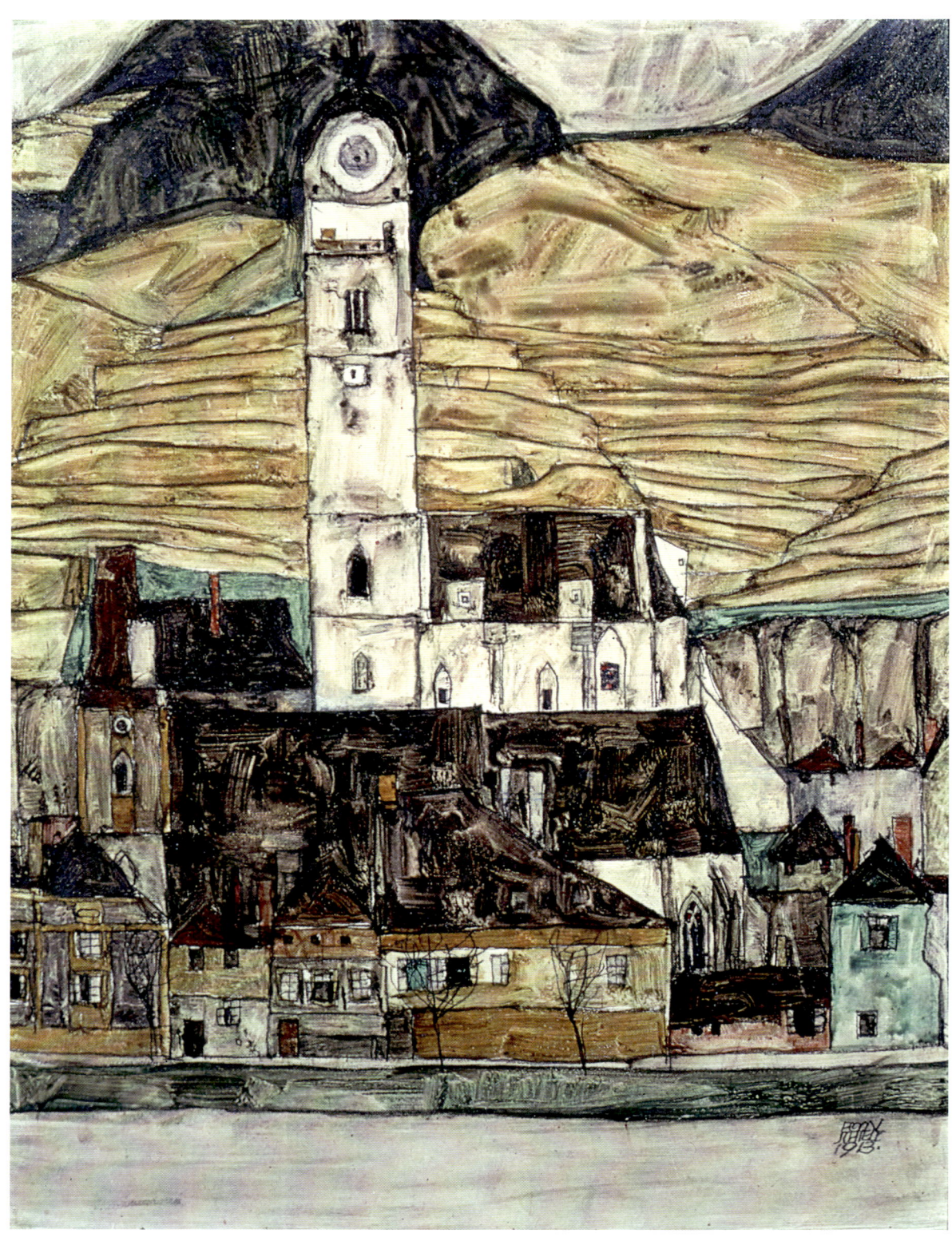

55. STEIN ON THE DANUBE, SEEN FROM THE SOUTH (SMALL), 1913

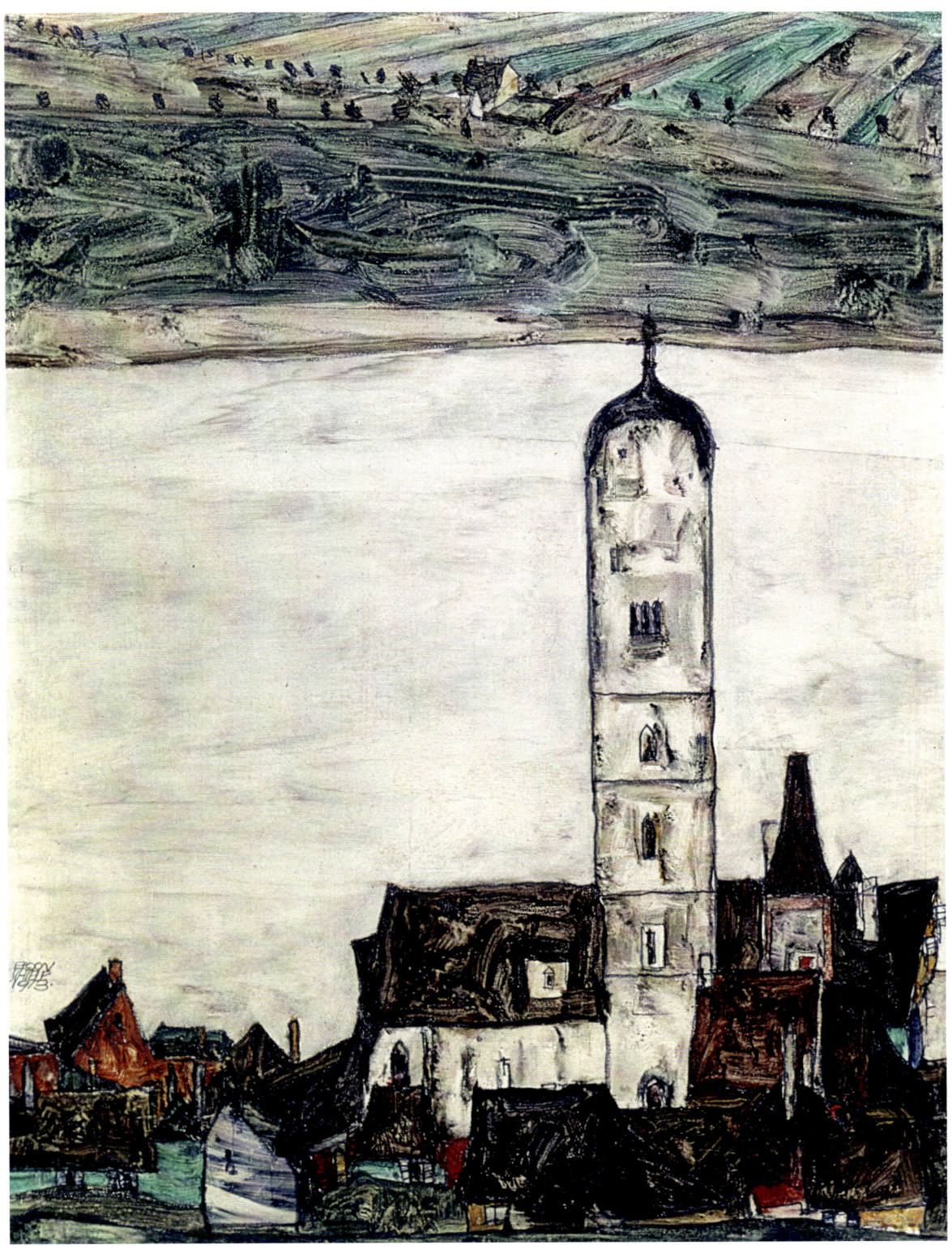

56. STEIN ON THE DANUBE, SEEN FROM THE KREUZBERG (SMALL), 1913

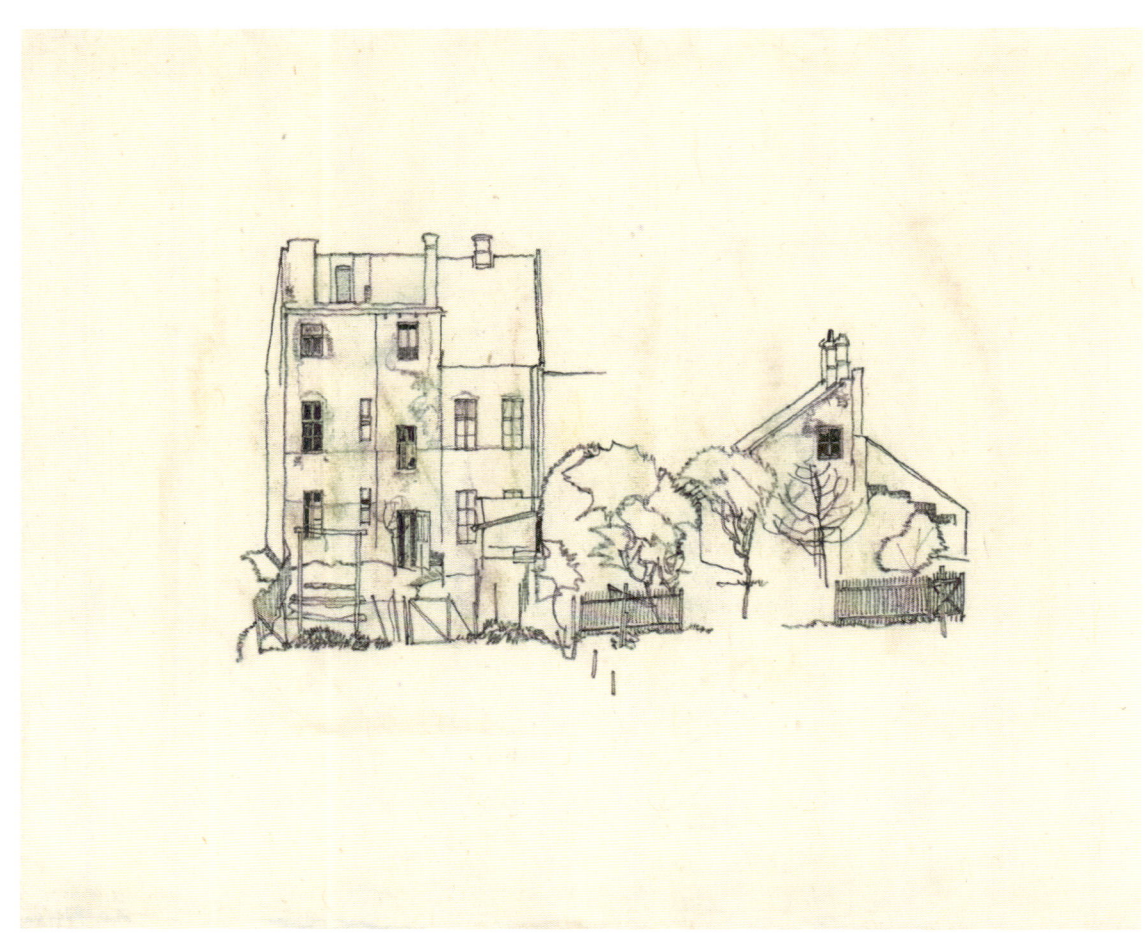

57. LAST HOUSES (AT THE EDGE OF TOWN), 1915

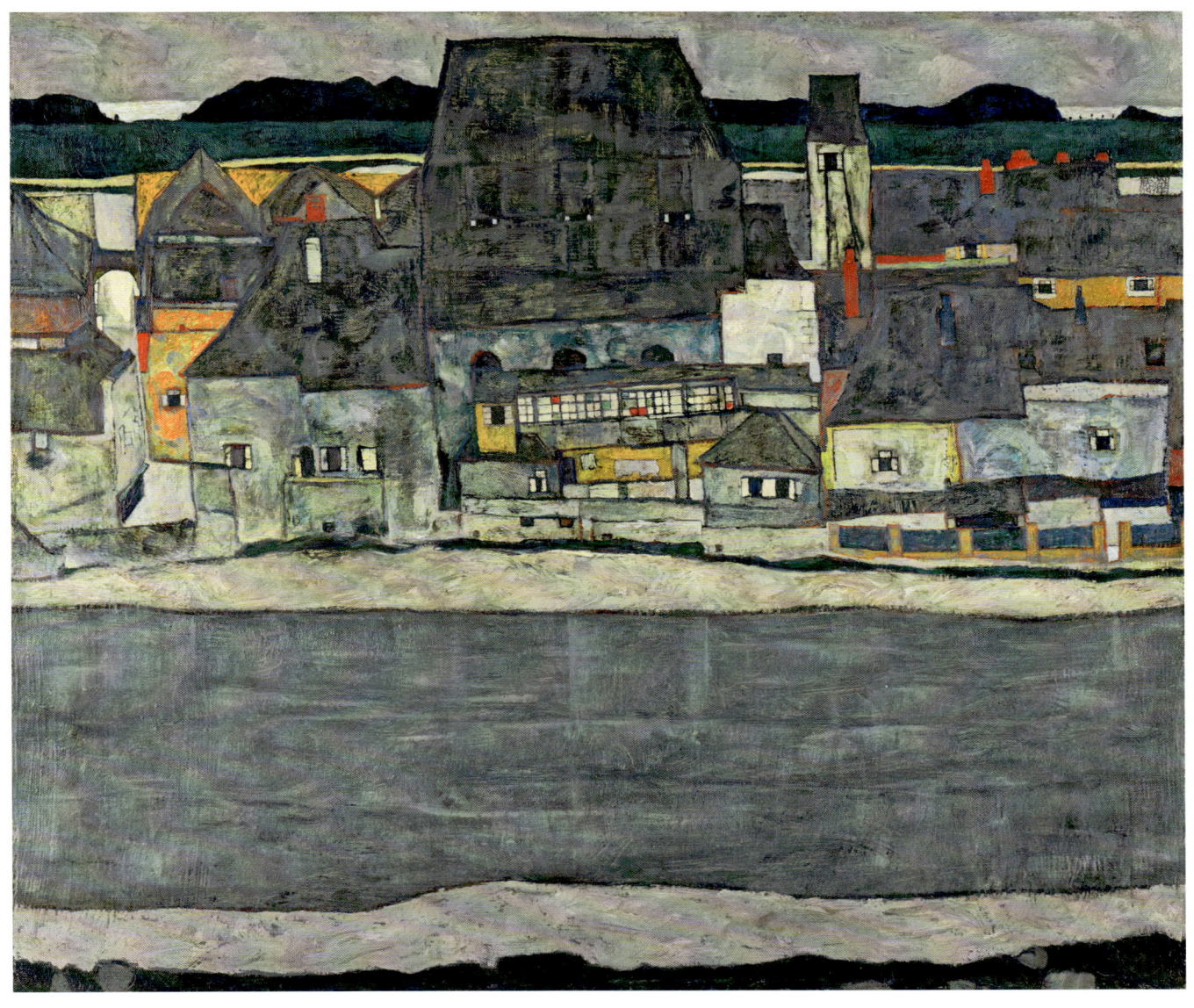

58. HOUSES BY THE RIVER II (THE OLD CITY II), 1914

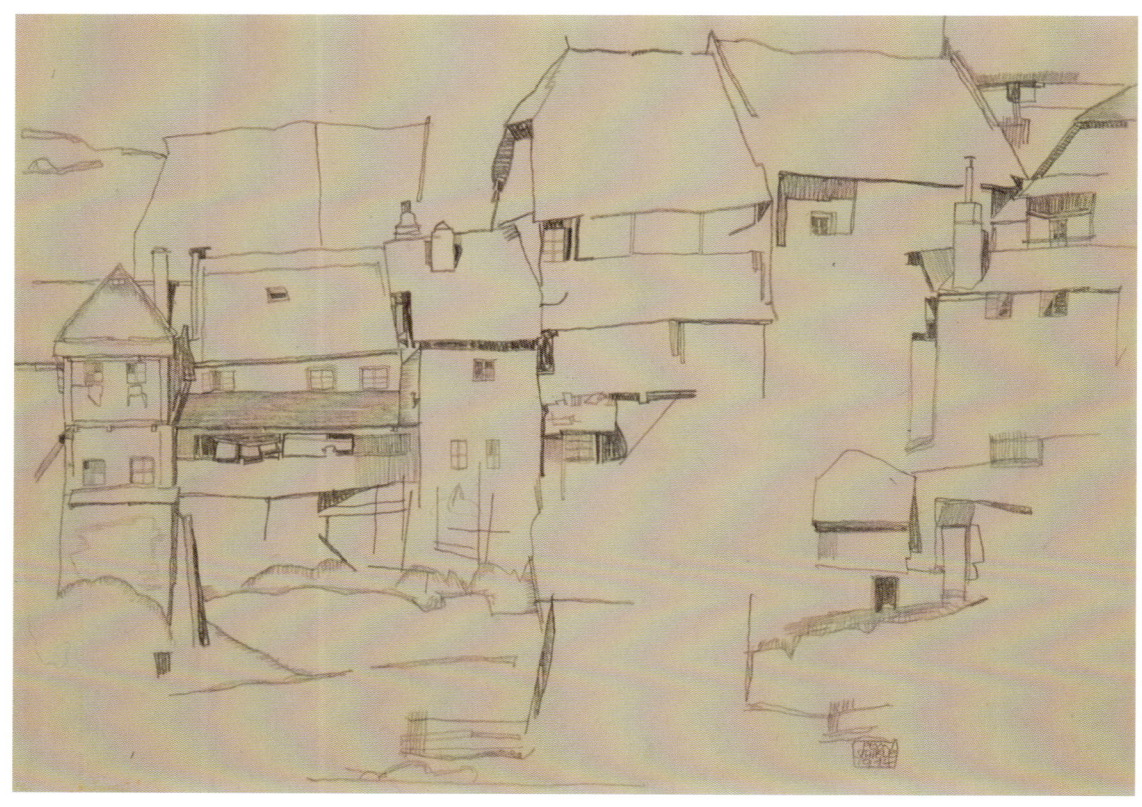

59. OLD HOUSES IN KRUMAU, 1914

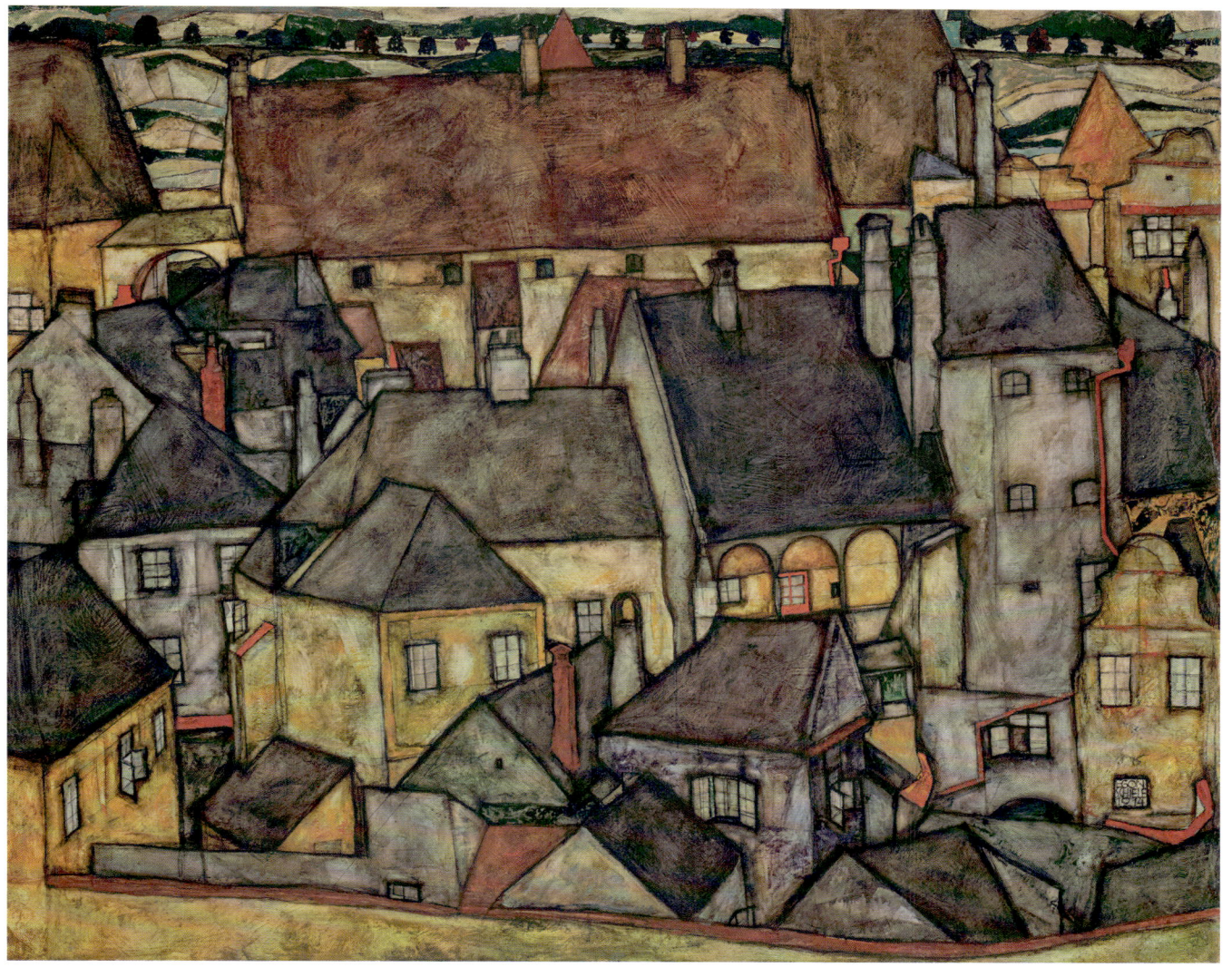

60. YELLOW TOWN, 1914

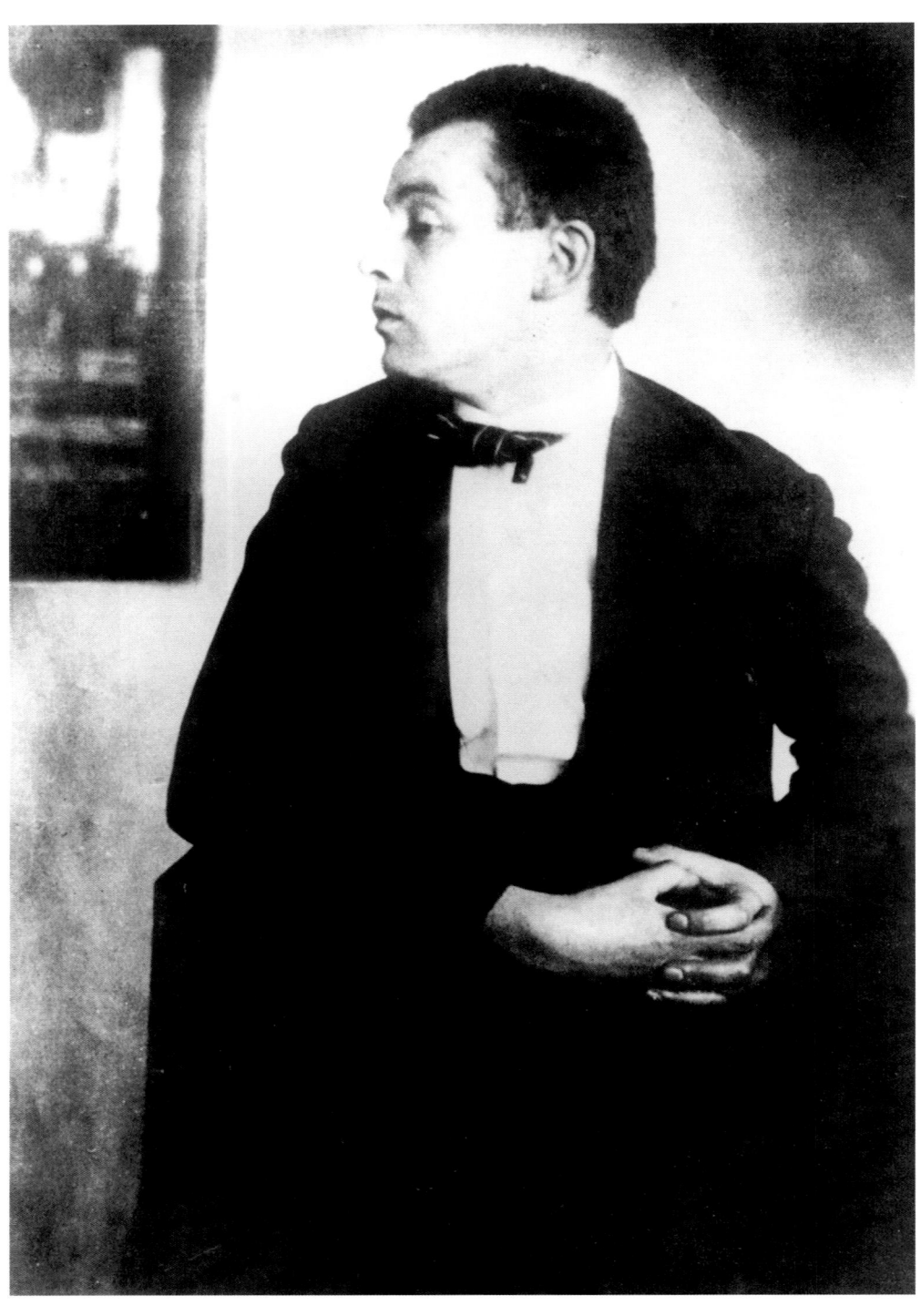

61. EGON SCHIELE, WITH *HOUSES BY THE SEA (ROW OF HOUSES)* IN THE BACKGROUND, 1914

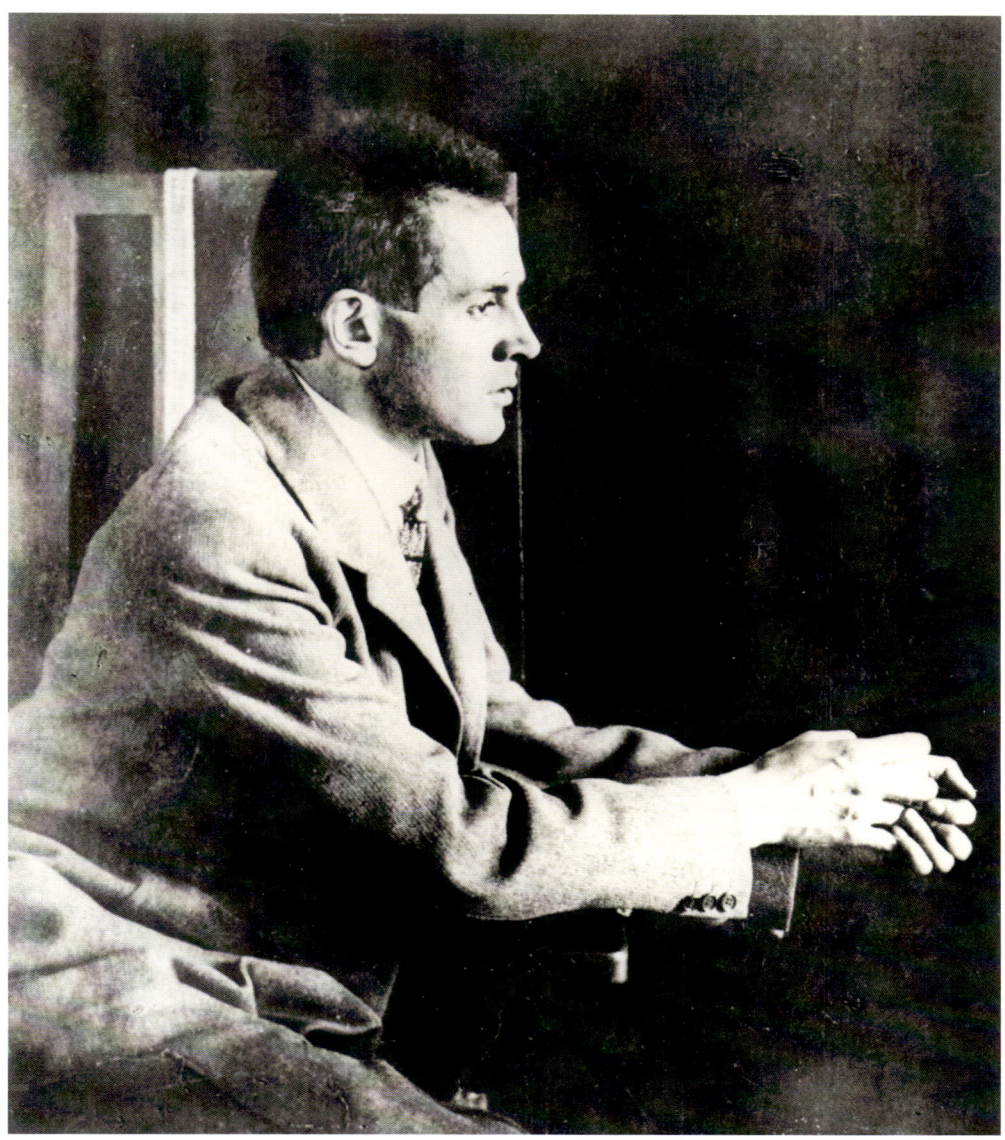

62. EGON SCHIELE, 1915

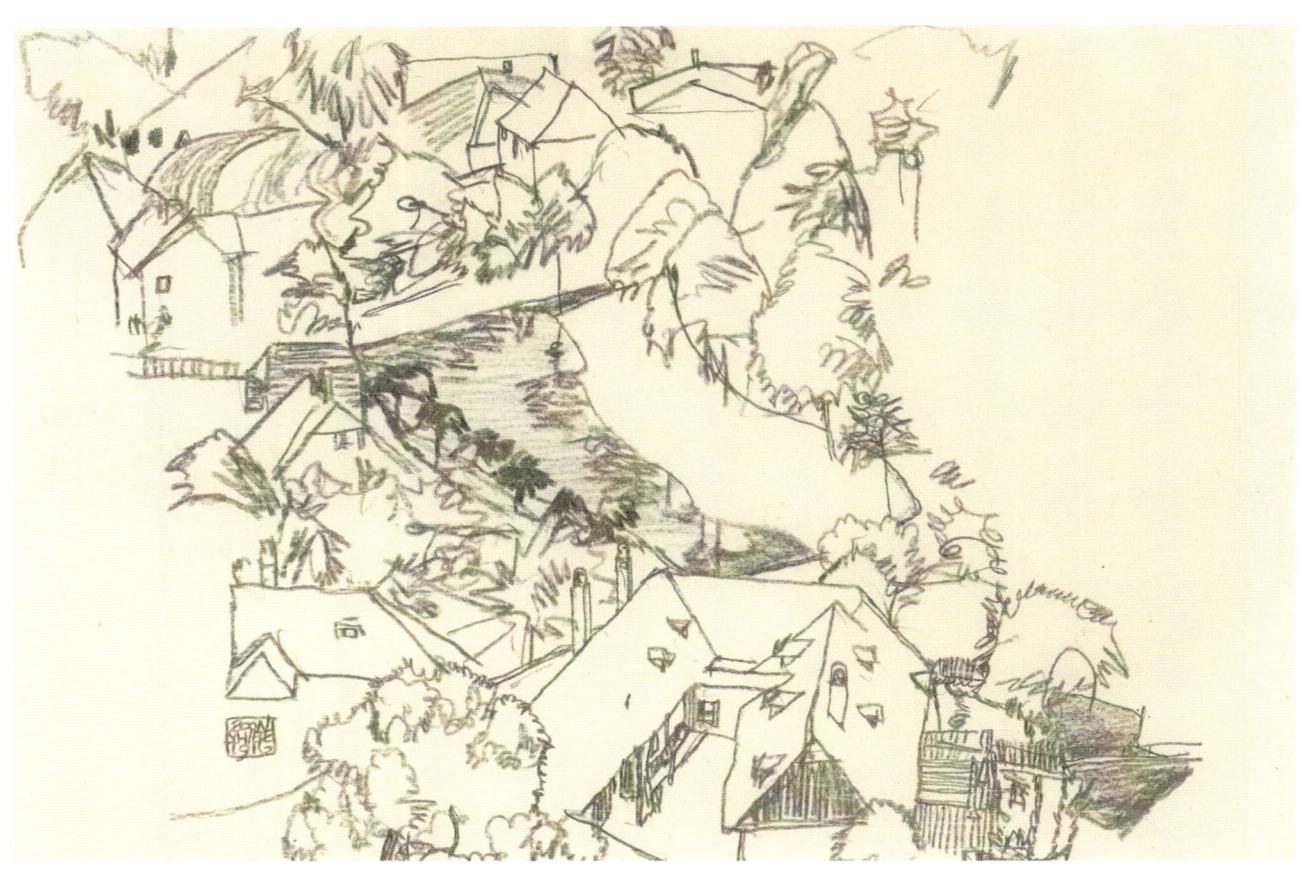

63. KRUMAU TOWN CRESCENT (TOWN ON A RIVER), 1916

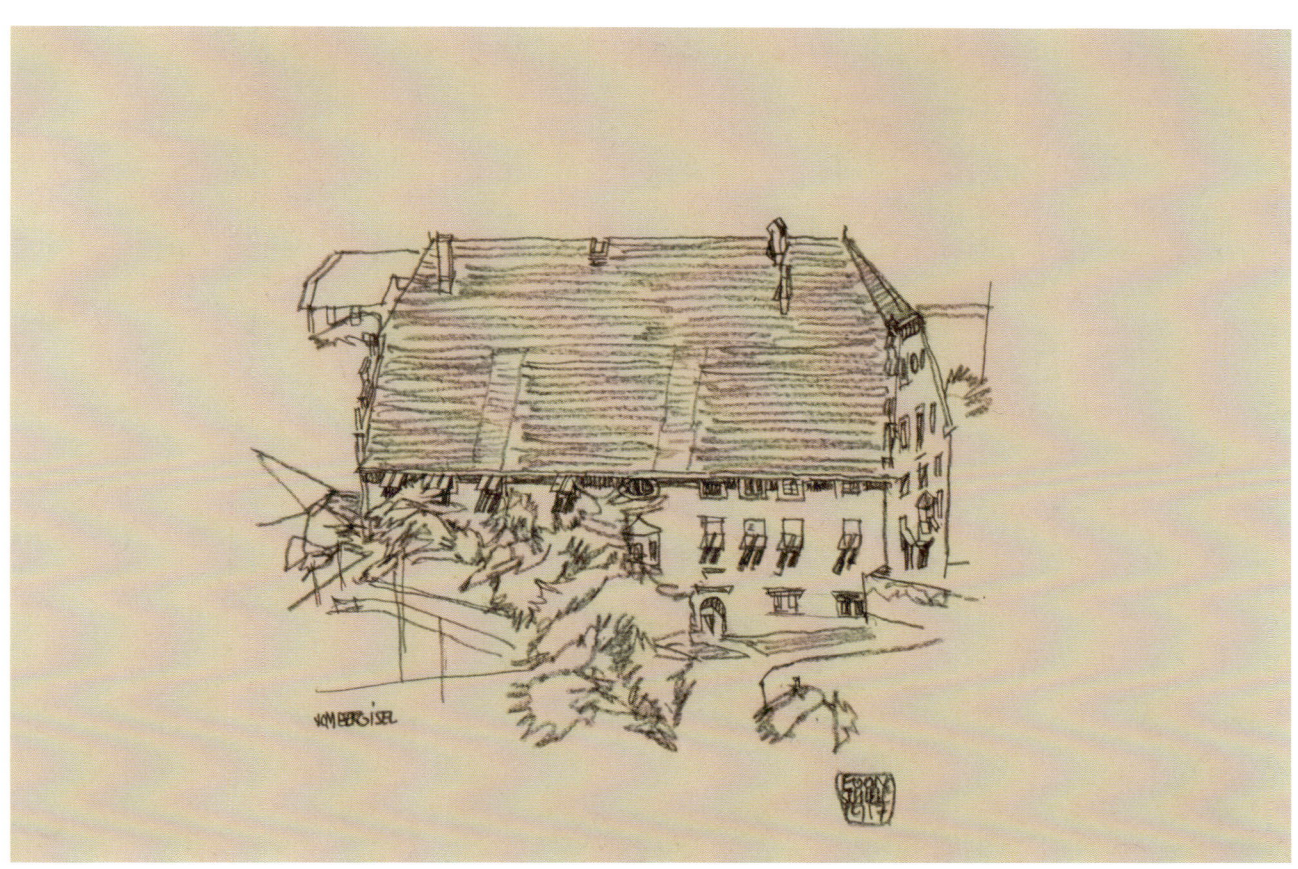

64. FARMHOUSE AT ISEL MOUNTAIN, 1917

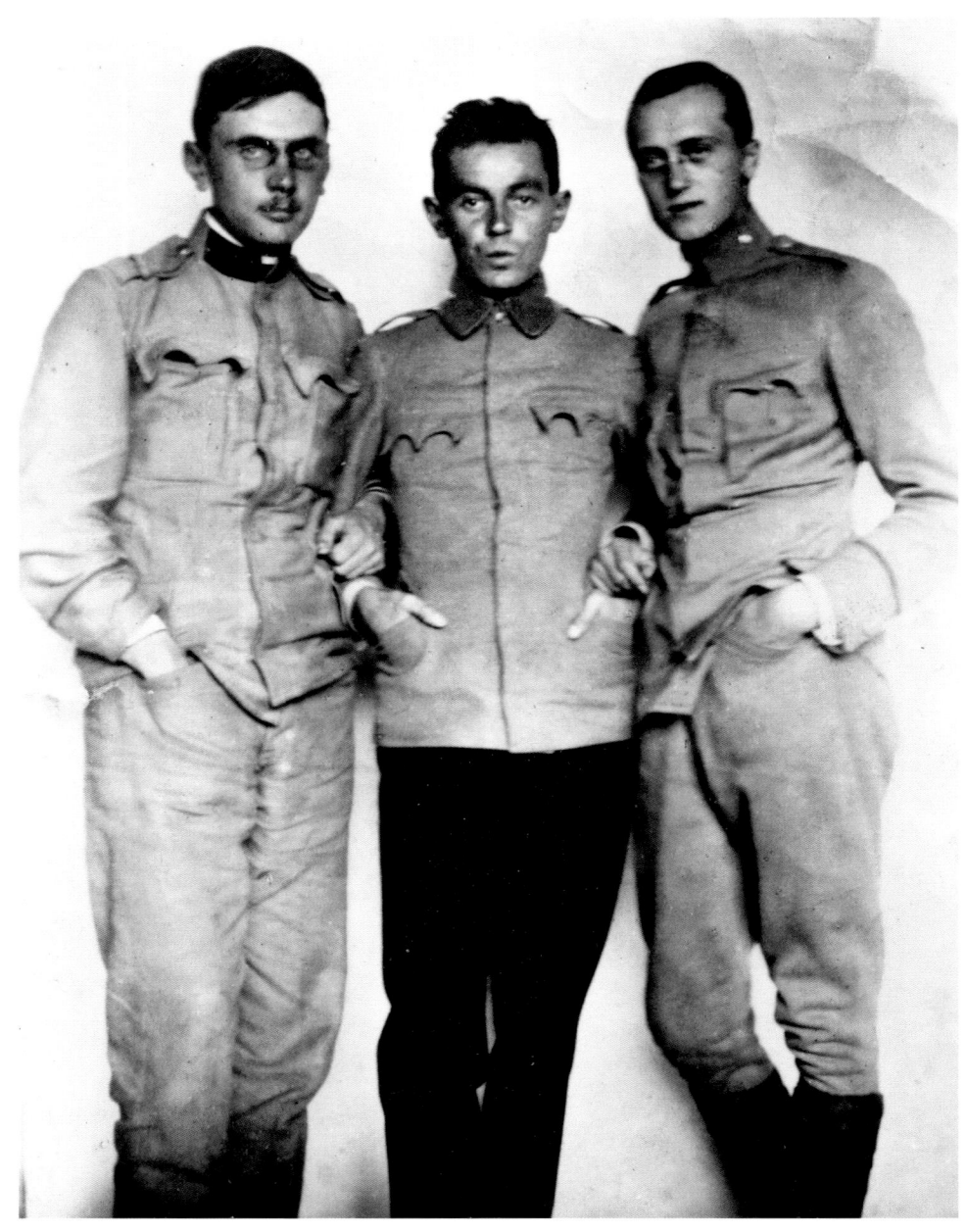

65. EGON SCHIELE (CENTER) AND FELLOW SOLDIERS AT THE PRISONER-OF-WAR CAMP FOR RUSSIAN OFFICERS IN MÜHLING NEAR WIESELBURG, 1916

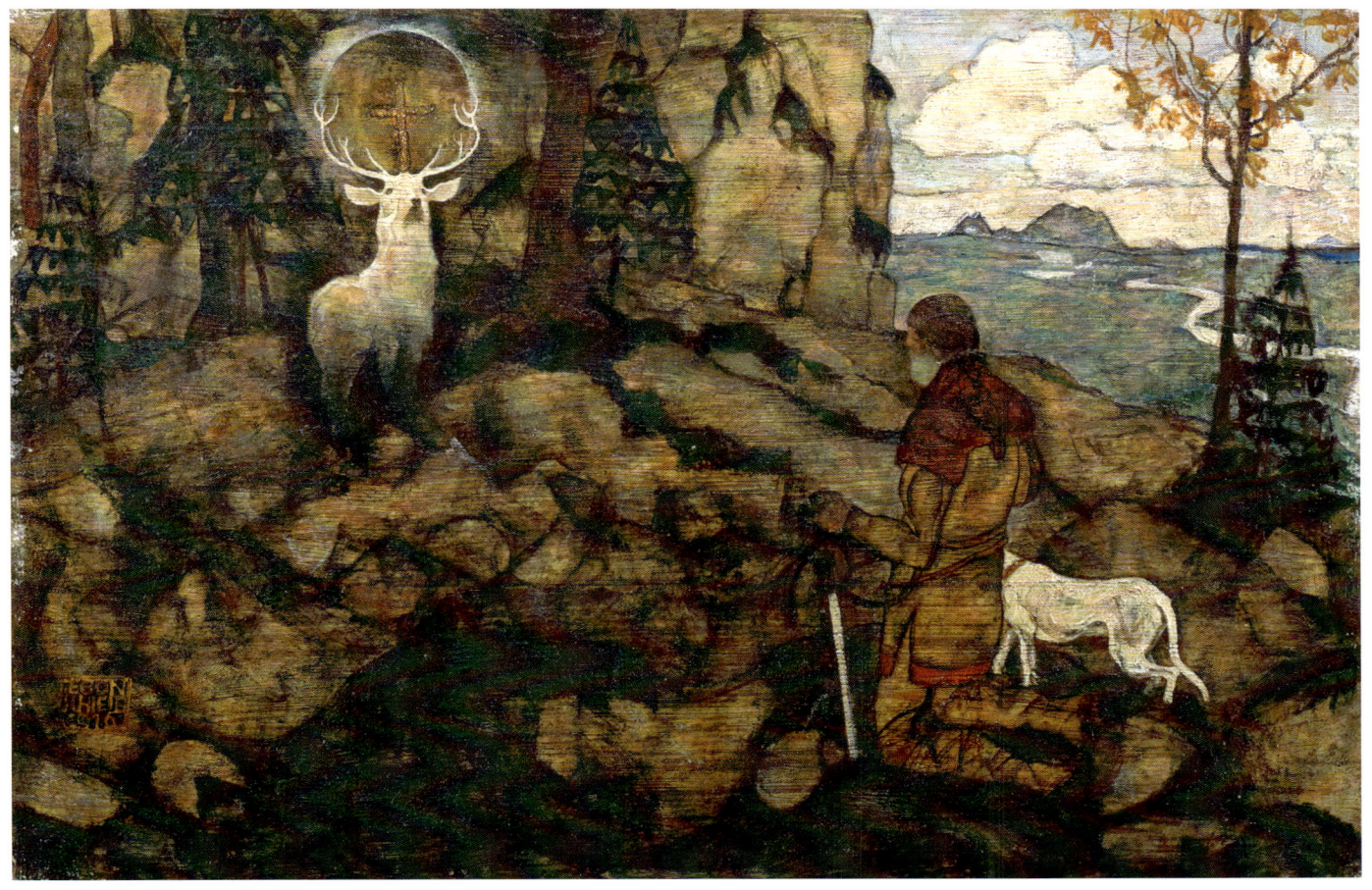

66. THE VISION OF ST. HUBERT, 1916

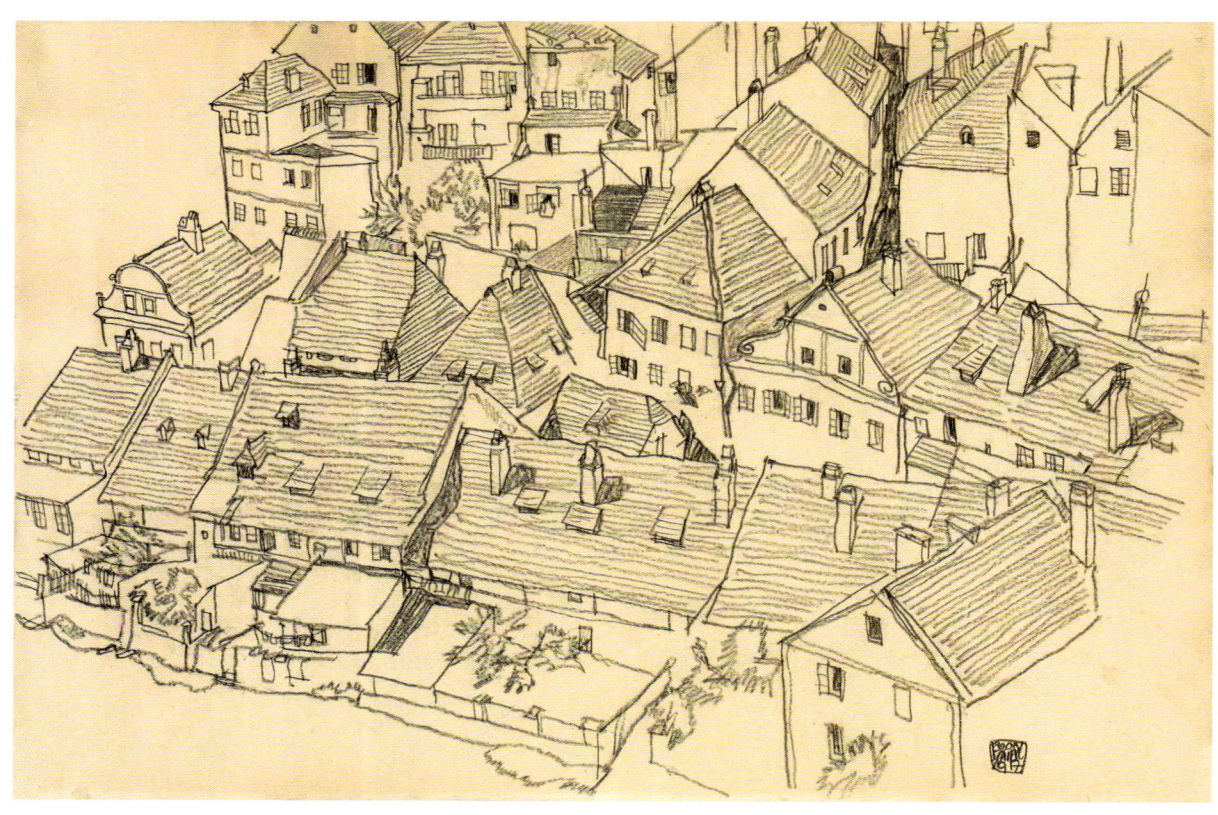

67. HOUSES IN KRUMAU, 1917

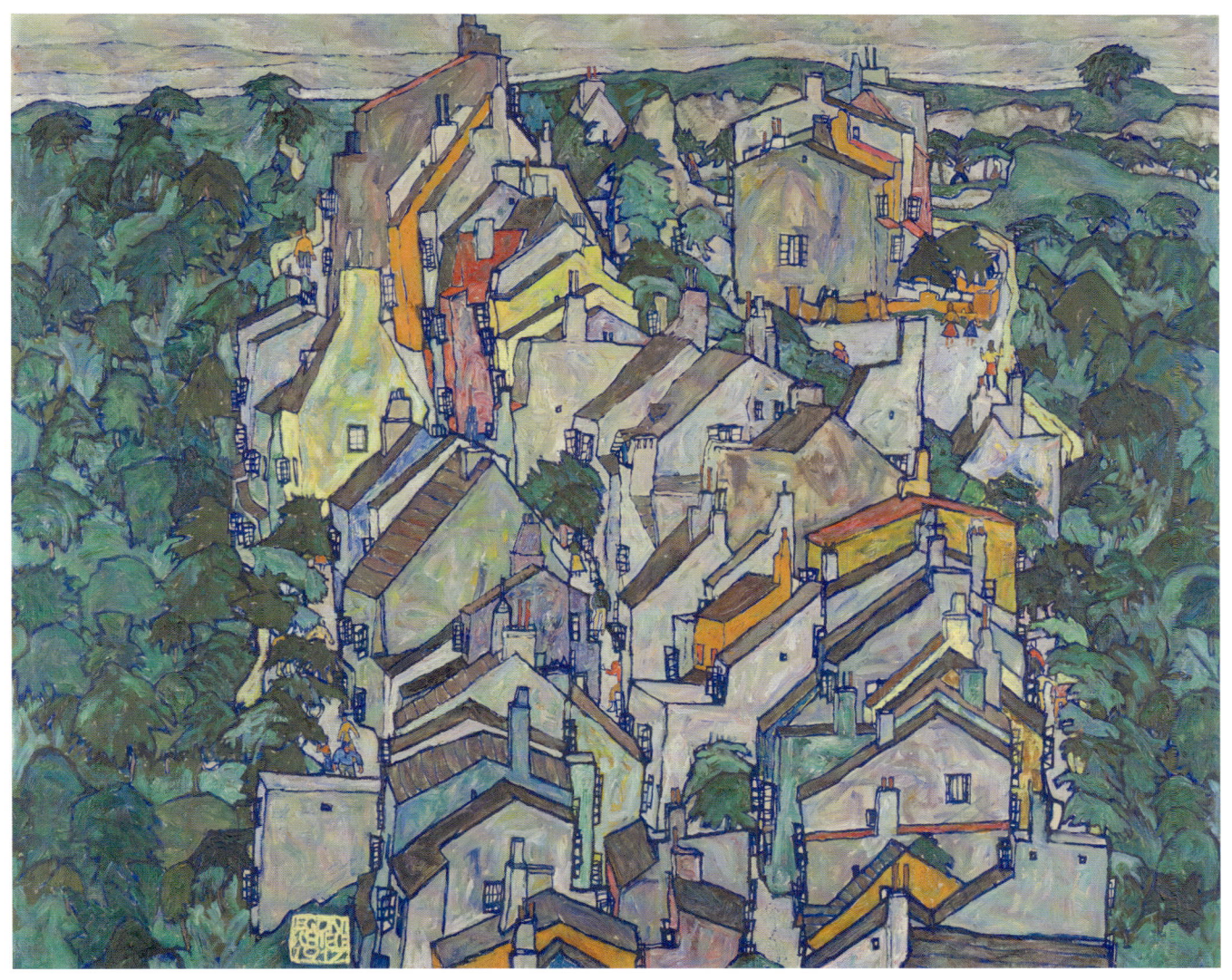

68. TOWN AMONG GREENERY (THE OLD CITY III), 1917

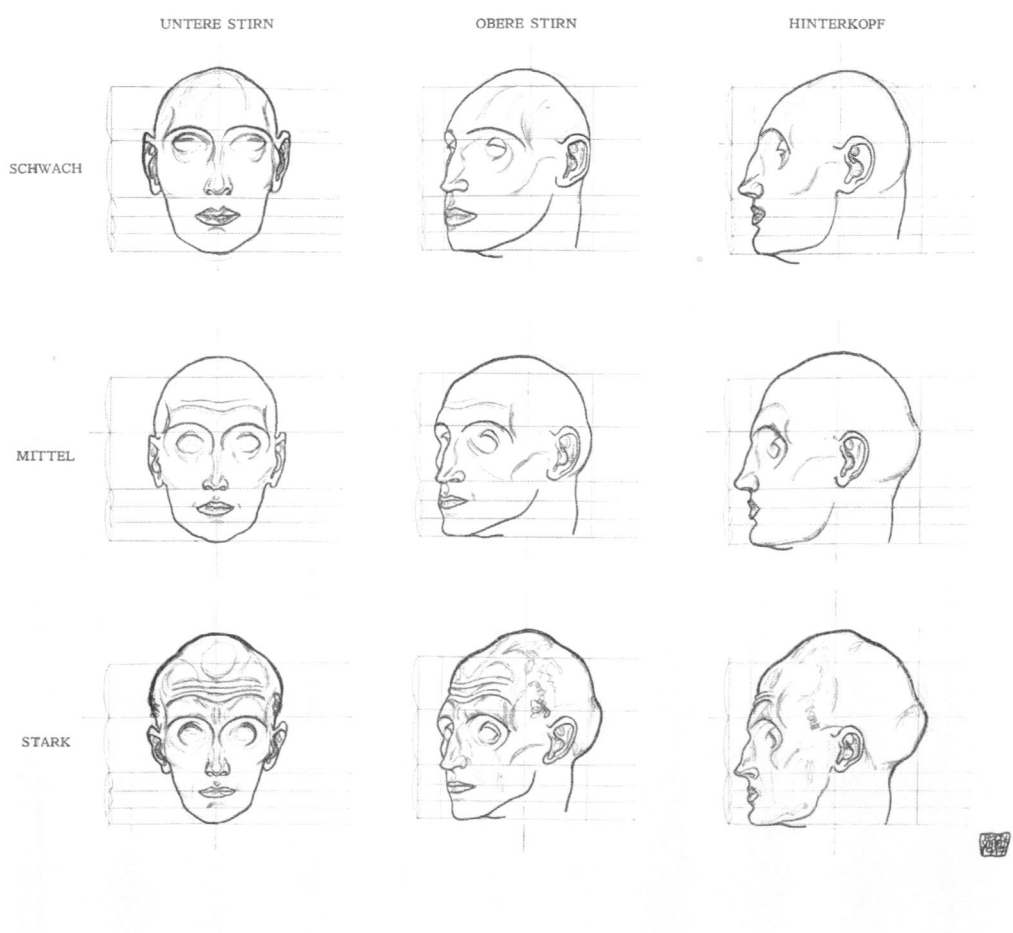

69. HEAD STUDIES ILLUSTRATION FOR ERWIN HANSLIK'S
THE ESSENCE OF HUMANITY, 1917

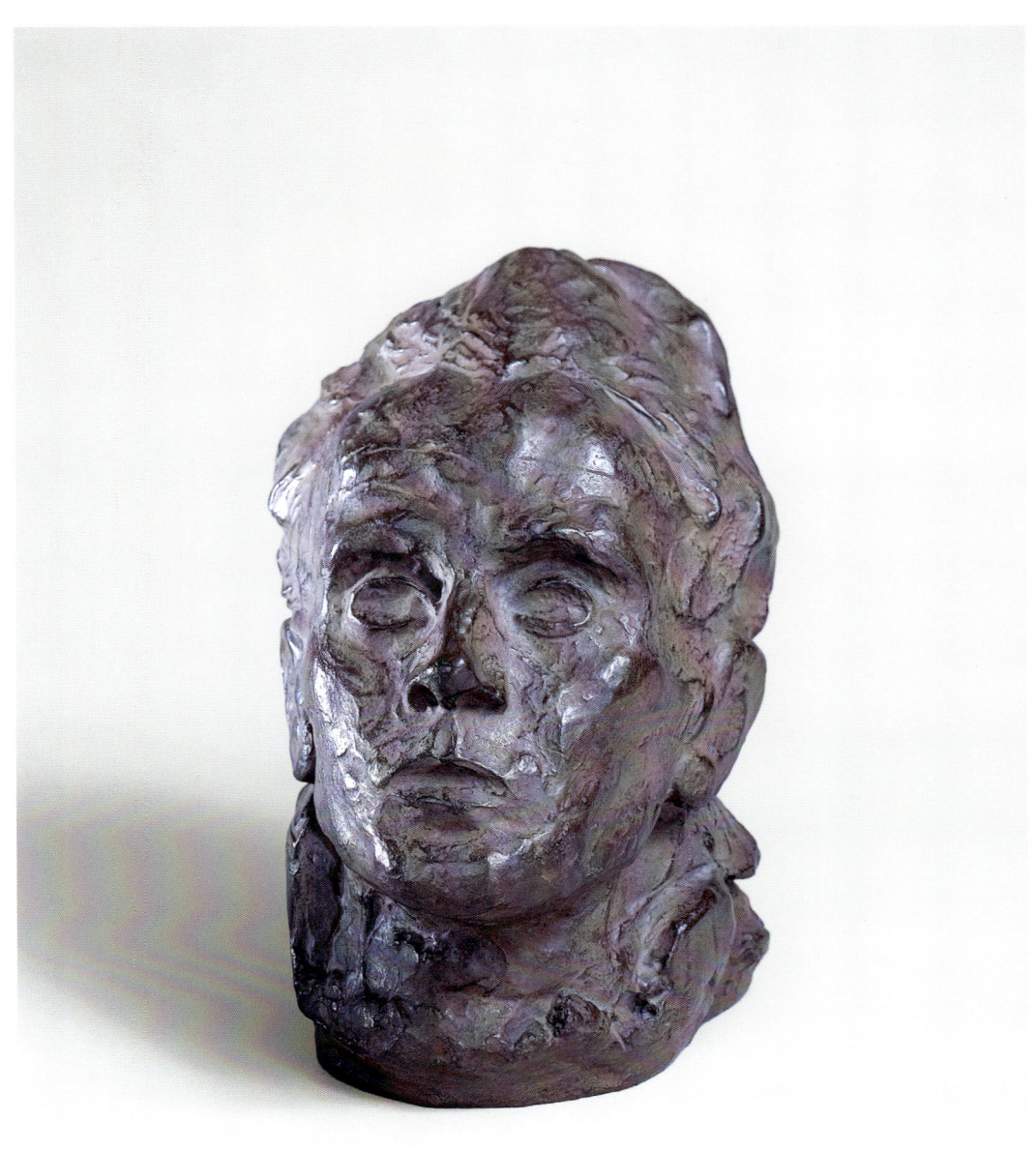

70. SELF-PORTRAIT, CA. 1917

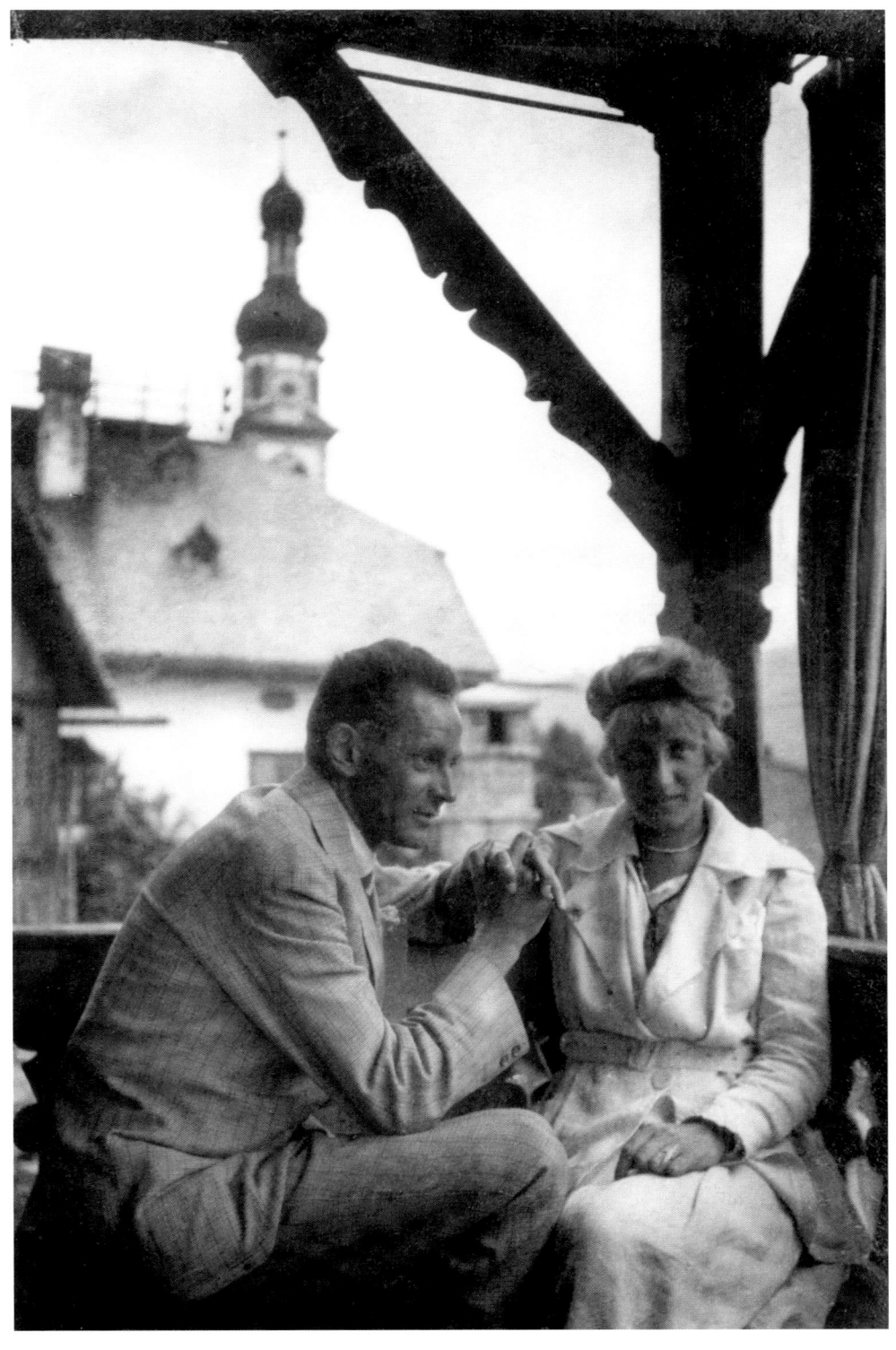

71. EGON AND EDITH SCHIELE IN FULPMES, TYROL, AUGUST 1917

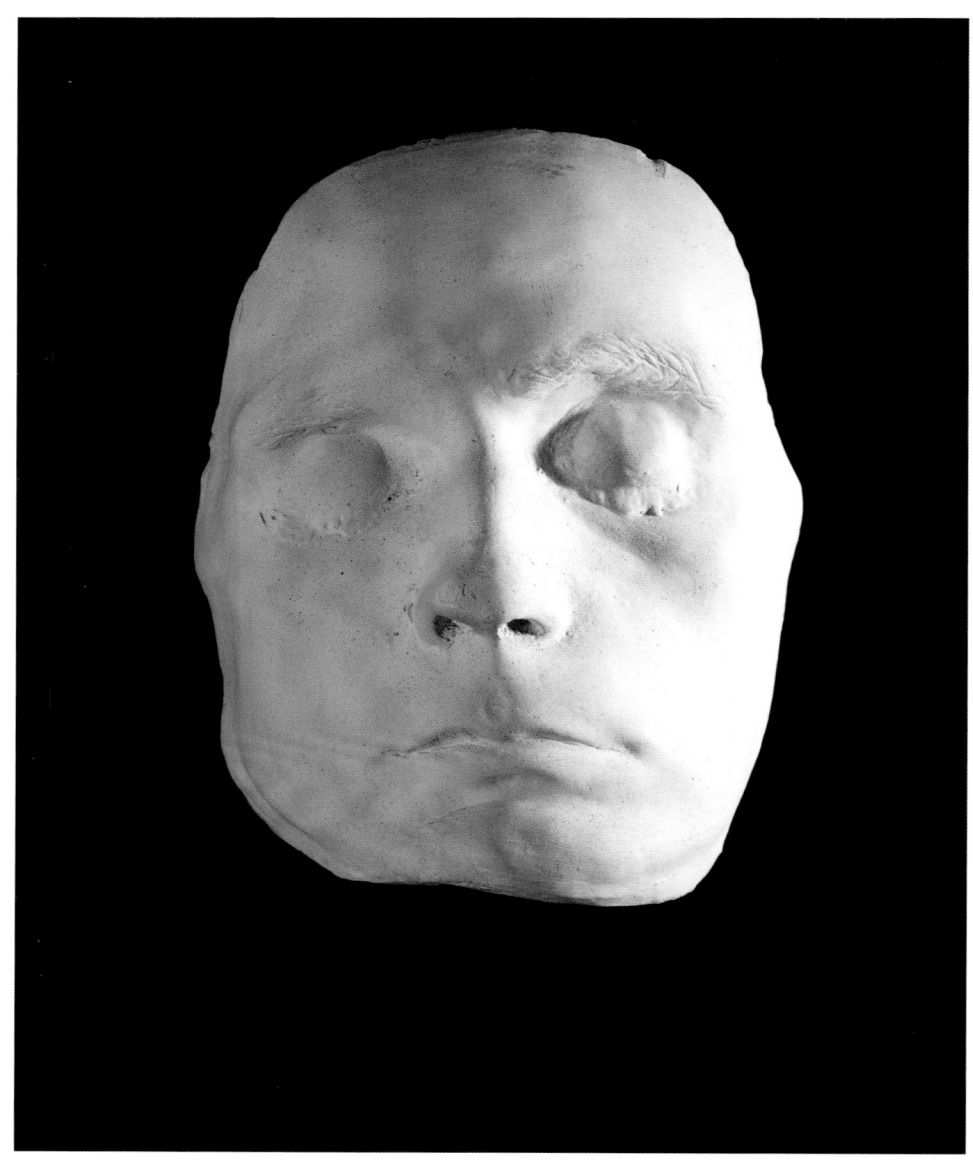

72. DEATH MASK OF EGON SCHIELE, 1918

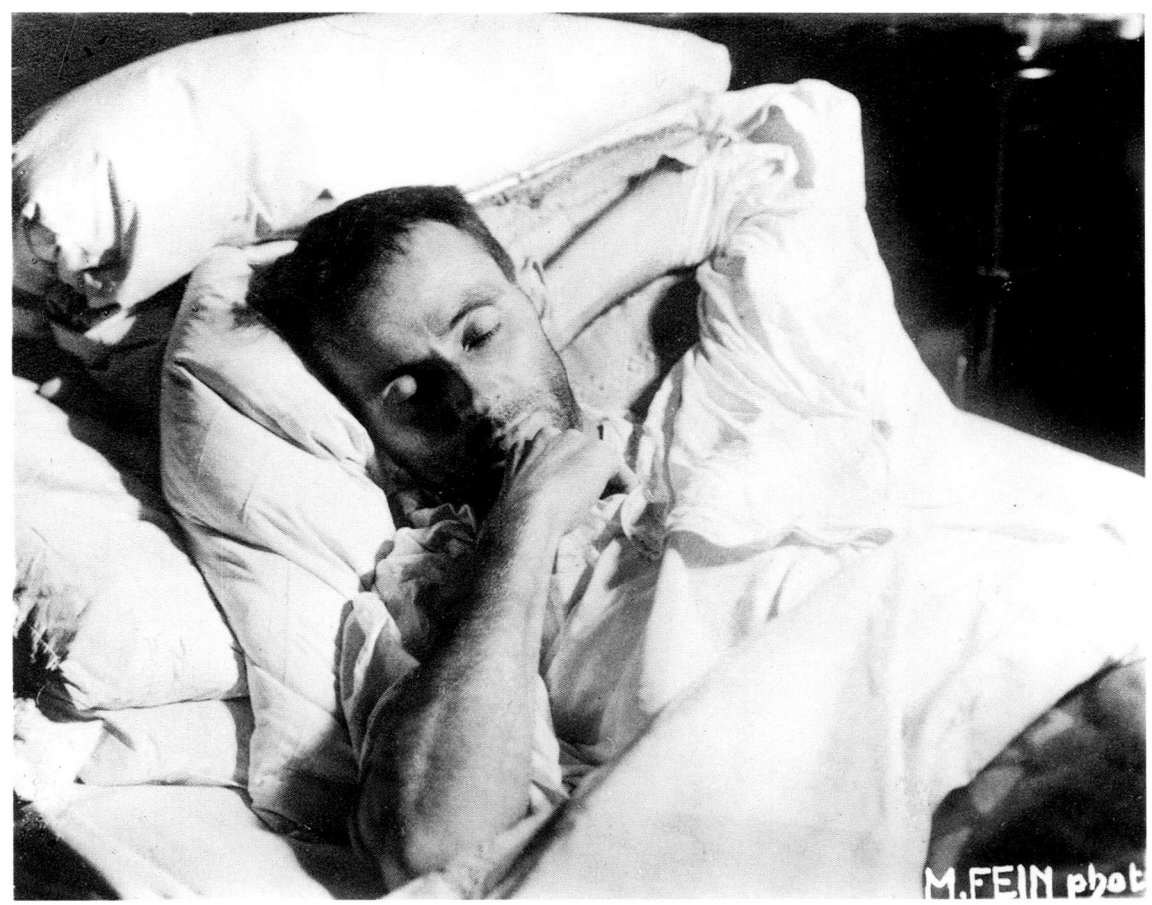

73. EGON SCHIELE ON HIS DEATHBED, OCTOBER 31, 1918

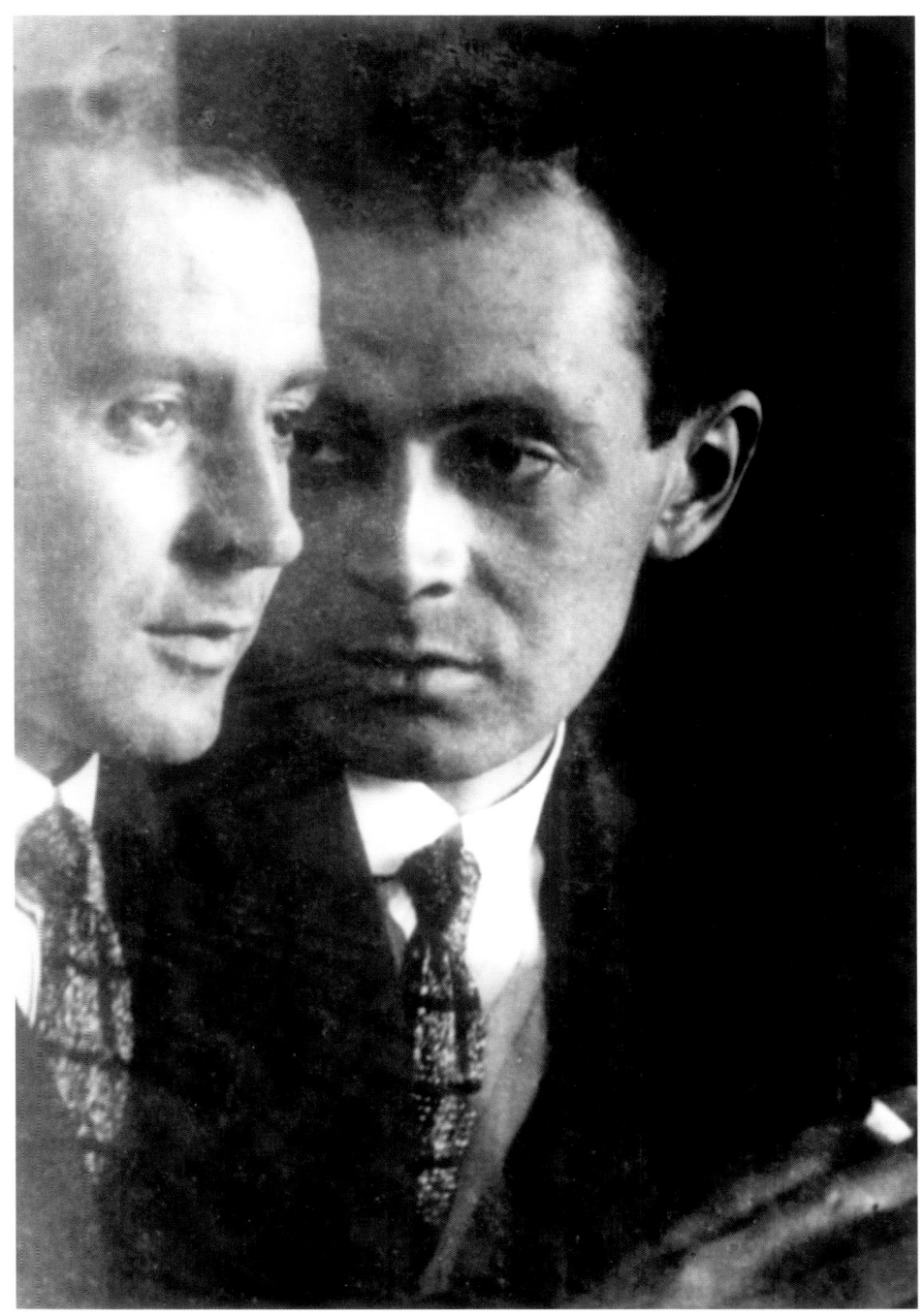

74. DOUBLE EXPOSURE PORTRAIT OF EGON SCHIELE WITH CIGARETTE, 1915

CHECKLIST

1

Egon Schiele with palette as a first-year student at Vienna's Academy of Fine Arts, September 1906
Photographer: Adolf Bernhard
Brandstätter Archive

2

Sketchbook, late spring / summer 1906
Pencil, ink and watercolor on paper in a cloth-bound notebook
13.5 x 20.5 cm (5 3/8 x 8 1/8 in.)
Private Collection
Kallir Sk2

3

Through Europe by Night, ca. 1906
(Durch Europa bei Nacht)
Watercolor and ink on paper
9.5 x 39.2 cm (3 3/4 x 15 3/8 in.)
Landessammlungen Niederösterreich, St. Pölten
Kallir D76

4

Silhouette of Klosterneuburg, ca. 1906
(Silhouette von Klosterneuburg)
Watercolor and ink on paper
9.5 x 13.9 cm (3 3/4 x 5 1/2 in.)
Landessammlungen Niederösterreich, St. Pölten
Kallir D55

5

Klosterneuburg in Fog, 1907
(Klosterneuburg im Nebel)
Oil on canvas
58.5 x 73.7 cm (23 x 29 in.)
Stadtgemeinde Tulln
Kallir P90

6

Houses in the Suburbs, 1907
(Vorstadthäuser)
Oil on cardboard
20.2 x 24.5 cm (7 7/8 x 9 5/8 in.)
Private Collection, courtesy Kallir Research Institute, New York
Kallir P62

7

Meadow with Village in Background I, 1907
(Wiese mit Dorf im Hintergrund I)
Oil on cardboard
26.3 x 38 cm (10 3/8 x 15 in.)
Private Collection, courtesy Kallir Research Institute, New York
Kallir P63

8

The Blacksmith's Courtyard in Klosterneuburg, 1906
(Der Schmiedehof in Klosterneuburg)
Gouache and watercolor on paper
36.9 x 47.6 cm (14 1/2 x 18 3/4 in.)
Stiftsmuseum Klosterneuburg
Kallir P6

9

Courtyard of the Abbey Carpentry Shop, Klosterneuburg, 1907
(Hof der Stiftstischlerei, Klosterneuburg)
Oil and pencil on paper
24.5 x 32.9 cm (9 5/8 x 13 in.).
Stiftsmuseum Klosterneuburg
Kallir P70

10

Summer Night, 1907
(Sommernacht)
Oil on cardboard
20.2 x 20.2 cm (8 x 8 in.)
Private Collection, courtesy Kallir Research Institute, New York
Kallir P93

11

Forest, Hirschbergen, 1908
(Waldstück, Hirschbergen)
Gouache on paper
19 x 19.7 cm (7 3/8 x 7 3/4 in.)
Private Collection, courtesy Kallir Research Institute, New York
Kallir P137

12

Orchard in Spring, 1907
(Obstgarden im Frühling)
Oil on cardboard
35.7 x 25.4 cm (14 x 10 in.)
Private Collection, courtesy Kallir Research Institute, New York
Kallir P44

13

Shrines in the Forest I, 1907
(Waldandacht I)
Oil on board
29.8 x 22.8 cm (11 3/4 x 9 in.)
Landessammlungen Niederösterreich, St. Pölten
Kallir P51

14

Students from Vienna's Academy of Fine Arts at the Schillerplatz, June 1907. Second row, from right: Anton Faistauer and Egon Schiele.
Photographer: Unknown
Private Collection

15

Boats in the Harbor (Trieste), 1908
(Boote im Hafen [Triest])
Oil and pencil on board
29 x 21 cm (11 3/8 x 8 1/4 in.)
Landessammlungen Niederösterreich, St. Pölten
Kallir P113

16

Egon Schiele in a haystack with his uncle Leopold Czihaczek, while hiking from Neulengbach to Hegerberg Mountain near Böheimkirchen, July 15, 1908
Photographer: Gottfried Hoffmann
Brandstätter Archive

17

Egon Schiele with his uncle Leopold Czihaczek and his dog Miro (Murl) hiking from the Villa Wundsam in Neulengbach to the Buchberg Mountain, July 11, 1908
Photographer: Gottfried Hoffmann
Leopold Museum, Vienna

18
Drying Laundry, 1908
(Trocknende Wäsche)
Oil on cardboard
18.5 x 18.1 cm (7 1/4 x 7 1/8 in.)
Kallir Family Foundation
Kallir P141

19
Study of Houses (Hofkirchnergasse, Klosterneuburg), 1908
(Häuserstudie [Hofkirchnergasse, Klosterneuburg])
Oil on cardboard
26.7 x 25.4 cm (10 1/2 x 10 in.)
Stiftsmuseum Klosterneuburg
Kallir P128

20
Letter to Josef Hoffmann, September 20, 1910
Ink on paper
Private Collection

21
A Self-Portrait, May 1910
(Ein Selbstbildnis)
Ink on paper
Private Collection

22
Thunderstorm, July 1910
(Gewitteranzug)
Pencil on paper
30 x 19 cm (11 3/4 x 7 1/2 in.)
Private Collection

23
Egon Schiele's garden house in Krumau, 1911
Photographer: possibly Egon Schiele
Brandstätter Archive

24
City on the Blue River II, 1911
(Stadt am blauen Fluss II)
Pencil, gouache, oil and pencil on wood
37.2 x 29.8 cm (14 5/8 x 11 3/4 in.)
Belvedere, Vienna
Kallir P212

25
Sunflower I, 1908
(Sonnenblume I)
Oil on board
44 x 33 cm (17 3/8 x 13 in.)
Landessammlungen Niederösterreich, St. Pölten
Kallir P144

26
Egon Schiele, 1909
Photographer: Unknown
Private Collection

27
Wilted Sunflower, 1912
(Welke Sonnenblume)
Gouache and pencil on paper
45 x 29.9 cm (17 3/4 x 11 3/4 in.)
Private Collection, courtesy Kallir Research Institute, New York
Kallir D1212

28
Sunflowers, 1911
(Sonnenblumen)
Oil on canvas
90 x 80.3 cm (35 5/8 x 31 5/8 in.)
Belvedere, Vienna
Kallir P221

29
Single Houses (Houses with Mountains), 1915
Einzelne Häuser (Häuser mit Bergen)
Oil on canvas
109.8 × 139.8 cm (431 × 55 in.)
Private Collection
Kallir P292

30
Wilted Sunflowers (Autumn Sun II), 1914
(Welke Sonnenblumen [Herbstsonne II])
Oil on canvas
100 x 120.5 cm (39 3/8 x 47 1/2 in.)
Private Collection,
Courtesy Eykyn Maclean
Kallir P280

31
Little Tree (Chestnut Tree at Lake Constance), 1912
(Bäumchen [Kastanienbaum am Bodensee])
Watercolor and pencil on paper
45.8 x 29.5 cm (18 x 11 5/8 in.)
Kallir Family Foundation
Kallir D1215

32
Group of Houses on a Mountain, 1912
(Häusergruppe am Berg)
Pencil, watercolor, and gouache on primed Strathmore Japan paper
31.8 × 48 cm (12 1/2 x 18 7/8 in.)
The Albertina Museum, Vienna
Kallir D1218

33
City Houses (Krumau Ringplatz), 1911
(Stadthäuser [Krumau Ringplatz])
Pencil on buff wove paper
44.4 x 31.8 cm (17 3/8 x 12 1/2 in.)
Kallir Family Foundation
Kallir D982

34
Ringplatz, Krumau, 1910
(Ringplatz, Krumau)
Watercolor and black crayon on paper
31.4 x 44.5 cm (12 3/8 x 17 1/2 in.)
Private Collection
Kallir D740

35
Red Earth, 1910
(Rote Erde)
Oil on canvas mounted on pressed wood
52.1 x 49.9 cm (20 1/2 x 19 5/8 in.)
Private Collection, courtesy Kallir Research Institute, New York
Kallir P188

36
Krumau Townscape (St. Vitus's Church with Houses) (Meadow, Church, and Houses), 1912
Stadtbild von Krumau (St.-Veit-Kirch mit Häusern) (Wiese, Kirche, und Häuser)
Oil on panel
36.8 x 29.3 cm (14 1/2 x 11 1/2 in.)
Private Collection
Kallir P243

37

Current of Youth (Danaë), 1903

(Danaë [Jugendströmung])

Oil and metallic paint on canvas

80 x 125.4 cm (31 1/2 x 49 3/8 in.)

The Lewis Collection

Kallir P148

38

Portrait of Gerti Schiele, 1909

(Bildnis Gerti Schiele)

Oil, silver, gold-bronze paint,

and pencil on canvas

139.5 x 140.5 cm (55 x 55 1/4 in.)

The Museum of Modern Art, New York.

Purchase and partial gift of the Lauder

family, 1982, and private collection

Kallir P155

39

Portrait of the Painter Karl Zakovšek, 1910

(Bildnis des Malers Karl Zakovšek)

Oil, gouache, and charcoal on canvas

100 x 89.9 cm (39 3/8 x 35 3/8 in.)

Private Collection

RSL.4734

40

Self-Portrait with Peacock Waistcoat, Standing, 1911

(Selbstbildnis mit Pfauenweste, stehend)

Gouache, watercolor, and black crayon

on paper, mounted on cardboard

51.5 x 34.5 cm (20 1/4 x 13 5/8 in.)

Ernst Ploil, Vienna

Kallir P189

41

Procession, 1911

(Prozession)

Oil on canvas

100 x 100.5 cm (39 3/8 x 39 5/8 in.)

Ernst Ploil, Vienna

Kallir P198

42

Man and Woman I (Lovers I), 1914

(Mann und Frau I [Liebespaar I])

Oil on canvas

121.3 x 140.5 cm (47 5/8 x 55 1/4 in.)

Private Collection

Kallir P275

43

Egon Schiele and Anton Peschka in Krumau, 1910

Photographer: possibly Erwin Osen

Leopold Museum, Vienna

44

City on the Blue River I (Dead City I)

(Stadt am blauen Fluss I [Tote Stadt I])

Gouache with glue and black crayon

on paper

41.2 x 30.8 cm (16 1/4 x 12 1/8 in.)

Private Collection

Kallir P183

45

The Small City I (Dead City VI), 1912

(Die kleine Stadt I [Tote Stadt VI])

Oil on canvas

80.2 x 80.2 cm (31 1/2 x 31 1/2 in.)

Kunsthaus Zürich

Kallir P246

46

The Bridge, 1913

(Die Brücke)

Gouache, watercolor, and pencil

on paper

31.7 x 48.2 cm (12 1/2 x 19 in.)

Kallir Family Foundation

Kallir D1463

47

The Bridge, 1913

(Die Brücke)

Oil on canvas

89.7 x 90 cm (35 3/8 x 35 3/8 in.)

Kallir Family Foundation

Kallir P262

48

Hay Racks, 1914

(Heuhütten)

Pencil on paper

28 x 45.1 cm (11 x 17 3/4 in.)

Inv. no. 12.4892

Private Collection

Kallir D1682a

49

Sawmill, 1913

(Sägewerk)

Oil on canvas

80.1 x 89.8 cm (31 1/2 x 35 3/8 in.)

Kallir Family Foundation

Kallir P271

50

Carinthian Landscape, 1914

(Kärntner Landschaft)

Pencil, watercolor, and gouache

on Japan paper

31 × 47.9 cm (12 1/4 x 18 7/8 in.)

The Albertina Museum, Vienna

Kallir D1684

51

River Landscape with Two Trees, 1913

(Flusslandschaft mit zwei Bäumen)

Oil on canvas

88.9 x 89.9 cm (35 x 35 3/8 in.)

Private Collection

Kallir P264

52

Egon Schiele and Arthur Roessler in front of Orth Castle in Gmunden on Lake Traun, Salzkammergut, 1913

Photographer: Unknown

Gelatin silver photograph mounted

on cardboard with a pen and ink drawing

by József Divéky

Wien Museum, Vienna

53

Egon Schiele and Walburga (Wally) Neuzil on Lake Traun, 1913

Photographer: probably Arthur Roessler

Brandstätter Archive

54

Stein on the Danube, Seen from the South (Large), 1913

(Stein an der Donau, vom Süden gesehen [gross])

Oil and pencil on canvas

89.9 x 89.6 cm (35 3/8 x 35 1/4 in.)

This work is part of the collection

of Estée Lauder and was made available

through the generosity of Estée Lauder

Kallir P268

55

Stein on the Danube, Seen from the South (Small), 1913
(Stein an der Donau, vom Süden gesehen [klein])
Oil and pencil on panel
39.8 x 31.6 cm (15 $^5/_8$ x 12 $^1/_2$ in.)
Private Collection
Kallir P266

56

Stein on the Danube, Seen from the Kreuzberg (Small), 1913
(Stein an der Donau, vom Kreuzberg aus gesehen [klein])
Oil and pencil on panel
39.7 x 31.5 cm (15 $^5/_8$ x 12 $^3/_8$ in.)
Private Collection
Kallir P267

57

Last Houses (At the Edge of Town), 1915
(Letzte Häuser [am Stadtrand]), 1915
Pencil on Japan paper
32.8 × 40.5 cm (12 $^7/_8$ × 16 in.)
The Albertina Museum, Vienna
Kallir D1806

58

Houses by the River II (The Old City II), 1914
(Häuser am Fluss II [Die alte Stadt II])
Oil on canvas
100 x 120.5 cm (39 $^3/_8$ x 47 $^1/_2$ in.)
Museo Nacional Thyssen-Bornemisza, Madrid
Kallir P279

59

Old Houses in Krumau, 1914
(Alte Häuser in Krumau)
Pencil on paper
32.3 x 48 cm (12 $^3/_4$ x 18 $^7/_8$ in.)
Landessammlungen Niederösterreich St. Pölten
Kallir D1690

60

Yellow Town, 1914
(Gelbe Stadt)
Oil on canvas
110 x 140 cm (43 $^1/_4$ x 55 $^1/_8$ in.)
YAGEO Foundation Collection, Taiwan
Kallir P286

61

Egon Schiele with *Houses by the Sea (Row of Houses)* in the background, 1914
Photographer: Johannes Fischer (?)
Private Collection

62

Egon Schiele, 1915
Photographer: Johannes Fischer
Private Collection

63

Krumau Town Crescent (Town on a River), 1916
Pencil on paper
28.6 x 66.7 cm (11 $^3/_{16}$ x 26 $^5/_{16}$ in.)
Private Collection
Kallir D1867a

64

Farmhouse at Isel Mountain, 1917
(Bauernhaus am Berg Isel)
Black crayon on paper
27.3 x 42.8 cm (10 $^3/_4$ x 16 $^7/_8$ in.)
Private Collection
Kallir D2137

65

Egon Schiele (center) and fellow soldiers at the prisoner-of-war camp for Russian officers in Mühling near Wieselburg, 1916
Photographer: Unknown
Brandstätter Archive

66

The Vision of St. Hubert, 1916
(Die Vision des heiligen Hubertus)
Oil on panel
26.5 x 46 cm (10 $^3/_8$ x 18 $^1/_8$ in.)
Private Collection, Courtesy Richard Nagy Ltd., London
Kallir P302

67

Houses in Krumau, 1917
(Häuser in Krumau)
Black chalk on paper
29.8 × 45.8 cm (28 $^5/_8$ × 10 $^1/_2$ in.)
Anonymous Lender
Kallir D2135a

68

Town among Greenery (The Old City III), 1917
(Stadt im Grünen [Die alte Stadt III])
Oil on canvas
110.7 x 140.1 cm (43 $^5/_8$ x 55 $^1/_8$ in.)
Neue Galerie New York, in memory of Otto and Marguerite Manley, given as a bequest from the Estate of Marguerite Manley
Kallir P313
Photo: Shawn Digney-Peer

69

Head studies illustration for Erwin Hanslik's *Wesen des Menschheit* (The Essence of Humanity), 1917
Publisher: Vienna: Verlag Institut für Kulturforschung
23.9 × 24.7 cm (9 $^3/_8$ x 9 $^3/_4$ in.)
The Albertina Museum, Vienna
Donated by Dipl. Ing. Wolfgang Zittel, Rösrath

70

Self-Portrait, ca. 1917
[this series from 1965, no. 6 from a numbered edition of 7]
Cast stone, brownish-gray patina
28.4 x 16.8 x 22.2 cm (11 $^1/_8$ x 6 $^5/_8$ x 8 $^3/_4$ in.)
Private Collection
Kallir S4e

71

Egon and Edith Schiele in Fulpmes, Tyrol, August 1917
Photographer: Unknown
Private Collection

72

Death mask of Egon Schiele, 1918
Plaster
Cast taken by Anton Sandig
17.8 x 15.6 x 9.5 cm (7 x 6 $^1/_8$ x 3 $^3/_4$ in.)
Neue Galerie New York. Gift of Alessandra Comini

73

Egon Schiele on his deathbed, October 31, 1918
Photographer: Martha Fein
Brandstätter Archive

74

Double exposure portrait of Egon Schiele with cigarette, 1915
Photographer: Johannes Fischer
Private Collection

INDEX

PHOTOGRAPH
AND COPYRIGHT CREDITS

We wish to thank the museums, galleries, and individuals named in the captions of plates and text illustrations
for supplying the photographic materials in this publication.

akg-images: 17 (Kunsthaus Zug), 19 (Tiroler Landesmuseen, Innsbruck), 21 (Neue Galerie, Joanneum, Graz), 104
The Albertina Museum, Vienna: 43, 68, 95, 100, 163, 182, 190, 202
Archives of the Liljevalchs Konsthall, Stockholm: 46, 47
Artefact / Alamy Stock Photo: 31 (Landessammlungen Niederösterreich, St. Polten), 32
ARTOTHEK: 62 top left (Museum Folkwang, Essen), 65 right (Neue Pinakothek, Bayrische Staatsgemäldesammlungen)
Art Resource, New York: 67 (Erich Lessing), 78 (Israel Museum, Jerusalem), 169 (© The Museum of Modern Art/Licensed by SCALA)
Belvedere, Vienna: 18 bottom, 25, 39 (Johannes Stoll), 60 (Johannes Stoll), 69 (Johannes Stoll), 75 (Johannes Stoll), 155, 159 (Johannes Stoll)
Brandstätter Archive: 7, 13, 115, 144, 154, 185, 198, 207
Courtesy Leopold Fine Arts, Vienna: 105
Courtesy Richard Nagy Ltd., London: 199
© Christie's Images Limited: 160
Ernst Ploil, Vienna: back cover, 171, 172
Galleria Doria Pamphilij, Rome: 65 left
Josef Schütz, Vienna: 64 top
Kallir Research Institute, New York: 18 top, 26, 58, 85, 134, 135, 138-140, 146, 158, 162, 164, 166, 178, 179, 181, 188, 189
© Kungliga Biblioteket, Stockholm: 86
Kunsthaus Zürich: 177
Kunsthistorisches Museum, Gemäldegalerie, Vienna: 66
Landesgalerie Niederösterreich, Krems: 38
Landessammlungen Niederösterreich, St. Polten: 22, 131, 132, 141, 143, 156, 192
Courtesy Leopold Fine Arts, Vienna: 105
Leopold Museum, Vienna: 15, 16, 20, 37, 40-42, 44, 51, 53, 55, 57, 59, 61, 64 bottom, 77, 81, 88, 97-99, 102, 107, 145, 174
The Lewis Collection: 168
Liljevalchs Konsthall, Stockholm: 46, 47, 87, 89
© MAK – Museum of Applied Arts, Vienna: 62 top
Minneapolis Institute of Art: 24
© Museo Nacional Thyssen-Bornemisza, Madrid: 191
© Neue Galerie New York: 9 (Hulya Kolabas), 112-113 (Shawn Digney-Peer), 187 (Hulya Kolabas), 201
   (Shawn Digney-Peer), 206, 224
National Museum, Poznań: 56 bottom
Salzburg Museum: 62 bottom (Zander & Labisch)
Stadtgemeinde Tulln: 133
Stiftmuseum Klosterneuburg: 136, 137, 147
Wien Museum, Vienna: 23, 45 (Birgit and Peter Kainz), 56, 63, 184
YAGEO Foundation Collection, Taiwan: 193

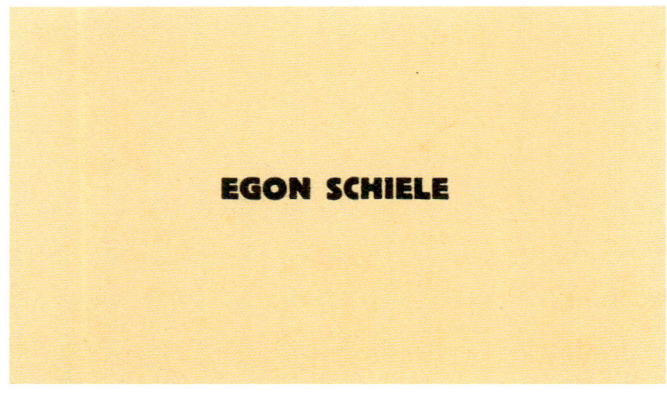

Egon Schiele, calling card, ca. 1905–18, printed paper. Neue Galerie New York.
Gift of Alessandra Comini